# AMERICA'S FIRST CRISIS

# AMERICA'S FIRST CRISIS
## The War of 1812

ROBERT P. WATSON

excelsior editions
State University of New York Press
Albany, New York

*The Action between United States and Macedonian in the mid-Atlantic, 25th October, 1812*
by Derek G. M. Gardner, RSMA.

Image courtesy of Jack Fine Art by permission of Mrs. Mary Gardner.

Published by State University of New York Press, Albany

Printed in the United States of America

Excelsior Editions is an imprint of State University of New York Press

For information, contact State University of New York Press, Albany, NY
www.sunypress.edu

Production by Jenn Bennett
Marketing by Fran Keneston

**Library of Congress Cataloging-in-Publication Data**

Watson, Robert P., 1962–
   America's first crisis : the War of 1812 / Robert P. Watson.
       pages cm. — (Excelsior editions)
   Includes bibliographical references and index.
   ISBN 978-1-4384-5134-3 (pbk. : alk. paper) 1. United States—History—War of 1812.
I. Title.  II. Title: War of 1812.

   E354.W396 2014
   973.5'2—dc23                                                    2013021831

10 9 8 7 6 5 4 3 2 1

# CONTENTS

## 1813

## THE HIGH SEAS

## THE GREAT LAKES THEATER

## 1814

# TURNING POINTS

# ECHOES

# PREFACE

I grew up not far from Gettysburg and Valley Forge in Pennsylvania, sites of two of the most important events in American military history. I recall visiting them when I was a child and suppose in some way these experiences helped fashion in me a lifelong love of history. As a professor, part of my job is to promote civic and history education. To that end, it was apparent to me that the War of 1812 has remained an under-appreciated conflict. Few people—reporters, students, politicians, or the general public—know very much about this fascinating war, one that played a significant role in shaping American history but one that was also accurately described by President Harry Truman as America's "silliest damned war."

However, the years 2012 through 2015 mark the bicentennial of the War of 1812 and I am optimistic that the events throughout Canada, the United States, and even in Britain have helped to raise awareness. Sadly, there remains a remarkable disconnect in America over the war and its causes and consequences, less so than in Canada where the war is a source of national pride. Sandra Shaul, a city administrator in Canada working on various bicentennial projects, noted that she was "a little surprised" that Americans knew so little about a war so important to their homeland, adding "They have their perspective and we have ours. It's a question of emphasis: They emphasize their version of the story . . . and of course we emphasize ours." But it is more than just a question of perspective, it is a matter of an important chapter in the life of a country that is all but forgotten.

Therefore, a goal of the book is to help promote awareness of the people, places, and events of the war during the bicentennial celebration of this "forgotten" conflict. The book tells the story of the heroes and villains of the war, discusses the war's causes and consequences, and uncovers its role in shaping the continent's history and forging a sense of nationalism among both Americans and Canadians. Relatedly, rather than explore a single major battle or facet of the War of 1812, the following pages present the highlights and lowpoints of all the major theaters of the war, from America's repeated efforts to invade Canada and the colossal ineptitude in that theater of the war, to naval fights for the Great Lakes and on the open oceans, to raids in the "northwestern" territory and the ongoing Indian conflict, to the British invasions of the Chesapeake and Gulf Coast.

But one does not have to be a military historian to follow the battles. In an effort to bring the war and those who fought it to life, I made the difficult decision to remove details such as the name of every unit engaged in each battle and the specific types of weaponry used in hopes of enhancing the readability of the book. However, I included the names of the generals and figures on the casualty counts, troop strength, and topography for each battle. Therefore, every effort was made to produce an accessible, readable account of the war for a wide audience.

I would like to thank Michael Rinella, Jenn Bennett, Fran Keneston, and the staff at SUNY Press for their confidence in my initial proposal and manuscript, and their assistance in publishing this book. I have had the pleasure of publishing three other books with SUNY. University presses such as SUNY provide such rich cultural, literary, and scholarly contributions to society and I am always grateful for their work. Thanks also to my friends Steve West, Doris Davidoff, and Bob Terpstra for reading early drafts of this book and providing helpful feedback, and to my excellent student Mimi Trinh for generously digging up facts on some of the commanders of the war. Lastly and most importantly, I acknowledge my family—Claudia, Alessandro, and Isabella—for their support and patience during the many long days and nights I spent researching and writing this book.

I hope you enjoy the book and find it to be informative and exciting. I also encourage you to visit the many fun and helpful battlefield sites and Websites associated with the War of 1812.

Robert P. Watson
Boca Raton, Florida

# THE FORGOTTEN WAR

"Impressment of American seamen by the British Navy." Acknowledgment: By Howard Pyle, 1814; U.S. Library of Congress, Washington, DC (USZ62-75535/75537)

# 1

# "THE SILLIEST DAMNED WAR"

## A CURIOUS AFFAIR

Quite simply, the War of 1812 was a curious affair. Had the war been lost, it is possible Americans would have once again become British subjects. Had it been won, it is possible Canada would be part of the United States. But it ended in a costly and complicated tie.

At the time it was fought it was also disparagingly referred to as "Mr. Madison's War," a reference to President James Madison who, ironically enough, tried to avoid the war. President Harry S. Truman was even less charitable in his description of the conflict, deeming it, with characteristic bluntness, to be "the silliest damned war we ever had." It has even been hailed as America's "Second War for Independence." Interestingly, all three descriptions of the war are accurate. What is inaccurate is the title. It was a war that lasted two-and-one-half years but was named for only one of them. It can also be said that the War of 1812 is perhaps America's least well known war.[1]

America's "forgotten war" is one that should be remembered for several reasons. It was, simultaneously, one of the most unusual, one of the most unnecessary, and one of the most important wars in the country's history. As such, it was a war of great contradictions and ironies. At the highest levels of government and military leadership on both sides of the conflict, cowardice and incompetence undermined the sacrifices of the soldiers and sailors who did the fighting. Yet, the war produced several remarkable heroes and was the proving grounds for seven future American presidents. It also marked the only time that an invading enemy fought its way deep into American territory and even burned the building known today as the White House. Indeed, President Madison was within a battle or two of losing the United States. The War of 1812 was therefore America's most dangerous war.

It was a war fought by an inexperienced American army supplemented by undisciplined state militias. In addition to the destruction of forts and deaths of thousands of soldiers, the war's violence and mismanagement spilled over into civilian populations. Commercial ships were sunk, peaceful villages sacked, and unarmed locals harassed. On numerous occasions, marauding armies turned women, children, and the aged out of their homes in the middle of the night and dead of winter. On the frontier, surrendering soldiers were massacred in cold blood by Indian warriors allied with both sides. Even the capitals of both the United States and Upper Canada were put to the torch during the war. Such hostilities and tit-for-tat raids against civilian populations by both armies marred any glory from the fighting.

## ESCALATING TENSIONS

The War of 1812 was a rematch of the war for American independence, pitting the new nation against her former colonial master. As was the case during the first conflict, the American and British people were divided in their views about the necessity of war. Most people living in Britain had suffered through shortages of food and other essential products on account of the Napoleonic wars in Europe at the dawn of the nineteenth century. By necessity, commerce and trade were restricted by the ongoing conflict and the prospect of another war in North America meant further sacrifices and additional restrictions. Therefore, even though relations between the two nations remained strained ever since the Revolutionary War and some military and political leaders in Britain longed to exact revenge on the former colonies (and others even wished to reclaim them), many Britons did not want war.

President Thomas Jefferson and his successor, James Madison, also sought to avoid war. But the matter of "impressment"—the act of Britain forcing American sailors into service with the Royal Navy—undermined any goodwill between the two nations. Because Britain viewed no country as neutral in their war with Napoleon, they believed they had the right to stop any ship on the seas and search it. This included American ships which were searched and seized for goods that might be traded with France and for British subjects who were sailing with American crews.

Having coastal ports and communities blockaded by the powerful British navy did little to quell the drumbeat for war. Yet, the blockade was seen by the British as a necessary outgrowth of the policy to blockade France's ports from 1803 to 1807. In fact, after 1805, in what was known as the "Essex Decision," Britain unilaterally decreed that the United States could not trade with France. In 1807, a faction of conservative Tories came to power in Britain and imposed even tougher trade restrictions on France and neutral nations, all in an effort to starve opponents into submission.[2] At the same time, Napoleon's fleet was struggling with blockades of the French coast and British naval power on the open seas, so the emperor demanded that neutral nations boycott British goods and attempted to interfere with anyone who traded with Britain. The United States found itself caught in the middle of a growing "crisis in foreign affairs."[3]

Tensions between the two nations had also been escalating over British efforts to incite Indian raids on the American frontier. Attacks against white settlers on the frontier fueled anti-British sentiment across the land, just as the blockades and impressment angered villages up and down the eastern seaboard. America's eagerness to expand westward was threatened, while coastal communities dependent on shipping for their livelihood suffered mightily. Even so, war was avoidable.

Most American sailors hailed from New England. Yet, these states and their northern neighbors generally opposed going to war with Britain. The war's early rally cry of "Free trade and sailor's rights!" failed to move most northern citizens to arms. Only in the South and on the frontier—ironically, the regions least impacted by the trade restrictions and impressment—was there real passion for war. To be sure, it was British policies that caused the war, but the inflammatory rhetoric of Congressman Henry Clay of Kentucky and his coalition of frontier and southern "War Hawks," played into American fears and passions while undercutting the voices of reason and peace. Indeed, these warmongers demanded that President Madison punish Britain while also using the "British problem" as an excuse to invade Canada. Some politicians from the frontier-southern war coalition even advocated attacking and invading other countries.

Americans had many legitimate complaints about British policies—impressment of American sailors, seizing American commercial ships, and provoking Indian raids in the frontier. Any one of these may have constituted grounds for war, but there was, until the final moment, an opportunity to avoid a war the United States was ill-prepared to fight. But Henry Clay and his fellow hot-heads were in no mood for negotiation or peace. Said Henry Adams, the noted historian: "Many nations have gone to war in pure gayety of heart, but perhaps the United States were first to force themselves into a war they dreaded, in the hope that the war itself might create the spirit they lacked."[4]

Indeed, neither nation desired war, but both foolishly "drifted" into it. In Britain, one misguided and heavy-handed decision followed another. In America, cooler heads nearly prevailed. But war came.[5]

# 2

# STUMBLING TOWARD WAR

## WAR PREPARATIONS?

In the year 1812, the United States was utterly and completely unprepared for war. As of that January, the army consisted of only about 4,000 poorly-trained and ill-equipped soldiers. With conflict already simmering both on the seas against the British and on the frontier against several Indian nations, war seemed imminent. The time for preparation had come and gone, and yet it took until that same winter before Congress hesitantly authorized funds to increase the size of the military to just over 35,000 troops. Rather than rely almost entirely on state militias, which during the American Revolution proved to be problematic, Congress and the War Department wisely decided to enlist soldiers for five-year tours of duty. Yet, because of gross incompetence by the War Department and Congress, virtually nothing happened.[1]

There also remained considerable opposition to the idea of a large, standing Federal army among some states' rights advocates, southern and frontier politicians, and a few governors. Ironically, many of them were the same War Hawks who agitated for war. Remarkably, representatives in Congress from these regions refused to fund the war they sought!

By the spring of 1812, the Army was still a third-rate fighting force incapable of even defending a single state, much less the vast wilderness that separated the United States from Canada, the lengthy eastern seaboard, and the western border. So Congress began debating emergency, single-year enlistments. That April, Congress authorized the President to add 15,000 soldiers serving eighteen-month tours to the Army. Governors were also asked to increase the size of state militias. Some complied and some did not. As a result, as the nation stumbled toward war that summer, troop strength was still less than 7,000 regulars.

Things were no better on the seas. The Navy had only five frigates, three sloops, and seven brigs, along with a handful of gunboats and glorified dinghies manned by approximately 4,000 sailors. President James Madison, who struggled to prevent war while simultaneously trying to prepare for it, was in a pinch. He asked Congress to fund the immediate acquisition of a dozen large warships and twenty new frigates. However, the same War Hawks who beat the drums for war in Congress once again voted down the request.[2]

Madison also had to contend with logistical limitations and political opposition for the war at home. In 1812, the country was less a nation than a loose collection of eighteen sparsely populated states, each one an independent entity. In some instances, political leaders did not even want men from their home states fighting under the command of an officer from another state, or for the militia from another state to march through their state. When the United States declared war and attempted to invade Canada, many of her citizens opposed the war, while militiamen from New York and New England refused the orders of commanders to march into Canada, instead remaining on the American side of the border or simply abandoning their units to return home. Many northern and New England merchants and shippers in the region refused to stop trading with Britain or Canada, believing there was more to lose than to gain from the fighting.

Some astute American politicians opposed war with Britain because of Napoleon, viewing the British as the only thing that stood between the ambitious dictator, who had designs on Louisiana and the American West, and being overrun themselves. Britain was the lesser of the two evils. President Thomas Jefferson, although leery of both the British and French, even referred to Napoleon as "The Attila of the age."[3] Similarly, some British politicians and military planners favored a peaceful alliance with the United States as yet another way to oppose France and Napoleon, which they rightly saw as a far more lethal threat than the upstart Americans. Parliament even debated the repeal of impressment and normalization of trade with the United States. Had they done so, war might have been prevented.

Unfortunately, such rational voices on both sides were in the minority. The only good news for the Americans, who were utterly unprepared for war, was that British forces in Canada were equally unprepared for war.

## BRITAIN'S CANADA

When the war started, Britain had just shy of 4,500 troops in her vast Crown colony on America's northern border. The under-manned British forces in Canada, like their American opponents, lacked proper armaments and sufficient amounts of food and supplies. Canada was simply not a priority for the British, who instead focused on their massive military mobilization in continental Europe in order to defeat Napoleon. Britain's more serious conflict closer to home took precedent even when some British commanders in Canada warned that French Canadians and recent immigrants from the United States might side with America or welcome their southern neighbors into Canada. One or more Canadian provinces could be lost. [4] But, across the "pond," the War of 1812 was viewed, in the words of one historian, as a "sideshow."[5] For Americans, this was good fortune. Had the British brought the full capabilities of their military to bear on the unprepared states, America likely would have been crushed in 1812 and may even have ceased to be a nation.

Canada was, of course, an immense nation with a very small population scattered among the thickly forested countryside. As such, the matter of how Britain would defend the large, unprotected border with the United States was of great concern among British and Canadian politicians and generals. Likewise, the logistics of moving an army through the vast wilderness—one full of mosquitoes, rivers, mountains, wild animals, hostile Indians, and very cold, snowy winters—was worrisome. This liability would, ironically, later prove to be an asset. The Canadian wilds limited the mobility of the invading American army too.

While some Britons believed America's grand experiment in democracy would end bitterly in "mobocracy," a vocal faction in America were angered that Britain still controlled Canada. They had always worried that the British might try to re-conquer America from Canada. It did not help allay concerns when Britain delayed by a decade their agreement to withdraw from outposts along the American side of the Great Lakes. Ever since the end of the Revolutionary War, both nations eyed the vast and rich American West.[6]

## A CONTINENTAL CRISIS

The War of 1812 marked America's first invasion of another country—Canada. Much of the war took place in and along the Canadian border, particularly in Ontario, which was then known as "Upper Canada." Some Americans, including President Thomas Jefferson and Congressman Henry Clay, believed that an invasion of Canada would be a matter of the American military simply marching north. Clay's fellow Kentuckians even boasted that the Kentucky militia could claim victory simply by showing up. They were wrong.

The invasion turned out to be anything but easy. The American military lost many battles, including several decisive and disastrous ones. By the end of the war, American forces were not only pushed out of Canada but were fighting for the very survival of their own nation against a vastly superior British army, fresh off victory over Napoleon in Europe. The zealous fever of invasion that swept much of the rural American South and frontier would soon be silenced when the country found itself facing invading armies from its northern and southern borders and on the Chesapeake in the heart of the nation. By 1814, when the British marched on the capital city of Washington, America was fighting for her very existence. Remarkably, during the course of the war, there would be a total of thirteen invasions of the United States and Canada by the two warring sides.[7]

It was also a continent-wide conflict. Fighting raged in the American "northwest" near Lakes Huron and Michigan. Armies crossed the Canadian border, up and down the Niagara and St. Lawrence Rivers, and battled on Lakes Champlain, Erie, and Ontario. The hostilities stretched southward to the Chesapeake Bay and even to the mouth of the mighty Mississippi River. There were naval engagements throughout the Atlantic and far reaches of the Pacific Ocean, as warships from the United States and Britain engaged one another in waters by the Azores, Brazil, British Guyana, Cuba, and Ireland. And yet, most battles had little or no impact on one another. In fact, because of rudimentary communication and transportation systems as well as incompetence by many generals and admirals, most soldiers and even many commanders had no idea what was happening in those other theaters of operation.

Another casualty of the war was the future of the First Americans on the continent. American Indian nations, often in conflict with one another and divided over their loyalties to the two warring powers, found themselves in the middle of the fighting. As the war spread, entire Indian nations were pushed off ancestral lands and survivors were ultimately forced to pick sides. It was a no-win situation for Indian leaders. This war also took the life of the great Indian unifier, Tecumseh. With his death during a battle against the American army, any hope of Indian self-determination and intertribal cooperation on the continent vanished.

The United States found itself on the receiving end of much of the fighting. However, after getting badly beaten in countless battles, the war ended with a string of triumphant American victories. Ironically, perhaps the most decisive and glorious American victory—the Battle of New Orleans—occurred in January of 1815. But, because news that a peace treaty had been signed had yet to arrive, this final battle actually occurred after the war had officially ended!

By the end of the conflict, many had forgotten why the war was fought in the first place and the issue of impressment, which started the war, was not even a part of the peace negotiations that ended the war.

# 3

# THE CHESAPEAKE AFFAIR

## FIRST SHOTS

The first shots of the war were fired not in 1812, but in 1807. It all started with the attack on the American warship the USS *Chesapeake*. When the war commenced a few years later, outrage over the attack and the British attitude that it could board American ships at will, were among the main sparks that ignited the conflict. The circumstances surrounding the attack involved the British policy of "impressment."

Throughout the early 1800s, British warships sailed just off the coast of the United States, often anchoring in American waters. They even brazenly sailed within sight of the capital city, cruised along the coast of Maryland and Virginia, and through the Chesapeake into the Potomac River. British warships blocked U.S. trade routes, harassed commercial ships, and seized American sailors suspected by the Royal Navy of being British citizens. The Royal Navy claimed they had the right to do as they pleased on the high seas. Respect for the integrity of American ships was nonexistent. The British simply boarded American ships at will. Permission was not requested from British naval commanders to board U.S. ships and to refuse a request to be boarded and searched was to risk being fired upon. The captured American sailors were then pressed into the service of His Majesty's Royal Navy or a British commercial ship.

The most infamous seizure of a ship under Britain's impressment policy occurred a few years before the War of 1812. It was in June of 1807 in the second term of Thomas Jefferson's presidency.

The HMS *Melampus*, a heavily armed warship, was part of a larger squadron of British ships anchored off the mouth of Chesapeake Bay. The *Melampus* was waiting for a French warship which had taken shelter in the American port during a storm. Although the United States was neutral in

12

the Anglo-Franco conflict raging in Europe and on the world's oceans, the presence of a British warship in American waters smacked of aggression. While the *Melampus* awaited their French foe in early June of 1807, several of her own crew members appear to have deserted. The British claimed the sailors even confiscated one of the captain's rowboats in the process.

The deserters, it was alleged, made their way to the Washington Naval Yards to work. Meanwhile, in nearby Norfolk, the frigate USS *Chesapeake* was being readied for service against the Barbary pirates who had been attacking western shipping in the Mediterranean Sea. It was rumored that three of the deserters from the *Melampus*—Daniel Martin, John Strachan ("Strahan" in some historical documents), and William Ware—made their way to the *Chesapeake* to enlist with the crew of the American warship. Based on this hearsay, the Royal Navy formally demanded that the men turn themselves in or that U.S. authorities give them up.[1]

In response to British demands, the U.S. State Department, which dealt with such maritime claims and cases of impressment, made inquiries into the matter of the three deserters. Their finding was that Strachan had likely been born in Maryland, while Martin was taken to Massachusetts from Britain at the age of six and had served for an unspecified period of time as an indentured servant. The third man, Ware, who was black, had been born in either Maryland or Massachusetts. All three men claimed to have been pressed into service against their will by the Royal Navy. Because they all had some legal grounds to claim U.S. citizenship, Secretary of State James Madison rejected the Royal Navy's demand. America would not hand the men over and Madison also ruled that the three men be allowed to serve as crewmembers aboard American ships, including the USS *Chesapeake*.[2]

The case of the deserters from the *Melampus* took on a sense of urgency. From his command in Nova Scotia, Vice Admiral George Cranfield Berkeley, the British commander in Canada, had just distributed orders throughout his fleet that all British warships were to detain and search American ships, especially those in and around the Chesapeake Bay. One of the ships that received the orders was the HMS *Leopard*, a powerful, 56-gun frigate commanded by Captain Salisbury P. Humphreys.

The *Leopard*, with orders to seize and search American ships, arrived off the U.S. coast on June 21, 1807. As fate would have it, the next day the *Chesapeake* set sail for an extended tour to the Mediterranean. A 38-gun frigate, the USS *Chesapeake* was a capable ship captained by Charles Gordon. It also served as the flagship of Commodore James Barron's command, which included a small squadron of ships patrolling the pirate-infested southern Mediterranean and North African coast. Accordingly, the *Chesapeake* was a high-profile ship on an important mission. However, as soon as the *Chesapeake* sailed out of port it was hunted by the HMS *Leopard*. The incident that followed would change history.

## TOTAL WAR

Impressment had a long history, but the roots of the crisis plaguing American shipping in the early 1800s can be traced to Britain's war with the French emperor Napoleon Bonaparte. The conflict ran from 1793 until 1802. Then, after a brief reprieve in 1803, war broke out again and continued through the start of the War of 1812.

Napoleon had made himself emperor of France and was intent on conquering most of Europe. Indeed, through the early 1800s he appeared to be well on his way to accomplishing this goal. The French were on the march across Europe and the British found themselves fighting Napoleon in Portugal, Spain, France, and elsewhere. France also won important battles against the Austrian and Russian armies at Austerlitz; they defeated the Prussians at Jena, and beat the Russians at Friesland. All of Europe continued to be pulled into the war, which also spilled over into Britain's relations with the United States.[3]

In late 1806, Napoleon issued the Berlin Decree, stating that all commerce with Britain from any country was heretofore illegal. His Milan Decree a year later deemed any ship that traded with Britain or even visited a British port to be an enemy of France and could be seized or attacked. King George III and Parliament responded with Orders in Council, a series of rules that established a massive naval blockade. It sealed off ports throughout Europe and required all foreign shipping to stop at British ports or trade first with Britain. It also placed customs on shipping. This blockade was aimed at French shipping, but had the effect of also denying neutral ships from loading or unloading goods in any port controlled by the French or a port that might benefit Napoleon's war efforts. In effect, it was "total war" and all British policies—including impressment—were in the service of the effort to defeat the emperor. The British and French forced the world to pick sides and the continent-wide war took on global dimensions.

These policies worked in concert with the longstanding "Rule of 1756," which recognized the necessity of cutting off trade with an enemy and limiting an enemy's ability to trade on the seas. American traders had been making money off the conflict in Europe, selling cotton, grain, tobacco, wheat, and wood to both the British and French militaries. As such, U.S. ships were targeted by both warring nations: They were forced to pay customs, were denied trade and safe harbor, and were boarded by British warships looking to press sailors into the service of the Royal Navy.

Such provocations were not entirely new—British and French ships had long harassed American ships. Most governments recognized the right of ships to search for contraband on the high seas. The Barbary pirates routinely demanded ransoms from ships off the coast of North Africa. However, the frequency and boldness of British impressment of U.S. sailors humiliated and angered Americans, and the bad blood between the former colony and the Crown increased.

## IMPRESSMENT

The grand economic blockades by Britain and France were very expensive for their taxpayers. They also required very large navies. As a result, the Royal Navy was strengthened to more than 1,000 ships. But there was still the matter of Britain finding enough sailors. The Royal Navy had roughly 150,000 sailors and it needed every one of them to defeat Napoleon and sustain a global blockade. But Britain could not crew her ships solely with volunteers. As such, they pursued a policy of impressment on the world's oceans. On the eve of the War of 1812, President James Madison reported that, from November of 1807 until June of 1812, Britain had seized 389 American ships and the French had stopped 558 American vessels. However, the French did not press U.S. sailors into service.[4]

Despite the contempt for impressment, some in America accepted the practice, especially those living in port cities where deserters from the Royal Navy were seen as competing for American jobs. British sailors were far better trained, which made them more attractive to U.S. commercial shippers. Life in the Royal Navy was brutally tough and sailors were often away from home for months or years at a time. British law allowed for any able-bodied man to be drafted for service and the Royal Navy worked its sailors mercilessly. As such, British sailors preferred service aboard an American ship and were willing to work for lower wages.[5]

At the same time, even though the Royal Navy needed the recruits, many British captains were less than enthusiastic about impressment.

Believing that foreign sailors were undisciplined, disloyal, and less willing to fight for Britain than their own British crews, some officers in the Royal Navy opposed the policy.

American ships, by law, carried lists of crew members that included their names and places of birth. However, these lists were ignored by British captains and boarding parties, who displayed contempt for American laws and claimed the certificates of American citizenship were oftentimes frauds. It was joked that it was "by no means uncommon for a man with blue eyes and sandy hair to carry about with him a collector's certificate describing a mulatto."[6] American law during the late eighteenth and early nineteenth centuries allowed people to become full citizens after only a few years of residency. It also permitted citizens to leave the country and vacate their citizenship. British law was not as accommodating. Even if countries had naturalization laws to make someone their citizen, the Crown believed that "once an Englishman, always an Englishman." An individual could not simply or willfully abandon citizenship; only the monarch could sever the allegiance.

At the same time, when a British warship was short-handed, the captain would simply pursue another country's ship. After firing a warning shot, a British boarding party known as a "press gang" was dispatched in a rowboat to grab any suspected deserters. British warships had standing orders for interrogations and impressment, which included detailed guidelines for interrogating sailors. In all, there were thirty-four questions, each with several sub-questions, required of this excessively bureaucratic order. They read:

> Any person . . . shall be seized or taken as Prize by any of His Majesty's Ships or Vessels, which have or shall have Commissions or Letters of Marque and Reprisals, concerning such captured Ships, Vessels, or any Goods, Wares, and Merchandizes on board the same. . . .

The interrogation included such questions as: Where were you born? Where have you lived? Are you married? Where does your family reside? Were you present at the time of the taking of the ship? Was the ship seized? Were guns fired in capture? Who is the commander of the ship? What is the ship's tonnage? What is the name of ship? How long was it at sea?[7]

These press gangs also routinely went ashore to round up such unwilling "recruits" as drunks at pubs, inmates at jails, and customers at brothels.

Many of the new recruits were Americans. It is impossible to determine an accurate number, but it is probable that thousands of Americans were forced into the service of the Royal Navy during the years leading up to the War of 1812. Making matters worse, the press gangs did not require a trial, compensation, or notification of the U.S. authorities.

President Jefferson condemned impressment, Secretary of State Madison called it "abominable," and John Quincy Adams was so appalled by his political party (the Federalists) for attempting to appease the British that he switched and became a Democratic-Republican in part because of the issue.[8] Naturalization was thus an ongoing point of political disagreement between the Americans and British, with the Crown refusing to recognize the citizenship that any foreign nation might bestow on British subjects.[9]

And so it was when a few sailors deserted from the HMS *Melampus*.

# 4

# "LEOPARDIZED"

## GENERAL QUARTERS

Tensions between the Royal Navy and U.S. sailors came to blows on June 22, 1807. Around mid-day, the HMS *Leopard* intercepted the USS *Chesapeake* off the Virginia coast as she sailed past Cape Henry. The British warship signaled the American frigate to "heave to" and sent a messenger on a small boat who delivered an order stating that American ships were to be boarded and searched for deserters. The ranking officer of the *Chesapeake*, Commodore Barron, pleaded ignorance of the entire matter and refused the demand by his British counterpart, ordering the British messenger and boarding party off his ship. Barron then issued the call for "general quarters," preparing the ship for battle. However, he did so "without the beat of the drum" so as to not alarm the British. His order also lacked the urgency that it should have had and the *Chesapeake*, unlike the *Leopard*, did not fully prepare for battle. Both commanders—Barron and Humphreys—proceeded to engage in a shouting match from their respective ships, speaking into "trumpets," as early bullhorns were called.[1]

Shockingly, Commodore Barron, who was a veteran of the Barbary pirate campaigns, was sailing with his gun ports closed even after observing the *Leopard* pursuing him and despite rumors that American ships were being boarded. He failed to take the necessary precautions or alter his course to avoid engagement. In short, the *Chesapeake* was utterly unprepared to fight, its decks cluttered with supplies still being stored for the long voyage to the Mediterranean.

After the British boarding party had rowed back to the *Leopard*, her captain ordered a warming shot be fired across the *Chesapeake's* bow. After no response from Commodore Barron, the British warship unloaded several broadsides into the *Chesapeake*. The *Chesapeake*, still sailing without its cannons readied or with armed marines on deck at the ready, was hit hard.[2]

Three American sailors were killed instantly and another eighteen were injured—eight of them seriously so. One of those wounded was Commodore Barron. The *Chesapeake* had sustained serious damage. Perhaps because of his injuries, Barron quickly struck his colors, indicating his surrender. One of the few crew members in Barron's command who reacted was Lieutenant W. H. Allen, who grabbed hot coal and ran with it in order to light one of the cannons to fire back at the *Leopard*. But the *Chesapeake* struck her colors without firing back.

The victorious British commander, Captain Humphreys, ordered a second boarding party to search for the suspected deserters—Martin, Strachan, and Ware. It was successful. The British returned from the crippled American warship having taken three men they claimed were the deserters and a fourth prisoner named John Wilson, who went by the alias Jenkin Ratford and had often boasted that he had escaped from the British. After the *Leopard* sailed back to the base at Halifax, Wilson, a British subject, was hanged.

Captain Humphreys wisely did not take the *Chesapeake* as a prize. To do so might have started the war in 1807. Rather, he let it float dead in the water. The leaking wreck was repaired enough to sail under her own power back to Hampton Roads, Virginia, her hull half full of water. The *Chesapeake*'s arrival was greeted by the Americans as a triumph, but the sight of dead sailors being carried off the ship along with their wounded commander began talk of war.

The three Americans taken from the ship were arrested and sentenced to death, but later were released in an effort by the British to downplay the entire incident, which by then had received condemnation from both sides of the Atlantic. Britain was forced to disavow the actions of the commander of the *Leopard* and both Captain Humphreys and Vice Admiral Berkeley, who issued the orders to seize deserters, were recalled by the Crown. They came under intense criticism back in Britain and Humphreys was formally reprimanded. Although Britain scaled back its seizure and impressment policies, the Royal Navy did not offer restitution and refused to abandon such efforts.[3]

## POURING SALT IN AN OPEN WOUND

President Jefferson demanded an apology and reparations. Secretary of State Madison acted on Jefferson's order, meeting with the British minister to the United States, David Montague Erskine, to work out some resolution for the attack and a possible repeal of the Orders in Council for impressment. Madison even pushed to resume normal trade with Britain. However, just when it appeared progress might be made and an understanding reached that could have averted continued hostilities, the Crown recalled their minister.

The man they replaced him with was Francis James Jackson, possibly the worst man for the task of diplomacy. It was none other than the notorious Jackson who, in 1807, had overseen the burning of the entire Danish fleet at Copenhagen by the Royal Navy rather than risk it being captured by Napoleon, earning for him the nickname "Copenhagen Jackson" by the American press. Jackson proved to be crude, belligerent, and unwilling to offer any resolution to the problem. Ultimately, Jackson was replaced and the new British minister did arrange for reparations for the *Chesapeake*, but not before further eroding any sense of goodwill between the two nations. The damage had been done.

Once the furor over the attack on the *Chesapeake* quieted down, Americans expressed disgust with Commodore Barron's lack of preparation for battle and his cowardice. Critics wondered why such a powerful warship was unprepared for engagement, did not attempt to flee, and was unwilling to fight. Barron was tried for neglect of duty, convicted, and removed from command for five years. It was a far lighter sentence than most thought he deserved.[4] Barron would later challenge to a duel and kill one of the war's most heroic naval commanders who rightly questioned his actions.

Another of Barron's critics was a young naval officer named Oliver Hazard Perry who, during the coming war, would distinguish himself as one of the great naval heroes of American history. Itching for a fight, Perry declared:

> The utmost spirit prevails throughout the United States in preparing for an event which is thought inevitable, and our officers wait with impatience for the signal to be given to wipe away the stain which the misconduct of the one has cast on our flag.[5]

It was later discovered that only one of the men seized by the Royal Navy that fateful day had truly been a British deserter. Many Americans would not forget the brazen attack. Similar to the cry "Remember the Alamo!" American sailors remembered the *Chesapeake* and American naval officers vowed never again to be "Leopardized."[6]

The *Chesapeake* was later repaired and would eventually play a role in the war with Britain. Meanwhile, U.S. ships and their commanders learned their lesson and began preparing for confrontations with the Royal Navy. Indeed, the *Leopard*'s attack did more to unite the nation than any act or individual since George Washington. Had cooler heads not prevailed, the War of 1812 might very well have been the War of 1807. But war was averted, for the time being.

## EMBARGO

Although President Thomas Jefferson deserves praise for avoiding war with Britain over the *Chesapeake* incident, his response to it and the larger matter of impressment did not succeed in repairing tensions between the two nations. Jefferson only delayed the call to arms and his policies ultimately hurt the American economy. Complained Jefferson of the attack on the USS *Chesapeake* and the prospect of war:

> God knows, [the British have] given us cause for war before; but it has been on points which would not have united the nation. But now they have touched a chord which vibrates in every heart.[7]

Even John Adams, whose northern Federalists generally opposed the idea of war, affirmed that "No nation can be Independent which suffers her Citizens to be stolen from her at the discretion of the Navy or military officers of another."[8] Nevertheless, knowing the country was unprepared for war with the most powerful military on earth, Jefferson temporarily stopped the mad rush to war. The American military needed training, ships, men, and guns. But, reasoned Jefferson, it had the advantage of time. The President maintained that Britain's conflict with France would, over time, weaken and distract them. So, Jefferson initially tried to downplay the *Chesapeake* affair in order to buy himself time. The course the President preferred involved negotiations with the British, but the talks floundered and his own countrymen demanded a more muscular response.

Congress was also split as to whether or not to go to war over the attack on the *Chesapeake* and the ongoing crisis of impressment. The

Foreign Affairs Committee in the U.S. House of Representatives debated a bill leveling a fine of $1,000 on any commander of an American warship harboring foreign sailors in his crew. The bill was seen as a possible means of avoiding conflict but was defeated by a single vote in Congress.[9]

As an alternative to war, Jefferson and his secretary of state and successor as president, James Madison, used trade and the economy as weapons against the British. On December 22, 1807, the Embargo Act was signed into law. It forbade any trade with Britain and prohibited any American ship to embark for a British port or any British ship to use an American port. The new law also made illegal all international trade. Jefferson's intention was to resolve the impressment and seizure controversies by having the British and French (and by proxy, the world) recognize the necessity of trading with the United States. Because their economies benefited by trading with the United States, Jefferson suggested, the British and French would come to the negotiating table to discuss America's right to trade and the rights of American sailors. Neither happened.[10]

## A MINI COLD WAR

The United States was also dependent on shipping. The fledgling nation produced very few of the products and goods it needed. Farmers bought their plows and seed from Britain and exported their crops to Britain, while merchants imported everything from paint and iron to paper and ink. The economies of regions such as New England and most coastal communities were completely tied to trade and shipping. For them the embargo was a disaster. Trade collapsed, imports dropped precipitously, and, paradoxically, many Americans sought ways around the embargo. They traded illegally with the same folks they claimed to despise. A black market flourished as did the practice of piracy. American ships resorted to "sneaking out" at night, hiding goods destined for Europe under their own supplies, or stating they were headed to other U.S. ports only to "get blown off course" and end up in the Caribbean, at a European port, or at a prearranged, mid-sea rendezvous with a British or French trader.[11]

It also hurt Britain. A relatively small, resource-poor island, Britain needed meats, hardwoods, furs, and other natural resources from America. Its merchants needed the profits they enjoyed from selling their goods to America and the British people, suffering from shortages of food and products, pleaded for the embargoes to be lifted. The Crown and Parliament refused to do so.

The embargoes also only heightened citizens' distrust of the British. The United States and Britain had signed a peace treaty after the American Revolution, which began in 1775 and ended in 1783. Yet, many Americans remained angry at the British long after the war and despite the treaties. Some even felt Britain should abandon the continent entirely, while other Americans—particularly those in the South and western regions—long wanted to annex Canada, an area they felt should have been conquered during or after the American Revolution. Some even wanted Mexico too.[12] Despite the threats and temptations on both sides of the conflict, however, the United States officially chose to ignore the British and French maritime decrees and remain neutral. For the time being.[13]

The embargo was repealed by Congress in 1809, during the final days of Jefferson's presidency. It was replaced with the Non-Intercourse Act, a less aggressive prohibition on trade that pertained only to Britain and France. Jefferson sought compromise, but it did not sit well with anyone. Southern and western War Hawks, wanting more, continued to saber rattle, while northern merchants continued to feel the economic pinch even under the limited embargo.[14] The Non-Intercourse Act expired in 1810, during James Madison's second year in office. Madison shared Jefferson's views on the handling of the crisis. Thus, when France revoked its policies, Madison revoked the Non-Intercourse policy on France. But Madison was criticized by the War Hawks for acting too quickly and for what they saw as weakness, and by northern Federalists for trusting Napoleon. It was an impossible situation that would continue until war was declared.[15]

## SWEET REVENGE

Real satisfaction for America came in May of 1811 when Commodore John Rodgers, commanding the American frigate USS *President*, won a naval engagement with a British warship. The confrontation occurred roughly four years after the USS *Chesapeake*'s deadly encounter with the HMS *Leopard*.

The impetus for the naval battle was the actions of the British warship HMS *Guerriere*, which seized an American commercial ship off the coast of New York. As per British protocol, the *Guerriere* sent a "press gang" to board the American craft and pressed into service an American sailor from Maine. Captain Rodgers heard about the incident and ordered the *President* to hunt the *Guerriere*. Soon afterward, the crew of the *President* spotted a British warship and gave pursuit. Rodgers caught the ship he thought to be the *Guerriere* outside New York harbor at night. However, in the darkness, Rodgers had followed the wrong ship. The ship turned out to be the HMS *Little Belt*, a British sloop. It did not matter to Rodgers.

When the *Little Belt* fired a broadside at the larger American warship, Rodgers ordered his massive guns to open fire. The powerful *President* easily bested the *Little Belt*, inflicting serious damage to the extent that the sloop could not fight back. Nine of her sailors were dead and another twenty-three wounded. It was a decisive victory for the Americans. Rodgers wisely did not sink his foe. Rather, he offered the ship assistance but the proud British captain refused. Rodgers then allowed the *Little Belt* to repair herself and limp back to Halifax.

The American public rejoiced at the news of the *President*'s victory, even if it was against the wrong ship. Many saw it as long overdue retribution for the *Chesapeake* affair. But, the conflict only falsely emboldened the United States and angered Britain, constituting a loud drum beat by both sides for war.

However, the roots of the war can be traced to events a decade prior.

# DRUMBEATS

*"The Hummingbird" ("The Way to Avoid War")*

*The only way to keep off war,*
*And guard 'gainst persecution*
*Is always to be well prepar'd*
*With hearts of resolution.*
*Yankee Doodle, let's unite,*
*Yankee Doodle dandy;*
*As patriots still maintain our rights,*
*Yankee Doodle dandy.*

—Song written in Boston in 1798
and sung before and during the War of 1812

"The Prophet at the Battle of Tippecanoe." Acknowledgment: By Alonzo Chappel, 1859; U.S. Library of Congress, Washington, DC (USZ62-52118)

# 5

# LAND, EMPIRE, AND INTRIGUE

## GROWING PAINS

In 1787, even as the U.S. Constitution was being debated, the Congress established the Northwest Territory, which extended from the Great Lakes to the Mississippi River. That same year, the Northwest Ordinance was created in order to provide some form of governance in the region and manage the settlement of the vast area. To qualify as a territory, the region had to have at least 5,000 men, who settled in the region and were eligible to vote. At that point, they could request to be a separate territory and, providing settlement continued and a system of government existed both loyal to and consistent with the U.S. federal government, the territory could then request to become a state.[1]

From its founding, the United States had expansionistic desires and many leaders yearned for an American empire. For instance, ever since the American Revolution there had been a strong interest to settle or take Mexico, Canada, and the West. The issue was partially addressed by the Jay Treaty of 1794, named for the Founder, John Jay, which formalized relations with Britain. Jay, a Federalist in the political mold of George Washington, John Adams, and Alexander Hamilton, favored trade and relations with the British, but prohibited British forts and soldiers on the American side of the Great Lakes. It was, thus, an early effort to establish a firm northern boundary for the United States. Obviously, it did not please everyone . . . on either side of the boundary.[2] In subsequent years, tensions arose with the British, French, Spanish, and Native Indians on the continent over the questions of expansion and settlement.

At the time of the outbreak of the War of 1812, America was a vast land with few inhabitants. No white man had stepped foot on much of the continent and little was known about regions to the west. Indeed, when Meriwether Lewis and William Clark were sent westward by Thomas Jefferson in May of 1804, it was the nineteenth-century equivalent of the moon shot. Accordingly, the famous expedition had many objectives, but among them were the tasks of surveying exactly what secrets the West held and what it was the president had just purchased.[3]

The Napoleonic war presented an opportunity for the United States. Britain was defeating France on the sea, which discouraged Napoleon from his imperialistic designs on North America. Therefore, a year prior to Lewis and Clark, France, whose army was overextended in Europe and in need of revenues, was forced to sell the Louisiana Territory to the United States. It was a massive piece of real estate, roughly one-third the size of the present United States and Napoleon sold it on the cheap—fifteen million dollars. He needed the money. Jefferson moved with much haste, signing the deal, which doubled the size of the country, on April 12, 1803. It was a land deal beyond even William Seward's purchase several decades later of Alaska or King Charles II's authorization of the Charter of the Hudson Bay Company. In all instances, critics expressed shock over what they saw as folly. They were proven wrong three times.

However, the sale did not mean that Napoleon was now disinterested in the region. Rather, there were concerns that he would simply retake it at gunpoint after he defeated the British in Europe. Others worried that the western region would be sympathetic to the emperor's cause. Still others worried that the United States would soon find itself defending the western frontier against whichever side won the war in Europe. Indeed, the entrance into the game of empire and land acquisition by the United States alarmed the British, who still had their own designs on the continent.[4]

Americans were also divided at home. Jefferson was criticized for the Louisiana Purchase, while voices in the South and on the frontier were arguing that the United States should simply seize the entire region without paying for it. During the debate over the Louisiana Purchase in the U.S. Senate, John Breckenridge warned colleagues that if the United States did not purchase Louisiana, the entire region would leave France by force and form a separate nation. Even Alexander Hamilton was looking southward and westward in the founding days of the Republic, believing that there were advantages to taking Florida and Louisiana, while also even suggesting that "we ought to squint at South America."[5]

The Louisiana Purchase was, in the course of history, a grand and glorious moment for the United States. But, in addition to greatly expanding the size of the young nation, the Purchase signaled the beginning of the end for American Indian self-determination. It also compounded tensions between North and South, as both sides debated what to do with the new territory. Political power had always been split in the United States both by political design and geographic necessity. The North/South and East/West rifts in the socioeconomic and political fabric of American society started early and festered in the years leading up to the War of 1812. Northern and Eastern interests favored a stronger role for government, including a professional military, policies to allow government to collect taxes and pay off the Revolutionary debts, and peaceful relations with the European powers predicated on trade among the many merchants and shippers who dominated elected offices in the regions. Southern and Western interests, however, preferred less government and opposed both taxes and establishing a stronger military. They did not want relations with the European powers. Rather, they hungered for empire at home and a continuation of slavery and an agricultural-based economy. The split was apparent when it came time for a vote for war, with New England Federalists in Congress voting against the war and Southern and frontier representatives voting for it. In Kentucky and South Carolina, there was even a cry for war against both Britain and France.[6]

It must also be remembered that, in the early nineteenth century, the United States was a nation in name only. A confederation in practice, it was even common at the time to write "United States" with a small letter "u" and a capital "S" as if "united" was an adjective. As early as 1792, Thomas Jefferson, then serving as secretary of state, warned President George Washington that southerners might secede over their opposition to Secretary of the Treasury Alexander Hamilton's plans for an active federal role in the economy and the assumption of the Revolutionary War debt.[7]

## THE NOTORIOUS JAMES WILKINSON

New Orleans, nestled along the Gulf of Mexico and sitting at the mouth of the Mississippi River, was a vitally important port. Accordingly, America needed—at the least—a symbolic presence in the region to deter the Spanish, French, and British, and to signal the formal acquisition of the Louisiana Territory. President Jefferson thus appointed a new governor, William Claiborne, to take control of the city on December 20, 1803, and then sent a force of 450 soldiers to occupy New Orleans. But the President made a terrible mistake that nearly undermined the entire purchase. He appointed

Brigadier General James Wilkinson to receive Louisiana from the French and then named him to head the small army garrisoned there.

If ever there was a wrong person for a job, it was Wilkinson. The general was either the most unlucky soldier in history, a victim of the worst press ever, or a real scoundrel. The answer is likely the latter. Born in Calvert County, Maryland, in 1757, a young Wilkinson intended to pursue the study of medicine. However, when the American Revolution started, he abandoned that career and joined the Continental Army. Chronically depressed and prone to fits of anger, Wilkinson had a penchant for blaming others for his failures and scheming to make money. His military career was soiled by an array of blunders and treasonous actions, not the least of which was his association with the notorious traitor General Benedict Arnold, who conspired with the British in September of 1780 to hand over the fort at West Point, New York, and thereby control the strategic Hudson River.

During the American Revolution, Wilkinson also worked for General Horatio Gates in 1777 and 1778, where he gained the title adjutant-general of the northern War Board. However, when Wilkinson was summoned by Congress to report on the success of Gates against General Burgoyne, the adjutant-general arrived late and was both disrespectful and sarcastic in his demeanor. Such behavior was not unusual for Wilkinson. However, the unworthy Wilkinson managed to be promoted to brigadier general when a miscommunication attributed the heroics of another officer to him.[8]

Wilkinson was also knee-deep in another scandal. During the autumn of 1777, a group of leading revolutionaries began conspiring to remove Washington as commander. General Gates, the esteemed physician Benjamin Rush, several hot-headed members of Congress including Samuel Adams, Thomas Mifflin, and Richard Henry Lee, as well as a foreign officer named Thomas Conway formed what is known as "The Conway Cabal." With the war going poorly, General Washington's command was at a low point. Gates's star, however, was rising. As such, Conway and his co-conspirators began promoting Gates or Conway as a replacement for Washington. Their scheming came to a head when a letter written by Conway to Gates leaked. It read: "Heaven has been determined to save your Country; or a weak General and bad Councilors would have ruined it." Conway also boasted to anyone who would listen that, "as to his [Washington's] talents for the command of an Army, they were miserable indeed."[9]

The source of the leak was a drunken James Wilkinson, who blabbed about the letter and cabal to fellow officers in Lord Stirling's (aka General Alexander) command. Stirling told Washington, who survived the attempted coup. Wilkinson managed to anger not only Washington's allies on account of his complicity in the cabal, but also the likes of General Gates and the conspirators because of his loose tongue. He also nearly lost his life when Gates challenged him to a duel. The cowardly Wilkinson declined and resigned his commission in 1778.

Discredited, Wilkinson, like many other army officers, turned his attention to the frontier. In 1784, he moved to present-day Louisville, where he was a merchant and made a considerable amount of money. Wilkinson's financial success was a result of an oath of allegiance he swore to Spain in 1787. It turns out that he was paid a substantial amount of money each year by British and Spanish agents for functioning not only as a supplier and trader of goods, but as their spy. To the Spanish, he was "Number Thirteen," a code name revealed in surviving correspondence. Wilkinson thus enjoyed preferential treatment—including trade and bribes of Spanish gold—from the Spanish and British governments to the extent that he brazenly even attempted to detach Kentucky and other western settlements from the United States and have them join either Spain or France. The corrupt former general also assisted his close friend, Vicente Folch, the Spanish governor of West Florida, in preventing the United States from annexing Florida.

In an effort to cover his tracks, in 1791 Wilkinson rejoined the army, this time with the rank of Lieutenant Colonel, and was a part of disastrous engagements against the Indians on the frontier and Louisiana Territory. Once again, despite his incompetence and deviousness, Wilkinson landed on his feet. He was promoted to brigadier general in March of 1792 and served as second in command to the famed Indian fighter, General Anthony "Mad" Wayne.

As he had done earlier in his career, Wilkinson conspired among fellow Kentuckians to supplant the command of General Wayne. He was unsuccessful. But that did not stop Wilkinson from basking in the glow of Wayne's decisive victories against the Indians in 1794. The campaign earned for Wilkinson great fame, as he was happy to claim credit for Wayne's successes. When Wayne died in 1796, it was the undeserving Wilkinson who was given command of Wayne's army. In this capacity, Wilkinson continued to pursue back-channel deals with Indians and the Spanish to benefit himself financially.

As such, it was a shock to many when Jefferson appointed Wilkinson to command the new forces at New Orleans. Wilkinson had few support-ers remaining "back East" but Jefferson liked him. It seems Wilkinson took care to endear himself to Jefferson, sending him a regular stream of complimentary letters. The corrupt general also sided with the president in his quarrels with other politicians. Jefferson continued to reward Wilkinson for his "loyalty." In 1805, he made the corrupt general both commander and governor of the region above the 33rd parallel, which was known as Upper Louisiana. It was in this capacity that Wilkinson set up headquarters in St. Louis and began conspiring to conquer Mexico and betray all of Louisiana.[10]

## A WESTERN EMPIRE . . . ONE WAY OR ANOTHER

For the task of exploring Mexico, Wilkinson dispatched a competent military officer named Zebulon Pike, who later commanded troops in the War of 1812. One of Wilkinson's ulterior motives was to design a route for his planned invasion of the Southwest. His accomplice was Aaron Burr. The two had served together during the Revolutionary War, where both were, perhaps fittingly, officers under Benedict Arnold and had participated in the disastrous campaign into Quebec.

Burr, born in 1756 in New Jersey, showed great promise as a child, even graduating from the College of New Jersey (which became Princeton) at the age of sixteen (in theology of all subjects!). By the age of twenty-one, he had distinguished himself in battle during the Revolutionary War and was a well-regarded officer, although he was involved on the periphery of the Conway Cabal and displayed troublesome characteristics.

Burr's political career included stints in the New York state legislature and the U.S. Senate. He was designated to be Jefferson's vice president in the 1800 election against incumbent President John Adams. However, due to an unforeseen glitch in the Electoral College, both Jefferson and his "running-mate" Burr, while besting Adams, ended up tied in the electoral vote. Each candidate received seventy-three votes. At the time, each elector was given two votes but could not cast them both for the same person. With little guidance from the Constitution about what to do in the event of a tie, Burr decided he would challenge Jefferson for the presidency rather than settle for vice president. And so a tie-breaker vote was held. It too ended without either candidate getting a majority. In fact, it took thirty-six ballots to break the gridlock and select a president.

It was the influence of Alexander Hamilton that partly helped break the tie. Even though Hamilton and Jefferson were avowed political enemies—the two served in Washington's cabinet, Hamilton as secretary of treasury and Jefferson as secretary of state, where they fought regularly until Jefferson resigned his position—Hamilton, like so many others including Jefferson, distrusted Burr. Thus, the ongoing Burr-Hamilton feud continued to smolder. The two men fought over politics, competed in their law practices in New York City, and even engaged in an adolescent match over who was more of a womanizer. Disgruntled and embarrassed by the 1800 election, Burr none-theless remained in the Jefferson administration as vice president until 1805. In 1804, Burr was nearly elected governor of New York but, once again, the influence of Hamilton helped defeat him and elect Morgan Lewis.[11]

Ultimately, the two men exchanged nasty words and highly public letters which led Burr to challenge Hamilton to a duel. Hamilton reluc-tantly agreed and, on July 11, 1804, in Weehawken, New Jersey, Burr shot and killed his nemesis. Even though he survived the duel, Burr's already spotty reputation took a major hit. From that point on, he was a political pariah to many.

It was then that Burr began conspiring with Wilkinson to invade Louisiana, the Southwest, and even Mexico. The two men wasted no time in accepting bribes from the Spanish and British as well as shadowy figures in the frontier. One case in point occurred on August 6, 1804, when the British ambassador to the United States, Anthony Merry, sent a commu-nication to the British foreign secretary, saying:

> I have just received an offer from Mr. Burr the actual vice president of the United States (which Situation he is about to resign), to lend his assistance to His Majesty's Government in any Manner in which they may think fit to employ him, particularly in endeavoring to effect a Separation of the Western Part of the United States from that which lies between the Atlantic and the Mountains, in its whole Extent.[12]

The conniving's of Burr and Wilkinson were about to become even more of a soap opera.

## CONSPIRATORS

Burr had completely worn out his welcome in Washington but was still admired in the West and in parts of the South, where he was hailed for his lust for empire. One of those in the West with whom Burr and Wilkinson conspired was Harman Blennerhassett, the son of English nobility, whose ancestors moved to Ireland. Blennerhassett was born in the Emerald Island in either 1764 or 1765 and married his statuesquely tall and stunningly beautiful cousin, Margaret Agnew, when she was just a teenager. Shortly after marriage, he sold his estate in Ireland and sailed to New York, arriving in August of 1786. In no time, Blennerhassett had turned his fortune into even more riches.

After visiting New York City and Philadelphia, Blennerhassett became intrigued with the American frontier and sailed on the Ohio River to a small island near Marietta that reminded him of Ireland. It was there, in 1797, that he purchased land and built a mansion. So successful was he that the area became known as Blennerhassett Island. It was also at Blennerhassett Island that the lord received visits from Aaron Burr, who enticed Blennerhassett to bankroll his plan for empire. Said Blennerhassett to his new accomplice:

> Having thus advised you of my desire and motives to pursue a change of life, to engage in any thing which may suit my circumstances . . . I should be honored in being associated with you in any contemplated enterprise you would permit me to participate in.[13]

In May and June of 1805, Burr visited Andrew Jackson in Nashville in an effort to enlist his support in the conspiracy. The man, who would later emerge as the most celebrated hero of the War of 1812, had much in common with Burr. Jackson was a fellow duelist, a believer in American manifest destiny, and a man who had abandoned the East for the frontier. Jackson also shared Burr's vision of pushing the Spanish off the Continent, especially in Florida and Texas. As such, Jackson supported Burr . . . initially. However, Jackson, like many others, soon came to distrust Burr and Wilkinson. Burr visited Jackson again in December of 1806 to calm any concerns, and it appears to have temporarily worked. He bought two boats from Jackson, and set sail to gather additional supplies and men for the invasion.

Ultimately, when the full extent of the Burr-Wilkinson plan to seize New Orleans as the beginning of a vast southern and western empire were revealed to Jackson by Burr's associate, Captain John A. Fort, the Tennessee lawyer ended his association with the two men. It was Jackson who helped unmask the two schemers by writing letters to friends and politicians in Washington informing them of the dubious plan. One of the letters Jackson penned was written to President Jefferson. Zebulon Pike, the officer sent by Governor Wilkinson to detail the path of the invasion, also betrayed Wilkinson to the president.[14]

Jefferson, worried about a full military coup by Burr and Wilkinson as well as potential damage to U.S. relations with Spain, moved quickly. He signed the Neutral Ground Agreement with Spain and ordered by presidential proclamation that New Orleans be placed under martial law. Jefferson also ordered that Wilkinson, Burr, and their accomplices in the Louisiana-Mexico empire scheme be apprehended. In 1807, Burr was arrested. Trials of Burr and a few of his co-conspirators took place in Frankfort, Kentucky, and Richmond, Virginia, where charges of treason and conspiracy for illegally raising an army were made. Burr's lawyer was Henry Clay, the powerful political leader of Kentucky, who shared Burr's vision for empire. Clay argued that no breach of law or act of violence had occurred, and ultimately the charges were dismissed. Chief Justice John Marshall, although disgusted by Burr's actions, did not feel it was truly an act of war to overthrow the Spanish in Mexico. Just five years later, Congressman Clay would trumpet the loudest call for war with Britain.

Burr's co-conspirators turned against him to save their own hides. Harmon Blennerhassett was arrested and jailed for a few weeks in Richmond. But he testified that he had no idea about Burr's grand plans for an invasion and all charges were ultimately dropped against Blennerhassett. But his reputation was soiled. During the frontier conflicts of the War of 1812, local militia seized his beloved mansion at Blennerhassett Island and destroyed much of it. Jackson, also in hot water, accused Burr of deviousness. Suggesting he was duped, Jackson fumed "I am more convinced than ever that reason never was intended by Burr, but if ever it was you know my wishes that he may be hung."[15]

Wilkinson was court-martialed and investigated by Congress. However, Wilkinson had again anticipated that his devilishness might catch up with him. The treacherous general had covered up much of his own complicity in the schemes, played all sides during the affair, and ultimately double-crossed Burr. He even served as the main witness against Burr in the trial, testifying that he helped stop Burr because of his love of country! The self-serving Wilkinson boasted, "I perceive the plot thickens; yet all but those concerned sleep profoundly. My God! What a situation has our country reached."[16]

Like a cat with nine lives, Wilkinson survived the ordeal. He even landed on his feet when Jefferson again entrusted to him the charge of governing the Louisiana Territory, the very region he tried to invade. In another incredible irony, during the War of 1812 Wilkinson commanded American forces in New Orleans. He was even promoted to Major General. However, Wilkinson could not escape his character. He would go on to preside over disastrous debacles during the war, including a botched effort to invade Montreal. Wilkinson was ultimately stripped of his command, a dishonorable end to a dishonorable career. His death was equally ironic. After his military career, Wilkinson sold his services to the American Bible Society, representing their application for a land grant in Mexico. While in Mexico City attempting to swindle the Mexican government, Wilkinson died. He passed on December 28, 1815, from a local illness he contracted after a debilitating opium addiction.

America's growing pains were apparent in the early 1800s, even if plans to invade Mexico and sell Louisiana to the Spanish or French never came to fruition. The restless lust for empire felt by many in the West and South continued to fester and the "Burr Conspiracy" was but an omen of things to come during the War of 1812.

# 6

# THE INDIAN QUESTION

## THE BEGINNING OF THE END

The so-called "Indian question" also factored into the drumbeats for war in 1812. As white settlers expanded westward they came into contact with the Indigenous inhabitants, many of whom were threatened by the rapid encroachment upon their ancestral lands. Some Indian nations on America's frontier were loyal to the British, dating from the colonial period when they fought alongside the British. Others traded with the French and preferred them as the lesser evil. This only emboldened American efforts to eradicate them.

Tragically, there were many hostile encounters on both sides, as scalping, murders, and raids become increasingly common. Settlers not only complained about their safety but alleged that it was the British who were both arming Indian communities with guns and inciting the violence on the frontier. This appears to have been the case, although the degree to which the British aided and abetted the Indians was overstated. The small British forces in Canada were very poorly equipped and, while they did trade with several Indian nations, they had only minimal armaments to sell. Nonetheless, settlers were dying on the frontier and demanding something be done. The War Hawks in Congress used this as an excuse to march on the British in Canada and against the Indians on the frontier.

The U.S. army responded with search-and-destroy missions against the Indians. One of the most famous had occurred a few years prior in 1794 when the new nation dispatched the Revolutionary War hero, General "Mad" Anthony Wayne to deal with the Indians. Deal with them he did. Wayne marched an army of roughly 1,650 regulars supplemented with almost as many members of the Kentucky militia to the present site of Ohio and Indiana to engage warriors from several Indian nations. This extensive confederation—which included the Delaware, Miami, Ottawa, and Shawnee nations—not only posed a serious threat to any white settlers in the region, but demonstrated the possibility of a grand alliance united in opposition to the expansionist tendencies of the United States.

General "Mad" Wayne's army built forts throughout the region. Then, on August 20, 1794, they met the confederation of over 1,000 warriors led by Chief Little Turtle and other chiefs. The armies clashed just north of the Maumee River in the Battle of Fallen Timbers, a site named for the trees that had been toppled by a recent tornado. Both sides suffered about 100 casualties each, but the victory was Wayne's in what has been deemed "The Last Battle of the American Revolution" because of its significance in ending the Indian threat in the region and active Indian support for the British still in Canada.[1]

The following year, the Americans negotiated the Treaty of Greenville, which reorganized the land in the region, taking much of Illinois, Indiana, Michigan, Ohio, and Wisconsin for the United States. The battle and subsequent treaty dampened British hopes for the region and marked a dark period for the Native inhabitants. It also produced a minor land rush among white settlers. By 1803, Ohio had become a state, while statehood for Indiana was pending.

The Wayne campaign would end up shaping the War of 1812 and future of the nation. Two of the participants in the conflict were a young Shawnee brave named Tecumseh and a 21-year-old officer in Wayne's army named William Henry Harrison.


# HARRISON

Born on February 9, 1773 in Virginia, William Henry Harrison was a member of one of America's foremost families. His father, Benjamin Harrison V, had signed the Declaration of Independence and served for two terms as the governor of Virginia. His ancestor, Benjamin II, served in the Virginia House of Burgesses; Benjamin III was the colony's attorney general, treasurer, and speaker of the House of Burgesses; and Benjamin IV was also a member of the House Burgesses. Despite his family lineage, young William was plain-spoken and had few hobbies or interests. Of average height, build, and intellect, he was an unremarkable youth.

William grew up on the massive family plantation, Berkeley, and was sent at the age of fourteen to study medicine at Hampden-Sydney College. But Harrison grew to dislike medicine and rejected the school's association with the Methodist faith (he was an Episcopalian). So, he transferred to the University of Pennsylvania in Philadelphia, where he studied medicine under the most celebrated physician in the country, Dr. Benjamin Rush. However, his true passion was for military history and Harrison left school to join the army in August of 1791.

Having served as General "Mad" Wayne's aide-de-camp from 1793 to 1796, Harrison was familiar with the delicate matter of the Indian question. In fact, it was a young Harrison who counseled Wayne not to rush into battles, as was his style, but rather to adopt a slow, methodical approach that relied on time and overwhelming force to defeat the Indians. It was a strategy that worked and Harrison would later take his own advice against the Indians.

Harrison's star began to rise when, in 1798, President John Adams appointed Harrison as secretary of the Northwest Territory and he also served as a delegate to the U.S. House of Representatives from the Northwest Territory in 1799 and 1800. In 1800, when Indiana became its own territory, Harrison became governor, a position he held until the start of the War of 1812.

The military officer-turned-politician quickly gained a reputation for his ability to suppress Indian rebellion and amass rich lands for white settlers and the government. Harrison shrewdly used whiskey and bribes to play one Indian nation against another, supported more pro-government tribes over their enemies, and ruthlessly intimidated tribes into forfeiting land during negotiations. In one such instance in 1809, known as the Treaty of Fort Wayne in Indiana, he managed to get leaders of the Delaware, Kickapoo, Miami, and other nations to give up millions of acres of land. Ultimately, the government bought it for less than a penny an acre in cost, along with some basic promises and a few supplies. Harrison then sold the land for dollars on the acre to settlers and farmers. Said Harrison of the enterprise in an understated tone, "I think upon the whole that the bargain is a better one than any made by me for lands south of the Wabash."[2]

All the while, Harrison was efficiently destroying any solidarity among Indians and strategically acquiring lands for settlers. However, a particular piece of land eluded Harrison. The general-governor had his eye on the Wabash River, which he called "one of the fairest portions of the globe."

Harrison was nearly fixated on this prize region. However, one Indian leader refused to cooperate.[3]

## TECUMSEH

One of the most gifted Indian leaders in history was the great Tecumseh (sometimes spelled Tecumthe, Tecumtha, or even Tecutha), which meant "shooting star" in Shawnee. Born in 1768 in a small, Shawnee Indian village near present-day Dayton in Ohio, Tecumseh had a difficult upbringing. The Shawnee had been driven out of their lands for generations, first by other Indians and later by whites. As such, they migrated long distances by necessity, settling lands from the western Carolinas and Georgia to western Pennsylvania and Ohio, and ultimately all the way to Indiana.[4]

When Tecumseh was a child, the Shawnee were fighting white settlers in the region and many from Tecumseh's village were attacked, had their crops and fields burned, or were killed. Tecumseh's own father was killed by whites in 1774 and his mother, a Muskogee Indian, abandoned him when he was only seven years old in order to relocate to Missouri with a group from the village. Consequently, Tecumseh was raised by his older sister, Tecumapease, who taught him the old ways of the Shawnee, and by his older brother, Cheeseekau, who instructed the young boy on how to fight and hunt. The young boy showed promise and was later adopted by the Shawnee chief, Blackfish.

At fourteen, Tecumseh became a warrior and participated in the Revolutionary War where he and Chief Blackfish sided with the British against the colonials. At the end of the war, he fought in the Battle of Fallen Timbers, which foreshadowed the end of Indian self-determination in the region. The consequences of the battle alarmed Tecumseh. It was also at Fallen Timbers where Tecumseh witnessed the death of an older brother, Sauwaseekau. His mentor and other older brother, Cheeseekau, was killed in a raid near Nashville in Tennessee.

While Tecumseh was raised to hate whites and certainly had ample reason to wage war against them, he was appalled by Indian atrocities against whites. Once, when taking part in a raiding party against white settlers traveling on boats down the Ohio River, he watched as a white man was tied to a stake and burned alive. Tecumseh understood the white settlers. He observed them, fought them, and as a young brave even tried to court a white woman. Tecumseh thus came to the realization that his people could not exist with the white man.[5]

As a young man, Tecumseh began using his gift for oratory to speak against war-related abuses both by and against his people. But he also began speaking out for Indian unity and self-determination. In doing so, Tecumseh found his voice and quickly emerged as a celebrated leader of his people, traveling far and wide on both raiding parties and diplomatic missions where he met chiefs of other nations. In 1792, while still a young man, Tecumseh was chosen as chief and announced his priority to oppose white settlement and rule in the Ohio River Valley. The charismatic young chief opposed treaties that gave away Indian lands and advocated the belief that the land was owned by all Indians. Therefore the land sold or bargained away by other chiefs was not theirs to give away. According to Tecumseh, all Indians needed to be consulted on such matters:

> These lands are ours, and no one has the right to remove us, because we were the first land owners, the Great Spirit above has appointed this place for us on which to light fires, and here we will remain. As to the boundaries, the Great Spirit above knows no boundaries, nor will his red people know any. . . .[6]

## THE GREAT SPIRIT AND THE GRAND CONFEDERATION

Not surprisingly, Harrison and other white leaders were disinclined to invite Tecumseh to attend many of the land and peace negotiations, and even if he was in attendance, he refused to sign or recognize the terms. Tecumseh famously broke with the "peace chiefs" at the conference to negotiate the Treaty of Greenville in August of 1795, criticizing his fellow Indians for giving away land that was not theirs to give and William Henry Harrison for taking land that was not his to take. Tecumseh never recognized any treaty, including Harrison's Treaty of Fort Wayne, which he deemed harmful to Indian sovereignty. He also spoke out against the Louisiana Purchase.

In place of white settlement, Tecumseh wanted free Indian lands from the Ohio River north through the Great Lakes and south down the Mississippi River. Because he opposed integration, these free lands, he argued, should be only for Indians. He also wanted his people to reject white culture, believing that many of his fellow chiefs were their own worst enemy. Tecumseh reminded these chiefs that they bargained away lands and their morals for the white man's alcohol, trinkets, and money. In his effort to maintain Indian culture, Tecumseh was messianic. He believed the Great Spirit of all Indians had selected him for the task.[7]

But, perhaps Tecumseh's grandest vision was for a continental Indian confederation, one based on the old ways that rejected white culture, and one capable of standing united to oppose continued white settlement. In Tecumseh's view:

> The Great Spirit said he gave this great island to his red children. He placed the whites on the other side of the big water, but they were not content with their own, and they came to take ours from us. They have driven us from the sea to the lakes: we can go no farther.[8]

With Indian nations united, Tecumseh felt he could slow or stop the expansion of whites by making it so bloody that other whites would not come west. The Great Chief needed a large alliance among warring Indian nations to accomplish this goal. He astutely observed that divided, warring Indian nations stood no chance, but recognized that white leaders were also often in disagreement with one another. Here, he drew inspiration from the fact that the British held Canada to the north, the Spanish were in Florida to the south, and there had been French influence in Louisiana. So, he reasoned, a grand alliance would allow Indians to retain control of the Mississippi River and Ohio regions.

Tecumseh had already established the "Red Stick" confederacy, an alliance of warriors who carried red war clubs and were known to use red sticks to compose a calendar.[9] But, Tecumseh needed more warriors and a broader political reach, so he traveled as far as Florida, New York, and present-day Iowa. He organized tribes into the beginnings of an alliance along the Gulf Coast and in the Northwest, convening great councils and putting to good use his natural charisma and oratorical skills. He even visited his old enemies, the Creeks, to try and unite with them.

Tecumseh's fame was growing and the idea of a grand confederation was becoming less of a dream. To some whites, Tecumseh was the Henry Clay of the Indians, a reference to the famed Kentucky politician and orator. To most others, such as William Henry Harrison, he was one of the nation's biggest threats. Tecumseh's vision would have serious ramifications on the coming war.[10]

## VINCENNES

In 1808, Tecumseh moved to Indiana with his brother, Tenskwatawa, who was known as "The Prophet" on account of his mystical ways and claim to have communicated with the "Master of Life." In Indiana, Tecumseh continued his efforts to get Indians to abandon the ways of the white man and to unite in opposition of white settlement. At the same time, Governor William Henry Harrison was expanding his conquest of the region and was interested in the fertile lands near the Wabash River. The two leaders were careening toward conflict.

To solidify his hold on Indian nations in the region and to attempt to avoid war with Tecumseh, Harrison proposed a meeting, believing he could bargain with the Shawnee chief the way he had done with other Indian chiefs. The meeting took place at Harrison's home, Grouseland, in 1810, but Tecumseh refused to recognize the legitimacy of the land treaties. Instead, he spoke of the many Indian nations that were similar to the seventeen U.S. states—which he called "seventeen fires"—that must be consulted on all matters impacting ancestral lands. Even though the two had squared off against one another at the Battle of Fallen Timbers, this face-to-face meeting resulted in a blood feud that would decide the fate of Indian self-determination on the continent during the War of 1812.

Harrison tried again one last time to persuade Tecumseh, calling for a conference at Vincennes, the capital of the territory. The meeting was held on August 12, 1810, and the Governor invited as his special guest Chief Tecumseh and no more than thirty braves. Not wanting to be caught unprepared in the event of violence, Harrison had 600 soldiers attend the meeting. During the talks, the governor offered terms to acquire Native lands for white settlement. But, Tecumseh, who showed up with an army of a few hundred warriors in a show of force, remained firm in his belief that Harrison did not have the right to buy Indian lands, just as any one Indian or even a group of them did not have the right to sell land belonging to all Native peoples. Said the great Indian leader at the Vincennes conference:

> I now wish you to listen to me. I tell you so because I alone am authorized by all the tribes to do so. I am the head of them all. We want to establish a principle that the lands should be considered common property and none sold without the consent of all.[11]

Tecumseh did more than reject Harrison at the meeting. He threatened him, demanding he cease all settlement and new surveys for land. Both knew that Tecumseh was making progress bringing together a grand Indian alliance to oppose Harrison and white settlement. Of Tecumseh, Harrison said:

> If it were not for the vicinity of the United States, he would perhaps be the founder of an empire that would rival in glory that of Mexico or Peru. No difficulties deter him. His activity and industry supply the want of letters. For four years he has been in constant motion. You see him today on the Wabash and in short time you hear of him on the shores of Lake Erie or Michigan, or on the banks of the Mississippi and wherever he goes he makes an impression favorable to his purposes. He is now upon the last round to put a finishing stroke to his work.[12]

Harrison knew he needed a treaty or military action, and needed it quickly. And he knew the first option was unlikely. But the general respected his formidable foe, describing him as follows:

> He is one of those uncommon geniuses which spring up occasionally to produce revolutions and overturn the established order of things. If it were not for the vicinity of the United States, he would perhaps be the founder of an empire. No difficulties deter him. Wherever he goes he makes and impression favorable to his purpose.[13]

The talks at Vincennes failed. The path to war was set. Tecumseh closed the meeting saying, "My brother, I do not see how we can remain at peace with you." And so it was.[14]

# TIPPECANOE AND
# THE COURSE OF HISTORY

## INDIAN ATTACKS

There were several battles with Indians during the War of 1812. Soon after the war commenced, a series of surprise Indian attacks occurred in September that harassed forts and units throughout Indiana. This was General William Henry Harrison's backyard. Harrison had for years bested numerous Indian nations in the region through both the sword and pen. So, he was not used to defeat. Moreover, at Tecumseh's urging more and more Indian nations were siding with the British.

The first of the attacks occurred on September 3, 1812 at the Pigeon Roost settlement, a small, frontier village that dated to 1809. Without detection, roughly a dozen Shawnee warriors began their raid by sneaking through the woods that surrounded the settlement. While doing so, they encountered two settlers and killed them both. Springing from the woods, the marauders then attacked three cabins at the edge of the settlement, visiting their wrath on all the occupants. Elias Payne, his wife Kesiah Bridewater, and their eight children were killed. Their relatives, Jeremiah and Sarah McCoy Payne, survived. It is likely they ran to hide in the woods. In the next cabin, John Morris along with his mother, wife, and child, were all killed. The Indian band then prepared to attack the cabin of William Collings, but Collings and his relative, Henry, counter-attacked. Their spirited defense resulted in three dead warriors. However, while William was fighting another Indian, Henry, his wife, and their seven children were killed.

The efforts by the Collings's men probably prevented the warriors from killing the remainder of the residents in the settlement. Rather, the war party set the cabins ablaze and then fled. One of the cabins they burned was the Biggs cabin. Mrs. John Biggs, her newborn, and two other children, however, were not in the cabin. By dumb luck, Mrs. Biggs had taken her three kids out into the fields to look for a cow that had wandered off. Seeing the warriors, she hid in the woods. The braves passed so close to the hiding place that she claimed she heard their footsteps. A few minutes later her newborn began to cry. Mrs. Biggs quickly placed her shawl tightly over the child's mouth. She inadvertently smothered the child.

There were so many tragedies that day. In all, twenty-four settlers were killed in less than one hour. But, several villagers managed to escape into the woods.[1]

The next day—September 4, 1812—a fort named, interesting enough, for William Henry Harrison was attacked. With the larger American force away, an obscure captain named Zachary Taylor commanded just a few soldiers, several of whom were ill. However, Taylor, whose heroism in the war would later propel him to the presidency, successfully held off wave after wave of attacks by Miami and Wea warriors. Others were not so fortunate. American forts in the region began to fall to the British and their Indian allies and the entire territory was under attack.

The surprise attacks continued the next day, when Indians in the region attacked Fort Madison, named for the American president. A fourth attack in as many days in Indiana occurred at Fort Wayne, named for General "Mad" Wayne. The fort, garrisoned by less than 100 men, sat on the frontier and had fallen into disrepair. The commander, Captain James Rhea, did not see fit to strengthen the fort or even maintain adequate armaments or supplies. As such, it was vulnerable.

Perhaps as many as 500 warriors from the Miami and Potawatomi nations under Chief Winamac surrounded the fort. After minor skirmishes, Chief Winamac and other chiefs were summoned to the fort by Captain Rhea for a discussion of peace. Inside the fort, the chiefs and the few braves guarding them found Rhea drunk. Captain Rhea offered his "guests" wine and appears to have offered terms that would save his own hide. Chief Winamac informed the American commander that all the forts in the region had fallen and stated, "You must expect to fall next, probably in a few days." Confident of success and seeing that the fort was poorly defended and its commander a drunk and a coward, Winamac and the chiefs rejected Rhea's terms. They departed and prepared to sack the fort.[2]

The attack began on September 5. Rhea took to his quarters drunk, claiming to be ill. For the next few days, the Indians made progress but were unable to overtake the fort. News of the siege reached Governor Harrison, who hastily assembled troops from area militia units to aid the beleaguered fort. Harrison also heard reports that Chief Tecumseh was on his way to Fort Wayne to join in the assault. Harrison thus ordered his men to rush to the fort, but along the way his militia units were harassed by Indian raids. The hit-and-run raids slowed Harrison's army. Finally, on September 12, General Harrison arrived with several hundred militiamen to reinforce the garrison. Upon seeing the approaching army, Chief Winamac and his warriors abandoned the invasion and melted back into the woods. Harrison and Rhea were fortunate that the reports about Tecumseh were not accurate.

Fort Wayne held and Harrison prevailed, but white settlers in the region were unnerved. Political leaders back East demanded the Indians be destroyed. Tecumseh, however, was not dissuaded by the growing American military presence in the region. He wanted to avenge the most pivotal battle of the conflict, which occurred a year earlier on November 7, 1811. It too involved Harrison and Tecumseh.

## THE PROPHET

The HMS *Leopard*'s attack on the USS *Chesapeake* in 1807 may have marked the first battle of what would become the War of 1812. If so, the Battle of Tippecanoe Creek essentially amounted to the second battle of the War of 1812, even though it occurred seven months prior to the formal declaration of war against Britain.

Running from the advancing white settlement and hoping to establish a base of operations for a grand Indian confederation, Chief Tecumseh and many Shawnee had moved to Indiana from Ohio. Among the leaders of the Shawnee nation was Tecumseh's brother, Lalawethika ("the rattle" in Shawnee), who would later be known as "The Prophet." A charismatic but rash holy man, he emerged as a spiritual leader in the larger opposition to white rule.

Lalawethika was born in 1775, making him seven years Tecumseh's junior. He was at a tender age when his mother abandoned the family to travel to Missouri. By all accounts, as a boy Lalawethika was a sickly child and weak physically. Unable to hunt, fight, or play like the other boys, Lalawethika also suffered from a wound to his right eye from an arrow. As such, he grew up an outcast and was always dependent on the charity of members of the tribe for his food and protection. As a young man, Lalawethika suffered from alcoholism and, in 1804, when the tribe's medicine man died, Lalawethika tried to establish himself in that role. However, he never mastered the art and magic of medicine and remained addicted to alcohol. The turning point in Lalawethika's life—one that established him as a prophet—came in April of 1805 when he fell into a deep trance, likely from excessive smoking of medicinal plants.

His fellow villagers believed Lalawethika to be dead. But when he awakened he claimed to have been visited by the Master of Life, a Shawnee deity, who had spoken to him and given him a vision. The vision that Lalawethika shared with his people, aided by his natural charisma, was that the white man's ways and Indian dependence on them angered the gods. They needed to return to traditional practices. Lalawethika changed his name to Tenskwatawa ("open door" in Shawnee). To other nations and to whites he would become known as The Prophet.

Even though some Indians distrusted The Prophet, others followed him when he established a Shawnee village in Ohio. The Prophet, like his older brother, began traveling and espousing the new vision of the traditional ways and Indian self-determination. He met leaders of the Ottawa, Seneca, Wyandot, and other tribes. Accordingly, he caught the attention of William Henry Harrison, who considered him nearly as powerful and thus as problematic as Tecumseh.

In an attempt to discredit the holy man, Harrison challenged The Prophet to perform miracles. In 1806, The Prophet predicted the eclipse of the Sun and it came to be, thus embarrassing Governor Harrison and enhancing his own image and base of power. It remains uncertain how The Prophet correctly predicted the eclipse, but some scholars note that many American scientists in the area were anticipating the event and Tecumseh had met with them in Ohio to talk about white settlements on Indian lands. So, it is likely Tecumseh informed his younger brother about the talks and the scientists' prediction. There is also an oral tradition that states that Tecumseh told The Prophet to make the prediction in order to enhance their cause with fellow Indians. Tecumseh, after all, often used his brother's mystical and religious appeal to promote his grand Indian confederation.[3]

The Prophet and his followers moved with Tecumseh in 1808 to Tippecanoe Creek in Indiana and their village became known as "Prophetstown." By 1811, the charismatic brothers had attracted so many Indians from across the country that the village had become an Indian stronghold and a powerful symbol of Indian resistance to the white government. The region included the fertile waters and fields of the Wabash, a site Governor Harrison had always wanted to settle. The Shawnee, Miami, and other nations began using the growing Indian community as a staging ground from which to attack American supply lines and settlers throughout the region. In time, Indians began considering this remote site to be both sacred and safe, and white settlers in Indiana began to demand that Governor Harrison do something about it.

Harrison knew that Tecumseh was strong and was continuing his successful effort to rally Indian nations from the Gulf of Mexico to the Great Lakes to join his grand confederation. If Tecumseh managed the impossible, Harrison understood that it would fundamentally change the balance of power between whites and Indians. The epicenter of Tecumseh's resistance would be in the Indiana territory Harrison governed. As such, Harrison needed to defeat Tecumseh immediately, before he had time to finalize his confederation.[4] The opportunity presented itself in November of 1811.

With Tecumseh away on another diplomatic mission, this time far to the south to meet with the chiefs of the Creeks, Harrison gathered an army of 1,100 regulars and militia, supplemented by the powerful Fourth Infantry, which was sent all the way from Pittsburgh for the express purpose of destroying the Indian stronghold. Tecumseh had left The Prophet in charge with orders not to attack until his return. The great chief did not want anything to unravel his grand confederation and wanted to deliver a decisive blow to Harrison and the armies of Indiana, one that would be achieved by a unified and massive army of many Indian nations.

Meanwhile, however, Harrison marched his army to Indian country and built Fort Harrison (it would come under attack one year later by Indians). He then marched to the Wabash River and Tippecanoe Creek, on the outskirts of Prophetstown.

## THE BATTLE OF TIPPECANOE CREEK

General Harrison followed the same path and tactics as his former commander, General "Mad" Wayne, who approached the Indian confederation at the Battle of Fallen Timbers with massive force but in a cautious manner. Harrison wisely deployed scouts far in advance, had riflemen at the ready, and had patrols on his flanks. Arriving near Prophetstown, Harrison met with chiefs from the village for a parley. They gathered about one mile from the village but nothing was accomplished, except that Harrison would later be criticized for exposing his troops to potential harm and for camping too close to the enemy stronghold. On the other hand, Harrison never wanted to appear to be the naked aggressor, so the meeting served the purpose of providing Harrison with political cover. Ultimately, The Prophet would play perfectly into Harrison's plans and hands.

On the night of November 6, 1811, Harrison ordered his men to build a camp on the banks of Tippecanoe Creek, about two miles distance from Prophetstown. He chose a small peninsula, surrounded on three sides by the creek and marshlands. The camp was organized in a quad formation with sentries wisely posted all around the site. The cautious Harrison even ordered his troops to sleep fully dressed and with their rifles loaded and fixed with bayonets. It was a cold, rainy night; but conditions were about to get worse.

Nearby in Prophetstown, hundreds of warriors were celebrating. Braves from the Chippewa, Huron, Kickapoo, Ottawa, Potawatomi, Shawnee, and other nations in Tecumseh's confederation had all come to Prophetstown, lured by the charisma of Tecumseh and The Prophet. The reason for the celebration that night was not the promise of confederation, but preparation for a great battle. With Tecumseh gone, The Prophet defied his brother's direct command *not* to engage the whites. Whipping the warriors into a frenzy, The Prophet told them of his dream that they would achieve a decisive victory under his leadership. He also conjured great magic, announcing to the war party that he had the power to render them invisible. Under the protection of The Prophet's magic, the soldiers' bullets would not harm the warriors because all their gunpowder had burned. Believing The Prophet's magic, the celebration lasted all night.[5]

Roughly two hours before sunrise on the morning of November 7, with most of General Harrison's army asleep, about 700 warriors attacked. Imbued with The Prophet's magic and the image of him standing high on a rock overlooking the battle, they rushed wildly into Harrison's encampment believing they were invisible and immune to the soldiers' bullets. The initial wave hit the northwest end of the camp. However, a sentry, Stephen Mars, heard the warriors and managed to fire a shot before being killed with a tomahawk blow to the head. With Indian screams filling the air, warriors poured into the camp. Groggy soldiers waking from the noise were killed instantly. In the chaos of darkness, the warriors initially enjoyed the upper hand, taking over the northwestern quad. However, the shot by Mars served as an alarm for the larger army, who quickly scrambled to their posts.

Harrison was awakened by the commotion and ran to mount a horse in order to organize a counter-attack. Legend holds that the first available horse was Major Waller Taylor's black stead rather than Harrison's own gray horse. There was no time to wait, so the general mounted Taylor's horse. Nearby, Colonel Abraham Owen charged forward on a gray horse, and was mistaken for General Harrison. He was immediately beset by screaming braves who apparently were looking for the hated General. Colonel Owen was savagely killed.[6]

Harrison and his army managed to push the advancing warriors back. He was aided by Major Waller Taylor who was riding Harrison's horse until the General advised him to get a different mount or be targeted![7] Interestingly, one of Harrison's officers who led the counterattack was Joseph Hamilton Davies, who had earlier served as the prosecutor of Aaron Burr during the trial over Burr's empire scheme. Davies was shot as he charged. But, the cavalry charge served its purpose and panicked the disorganized braves. In the face of a wave of horses and the realization that they were neither invisible nor immune to the bullets, the braves broke off the attack and fled back to Prophetstown.

As dawn emerged, Harrison's largely untested army proved up to the task. Their superior numbers and an organized cavalry charge succeeded in repelling the attack. The soldiers' trained muskets hit their mark, despite The Prophet's magic. After two hours of bloody, hand-to-hand fighting, Harrison had lost 37 men with another 126 wounded. Another 25 men would later die from their injuries. No reliable numbers exist for Indian casualties that night, but they were likely a lot worse, with a minimum of at least 200 casualties and probably much more.

Worse than the high casualty count, however, was the damage the defeat did to Tecumseh's grand hopes. Many warriors disappeared after the battle, abandoning The Prophet and Tecumseh's beloved confederation. The day clearly belonged to Harrison, as would history.[8]

## TURNING POINT

Harrison spent the day treating his wounded and preparing his defenses. He suspected that the predawn attack was but the first wave of a larger effort. However, no additional attack ever materialized.

The next morning, on November 8, the American army marched on Prophetstown, which by then was a ghost town with only a few women, children, and the elderly still remaining. The warriors had abandoned the village, The Prophet, and Tecumseh's confederation. The army proceeded to burn the village to the ground. Every dwelling was destroyed, the fields of corn were burned, graves dug up, and corpses were piled high and set afire. The vital stores of supplies the Indians would need not only for the coming winter but for Tecumseh's alliance were confiscated or destroyed. Also, in the process of searching the village, Harrison's men found muskets, which had likely been sold or given to them by the British. To Harrison and later to the same politicians clamoring for war, this was direct evidence that the British were continuing to incite Indian violence. Moreover, they were arming the gravest threat to America—Tecumseh.

News of the battle and the cache of weapons captured spread across the country. Newspapers and politicians spewed anti-British sentiment and the call for war spiraled out of control. After burning Prophetstown, Harrison marched his army to Vincennes, the capital of the territory, to be received as a hero. The victory was far more than one on the battlefield for Harrison. The Shawnees and their allies were demoralized and The Prophet utterly discredited as a charlatan. The people of Prophetstown rose up against the Prophet, angry because his magic was weak. Many of his warriors even threatened to kill him. When Tecumseh arrived home three months later, he was outraged that his command had been ignored and violently struck his brother, knocking him to the ground. Tecumseh forever banished The Prophet, who moved far to the west to a place called Wildcat Creek. With a small band of loyalists, the holy man then traveled through the Northwest and Canada during the War of 1812. The Prophet died in Wyandotte, Kansas in November of 1834. Of the battle which ended his dream, a dejected Tecumseh stated flatly:

> Governor Harrison made war on my people in my absence. On my return I found great destruction and havoc—the fruits of our labor destroyed, the bodies of my friends laying in the dust, and our village burnt to the ground by the Big Knives.[9]

As word of the disaster spread, it had the effect of proving Tecumseh, who had been hundreds of miles to the south, to be both vulnerable and incapable of governing his own people. The defeat undermined confidence in the grand confederation. Nations contemplating the confederation backed down, many worrying that Harrison's army would march on their villages next. The grand vision of an Indian confederation capable of securing Indian self-determination was ended. The defeat, however, firmly pushed many Indian chiefs, including Tecumseh, who now realized he could only defeat the Americans through the British, into siding with

Britain in the coming war. White settlers and pro-empire politicians were emboldened by the victory, which resulted in further settlement and talk of punishing the British.[10]

As for Harrison, his service in the coming war would be mixed, but the Battle at Tippecanoe Creek would eventually mark him as having presidential timber. This lop-sided skirmish, which was not a battle in the War of 1812, ended up shaping both the war and history.

# 8

# A DECLARATION OF WAR

## RISE OF THE WAR HAWKS

There was no single smoking gun that caused the War of 1812. Rather, a number of events, individuals, and historical and political forces converged at the right (or wrong) time to bring about the ill-considered war. American passions were stoked by several ham-fisted policies of the British, who continued to board American ships at will and incite Indian raids on white settlements in the west. At the same time, several ruthless politicians from the frontier and southern states came to power clamoring for war and expansion.

When Thomas Jefferson won the presidency in 1800, many saw the election of a southern slave owner as a victory for these interests. But, while Jefferson advocated states' rights and expanded the nation with the Louisiana Purchase, he also sought treaties with Europe in an effort to avoid war. Likewise, when James Madison followed Jefferson in the presidency, southern and western interests had hopes the new president would champion their causes. But Madison, like Jefferson, was also eager to prevent war with Britain or other European powers.[1]

It was the congressional elections in the early 1800s that swept into power a new generation of politician, advocating cuts to the size of government but American expansionism. In particular, the election of 1810 was a watershed election that brought to power radical anti-Federalist (the so-called Democratic-Republican Party) leaders from the western and southern states. These firebrands aggressively limited the role of government, cut the military, cut taxes, clamored for conflict with Europe, and yearned for all of North America to be part of the United States. New Englanders and the Federalists worried about the negative impacts on the economy of these policies and opposed war, but their voices were drowned out. Even though the new radicals in Congress were members of Madison's own political party, he was unable to control them and they outmaneuvered him politically on the matters of war and expansion.

It was Thomas Jefferson who coined the term "War Hawks" to describe pro-war politicians during the presidency of John Adams, who managed to prevent war with France. In a letter to James Madison in 1798, Jefferson complained: "At present the war hawks talk of war with France. . . ."[2]

Among the leaders of the War Hawks were Henry Clay of Kentucky and John C. Calhoun of South Carolina, along with a few others including Richard Mentor Johnson of Kentucky, William Rufus King of North Carolina and, later, Alabama, and Felix Grundy and George Troup of Georgia. Many of them were under the age of thirty-five and had therefore not fought in the Revolutionary War. Most of them had never seen combat but showed complete contempt for the Revolutionary generation and, frankly, anyone who dared disagree with them. They even ignored advice from Jefferson, Madison, and other Founders.

Their political *modus operandi* was to intimidate and attack opponents, while relying on inflammatory and impassioned rhetoric to manipulate public opinion. Ambitious and determined, the War Hawks succeeded in promoting their vision of manifest destiny through ingenious but despicable methods such as decrying advocates of peace as unpatriotic, claiming opponents wanted "European appeasement," and whipping up fear of Indian attacks. The public fell prey to this new brand of divisive politics.[3]

When the Twelfth Congress convened after the 1810 elections, the House of Representatives selected as their leaders these young, hawkish members. It was one of the biggest political upheavals in American history, sweeping out the old, Revolutionary guard, limiting the Federalists' power, and placing into leadership men with little political or military experience. The American public essentially voted for war in the 1810 midterm elections: Of the 142 members of the House of Representatives, fully sixty-one were newly elected in 1810 and about half of them were staunchly in favor of war.

The stars aligned in just the right way for these young hawks. First, the former speaker of the House, Joseph B. Varnum of Massachusetts, a Revolutionary War general, decided to resign in order to serve in the U.S. Senate. His heir apparent as speaker was Nathaniel Macon of North Carolina, another veteran of the war and of politics. However, the young Republicans orchestrated a coup that pushed Macon aside for Henry Clay of Kentucky. Under the eloquent but dictatorial Clay and his well-organized and aggressive supporters (the large freshman class backed Clay and the Democratic-Republicans had sizeable majorities in both houses), the House dominated the Senate to the point where the senior chamber barely functioned or played any balancing role. Gone with the experienced legislators was any respect for tradition or civility; or any viable opposition to war. Clay packed key committees with southern and frontier firebrands so that Clay's Twelfth Congress became known as the War Congress, leading the elder statesman John Randolph of Virginia to complain that "We have heard but one word—like the whip-poor-will, but one eternal monotonous tone—Canada! Canada! Canada!"[4]

## CLAY

Henry Clay was born in Virginia on April 12, 1777, the seventh of nine children born to Reverend John and Elizabeth Hudson Clay. When Clay was only three, the British attacked the village where he lived and ransacked the family home, which formed in him a lifelong hatred of the British. Clay pursued a career in the law and was admitted to the Virginia bar in 1797, but soon afterward moved to Lexington, Kentucky to seek the vast opportunities of the west.

His meteoric rise to power included two partial terms in the Senate in his twenties, even though Clay was not of the age mandated by the Constitution (30) to be able to do so. He was only thirty-four when he became the speaker. A workaholic, Clay was also vain and hyper-conscious of his appearance and image. Tall and thin with light hair and a high forehead, Clay possessed the natural gift of charisma. He was a great conversationalist who could be quite charming when he wanted to be. But Clay's admirable traits produced a dangerous cocktail when combined with his massive ego and disregard for advice. Not known for being a listener or for self-reflection, Clay was utterly unencumbered by the consequences of his actions and was a zealot who was disinterested in compromise.[5] He was also not without numerous vices and character flaws including a passion for horse racing, poker games, cigars, drinking, and carousing at taverns. Clay was also not that intelligent, although he believed he was, leading John Quincy Adams to dismiss him as "only half educated."[6]

Clay placed war and expansion atop his political priorities. As Speaker, Clay now had a national platform and the official power to agitate for seizing Canada and defeating the Indians. He was the man, after all, who had earlier defended Aaron Burr during the trial over the scheme to seize Mexico and the Southwest. Clay made clear from the start his position on the debate over expansion and war: "I would take the whole continent from Britain. I wish never to see peace until we do."[7]

By the fall of 1811, Clay's War Hawks were calling for an invasion of Canada. To his supporters and fellow countrymen, Clay promised it would be a quick and easy war. He even boasted to President Madison: "I trust I shall not be presumptuous when I state that I verily believe that the militia of Kentucky alone are competent to place Montreal and Upper Canada at your feet." The Speaker predicted the victory would take less than four weeks and would be but a matter of Kentuckians marching to Canada.[8]

As the country drifted toward war, however, only a few hundred Kentuckians volunteered for the effort. The War Hawks in Congress turned out to be better at talking about war than actually preparing for war. After voting for war, congressional War Hawks failed to adequately fund equipment and supplies, and defeated bills to increase the size of the Navy and Army. Governors and legislatures from the same frontier and southern states sent poorly equipped militiamen without winter clothing, many of whom froze to death during the first winter of the fighting on the Canadian border.

In 1812, when war was declared, only about 7,000 men had volunteered for the army and been equipped. And many of those were underequipped and utterly untrained. The army that prepared to do battle with the world's strongest military was led by old men from the Revolution and young politicians lacking military experience. The war would be anything but the quick and simple affair, as predicted by Clay and the War Hawks.

## "MR. MADISON'S WAR"

James Madison, America's Fourth President, was part of the Virginia dynasty that played such a prominent role in the nation's founding. Madison was a key voice during the Continental Congress, one of the architects at the Constitutional Convention in 1787, and Thomas Jefferson's secretary of state. But none of that stopped the ribbing Madison took from opponents and the press, often on account of his diminutive stature. Standing just 5'4" in height and weighing just over 100 pounds, Madison's enemies labeled him a "pygmy" or "Little Jimmy" and even to his allies he was the

"Great Little Madison." It was said of the patriot from Montpelier that he possessed "so much mind [but] so little matter." But whatever Madison lacked in physical stature, he more than made up for in intellect.

In 1808, Madison defeated Charles Pinckney, the Federalist candidate whose party was fast becoming irrelevant in American politics, and in so doing became the first president to ask Congress to declare war.[9] Madison tried to avoid war by calling Congress into session one month early on November 4, 1811, but he was overrun by Speaker Clay and the War Hawks, who played poker to Madison's political chess and turned the session into the "War Congress."

While he lacked the charisma of some of the other Framers and his health had kept him out of the fighting during the Revolutionary War, Madison was known to outwork those around him. Madison was also one of the most intelligent members of the Virginia House of Burgesses, but he rarely ever spoke. Indeed, when he did speak, it was so softly that few people even heard his comments. It was even something of a Washington joke to cup one's hand to the ear when Madison was speaking. He was shy, did not smoke or drink, and avoided "chummy" political gatherings, but he did once joke that "I nearly lost my nose in the service of my country," a reference to an incident when he was working in freezing weather and thereby suffered frostbite.[10]

In short, the scholarly Madison who avoided back-slapping politicos was polar opposite of the feisty and loud Henry Clay, John Calhoun, and other War Hawks in Congress. As the politician and author, Richard Thompson, said of the President: "It seemed to me, each time I observed him, that I had rarely seen a face in which more benignity and quiet composure was expressed. It was a complete personification of gentleness and benevolence."[11] These comments were echoed by Margaret Bayard Smith, friend of Thomas Jefferson and chronicler of the social scene in early Washington, who noted of Madison: "His little, blue eyes sparkled like stars from under his bushy gray eye-brows and amidst the wrinkles of his poor, thin fact" . . . and his conversation was "a stream of history . . . so rich in sentiment and facts, so enlivened by anecdotes and epigrammatic remarks."[12] But Madison was steamrolled by Clay.

On April 20, in the midst of the debate over war, Madison's vice president, George Clinton, died. It appeared that Madison would not be reelected in the fall election on account of the war. Voters in the South and frontier were angry that the president vacillated on going to war, while voters in the North and New England decried the rush to war as "Madison's War." That fall Madison defeated the anti-war nominee, DeWitt Clinton of New York, by only thirty-nine electoral votes.

Through the winter and spring of 1812, Madison held off the War Hawks as long as he thought he could. But it was a losing proposition. The President knew the United States was completely unprepared. His predecessor, Thomas Jefferson, had put his faith in small, cheap gunboats, which could only patrol shallow coasts and inlets and limited the standing army to but a few thousand men. Despite the turbulence in Europe and repeated harassment of U.S. ships off the coast of Tripoli, Madison had been unable during his first four years in office to get Congress to fund a larger military.[13] Madison complained about congressional inaction:

> To enable the Executive to step at once into Canada they have provided after two months parlay for a regular force requiring twelve to raise it, and after three months for a volunteer force, on terms not likely to raise it at all. . . .[14]

An article in *The Boston Patriot* from the week the war started seems to sum up the situation. It described an American public tired of waiting for unsuccessful diplomatic overtures. The journal noted:

> Americans are the worst people in the world to be kept in a state of inaction. A slow remedy for evil, however certain, suits not their nature. They could better contend with greater dangers that were to be encountered by energy and action, than smaller ones which were to be overcome merely by patience and delay.[15]

## WAR, AT LAST

In a last ditch effort to avoid war, Madison sent a diplomatic mission to Europe. But, Clay, who was rabidly anti-Indian and pro-war, was a part of the peace delegation. The frontier orator was a strange choice for another reason. It was the first time Clay had ever seen, much less traveled on the ocean. As a result, the *New York Spectator* opined: "It will amuse Old Neptune, to find for the first time in the limits of his domain, the man who, as lord paramount of the backwoodsmen, has held so extensive an authority over it."[16]

Clay ruled out the possibility for peace, declaring "I am not for stopping at Quebec or anywhere else. I would take the entire continent."[17] Declared William Armistead Burwell, Jefferson's former private secretary and member of Congress from Virginia who was part of the pro-war faction, "The expulsion of the British from Canada has always been deemed an object of the first importance to the peace of the United States."[18] In yet another bitter irony of the war, just two days before the war, the British repealed the policy of impressment, which had been a main cause of the war. On June 23, Britain also revoked their restrictions on American commerce. However, because of rudimentary communication and transportation systems, word of the repeal did not arrive in the United States or to British commanders in Canada in time. Even if word had arrived, however, the War Hawks would likely not have been dissuaded from war.

A reluctant President delivered his message for war to Congress on June 1, 1812, citing Britain's repeated violations of the rights of American sailors, British complicity in inciting Indian raids on the American frontier, and his own attempts at peace. The President's message to both chambers of Congress read, "The conduct of the [British] Government presents a series of acts hostile to the United Sates as an independent and neutral nation." It continued:

> British cruisers have been in the continued practice of violating the American flag on the great highway of nations, and of seizing and carrying off persons sailing under it, not in the exercise of a belligerent right founded on the law of nations against an enemy, but of a municipal prerogative over British subjects . . .
>
> British cruisers have been in the practice also of violating our entering and departing commerce. To the most insulting pretensions they have added the most lawless proceedings in our very harbors, and have wantonly spilled American blood within the sanctuary of our territorial jurisdiction. . . .[19]

Madison reminded Congress, his countrymen, and the world that he sought peace and attempted to negotiate several times, but all efforts failed. Therefore, "We hold, in fine, on the side of Great Britain a state of war against the United States, and on the side of the United States a state of peace toward Great Britain." The President ended his message, obviously aware of the historic moment before him:

> Whether the United States shall continue passive under these progressive usurpations and these accumulating wrongs, or, opposing force to force in defense of their national rights, shall commit a just cause into the hands of the Almighty Disposer of Events . . . is a solemn question which the Constitution wisely confides to the legislative department of the Government. In recommending it to their early deliberations I am happy in the assurance that the decision will be worthy of the enlightened and patriotic councils of a virtuous, a free, and a powerful nation.[20]

Led by Speaker Clay, the House of Representatives acted with haste, passing a bill for war by a 79–49 margin on June 4, 1812. Clay rode roughshod over Federalists who clamored for additional time for debate or even public hearings on the war. Josiah, Bartlett, a congressman from New Hampshire, said simply, "I think the business was too hasty."[21] In the Senate, a motion was added to the war declaration to promote the authorization of privateers to raid British shipping. It passed 17–13. But the full bill was tied at sixteen votes apiece, in part because the bill called for a limited war and the War Hawks wanted a full war. Additional measures were introduced, including the call for war against both British and French shipping. That measure was narrowly defeated by a vote of 15–17. Ultimately, a clean bill for war against Britain was introduced to the Senate on June 17. The next day, with thirty-two of the thirty-six senators present, the vote was 19–13 for war. It was the closest war vote in American history.

Delegations from the South and West, as expected, voted for the war with Kentucky, Georgia, and South Carolina leading the way. New York and New England opposed war, with the delegations from Connecticut, Rhode Island, and Delaware voting unanimously against the war declaration. However, in the Senate, the Federalists held only six of the thirty-six seats, so there was little they could do to stop the war. Every federalist in Congress voted against it.

The famed orator, Daniel Webster, summed up the debate over the war, addressing his remarks to the War Hawks:

Whoever would discover the causes which have produced the present state of things, must look for them, not in the efforts of the opposition, but in the nature of the war in which we are engaged . . . Quite too small a portion of public opinion was in favor of war to justify it originally. A much smaller portion is in favor of the mode in which it has been conducted . . . Public opinion, strong and united, is not with you in your Canada project . . . The acquisition of the country is not an object generally desired by the people . . . You are you say, at war for maritime rights, and free trade. But they see you lock up your commerce and abandon the ocean. They see you invade an interior province of the enemy. They see you involve yourselves in a bloody war with native savages; and they ask you if you have, in truth, a maritime controversy with the Western Indians, and are really contending for sailors' rights with the tribes of the Prophet.[22]

It has been speculated that the President thought the Senate vote might save him and the nation from war.[23] It did not happen and Madison, whose face was "white as a sheet," signed the measure on June 19, 1812. The United States was officially at war against Britain. Across the Atlantic, the King had grown tired of the rancor from the upstart Americans and, the day prior, declared war against the United States. War came not with the blast of cannons at sea or an invasion on the frontier, but with the stroke of a pen.

# "ON TO CANADA"

*"She Comes"*

*She comes! The proud invader comes*
*To waste our country, spoil our homes;*
*To lay our towns and cities low,*
*And bid our mothers' tears to flow;*
*Our wives lament, our orphans weep—*
*To seize the empire of the deep!*

—Old poem about the War of 1812 by Angus Umphraville

"Push on, brave York volunteers"/"General Brock at the Battle of Queenston Heights." Acknowledgment: By John David Kelly, 1896; Library Archives, Canada (1954-1-53-1)

# 9

# THE INVASION BEGINS

## BARELY AN ARMY

With Napoleon on the rampage in Europe, the British had no plans to offer support for the defense of Canada even though they had declared war. The sparsely populated villages just north of the U.S. border and the isolated population living in the vast northern frontier were on their own. Canada, which encompassed four mainland Crown provinces—Lower Canada, Upper Canada, New Brunswick, and Nova Scotia—seemed ripe for the taking.[1]

The royal governor was Sir George Prevost, an uninspiring man who had only arrived in Canada on October 12, 1811, to assume his duties which included serving as commander in chief of all British and Canadian forces in North America. Born in 1767, he had served the Crown previously as a governor in the West Indies. His Swiss father had been a soldier for the British and Prevost was sent to a military academy in London, later receiving a commission in the infantry in 1779. Prevost served in the West Indies, commanded forces in the Crown's Caribbean holdings, and helped capture Martinique in 1809. Although he rose through the military ranks quickly and proved to be an efficient administrator, Prevost lacked real talent for military command. He also inherited an army numbering less than 5,600 regulars in all of Canada, with only 1,200 stationed in Upper Canada where the fighting was most likely to occur.[2]

However, a number of factors would intervene to save Canada. Most notably, Prevost was fortunate that the American commanders charged with invading Canada were fantastically inept. Prevost's lax governing style was such that he alienated his advisory councils and delegated much of the actual governing to the lieutenant governors of the provinces. This would prove to be a blessing in disguise in the case of one of his lieutenant governors who would turn out to be perhaps the most gifted leader of the war.

Major General Isaac Brock was appointed military commander of Upper Canada on September 30, 1811 and, when the lieutenant governor of the province, Francis Gore, returned to Britain soon thereafter, Brock also assumed control of its government. A dashingly handsome, tall, and cerebral officer, Brock was ambitious and had yearned for command and glory. He therefore viewed his posting to Canada as a demotion. The real war was in Europe against Napoleon. That was the conflict that would define his times and forge Britain's great heroes. That was where the ambitious young officer belonged.[3]

All the good officers were engaged in the conflict with Napoleon, so Brock was given command of a small army in Upper Canada of a few thousand men mostly comprised of untrained militia units. It was led by inexperienced, unmotivated officers of questionable skill and even more questionable resolve to fight. In Brock's words, his army was "wretchedly officered."[4] He also had to contend with an army suffering from drunkenness and loneliness of epidemic proportions. Bitterly cold winters had taken their toll on the British soldiers garrisoning small, isolated outposts in the Canadian frontier. The major general was forced to rely on local recruits and militiamen, most of whom were willing to serve only short terms of enlistment, and whose loyalty to Britain was suspect. He also had no efficient system of communication in the vast Canadian frontier. In a letter to his brother back in Britain, Brock complained that "We got the rubbish of every department in the army. Any man whom the Duke [Wellington] deemed unfit for the Peninsula was considered as quite good enough for the Canadian market."[5]

Things were no better in the other provinces. Governor Prevost had an army of a few thousand militiamen in Lower Canada, which he described as "A mere posse, ill arm'd, and without discipline." Both Prevost and Brock suspected that many of their recruits, who were recent American immigrants, would join the American invaders as soon as the fighting started.[6] Much like their American counterparts, British commanders went to war with a lack of funds, little support from their government, and with farmers masquerading as militiamen, planning on returning home in time for the late summer harvest.[7]

But the British had Major General Brock.

## "CANADA! CANADA! CANADA!"

The United States entered the war without enough troops or equipment to achieve the goals of the war, which were still evolving when the fighting started. To the War Hawks, the war was about defending the nation's honor, promoting sovereignty over the seas, destroying the British (and maybe the French too), and, most importantly, conquering Canada and the Native Indians. Just a few weeks after signing the declaration of war, President Madison consented to their desire for a multi-theater war. From Canada to New York, from the Chesapeake to the Gulf Coast, and throughout the world's oceans, what resulted was several, separate and largely unrelated wars undertaken by a military ill-prepared to fight any one of them, much less all of them. And it started in Canada.

The Great Lakes and surrounding region were known as the "Old Northwest" in the nineteenth century. It was a densely wooded, sparsely populated area. In the year 1812, the population of the United States was only about 7.5 million, of which about 6 million were white and very few of them lived in the Old Northwest. Canada contained only about 500,000 people. To get to Fort Detroit from Lake Erie was a long and treacherous journey, but to travel between population centers in Canada was even more harrowing. There were few villages, fewer roads, and news traveled slowly, if at all, between them. The same was true in "Upper Canada" (which is now the Province of Ontario). Canada was an immense and rural country, much of it was controlled by Indian nations, and was divided geographically and politically. The roughly 100,000 whites living around Nova Scotia and New Brunswick were pro-British, but many (perhaps as many as 200,000 people) of those living in Lower Canada (Quebec) by the St. Lawrence River just north of the Great Lakes were Francophiles.

The Canadian population lived mostly along the St. Lawrence and Niagara Rivers in southeastern Canada between Quebec and Montreal, making this stretch of land the key to conquering Canada. Major General Brock understood this and thereby concentrated his limited forces there, while also guessing that the dense forests would slow the American military's mobility on land while the powerful Royal Navy would control the St. Lawrence, Great Lakes, and Atlantic. He doubted his ability to defend Upper Canada in the west, which was the region just north of the western Great Lakes, and worried that an American invasion there would eventually push north and east into the main population centers of Canada. In short, he was facing an impossible situation.

## "KILLING THE TREE"

But the U.S. military command struggled to piece together a clear plan for invading Canada. The basic strategy, hatched by Major General Henry Dearborn who had served as Jefferson's secretary of war, was for a three-pronged attack on Canada. All three attacks would occur simultaneously. Under Brigadier General William Hull, a western invasion would march to Upper Canada from Fort Detroit (from present-day Michigan and Ohio) and across Lake Huron to attack Amherstburg on the Canadian border. A second attack—the center prong—would be led by Major General Stephen Van Rensselaer. His army would cross the Niagara River and attack the capital city of York. A third army would invade from the east, by moving north to the St. Lawrence River from Lake Champlain in Vermont to invade both Montreal and Quebec. This prong would be led by Dearborn himself [see Map 2 in Appendix].

The basic idea was sound: to take the St. Lawrence River and Great Lakes in order to control trade and commerce. Commodore Isaac Chauncey, who commanded the small array of ships that were to function as the U.S. Navy, likened "taking and maintaining a position on the St. Lawrence" to "killing the tree" because America would first strangle the roots of the vast northern country.[8]

Invading from the St. Lawrence in the east and, to a lesser extent, the Great Lakes to the west presented a few problems. Brock centered his line of defense along the St. Lawrence and Quebec was heavily fortified. General Benedict Arnold had tried unsuccessfully to take the city and fort during the Revolutionary War. The campaign across the St. Lawrence would need to go through New England, a region that remained opposed to the war and unwilling to fully mobilize for war. As a result, the War Department moved much of the planned invasion westward into the frontier. But they foolishly failed to attempt to secure the Great Lakes beforehand and went to war with virtually no naval presence on the northern border. As a result, the initial invasion of Canada in 1812 was bogged down by long, treacherous travel through the thick forests along the border, cold weather and snow, and frequent Indian attacks. Without control of the waterways on the border, it would also be difficult to resupply and reinforce the army.

Nor was the American military prepared in any other way. The officers and soldiers were poorly trained and ill-equipped. When war was declared the War Department consisted of a secretary and only eight clerks, all of whom were overwhelmed by the prospects of planning a war against the world's greatest military. There was no general staff and Congress was forced to scramble to appoint a commissary system, ordinance departments, and a quartermaster to assure the army had supplies and weapons.[9]

President Madison was an intelligent patriot who had served well during the Founding era, but a charismatic commander in chief he was not. His secretary of war, William Eustis, was a Revolutionary War surgeon, but was a very poor leader whose day had passed. And the man appointed to command the army that would invade Canada, General Henry Dearborn, whose day had *long* since passed, suffered from timidity and insecurities. Augustus Forster, the British Minister, reported to his superiors quite succinctly about Dearborn, saying "He does not rank very high." The British correctly calculated that Dearborn and the American military were incapable of an effective military campaign.[10]

A descendent of one of the signers of the Constitution, Henry Dearborn was born in 1751 in Hampton, New Hampshire. Educated in medicine, Dearborn served as an officer and surgeon in the American Revolution, fighting at Bunker Hill in 1775 at the outset of the war. Dearborn also marched with General Benedict Arnold through the wilderness to Quebec where he was taken prisoner on New Year's Eve of 1775. Throughout the war he carried a small medicine case lashed together with his sword to his coat. Dearborn was eventually freed and went on to serve as deputy quartermaster-general of the army and in various appointed positions of political and military leadership over the early years of the new republic. While Dearborn had served his country admirably, he had grown soft in old age and was, at best, a hesitant and uncertain commander.[11]

The planned invasion force of 35,000 men was only 7,000 strong in June of 1812. Because of the extraordinary opportunity to own land and prosper in America, few men were willing to lay down their scythes and hoes to pick up muskets and join the military. Those recruits who did were reluctant to join for more than a three-month enlistment. The state governors still feuded about their men serving under the command of someone from another state or as part of a federal army and the political opposition to war in the northeast and New England further limited the number of recruits.

Still, war came. The cry throughout the American South and western frontier was "Canada! Canada! Canada!" When war was declared, it became

"On to Canada!" Canada, after all, had a seemingly infinite array of natural resources—fur, meat, hardwoods, and minerals—so the idea of Canada as a northern state of the United States was an attractive thought to many Americans. It was also hoped that Canadians would join the United States in the larger fights against Britain and the Indians. But, still others simply wanted conquest.[12] No less than Thomas Jefferson mused:

> The acquisition of Canada this year, as far as Quebec, will be a mere matter of marching, and will give us experience for the attack on Nova Scotia next, and the final expulsion of England from the American continent. Canada wants to enter the union.[13]

But President Madison was less optimistic and was joined in his concern about the invasion of Canada by his secretary of state, James Monroe, and secretary of war, William Eustis, both of whom opposed what was rapidly turning into a naked land grab. All three invasions ended up being poorly conceived, inadequately provisioned, and even less well managed on the ground. Because of poor communications, panicked generals,, and confusion in the wilderness, the coordinated, simultaneous attacks never happened. All three initial invasions of Canada would end up miserable failures.

## DISASTER

The first of the three-pronged invasion of Canada was already underway when the Declaration of War was signed. In the spring of 1812, militiamen from three Ohio regiments gathered at Dayton and marched north to join the Fourth Infantry Regiment under the command of Lieutenant Colonel James Miller. The Fourth Infantry was well-known throughout America because of their earlier victory over the Indian confederation led by The Prophet at Tippecanoe Creek. As such, when the troops assembled to march on Canada, they celebrated to cheers of "Tippecanoe—Glory!"[14] Indeed, with a force of nearly 2,500 battle-tested men with knowledge of the frontier, there was cause for optimism. However, President Madison doomed it to failure by appointing as their commander the governor of the Michigan Territory, William Hull.

A minor hero of the Revolutionary War, Hull had demonstrated sound judgment and rose to the rank of Lieutenant Colonel during that conflict.

Born in Massachusetts in 1753, Hull graduated from Yale at nineteen and, after contemplating a career in the ministry, became a lawyer. His career progressed at a sound rate and he was appointed the first governor of the Michigan Territory by President Jefferson in 1805.

When the War of 1812 started, Hull was fifty-nine and his critics said he was tired and weak. They were right. Still, Hull was made Brigadier General of the Army of the Northwest but was angered by the appointment because he had longed to be appointed secretary of war. Hull claimed he accepted the northwestern command only with "great reluctance." To keep his political options open, Hull arranged to remain as the territory's governor even while leading the army, much as General Harrison had done in Indiana.[15] It would prove to be too much for him.

Similar to William Henry Harrison, Hull had focused his governorship on the task of taking land from the Indians and was quite successful at it. The Indians of the region rightly despised Hull, perhaps second only to Harrison. However, unlike Harrison, Hull worried constantly that he would be the target of assassination or scalping and that Fort Detroit would be a prime objective of the Indians. This constant worrying caused Hull to become excessively cautious and consumed with his own safety. Hardly a heroic figure, why Hull was given a key command remains a mystery and blemish on President Madison's war-time leadership. Hull nearly single-handedly lost the battle for Canada.

General Hull's command was based in Detroit, a town of about 700 residents with a fort placed strategically on high ground not far from the Detroit River that separated the territory from Canada. Hull commanded roughly 2,500 troops in a region that was so rugged his men literally had to cut a road through Michigan and along the Maumee River in order to get to the fort. Another road needed to be built to later get into Canada.

Hull's entire offensive from Detroit was undermined because of a foolish mistake. With his army marching to Detroit, some of Hull's men boarded boats on the Maumee River. One of the ships was the schooner *Cuyahoga*, which carried Hull's personal correspondence with the War Department, the muster rolls for his troops, and his battle plans. The items were loaded into a large trunk. The remainder of the army marched through Black Swamp, crossed the River Raisin, and eventually arrived at Fort Detroit on July 11, 1812. The *Cuyahoga's* course on the river took it directly past British artillery stationed on the high ground at Fort Malden by the town of Amherstburg. News of the formal declaration of war had not yet reached the region in late June and early July. However, hostilities were imminent and the British were on alert. It was thus shocking that Hull believed the British would permit a warship loaded with soldiers to sail by. They did not. Soon after arriving at Fort Detroit, Hull received word that the British had captured the *Cuyahoga* and were in possession of all his war plans.

After hesitating, General Hull decided to go forward with his plans, marching his army across the river and into Upper Canada on July 12, 1812. It was the first wave of the American invasion of Canada. Rather than continuing his advance, the General, who had barely stepped foot into Canada, stopped the invasion force at the small village of Sandwich (Windsor today), located directly across the river from Detroit, and established headquarters at a farm house. Hull was supposed to attack the British fort at Amherstburg but he did not. Had he attacked Amherstburg and other forts and towns in the area, he would have caught the British unprepared.

Instead of attacking, General Hull issued his infamous warning titled: "Declaration for all Canadians." Rather pompously, it was addressed to "Inhabitants of Canada" and read:

> After thirty years of peace and prosperity, the united States have been driven to arms. The injuries and aggressions, the insults and indignities of Great Britain have once more left no alternative but manly resistance or unconditional submission. The army under my command has invaded your country. The standard of the union now waves over the territory of Canada. To the peaceful and unoffending inhabitants it brings neither danger nor difficulty. I come to find enemies, not to make them; I come to protect not to injure you. . . .[16]

## "HIS MAJESTY'S DOMAIN"

Within hours of crossing into Canada, Hull was showing signs that he knew little about military strategy and his troops immediately began to question his nerve and resolve. Many would later rightly question his decision to delay the attack. Rather than surround himself with talented officers, the General chose as his advisor and aide his own son, Captain Abraham F. Hull. While in camp, Hull's officers naively boasted that the British and Indians were likely already on the run and that enemy morale had been destroyed at the sight of a large army in Canadian soil. They cheered: "Our flag looks extremely well on His Majesty's domain!" But Hull and his officers greatly misjudged the situation.[17]

The people of Canada did not respond to Hull's decree. Hull thought the declaration would, on its own, end any resistance and he failed to plan beyond this contingency. Sufficient scouting parties or spying efforts had not been organized. Not seeing any sign of resistance, Hull eventually marched his army to British-controlled Fort Malden. But the grumbling from his troops continued and the Ohio militia units refused to go deeper into Canada, complaining that they signed up only to defend the United States and fight in their own country. Shockingly, Hull backed down and let a few hundred men return home.

Fort Malden (formerly known as Fort Amherstburg) on the outskirts of Amherstburg in Ontario thus loomed as the first major battle of the war. The fort, first garrisoned in 1796, was a small outpost but was strategically located where the Detroit River pours into Lake Erie. The earthen and wooden fort served as the British headquarters for the land and naval defenses of the western Great Lakes and it was from this outpost that the British recruited Indian allies.

Only a skeleton army stood in Hull's way. The British force had perhaps 100 British regulars supported by 300 Canadian militia and 150 Indians in the fort and surrounding vicinity of Amherstburg. But the defenders had two advantages. One was that the Indians were led by Chief Tecumseh, who put the word out among Indians that he was leading an attack against General Hull and the Americans. As Hull hesitated, a few hundred additional warriors rushed to join the great chief. The second advantage was that the commander of the British resistance was the very able General Sir Isaac Brock, one of the most able figures of the War of 1812—and one of the most tragic.

## THE COURAGEOUS BROCK

Brock was the eighth son of a leading family from Guernsey in the Channel Islands. He was born in 1769, a good year for military commanders, for it also produced Napoleon and Wellington. At age fifteen, Brock joined the Eighth Regiment, beginning a three-decade military career. He distinguished himself early and caught the attention of all around him after performing heroically during Nelson's attack on Copenhagen. At age twenty-eight, the then-Lieutenant Colonel in the 49th Regiment took it upon himself to transform the unit from an embarrassment to one of the most efficient and effective in the entire service.

However, in 1802, Brock was sent to Canada, where he was posted throughout the country, from Montreal to York (present-day Toronto), from Niagara to Quebec. It was a difficult time for the talented hero who was in his prime. A year before the war began, he wrote his brother of his situation in the wilderness: "You who have passed all your days in the bustle of London, can scarcely conceive the uninteresting and insipid life I am doomed to lead in this retirement." But Brock's professional misfortunes were Canada's advantage. He was only forty-two when the war started, was physically imposing, charismatic, and smart, had acquired a sophisticated understanding of the land, Indians, and people of Canada, and had the respect of everyone he encountered. In short, he was the opposite of his adversary, General Hull.[18]

In very short time, General Brock had taken a small army that was plagued by a lack of muskets, supplies, and morale and prepared it as well as anyone could have done. He organized defenses and trained his troops. There were only 5,200 British regulars in all of Canada when General Hull invaded, and Brock commanded only 1,200 of them in Upper Canada. But he organized roughly 11,000 Canadian militiamen to support his small army, nevertheless worrying that he would be lucky if one-third of them would actually fight.

Equally importantly, Brock earned the high admiration of Chief Tecumseh, who deemed it an honor to fight with the courageous British officer. Disgusted by the ways of the white man and white culture, Tecumseh's faith was momentarily restored by Brock's strength and honor as well as by his bold plan to lead an offensive against the superior American forces. In fact, after meeting Brock at Fort Malden near Amherstburg, Tecumseh gushed, "Now here is a man!"[19] Both men were instinctive and fearless warriors who quickly formed both a friendship and an alliance.

In addition to an inadequate army, Brock was hampered by Sir George Prevost, his superior who commanded all British political and military operations in Canada. The two men could not have been more different. Prevost was as political and cautious as Brock was bold and fearless. At a meeting in July at the capital city of York in Upper Canada, Governor Prevost and the legislature ignored Brock's repeated warning of a full-scale invasion. General Brock even urged Prevost to impose martial law but the governor

ordered Brock to not engage the Americans and avoid any offensive operations. But Brock had been tipped off on the details of the American invasion
from Detroit through Hull's confiscated letters aboard the *Cuyahoga*. He
thus acted quickly to take advantage of Hull's hesitation. Ignoring Governor
Prevost, Brock scrambled to organize 500 volunteers and, from his base at
York, rushed his small army to intercept the Americans and reinforce British
outposts on the border. With a skeleton detachment of 40 British regulars
and 250 militiamen, Brock arrived at Amherstburg on the night of August
13. His quick thinking and subsequent actions helped save Upper Canada.

## THE FORT MICHILIMACKINAC DEBACLE

While General Hull focused on the wording of his decree to all of Canada
and dallied near the border, he neglected the defense of American forts in
the Northwest Territories. Hull never imagined the British and their allies
would take the fight to him.

One of those American forts was Fort Michilimackinac located in
Michigan territory on the American side of the Canadian border. The fort's
name was from a Chippewa term that had been Anglicized to "Mackinac," which was also the name of the two-by-three-mile island strategically
nestled at the intersection of Lake Huron and Lake Michigan. The British
built the fort but it was later transferred to the United States after the Jay
Treaty of 1794, whereupon the Americans nicknamed it Fort Mackinac.
It was a strategically important fortification for the defense of trading and
commercial routes on several waterways, including the narrow straights
joining the two lakes (known as the Straits of Mackinac) and nearby St.
Mary's River which runs from Lake Michigan into Lake Huron.

Not far from Fort Mackinac was a small British outpost named for
the island where it was built—St. Joseph Island. The fort was commanded
by a young captain named Charles Roberts. Unlike the American general,
William Hull, General Brock dispatched couriers as soon as the war was
declared to alert all forts in the region. Captain Roberts was given bold
orders by Brock, who told him to immediately march a small cadre of men
from Fort St. Joseph to strike Fort Mackinac. Brock reasoned that Fort
Mackinac would be completely unprepared for the attack. He was right.

On July 15, 1812, forty-six British regulars and 180 Canadian voya-
geurs, supplemented by approximately 400 Indian allies—which Brock and

Roberts had wisely courted in anticipation of war—rushed to the American fort. The force trekked through dense forests and paddled in canoes to Mackinac Island, arriving on the evening of July 16. After coming ashore, they quietly positioned cannons on a nearby hill, as per Brock's orders. By morning they were in position around the fort.

Mackinac was commanded by Lieutenant Porter Hanks and garrisoned with only fifty-seven regulars. Hanks was accustomed to fur traders and Indians coming to the fort to trade, but had noticed an increase in the number of Indians and traders in area. So, he sent a fur trader named Michael Dousman out on the lake to investigate. Dousman was captured by the British and appears to have given up details on the fort and its defenses. On the morning of July 17, Lieutenant Hanks awakened to the sight of British cannons on the hill overlooking the fort. Hanks had not even heard that war had been declared!

At ten o'clock in the morning, Captain Roberts sent a messenger to the fort under the flag of truce. The message delivered to the Americans was: "Surrender or face the uncertain actions of our Indian allies!" Upon hearing that the war had been declared, the American commander is said to have gasped, "War! What war?"[20] Indian brutality was a frequent topic of conversation in the area, so the meaning of the threat was clear to Lieutenant Hanks. Moreover, Brock knew his American opponent, General Hull, was frightened by the prospects of Indian savagery. This threat would find its way to Hull and other American commanders and soldiers. The feisty young American officer in command of Fort Mackinac wanted to fight, but the fort was completely unprepared for war and he was outmanned, outgunned, and outmaneuvered. So, reluctantly, on July 17, Lieutenant Hanks ordered the surrender of Fort Mackinac. Hanks negotiated the terms of surrender so that he and his men were free to go unharmed by Britain's Indian allies, providing they pledge not to fight against the British for the duration of the new war.[21] Americans were shocked and outraged when the learned that Fort Mackinac had been captured without a shot being fired. The British now controlled access to two important lakes and renamed the outpost Fort George.

The Americans tried unsuccessfully to retake this strategically-located fort later during the war. When the War of 1812 ended, the U.S. military burned the fort to the ground despite its strategic location. It had come to represent an embarrassing failure.

## AMBUSH!

Back at Amherstburg, General Hull began to worry that he was exposed in enemy territory. Had he marched too quickly and too far into enemy territory? Would his army be cut off from their supply lines back to Ohio and Michigan? The fact of the matter was that Hull had barely crossed the border and had not encountered any serious opposition, but his natural hesitancy and fear of Indian raids unnerved him, as did the news of Fort Mackinac's fall. Nor did Hull make preparations to secure his vulnerable supply lines running miles through uninhabited forests and across rivers. These lines kept his men clothed, fed, and stocked with ammunition, something Chief Tecumseh recognized. He and his warriors began attacking the resupply caravans.

In early August, only six weeks after the start of the war, an American supply column led by Captain Brush was marching a herd of cattle through the wilderness to feed Hull's army. The small force stopped at River Raisin because the river road had been blockaded by Indians. A nervous Captain Brush dispatched a courier to inform General Hull that Chief Tecumseh, who had crossed the Detroit River and was attacking Americans, appeared to be in the area. Hull agreed to send reinforcements to escort the supply column and, on August 4, he ordered roughly 200 Ohio militiamen under the command of Major Thomas Van Horne to escort Brush's supply team.

However, Van Horne's troops ended up being ambushed by Tecumseh near Gibraltar and Brownstown in Michigan territory, roughly thirty-five miles south of Detroit. On August 5, with Van Horne's men exposed and vulnerable while crossing a creek, Tecumseh attacked. The Shawnee chief was joined by only twenty-four warriors, but he caught the Americans unprepared and his ambush was well planned. From the cover of the forest, the Indians opened fire, whooping and hollering. Van Horne gave the order to pull back. As the Americans fled from the creek, they believed incorrectly that Tecumseh had a large army and were likely joined by the British. The American retreat turned into a full panic. Van Horne lost control of his troops who fled all the way to Fort Lernout. Roughly eighteen Americans were killed, twelve were wounded in the ambush, and two were captured by their Indian attackers. These two were killed. Only one of Tecumseh's warriors—a fellow chief—was killed. But, more importantly for Tecumseh, seventy of the militiamen who fled went missing. Reports of the Indian raids reached Captain Brush, General Hull, and other American units and they began to panic.

Major Van Horne's escort force never made it to River Raisin to escort Captain Brush's supply convoy, so a nervous Brush ordered his men to high-tail it back to safety without resupplying Hull's army. Just three days later, on August 8, General Hull sent Lieutenant Colonel James Miller, to check on the whereabouts of Van Horne and the supply convoys near the border, as well as other units that went missing. However, Miller's comparatively large force of 600 men was also ambushed near the Indian village of Maguaga (or Manguagon), roughly fourteen miles from Detroit. The attack was led by Tecumseh and a British major named Adam Muir, who commanded seventy-five British regulars and sixty Canadian militiamen. Tecumseh brought over seventy braves and planned the brilliant ambush.

The surprise attack at Maguaga succeeded. The Americans lost eighteen men and had sixty-three wounded. Only one British soldier was killed and Major Muir's force suffered only about twenty-three wounded, but Tecumseh lost a few dozen braves. The ambush could have been far worse for the unprepared Americans, but in the thick of the woods the British fired mistakenly on their own Indian allies who Tecumseh sent to attack from the flank. This gave the American troops, with superior numbers, time to return fire and then retreat. But, on account of the ambush, the Americans never finished their mission.

The next day, on August 9, another unit of American soldiers was ambushed by a few British regulars and Canadian militiamen supported by Indians. The Americans managed to prevail this time and their attackers melted back into the forest. However, the frequency of the ambushes prevented American supply convoys from delivering the needed supplies. The loss of so many convoys and scouts also meant that General Hull's letters to the War Department were intercepted and given to General Brock, who used the intelligence gathered from them against Hull. The invasion of Canada was only days old but was going horribly for the Americans.


## THE FORT DEARBORN MASSACRE

But it was a tragedy at Fort Dearborn, near present-day Chicago on the southwestern shore of Lake Michigan, that had the effect of ending the first-prong of the invasion of Canada. Fort Dearborn had been under constant attack by Indians for months and the small outpost was running low on supplies. The fort was down to just fifty-four soldiers, making it extremely vulnerable. Rather than resupply or reinforce the outpost, General Hull sent a courier from Fort Detroit to order the fort's commander, Captain Nathan Heald, to abandon the post. By then, Hull was aware that Fort Mackinac had been lost and his supply convoys were ambushed. He began to panic.

Captain Heald did not want to abandon the fort, its provisions, or the nearby residents who were dependent on the fort for protection from Indian attacks. But Heald followed orders and departed with his men. He brought with him about forty civilians—mostly women and children, and a handful of traders—offering them protection. Hull had also ordered Heald to notify the local Indian villages of the abandonment of the fort and to give his provisions to Indians in the area. Hull naively assumed the gestures could serve as an exchange for safe passage. Heald opposed the order and did not trust the negotiator and Indians with whom he traded. But, he reluctantly complied with Hull's foolish decision. Sure enough, it only had the effect of notifying the Indians in the area of the exact time that the soldiers from the fort would be exposed while marching out of the fort.

On August 15, the small party headed south toward Fort Wayne, as per General Hull's orders. Heald and his men were escorted by a white man named William Wells who was a trader that had been captured by the Miami nation when he was young. Accordingly, Wells learned to speak the Miami's language and married the sister of the Miami chief, Little Turtle. Wells then went on to offer—or sell—his services to the highest bidder, working both for and against the Indians. Heald never trusted Wells, and for good reason. Wells was about to double-cross him.[22]

Heald had his men march with muskets ready in the event Wells and his thirty Miami escorts tried anything. Anticipating the worst, Heald's men even played the funeral march on their fife and drums as they abandoned the fort. The soldiers and civilians were only one mile from the fort by a series of large sandy dunes on the edge of Lake Michigan, when the shadowy Wells led the convoy directly into an ambush by a larger war party. The Potawatomi and Winnebago braves, hiding in the woods, swooped in on the group before Heald's men had time to organize defenses. Many of the Miami escorts fled at the site of the large war party, but others turned and started firing on the men they were supposed to be escorting.

Heald's soldiers rallied and succeeded in driving the Indian attackers back into the woods. However, many of the women and children in the party dropped what they had been carrying and ran. They headed into a flanking war party waiting for them in the woods opposite the scene of the slaughter. Loyal to Tecumseh and still smarting over the loss at Tippecanoe, the braves of all three nations wanted blood. They massacred the civilians, despite Captain Heald's attempt at the outset of the battle to parley with the Potawatomi chief, Black Bird, who led the ambush.

Heald lost roughly half the men in his command and most of the civilians. The battle was hopelessly lost so Heald ordered his men to run and he fled into the woods with his wife. Black Bird took the few surviving civilians prisoner. The large war party then burned the fort and surrounding homes to the ground. The fort and village were not rebuilt during the war, remaining as a charred reminder of the massacre. Fortunately for Captain Heald, he and his wife managed to escape and ran into a fur trader who lent them his canoe. Heald paddled for days until he arrived at Fort Mackinac. Unbeknownst to him, the fort had just days before been taken by the British and was now in the hands of Captain Charles Roberts. However, Roberts freed Heald and his wife, and even graciously provided them with a small boat, which the American captain sailed to Fort Detroit.

As for William Wells, many years earlier he had double-crossed the Miami and fought against them in the decisive American victory at Fallen Timbers led by General "Mad" Anthony Wayne. Wells was caught by the warriors during the massacre. They then double-crossed the double-crosser and promptly scalped and beheaded him. A similar fate awaited the civilian prisoners. Black Bird's warriors tortured and killed most of them. When an American scouting party eventually arrived at the scene of the carnage, they discovered the bodies of women and children "lying naked with principally all their heads off."[23]

## THE SURRENDER OF FORT DETROIT

Tired, in poor health, and now thoroughly unnerved, General Hull continued to make bad decisions. American outposts in the region were neither warned nor adequately garrisoned. Hull failed to account for the difficulty of transporting cannons through the dense wilderness and thus lacked the necessary artillery to bomb Fort Malden. By the time the assault on Fort Malden commenced, General Isaac Brock had already sacked Fort Mackinac and rushed his volunteers to reinforce Fort Malden and succeeded in beating back the American attack.

It was yet another embarrassment for Hull. News of the victories by Brock and Tecumseh—despite being greatly outnumbered—buoyed Canadian spirits and attracted additional recruits. An additional 600 Indian allies eagerly joined Tecumseh. Brock took advantage of the momentum and Hull's growing doubts by having Tecumseh perform additional attacks on Hull's supply lines, scouts, and even forts in American territory.

On July 28, General Hull worried that "The whole northern hordes of Indians will be let loose upon us."[24] Despite having superior numbers, Hull panicked and abandoned the invasion of Canada. He retreated all the way to Fort Detroit, which he presumed to be safe. By this time, Hull's command was in mutiny against him and urged Lieutenant Colonel Miller to demand the General's sword. But Miller was one of the few officers still loyal to Hull and declined his fellow officers' requests. Ironically, on hearing the news of the failures, the War Department and President Madison were furious and planned to have General Hull replaced by none other than Miller. However, word from the War Department to remove Hull arrived too late to save the army of the Northwest and Fort Detroit.[25]

Meanwhile, Brock rushed from his success at Fort Malden to audaciously pursue a far bigger prize—the main American fort in Detroit. Hull, now safely ensconced inside Fort Detroit, was horrified to learn that, seemingly out of nowhere, Brock and Tecumseh arrived on the shores of the Detroit River. On August 14, Brock began erecting cannon and mortar batteries. The siege of Fort Detroit began and Hull never saw it coming. In a full panic, Hull sent 350 of his best men out to try to find the missing supply lines and reinforcements. They were unsuccessful and the action served only to weaken the fort's defenses.

Detroit was not a large city. On the contrary, it was a town with only a few hundred people and roughly 150 homes. However, it contained the most important fort and stockade in the region. Moreover, it was on American soil and General Hull was inside with the largest American army in the territory. It was thus an irresistible target for the daring Brock. Using both deception and surprise, while playing on his opponent's fear of Indians, on August 15 Brock cleverly demanded Hull's immediate surrender. The British general warned that, if they fought and he won, he could not guarantee that Tecumseh and his Indian allies would refrain from scalping and then killing all inhabitants of the fort and town.[26] Brock's aide delivered a note to Hull that read:

> I require of you the immediate surrender of fort Detroit. It is far from my intention to join in a war of extermination; but you must be aware that the numerous body of Indians who have

attached themselves to my troops will be beyond my control the moment the contest commences.[27]

Of course, it was all a bluff. Brock had neither enough men nor artillery to lay siege to a large fort with over 2,000 defenders inside. Later that day, Brock ordered his few cannons to begin the bombardment of Fort Detroit. Among the townspeople of Detroit, was Lydia Bacon, who was caught in the fort during the bombardment. She described what she witnessed, writing "The cannon began to roar apparently with tenfold fury. A 24-pound shot cut two officers who were standing in the entry directly in two, their bowels gushing out."[28] Another one of the first cannonballs to explode in the fort hit and decapitated Lieutenant Porter Hanks, the officer who had reluctantly abandoned Fort Mackinac. The defenders inside the fort were alarmed by these gruesome scenes and read the bizarre coincidence as foreshadowing a terrible defeat.

Brock further unnerved the defenders inside the fort by ordering his Indians allies to scream terrifying cries during the first night of the siege. Brock correctly predicted that, at best, his ploy would cause Hull to panic and surrender or, at the least, the American army would head out to meet their opponents. On an open field, Brock knew that his well-trained soldiers and Tecumseh's warriors could best the larger army. Inside the fort, General Hull received word of additional ambushes and worried his reinforcements were not coming. His men talked of scalpings and beheadings at the hands of Tecumseh's braves. Brock's ruse worked perfectly.

Believing Brock had a huge army—which he did not—Hull, with at least a two-to-one advantage in troops and from the safety of the massive fort, ordered the surrender of Fort Detroit on August 16. The general sent his son, who served as his aide, across the river under a flag of truce to meet Brock. Inside the fort, Hull's officers, who were not even consulted by him on the surrender, were outraged at the cowardice of their commander. Three hours after the younger Hull met with General Brock, an army of over 2,000 Americans marched out of the fort. Brock had agreed to "control" his Indian allies and assure Hull and his men a safe surrender. By some accounts, Hull was nearly catatonic by the time of the surrender, saying only that "I have done what my conscience directed. I have saved Detroit and the Territory from the horrors of an Indian massacre." He also claimed he was low on ammunition; but it was courage that Hull lacked.[29]

Hull had not only given Brock the fort, but a hugely symbolic victory. Brock was also able to capture a cache of desperately needed cannons (thirty-three of them), muskets, powder, horses, supplies, and even a new ship from the fort. The British could now hope to defend Canada from additional American attacks. A triumphant Brock thanked Tecumseh by giving him a red military sash, which Tecumseh became well-known for wearing around his head. Tecumseh returned the gesture by giving the British general his beaded sash.

After the victory, which galvanized the defense of Canada, Brock posted a small detachment of men at the fort but rushed back to Canada in anticipation of the other waves of the invasion. He had before him the daunting task of trying to organize a defense of the entire Niagara region and Lake Erie. But, once again, General Brock was dressed down by Sir George Prevost, the governor of Canada, for refusing a direct order despite the mission's impressive success. Prevost ordered Brock to cease and desist from offensive engagements. Brock again ignored the order.

The British controlled the Michigan Territory and held Fort Detroit for over one year. They ultimately surrendered it to the Americans in late September of 1813. The Americans, still embarrassed by the disastrous loss a year earlier, renamed it Fort Shelby and succeeded in holding the fort for the remainder of the war. As for Hull, he was court-martialed and sentenced to death for his actions. However, the death penalty was overturned and Hull was awarded a stay on account of his prior service during the American Revolution. The cowardly general lived in disgrace until 1825.

# 10

# THE BATTLE OF
# QUEENSTON HEIGHTS

## A SECOND PRONG OF THE INVASION

Two months after the disastrous campaign into Canada by General William Hull, the Americans embarked on the second of the three-pronged invasion. This one was farther to the east in the present-day province of Ontario. The campaign was especially sensitive because relations between Americans and Canadians along the Niagara River separating the two countries had long been friendly. One story suggests that when news of the war arrived in the region, a group of American officers from Fort Niagara were dining with their British counterparts from nearby Fort George. On hearing about the war, the men exchanged courtesies, shook hands, and wished one another luck. The American officers then boarded a boat and crossed the river to prepare for attack.

New York and Canada are separated by the Niagara River. It runs just thirty-five miles from Lake Ontario in the east to Lake Erie, which is to the southwest. This compact region would end up being one of the most strategic theaters of the entire war [see Map 2 in Appendix]. Both countries had large populations on either side of the border and both lakes were vitally important trade routes. Once the war started both armies attempted to control the lakes and the Niagara River that separated them in order to transport supplies, troops, and armaments.

Two important forts commanded the region—Fort Niagara on the American side and Fort George on the Canadian side. Both forts would be engulfed in war and numerous battles were fought in the vicinity, including Chippewa, Grimsby, Lundy's Lane, Stoney Creek, and Thorold, along with naval engagements on the waters of Niagara, Ontario, and Erie. Whoever controlled these lakes and forts controlled the region. Perhaps not surprisingly, some of the most aggressive fighting of the war took place here.

The conflict along the Niagara and Lake Ontario actually started a bit farther to the northeast, on the St. Lawrence River, and would spark some of the action during the second prong. There were also cross-border raids in the region committed by both armies. The St. Lawrence, a major waterway in eastern Canada, connects the Atlantic Ocean in the east, via the Gulf of St. Lawrence, with Lake Ontario to the southwest. Upon the river's shores are the important cities of Quebec, Montreal, and Kingston, and the southern edge of the river serves as a border between New York and Canada.

## RAIDS

As soon as the war was declared, American soldiers from the garrison at Ogdensburg, New York began harassing shipping and villages on the Canadian side of the river. One such incident occurred on September 16, 1812, when a small group of Americans attacked Toussaint Island on the St. Lawrence.

The Americans sailed to the Island, which was known to house armaments, but were observed doing so by British soldiers who were on the river in small boats. The problem for the British was that they were transporting civilians, including women and children in the boats. Regardless of their "precious cargo," the British decided to engage the American invaders sailing the small boats to the shoreline. From the cover of trees, the Americans opened fire on the British while they attempted to land and join the fight. With women screaming, children bawling, and British officers trying to organize an attack, the boats ran aground and people poured out of them amid the American musket balls.

The son of one of the British officers, a boy named P. F. Finan, described the pandemonium he saw as well as a moment of levity that occurred in the midst of the mayhem. An older woman in one of the boats named Molly fell and hit her elbow on the side of the craft. Thinking she was shot, the woman cried out, "Oh, I'm shot! I'm shot!" A British soldier at her side examined her elbow and noted that it was red but that she had not been shot. However, the woman insisted, screaming, "Oh, bad luck to the Yankee rascals, they've done my job! I'm shot! I'm shot!" The soldier, finding humor in the moment, announced to all in the boat, "Faith, Molly, you're done now sure enough." Because the boat was an open target, the soldier then shoved Molly off the boat, proclaiming "But you had better get ashore as fast as you can!"[1]

Another woman caught in the melee, the wife of an officer stationed in Kingston, was rather overweight and in poor health. As such, she could not and would not get off the boat. An officer onboard rushed to help her off the craft. She agreed to be helped off but, despite the bullets flying overhead, her concern at that moment was not to get wet. So, the officer tried to carry her on his back. But, when they entered the shallow water, her weight was such that he sank down into the mud and became stuck. As others tried to help them, he said to the stout lady, " 'Pon my honor, Mrs., I'll be under the necessity of putting you down!" These two humorous moments seemed to reassure the British soldiers caught in the crossfire. They managed to jump off the boat and wade ashore to engage the Americans.

The fighting continued on the shore as civilian passengers from the boats ran for cover. Fortunately for the British, one of their gunboats from the garrison at Prescott appeared on the river. At the sight of the approaching gunboat, the American marauders fled back across the river without ever seizing the British armaments. The skirmish, like so many Indian raids, put women and children directly in the line of fire. This would not be the only time civilians became targets of the war.

One week after their failure to seize armaments on Toussaint Island, seventy soldiers of the American 1st Rifles set sail for another raid. From Sackets Harbor in New York, the raiding party sailed on small boats on Lake Ontario and the St. Lawrence. After three days they arrived at the Canadian village of Gananoque undetected thanks to the cover of many small islands and the skills of a few New York sailors who knew the waters. The small American force was led by Captain Benjamin Forsyth, a young, untested officer from North Carolina.

On September 21, 1812, they came ashore at a place called Sheriff's Point. However, two Canadian militiamen in the area spotted them and mounted their horses in order to race back to Gananoque to sound the alarm. The riflemen opened fire, killing one of the sentries. The other rider made it to the village. As the Americans headed down the main road to the village of Gananoque, they were met by a collection of townspeople who had been rustled out of their sleep, some still in night clothing. In all, there were sixty defenders of the village who took up formation across the road. Their leader was Colonel Joel Stone, one of the pioneers who founded the community. Stone had been born in Connecticut, but remained loyal to the Crown during the American Revolution, moving to Canada along with a group of like-minded Americans.

The colonel ordered his militia and townsmen to stand their ground. The Americans crept cautiously closer and Stone gave the order to fire. A great billow of smoke poured forth and a few members of the 1st U.S. Rifles fell. Foregoing a return volley, Captain Forsyth gave the order to charge. As the Americans rushed the village's defenders, the Canadians turned and fled. It was a quick and relatively bloodless rout.[2]

Unfortunately, the young Captain Forsyth permitted his men to plunder the town. While doing so, a stray bullet went into a home and, coincidentally, wounded Colonel Stone's wife. The Americans stayed just long enough to take muskets, ammunition, and a few prisoners, and burn a store. Then they hurried back to Sackets Harbor. British forces down river in Kingston were later alerted to the raid and gave chase, but never found the Americans. Although not very dramatic, this skirmish constituted the first "successful" American offensive operation of the war in Canada, but it was marred by the looting of civilian property. News of the Americans' behavior did not sit well with the British or Canadians.

## COSTLY DELAYS

It was on nearby Lake Ontario and the Niagara River, however, where the Americans focused the second prong of their invasion of Canada [see Map 2 in Appendix]. In October of 1812, an American force comprised of 900 regulars and 2,650 New York militiamen was organized in Lewiston. Their mission was to cross the Niagara and establish an American stronghold on the Canadian side of the border. The battle that followed was the first major conflict of the War of 1812.

This second prong of the invasion was led by General Stephen Van Rensselaer, a politician lacking adequate military experience and a poor choice to command an army. A Harvard graduate and one of the wealthiest men in America, Rensselaer was, ironically enough, also opposed to the war. Like General Hull, Van Rensselaer never had the respect of his officers or troops and went to war with a poorly trained, unruly army. His New

York militiamen ended up refusing to cross into Canada and his invasion ended in disaster.

Van Rensselaer was a leading Federalist candidate for governor of New York. The sitting governor, Daniel Tompkins, advocated in favor of Van Rensselaer's appointment as general, apparently so that he would be out of the way politically. It was also hoped that the appointment would limit Federalist opposition to the war. But, on account of the back-and-forth bickering and incompetence of so many involved, Van Rensselaer's appointment was not made until July 13, 1812. He therefore did not have time to execute the second prong of the invasion in time, which was further hampered by a lack of supplies and difficulties recruiting enough troops. Had this "central" prong of the invasion occurred simultaneously with Hull's western invasion as initially planned, the minimal British defenses may have been stretched far too thin. But the delay allowed General Isaac Brock, fresh off his victory at Detroit, to rush back to defend the Niagara River region.

Van Rensselaer's army was likely saved from complete annihilation when Sir George Prevost overruled Brock, who wanted to attack the Americans before they were at full strength. When September arrived—with the invasion still running behind schedule—Van Rensselaer had only 691 men of his army of roughly 3,500 ready. But Prevost's caution gave the Americans time to build a larger fighting force. Reportedly, Prevost delayed Brock because he still held out hope that peace negotiations would prevent further fighting. Prevost had sent word to the American commander of the three invasions, General Henry Dearborn, that he would be open to armistice talks. The United States rejected the idea. However, Prevost appears to have authorized Major General Sheaffe to commence talks with Van Rensselaer's cousin, Colonel Solomon Van Rensselaer, a veteran of the Indian campaign at Fallen Timbers.[3]

In effect, all the talks did was delay the fighting and give General Van Rensselaer time to staff his army and equip it with supplies. Brock simmered as he watched these events unfold. When they were ready to invade, the Americans simply ended the "armistice" talks on September 8, 1812. Even though Van Rensselaer had bought his army time, and Sir Prevost's diplomatic overtures had undermined Brock's planned offensive, the ongoing talks and delays did have the effect of alerting British and Canadian forces of the American invasion. The British had only about 1,500 soldiers, Canadian militiamen, and Mohawk Indian allies to defend the region. But Brock prepared them for the invaders.[4]

# THE CROSSING

Van Rennselaer's army of over 3,500 men camped at Lewiston, which bordered the Niagara River and sat opposite of Queenston Heights on the Canadian side [see Map 3 in Appendix]. They were to be joined by 1,700 troops under Brigadier General Alexander Smyth. However, the additional troops came with baggage. General Smyth detested General Van Rennselaer and refused to follow his orders. Even without Smyth's army, Van Rennselaer had more than enough men for the task. On the other side of the river, the British were seriously outnumbered.

Brock assumed the American attack would come in late summer, but by October the Americans still had not attacked. He also assumed the target would be Fort George, so Brock deployed most of his army there, and stationed grenadiers and militiamen in the vicinity to prevent any flanking attacks.

Finally, on October 9, the invasion began. It started when Lieutenant Jesse Elliot led a small American force to the head of the Niagara River, where they captured two British ships near Fort Erie. However, while sailing the two brigs back to be used in the invasion, one ran aground, perhaps foreboding the bad luck the Americans would have in the days to come. Elliot was forced to burn it rather than allow it to be recaptured by the British. When Brock heard this news, he assumed the Americans were preparing to strike on the Niagara near Buffalo. So the general dispatched part of his army there. However, Brock soon realized that the incident was unrelated to a direct attack and rushed the men back to base camp. Unfortunately for the Americans, their scouts reported to General Van Rennselaer that the British were still in Buffalo, leaving Queenston largely undefended.

General Van Rennselaer thus commenced the invasion on October 11, ordering the first wave of 3,500 men to cross the Niagara River at three o'clock in the morning. Van Rennselaer's cousin, Colonel Solomon Van Rennselaer, on whom the commander depended for military advice, was to lead this attack but he was suddenly taken ill. Confident of their success, the Americans went forward with the plan even without the general's cousin in command. While Van Rennselaer attacked Queenston Heights from Lewiston, General Smyth was ordered to simultaneously attack Fort George, a few miles away at Lake Ontario "with every possible dispatch." However, Smyth refused to follow the command. Van Rennselaer did not find out about Smyth's refusal until it was too late.

The first wave of Van Rensselaer's army boarded boats and began the crossing to Queenston. But the weather was foul. Heavy rains and thick mud made the roads impassable. Nearby and unknown to Van Rensselaer, General Smyth decided to march his army back to his base at Black Rock near Buffalo and wait for better weather. The Niagara was only 200 to 250 yards wide at the point of the crossing, so Van Rensselaer continued to send boats across. But the banks were steep and the swelling river flowed swiftly. Van Rensselaer's inexperienced army, now cold and wet, struggled mightily with the river and driving rain storm. Some of the boats were swept downriver far past the landing zone. Additionally, at the worst possible moment, a lieutenant by the name of Sims decided to desert. Sims simply paddled away in one of the boats, but the boat he picked contained the spare oars for the rest of the flotilla.[5]

## A SECOND CROSSING

Observing the disastrous crossing, Van Rensselaer halted the invasion. When the weather improved two days later, he tried it again, sending two columns each containing 300 men back across the river. Meanwhile, General Smyth wrote to Van Rensselaer that he was back in camp but would commence his invasion on October 14. Van Rensselaer's letter stating that the invasion would recommence on the 13th either did not arrive in time to alert Smyth, or it is also highly possible that the letter did arrive but the insubordinate general simply ignored it.[6]

The delay helped General Brock. On October 12, one of his officers from Fort George, Major Thomas Evans, was ordered to march under the flag of truce to negotiate a prisoner swap. Lieutenant Elliot had taken prisoners during his raid on Canada on the 9th. When Major Evans was in the American camp, he saw the tell-tale signs of the invasion, including a number of boats. All this was quickly reported to Brock, who immediately ordered his number two, Major General Sheaffe, who was in command at Fort George, to be prepared. Brock also reinforced the defenses at Queenston and put nearby locations such as Chippewa and Fort Erie on high alert.

Queenston was a small village of farmhouses, peach orchards, and large stone barracks nestled alongside the Niagara River. Just south of the village was a 300-foot-high bank known as Queenston Heights, which was covered in dense vegetation and sloped steeply down to the river. The village was defended by a small fort containing a company of soldiers led by Captain James Dennis and York militiamen under Captain George Chisholm. A small detachment of men was also positioned on the top of the Heights under the command of Captain John Williams, with a cannon dug in part way up the hill. Just north of the village at Vrooman's Point, Brock placed a company led by Captain Samuel Hatt and two militia companies under Captains Cameron and Heward. They guarded against flanking moves by the Americans or efforts to land the army upriver and then march it to Queenston. Two cannons looked out across the river at this point. Though seriously outnumbered, the Canadian border would be defended.

As the second attempt to cross the river began, a quarrel broke out between Colonel Solomon Van Rensselaer and Lieutenant Colonel John Chrystie about who should lead the crossing. This further delayed and strained the effort. It was decided to split the command, with Chrystie leading about 900 U.S. infantry regiments. Colonel Van Rensselaer led the New York militia regiments and a group of volunteer riflemen, comprising about 2,650 soldiers. Most of these men would never make it across the river.

On the shore that morning were twelve boats large enough to transport about thirty men each along with two larger boats capable of carrying eighty men and cannons, supplies, and wagons across the Niagara. At four o'clock in the morning of October 13, 1812, the crossing began with 300 men. Three of the first boats to push out into the river were immediately swept down river. One of them carried Colonel Chyrstie. Chrystie's boat and another managed to make their way back to the American side of the river, while the third boat was carried by the current far downriver.

Van Rensselaer managed to make it to the Canadian shoreline with about 200 men, but they were spotted by Captain Dennis's detachment. The Americans were thus pinned down on the muddy banks of the river from cannons and muskets firing from the high ground on and around the heights. Colonel Van Rensselaer was one of the first casualties. The wounded Colonel, struck by a musket ball, tried to rally his panicked troops on the muddy bank of the river, but he was hit five more times. With Colonel Van Rensselaer bleeding on the bank of the river and his men falling around him, panic set in. Amazingly, the Colonel lived through the battle but command was passed to his second-in-command, Captain John Wool.

As sunrise came, additional boats attempted to cross. But, with the break of daylight, the British began a deadly accurate bombardment of the American troops across the river at Lewiston. This unnerved the poorly trained militiamen. Many of them began refusing to get into boats. Others simply ran from the camp. Mass desertion now threatened the army.

Cannon fire also rained down on the boats trying to cross the swift river. American boats were hit or sunk; some boat pilots panicked and turned their craft back around. One of those boats was carrying a very frustrated Colonel Chrystie, who was still trying to get across the river to command the battle. Boats on either side of his were torn apart by artillery fire. Another boat carried Lieutenant Colonel John Fenwick, the former commander of Fort Niagara. It was carried far downriver. When Fenwick and his men finally made landfall, they found themselves surrounded by British soldiers on shoreline. Fenwick was shot in the face. He survived but he and his men were taken prisoner.

Things looked bleak for the Americans. However, the captain who assumed command when Colonel Van Rensselaer was shot numerous times proved to be a worthy officer. Though seriously wounded, Van Rensselaer ordered his second in command to "ascend the heights by the point of the rock, and storm the battery." If they could take the high ground and the large cannon there, they might yet salvage the battle.[7]

Only twenty-three, Captain John Wool encouraged his men to get off the banks, where they had been pinned down. He found a small trail that skirted the British defenses on Queenston Heights and climbed it using the thick underbrush as cover. Meanwhile, a few American boats managed to land, and Captain Dennis and his defenders were pushed off the banks of river and back into the village.

Just after sunrise, Captain Wool and his men emerged from the vegetation atop the Heights to surprise the British units there. After a quick skirmish, the British spiked their cannon and fled. Though the large cannon was inoperable, Wool now commanded the top of the Heights. From his point high atop the Heights, Wool was now in a position to change the dynamic of the battle.

## THE DEATH OF GENERAL BROCK

General Brock, who had been at Fort George, was awakened by cannon fire. Uncertain as to whether it was the main attack or just a diversion by the Americans, he decided to inspect the fighting at Queenston himself. Brock left his second in command, General Sheaffe, at Fort George. After galloping on his horse, Alfred, in the darkness, Brock arrived after dawn to discover the main invasion. As he arrived, Captain Wool was seizing the top of Queenston Heights.

As he rode through the fighting, Brock was cheered by his men. Captain Wool's men continued to rain musket balls down on the British from the high ground, but Brock encouraged the defenders to abandon their cover and join him in assaulting the hill. Brock led the assault on the Heights himself. Before beginning the assault, Brock sent riders to notify General Sheaffe at Fort George to bring most of his army to Queenston for a massive counterattack. Brock also ordered some of the British soldiers fleeing from the Heights to go and form a defensive position in the village because the Americans were now marching on the town. He kept roughly 100 of the men from the 49th Regiment for his assault on the redoubt atop the hill.

A hero and legend while still alive, and still wearing the garment given to him by Chief Tecumseh amid his red uniform and gold epaulettes, Brock looked the part. The General stood tall and rallied his men with the admonition, "This is the first time I have ever seen the 49th turn their backs! Surely the heroes of Egmont will not tarnish their record!"[8] Leading from the front, the dashing general was exposed and was shot first in the wrist, then in the chest, which knocked him off his mount. Legend suggests that his dying words were "Push on York Volunteers!" or "Push on, brave volunteers!" The authenticity of these words is uncertain, as the shot likely would have killed Brock instantly.[9]

The British continued the charge in the name of their fallen commander and nearly succeeded in pushing Captain Wool's men back. However, Lieutenant Colonel MacDonnell, commanding the British from the front as Brock would have done, had his horse shot out from under him. Picking himself up from the fall, MacDonnell was hit in the back. The other British officers, Captain Williams and Captain Dennis, were hit in the head and thigh, respectively. With their commanders knocked out of the fight, the British counterattack withered. Carrying their officers, the British retreated back down the hill. The American defenders were quickly reinforced and succeeded in holding the Heights.

## SNATCHING DEFEAT FROM THE JAWS OF VICTORY

By mid-morning it appeared that Queenston would be an American victory. With British riflemen and artillery batteries pushed back from the shoreline, a few hundred fresh American reinforcements made it across the river. The invaders held the high ground and had made it into the village. Only one British cannon was still harassing American boats attempting to cross the river—the 18-pounder nearby at Vrooman's Point.

At noon, General Van Rensselaer came ashore to inspect the progress of the battle. With him was Colonel Chrystie, who finally managed to cross the river. Van Rensselaer ordered the Heights be secured. Lieutenant Colonel Winfield Scott was put in charge of the defenses after spending much of the morning insisting that he be permitted to cross the river in order to save the debacle on the Canadian shore. Scott immediately set about reinforcing the Heights and securing the landing zones. Van Rensselaer appointed Brigadier General William Wadsworth to lead the New York militia into Queenston. The battle appeared to be won.

The real fighter among the officers leading the second prong of the invasion was Winfield Scott. The Lieutenant Colonel refused to serve under Colonel Solomon Van Rensselaer because he deemed him unfit. He also had a low opinion of General Van Rensselaer. Scott, twenty-six at the time, hailed from Virginia. It was there, in 1807, as a young attorney, that he watched the trial of Aaron Burr in Richmond on charges of conspiring against the government in his scheme to establish a western empire. Scott was disgusted by Burr and angered by Britain's policy of impressment. He was so outraged when he learned of the HMS *Leopard*'s attack on the USS *Chesapeake* that he abandoned his law practice to enlist in the military.

Scott was commissioned as a captain and served in New Orleans under General James Wilkinson, another corrupt and disloyal officer and politician. Ironically, Scott had observed Wilkinson attempt to save his own hide by turning on Burr at the trial. The fiery young officer publicly declared Wilkinson a "liar and scoundrel" and announced that he was as guilty as Burr in the conspiracy.[10] Scott was so vocal in his criticism of such senior officers that he was nearly court-martialed and pronounced guilty of displaying "conduct unbecoming of an officer and gentleman." But, the War Department reduced his punishment to a lesser offense, probably because Scott simply said what most felt about Wilkinson and other officers.[11] Scott was suspended from the service and returned to his law practice. However, when war broke out he again put on his uniform. Not surprisingly, given his experiences, Scott distrusted most American commanders and earned respect from the men he commanded because of his penchant for taking matters into his own hands.[12]

The American gains during the Battle for Queenston Heights were short lived. General Smyth, who had refused direct orders from Van Rensselaer, never did attack Fort George. This freed the British forces there to act on Brock's final dispatch and reinforce Queenston. The man Brock put in command at Fort George, Major General Roger Hale Sheaffe, arrived at the battle in the early afternoon with 600 men and 100 Mohawk Indian warriors. The York militia, that General Brock so admired, also rushed to the site of the fighting. They were joined by reinforcements from Fort Chippewa under Captain Richard Bullock and a small band of Mohawk warriors.

## SURRENDER

General Sheaffe brought with him batteries from the Royal Artillery, who immediately established positions for their two cannons. These cannons began pounding the American boats ferrying the main army across the river. Two boats were sunk and another was hit, prompting the sailors piloting the other boats to turn them around and head back to the American side of the river. General Van Rensselaer's main army never made it to Queenston's shoreline. Having limited the crossing, the Royal Artillerymen then aimed their cannons on Lewiston and the American staging area on the other side of the river. In short order, the British artillery knocked out the American artillery in Lewiston. The American forces at Lewiston were scurrying for cover or deserting down the road to town.

By mid-afternoon, the British counteroffensive had turned the battle. Most American positions in Queenston and on the Heights were overrun. General Van Rensselaer foolishly announced that he was crossing back over the river, allegedly to obtain more reinforcements and ammunition from Lewiston. This occasioned panic among his troops, who rushed the general's craft and began climbing into it. The boat nearly capsized and gave the impression of disorder, cowardice, and retreat. Nearby, other soldiers began running to the river and trying to cross back to Lewiston.

Safely back on the American shoreline, the general ordered his army to cross in order to reinforce the exhausted and wounded troops in Queenston. However, most units refused, including the large number of New York militiamen. The reports of great casualties from Queenston, the panic created by Van Rensselaer himself, and the Royal Artillery's bombardment of their camp at Lewiston cowed the army. At this same time, the British enacted one of General Brock's tactics and encouraged the Mohawk and Iroquois warriors across the river to start chanting and screaming. The large American camp was now in chaos, as entire units deserted.

The few hundred Americans already on Canadian soil were stuck and on their own. They were also unsupported by artillery. Van Rensselaer could not even muster enough boats to cross the river to evacuate his desperate army. Said the frustrated and inept general:

> I urged the men to pass over the river, but in vain. To my utter astonishment, I found that at the very moment when complete victory was in our hands, the ardor of the unengaged troops had entirely subsided. I rode in all directions—urged men by every consideration to pass over—but in vain.[13]

Van Rensselaer showed his indecisiveness when he then sent a message across the river to General Wadswoth and Colonel Scott informing them that the decision to stay and fight or abandon Queenston was theirs. It was a show of weakness and an attempt to try and avoid responsibility. Several hundred Americans were trapped on the Canadian side of the river. The message they received convinced them that the fight was over. Except for one officer.

On the Heights, Colonel Winfield Scott was outnumbered and surrounded. Wool had failed to hold the Heights. The British captains, John Norton and John Brant, with about 300 soldiers and Indian warriors, climbed the Heights to attack Scott, while the larger British force retook the town and established positions along the riverbank. Scott wanted to fight rather than surrender, so he ordered his men to cut the thick brush on the hill and build a sort of fencing that would allow his men some cover from which to fight. He hoped to hold off the British and work his way down the Heights. But volleys of shot poured into Scott's troops. The warriors then attacked from one flank while the British organized a bayonet charge on the other. It worked. Scott's men broke ranks and fled in all directions.

Scott barked orders and continued fighting his way down the Heights with his few remaining men. He managed to make it to the bottom of the hill, but there they found themselves stranded on the riverbank without boats or support. Nearby, General Wadsworth, with roughly 300 men, had also managed to flee to the river. But there were no reinforcements and no boats for evacuation there either. Scott tried to make a stand. But he was outgunned and his men were unwilling to fight. Two of his officers who tried to surrender were killed by Britain's Indian allies. Suspecting the same fate awaited his men, after thirty minutes Scott waived the white cravat he wore around his neck indicating his surrender to the British. Wadsworth joined him.

But it was then that Scott really became infuriated. As the surrender was taking place, a few hundred Americans along the riverbank, on the hill, and in town also surrendered. There had been enough men to take Queenston but they had been hiding rather than fighting!

# 11

# THREE-PRONGED DISASTER

## TWO STRIKES

After the Battle of Queenston Heights, General Sheaffe, who took command of the British and Canadian forces after the death of General Brock, offered a truce to his American adversaries. Both sides tended to their wounded. From the beginning through the end of the assault—with the exception of a brief moment when the Americans succeeded in capturing the Heights and pushing the British off the river's edge—Queenston had been an unmitigated disaster for the American army. American casualties included approximately 100 killed, 170 wounded, hundreds captured, and hundreds more were missing or deserted. Most of those captured were not militiamen but regulars in the army and were alleged to be the best soldiers the country had. Those militiamen who were captured were paroled and sent back to New York. America's misfortunes continued when thirty of the prisoners later died of their wounds. American supplies and cannons fell into British hands and a few top military commanders like General Wasdsworth and Colonel Scott were captured. British casualties at Queenston were far less, with estimates of perhaps twenty dead, eighty-five wounded, and twenty captured. A few Iroquois and Mohawk were killed and two wounded, but the warriors' chiefs were among the dead.

The first large battle of the War of 1812 resulted in a decisive and vitally symbolic British victory. This second prong of the American invasion of Canada had been beaten back. The defeat exposed a crisis of incompetence among America's generals. The leader of the debacle, General Van Rensselaer, who was dismissed by his own troops as "Van Bladder," was exposed as a coward and forced to resign his commission. American military and political leaders were embarrassed, the secretary of war resigned in disgrace that December, and several generals were reprimanded or forced out of the military.

Shockingly however, the War Department failed to learn an important lesson. Alexander Smyth, the insolent general who refused direct orders and, in not crossing the Niagara River, allowed General Sheaffe to reinforce Queenston and win the battle, was given Van Rensselaer's command.[1] Likewise, Henry Clay, the firebrand who pushed for war and claimed Canada would fall as soon as his Kentucky boys marched across the border, somehow remained in power in Congress.

As accounts of the defeat spread across the country, Americans began losing their appetite for invasion. Stories also spread of ferocious fighting by the British and their Indian allies. One American soldier described the battle as follows: "I thought hell had broken loose and let her dogs of war upon us."[2] This did not help recruiting efforts.

The British victory was bittersweet, however. The fighting claimed the life of the "Saviour of Upper Canada." The loss of General Brock, who was knighted posthumously, would end up having grave consequences for Britain's ability to wage war. Not only were there few gifted generals in America, but there were perhaps fewer in Canada. And none were as widely revered as Brock. Had the Americans defeated the army of Brock and Sheaffe at Queenston, they would have been able to march virtually unopposed through the middle of Canada. Or, had Brock lived, he might have continued his offensive into America's northern border. The War of 1812 might have had a far different ending and impact on the political geography of North America.

## THE "BATTLE" OF FRENCHMAN'S CREEK

Nevertheless, the second prong of the invasion was not yet over. Before the eastern assault commenced, Van Rensselaer's equally incompetent replacement, General Alexander Smyth, mounted another effort for Upper Canada. Smyth assumed Van Rensselaer's command on November 9, 1812, and the army now found themselves "out of the fire and into the frying pan." Smyth's grand invasion included plans for a force of about 3,000. While he raised troops, the new commander bought time through the same tactic as his predecessor—he pursued armistice discussions with the British.

Despite the series of failures by the American army, Smyth was able to muster roughly 4,500 men and plenty of boats and supplies for the attack. However, two problems would plague his campaign. On one hand, much of his army was composed of the same militia units from New York that earlier refused to cross into Canada with Van Rensselaer. On the other hand, from his headquarters at Black Rock near Buffalo, Smyth boasted so often and so loudly of his invasion that the British were prepared and awaiting him [see Map 3 in Appendix].

It is doubtful any American generals were serious about peace, but the British engaged them in talks. Then, however, they pulled a play out of the late General Brock's playbook and attacked the Americans first. Without warning, on November 17, British artillery pounded Smyth's headquarters. One of the targets hit was a powder magazine which blew up. The barracks and several buildings burned to the ground and supplies were lost. Nearby, a large cannonball crashed through the roof at the exact spot where Smyth's senior officer, General Peter Porter, was dining with other officers. It barely missed Porter. The surprise bombardment had the effect of further unnerving an already hesitant army. Many of Smyth's New York militiamen now changed their minds a second time about invading Canada.

Once Smyth had sufficient troops, he ended the talks with the British and announced on November 20 that he would cross the Niagara River and invade Canada. The invasion began on November 27. But many of his men were in no mood for fighting.

While the main army of 4,500 was still preparing for the invasion, under cover of darkness two small raiding parties crossed the river. One unit, led by Colonel William Winder, was assigned the task of destroying British artillery positions in advance of the main invasion. Under the command of Colonel Charles Boerstler, the other unit crossed the river and headed toward the bridge at Frenchman's Creek. The intention was to destroy the bridge so that the British could neither retreat nor reinforce their position.[3]

However, both advance raiding parties were met by the British, who were waiting for them. Under intense fire from the British and in the darkness, the American landings were chaotic and missed their assigned marks. Both sides shot wildly not knowing who was friend and who was foe. Somehow, Colonel Winder's team managed to land. In the darkness, they outflanked the British and seized one of the batteries. However, the point of attack was just over two miles from Fort Erie. The firing of muskets served as an alarm for the British army in the fort. Thus, as the Americans were spiking the cannons at the newly captured battery, they were attacked by British forces from Fort Erie led by Lieutenant Colonel Cecil Bisshop. The Americans fought but were pushed back to the shoreline.

Nearby, the other raiding party led by Colonel Boerstler also managed to come ashore. But, amid the hail of British musket balls, they inadvertently left the tools and axes they would need to wreck the bridge back in the boats. This second raiding party was also pushed back to the river. Almost forty men from the advance parties were captured and two of the U.S. boats were blown up. The Americans suffered nearly 100 dead or wounded, while the British lost only about half that number and had thirty-four men captured. The Americans failed to destroy the bridge and the British cannons. Both raiding parties fled back across the Niagara, accomplishing nothing except to alert the British that the invasion was beginning.

The main American army of 4,500 troops assembled on the morning of November 28 for the next attempt on Canada. However, the operation again ran well behind schedule and most of the militia units were refusing to cross the river. By noon, the officers and soldiers were still arguing with General Smyth and only about 1,200 men were prepared to cross over into Canada. Smyth had not learned the lessons from Van Rensselaer's failure at Queenston only a few weeks prior and proved to be equally as inept and weak. Desperate and without the support of those he commanded, the General organized a "war council" to resolve the matter. The decision was to again postpone the invasion!

Two days later, General Smyth again attempted to start the invasion but it too ran into serious opposition. Smyth called off the invasion. The American commander hunkered down for the winter and announced that he would take up the matter of the invasion in spring. The Battle of Frenchman's Creek was hardly a battle and marked the fourth failed attempt to invade Canada.

Smyth's senior commander, a very frustrated General Porter, the man who was nearly blown apart by a cannonball when the British bombarded the American headquarters, publicly called his superior a coward. Porter's accusation was printed in the *Buffalo Gazette* and gained much attention. A furious and embarrassed Smyth challenged Porter to a duel which, at the time, was considered by some to be the gentlemanly way of settling disputes. The two men met on nearby Grand Island and exchanged shots. However, they both missed (likely on purpose) and the duel was ended. Both felt they had retained their honor. But publicly and among the army, this was anything but the case.

By now, Smyth, like every other American commander—Hull, Van Rensselaer, and Dearborn—had lost his nerve. Despised by his men and officers, some of whom nearly mutinied, Smyth wrote to General Dearborn asking permission to go home to Virginia to visit his family. The cowardly general then slunk back to Virginia. Three months later he had had enough of the War of 1812 and asked to resign. Smyth was unceremoniously stripped of his command. In yet another ironic twist of fate during this war, the voters of Virginia elected Smyth to Congress. The former general even rose to chair the congressional committee charged with overseeing military affairs including the war he had earlier mismanaged.[4]

## "GRANNY" DEARBORN

The third prong of the invasion started no better. The man who designed the invasion—General Henry Dearborn—was alarmed by the failures of Hull in the West and Van Rensselaer along the Niagara. The news of their defeats unnerved Dearborn. Although Dearborn had been a Revolutionary War hero, the aged general was not the man he once was. Dearborn was even the brunt of jokes from his own soldiers, who nicknamed him "Granny."

Scheduled to lead the third prong of the invasion, Dearborn was supposed to have coordinated his eastern invasion with the other two efforts by Hull and Van Rensselaer, but the tired general dallied in New England to the extent that his leadership was described as "a miscarriage, without even the heroism of disaster."[5] General Dearborn would soon show that he had no stomach for leading the third invasion which, like the second prong before it, withered into inaction.

Dearborn's invasion was finally set for late November. However, given the delays, the army faced the daunting prospects of invading Canada in the cold of winter. In advance of what was to be Dearborn's major strike into Lower Canada, a force of 600 U.S. regulars crossed the Canadian border near the village of Champlain. In the early morning hours of November 20, the American advance force, led by Colonel Zebulon Pike, arrived at Lacolle Mills, rumored to have been used as a British base of operations along the border [see Map 2 in Appendix].

The first building they encountered was a large blockhouse. It was dark and visibility was limited, so the Americans were unable to determine whether British soldiers might be inside. The small force of Canadians in that town had actually pulled back from the blockhouse the night prior. A second American advance force comprised of untrained militiamen had marched from a different direction toward the village in order to surround what they thought would be a handful of British soldiers. But, rather than trap their foes in a pincer move, the second advance force began firing by mistake on Colonel Pike's army nearby.

The sound of musket fire alerted the small Canadian detachment now on the outskirts of the village. This group of Canadian volunteer riflemen, known during the war as "voltigeurs," and 300 Indians from the Caughnawaga nation, led by Major de Salaberry, rushed to attack the two American units. The Canadians caught the Americans unprepared and confused. While still trying to discern friend from foe, the Americans now came under fire from de Salaberry's force. The Canadian major then ordered his Indian allies to charge the American ranks. It worked. The American militia unit panicked and fled. Nearby, Colonel Pike realized what was happening and ordered his unit to pull back in order to regroup. However, the orderly withdrawal turned into disarray when many of Pike's soldiers ran. The American advance force retreated all the way back to Champlain.

The only consolation for the American army was that they suffered only five killed and another five wounded in the predawn volley. But the mishap at Lacolle Mills, as minor as it might have been, was just enough to weaken what little resolve the American forces and their hesitant commander, General Dearborn, still had. The seemingly insignificant spat at the village of Lacolle Mills ended up being the straw that broke the camel's back. The militia units from New York and Vermont, like other militia units in the new war, now refused to cross into Canada.[6] Some simply quit. Just three days later, General Dearborn withdrew his entire army to Plattsburgh, New York to establish a winter camp.

With all three prongs of the American invasion of Canada ending in defeat, surrender, or postponement, the secretary of war, William Eustis, was forced to resign. His departure on December 3, 1812, ended a very bad year for the Americans.[7]

## MEANWHILE, ON THE WESTERN FRONTIER . . .

Throughout history, fighting rarely took place in the dead of a cold winter. For good reason. This is a lesson that not all American commanders appreciated. In the Northwest, for example, William Henry Harrison was still having problems with Britain's Indian allies. Although he had delivered a massive blow to the larger Indian cause with his victory over The Prophet at Tippecanoe in 1811, small-scale Indian raids on white settlers continued.

One of the larger nations in the Ohio region was the Miami, many of whom sought an end to the violence. As such, chiefs from the Miami met with Harrison on October 12, 1812, to discuss peace. Rather than nurture the opportunity, the general-governor of the territory brazenly demanded the Miami surrender five chiefs to him as a sign of their sincerity. The chiefs never arrived, apparently distrusting Harrison. Meanwhile, Harrison, like other American commanders, was under pressure to produce a victory in the disastrous young war. He devised his own three-part plan of action with little consideration of the approaching winter.

The general assembled a large army that would simultaneously march on Detroit to liberate it from the British, invade Canada along the approach used unsuccessfully by General Hull a few weeks earlier, and subdue the Indians of the Northwest. It was an ambitious plan and involved several separate prongs of attack. It was doomed to failure.

Unfortunately for Harrison, two of the forces he sent to Detroit and into Canada became bogged down. One of the units, while marching along the Maumee River, ran into bad weather and a shortage of supplies. The army abandoned the invasion and made camp for the winter. The army of the second commander was ambushed by Indians, which delayed the attack by just enough time that he, too, decided to postpone the invasion until after the winter ended.

Harrison therefore turned his attention to the problem he knew best and the one closest geographically. He ordered an attack on Indian villages in the Ohio region. Writing to the then-secretary of war, William Eustis, Harrison referred to the continued Indian raids as a "severe chastisement." He recommended immediate action, suggesting, "It remains for the President to say what should be done with the Miami . . . [But] nothing could be more easy than to surprise the Miami village of Mississinewa with mounted men." While still waiting for a reply, Harrison began planning the attack.[8]

The village of Mississinewa was a key Indian stronghold near the Mississinewa and Wabash Rivers. Deemed by the Indians of the region to be one of the few safe communities, it is where the Miami nation stored their winter food supplies. It also served as a staging area for organizing raids on white settlements in the region and strikes against Fort Wayne. It was thus a perfect target for Harrison. Ultimately, however, the War Department selected a less-seasoned commander over Harrison's preferred choice, a decision that impacted the direction of the war in the region.

## THE BATTLE OF MISSISSINEWA

Lieutenant Colonel J. B. Campbell led the force charged with destroying the village of Mississinewa, and with it the Miami nation's ability to wage war. Harrison had little confidence in Campbell and therefore gave him specific orders regarding the attack. Among them were instructions to spare the lives of friendly Miami chiefs and handle the attack in a manner that would not bring shame to his command or embolden other Indian nations. This would allow Harrison to attempt to engage the conquered Miami and others in a peace treaty.

Marching from present-day Columbus, Ohio on November 25, the army arrived in what today is Dayton in mid-December. Like so many American attacks, the mission was behind schedule. After a slow start to the campaign, Campbell marched his men between twenty and forty miles a day in the final days in order to strike the village before the long winter set in. However, the decision only exhausted and demoralized Campbell's army.

The attack commenced on the morning of December 17, 1812, after a grueling all-night march. The exhausted soldiers formed careful lines outside the village, but for unknown reasons the men then broke ranks and charged wildly into the village. They poured into the Miami village, killing several Indians trying to flee from the charging army. The marauders then proceeded to kill the Miami's cattle and dogs, and loot the village. The army was out of control and burned the village to the ground. Amid the reckless attack, nearly all of the Miami warriors managed to mount their horses and escape.

Even though the warriors managed to escape, they abandoned women, children, and the elderly, many of whom were captured, wounded, or killed by Campbell's undisciplined troops. The Battle of Mississinewa was a disaster for both the Miami and for the Americans. Campbell's men not only failed to achieve the objective of eliminating the Miami's ability to wage war, they sparked an incident that both embarrassed Harrison and angered other Indian nations in the region. Discredited, Harrison was now unable to pursue peaceful options and treaties. Those Miami chiefs who had been contemplating peace now desired blood.

Campbell took prisoners from the Mississinewa campaign. But, the many women, children, and elderly Indians captured greatly hindered the army's progress in getting back to their fort. Already exhausted from their forced march to Mississinewa and now straining in the bitter December cold, Campbell's army moved slowly across Ohio. This gave the Indians time to regroup. Revenge came swiftly. Campbell's troops were caught in the open by a few hundred Miami warriors who attacked without warning. In the skirmish that followed, twelve soldiers were killed and sixty-five wounded. The Miami attackers suffered an estimated forty-five braves killed and perhaps seventy-five more wounded. The main setback for Campbell, however, was that the attacking warriors purposely targeted the army's horses, killing at least 100 in the attack. Campbell's cavalry units were eliminated and, without horses to pull wagons or scout the perimeter, the Americans' march back to their base was further slowed.

The weather worsened in late December and Campbell soon found himself leading an army of exhausted, wounded, and freezing soldiers. As a consequence, many of Campbell's men died on the march back, as did many of their Indian prisoners. A depleted army managed to eventually make it back to General Harrison's headquarters, but a few hundred of them were put out of action by frostbite. Mindful of the harm that had been done by Campbell's massacre and the fact that Indians in the region were now on the war path, Harrison attempted to "spin" the results by writing to the War Department with claims the campaign was a roaring success. It was anything but.[9]

The conflict with the Miami was a disastrous and fitting end to a tragic year for the Americans. The year 1812 had ended, but the war was far from over.

12

# "REMEMBER THE RAISIN"

## THE BATTLE OF FRENCHTOWN

On its way to Lake Erie, the brownish waters of River Raisin flow past a village known as Frenchtown, the present-day site of Monroe, Michigan. Although generally a peaceful waterway, the river once ran red with blood. Beginning on January 18, 1813, and lasting for six days, a terrible battle was waged on the north bank of the river as part of the larger campaign for control of Michigan and the western Great Lakes. It would be one of the largest battles ever fought in Michigan and ended in a devastating loss for the Americans.

The American military was faced with the matter of replacing the disgraced General William Hull, who had earlier surrendered Detroit to the British. Given the number of defeats suffered by the Americans and the suddenness of the resignations, the choice to replace Hull was both vitally important and urgent. Both the popular William Henry Harrison, the hero of Tippecanoe and governor of the Indiana Territory, and unpopular James Winchester wanted the command, and there was bad blood between the two men. The War Department waffled on the decision. Fortunately for the war effort, Harrison was selected by President Madison to command the Northwest Territory and given a massive army of roughly 10,000 men. However, the decision angered Brigadier General Winchester, who proceeded to disobey his new commander.[1]

Harrison acted quickly and showed promise in the new command. He reinforced Fort Wayne in northeast Indiana with 900 men. The small outpost had been under constant attack by Indian war parties. Harrison later arrived at the fort with about 2,000 men to begin a counteroffensive. After constant raids through the summer of 1812, American units finally began to secure the region in September. Indian war parties attacking Fort Harrison, which was commanded by a young captain and future president

107

named Zachary Taylor, and other small forts near the Wabash River and along the Upper Mississippi River were defeated in September. These rare victories were celebrated by the Americans and raised General Harrison's profile.[2] Not far away, Fort Madison had been under siege for several days in September. It started on September 5 when a soldier was caught, killed, and scalped. The next day, Indians placed his head and heart on pikes in front of the fort. News of the incident spread like wildfire across the region and alarmed Harrison, Taylor, and other commanders who worried that the entire region was about to come under attack.[3] However, the Americans held Fort Madison and beat back Indian raiding parties.

By the winter of 1812/1813, Harrison had succeeded in reinforcing many of the forts in the region. But he was eager to liberate Detroit and avenge the embarrassment of losing the major town and fort. Harrison decided to attack it in winter. The task required two columns, each with over 1,000 men, and would commence immediately. Harrison would lead one column along the Upper Sandusky River, while Winchester would lead the other column from the Maumee River near present-day Perrysburg in Ohio. The armies would converge on Detroit. At least that was the plan [see Map 2 in Appendix].

Winchester arrived at the Maumee and his instructions were to scout the area, stay put, and report back to Harrison. However, Winchester's camp was visited by two French traders who informed the general that a few British soldiers and Indians were nearby at Frenchtown, a small settlement on the River Raisin, halfway between the mouth of the Maumee River and Detroit. The British were alleged to have about 300 barrels of flour, corn, and wheat as well as other supplies for the winter stored there. These supplies were to be transported to the large British force at Fort Malden.

The report piqued Winchester's interest. The general also received complaints from civilians living along the Maumee that the British and Indians were occupying Frenchtown and had planned to destroy the village because the residents remained loyal to the United States. Directly violating General Harrison's orders, Winchester took the bait and sent part of his army to Frenchtown to attack the British and their Indian allies. Roughly 700 troops were led by Colonel William Lewis, who marched down the Maumee to the western shoreline of Lake Erie and up to River Raisin, which ran near Frenchtown.

Only a small force of British and Indians waited for the Americans at Frenchtown. However, most of Winchester's regulars and Kentucky volunteers, including those now under Colonel Lewis, had yet to taste combat and many were poorly trained. Nor had Winchester provided the force with sufficient intelligence, ammunition, or provisions, including food and warm clothing for a winter invasion.[4]

## "HOLD THE GROUND!"

On January 18, the Americans attacked the small group of British and Indians in Frenchtown and managed to drive them out of the village by the next day. Even if it was a skirmish, it marked one of the very few victories for the Americans. The Americans lost only twelve men, with fifty-five wounded. Confident, General Winchester ordered a small detachment of fewer than 300 men under the command of Colonel Samuel Wells to secure the village in order to prevent the British from returning. General Winchester then decided he would follow Colonel Wells and inspect the site of the victory. However, Winchester traveled at a leisurely pace in a carriage to the village, arriving on January 20. The general also sent a message to General Harrison explaining why he had violated direct orders. Winchester claimed he had to attack Frenchtown because his Kentucky volunteers were becoming a problem. They were both itching for a fight and threatening not to reenlist but to return home that winter when their six-month tours of duty ended.

When Colonel Wells arrived in Frenchtown he immediately realized the village was exposed and vulnerable. He pleaded with General Winchester to make immediate preparations for the defense of Frenchtown, which included deploying scouts to the surrounding areas and sending for more reinforcements. However, Winchester was tired from his carriage ride. He decided that the defense of Frenchtown could wait until the next day.

General Harrison, while angered by the failure to follow his orders, was pleased that Lewis was successful. America was desperate for a victory. Any victory. However, Harrison worried that Winchester did not send enough men to secure Frenchtown in the event of a British counterattack. The American commander began his march to rendezvous with Winchester's army in order to secure the prize. It is also likely that Harrison was concerned that his rival, Winchester, would get all the credit for one of the very few American victories of the young war. Harrison's army arrived at the Maumee River just moments after Winchester had departed for Frenchtown. Harrison, therefore, ordered 900 men to hurry to Frenchtown to reinforce the small unit Winchester stationed there. Harrison also sent Captain Nathaniel Hart on horseback to Frenchtown with orders for Winchester to stay put at Frenchtown and prepare to defend the village. Commanded Harrison, "Hold the ground."[5]

Captain Hart rushed into Frenchtown just as Winchester was getting settled in. Like Winchester's officer, Colonel Wells, he too was appalled by what he saw. Winchester was completely unprepared to defend the village. The troops were in disarray, had a limited amount of ammunition and supplies, and no defensive positions had been organized even though locals were warning that the Indians in the area were hostile. It was also rumored that a large British force was headed their way. When Captain Hart transmitted General Harrison's orders, Winchester dismissed the concerns as an overreaction, claiming that it would be "some days" before any British arrived.

Shockingly, Winchester ordered his small army to camp in an open field. He then commandeered a farmhouse for himself for the night, taking much of the ammunition and powder with him. This farmhouse was more than one mile away from his troops, too great a distance to be in operational command should an attack occur. He was joined there by his teenaged son and aides.

After the heroic General Isaac Brock was killed at Queenston Heights, the British replaced him with Colonel Henry Proctor. Like his predecessor, Proctor wasted no time in organizing a quick offensive against the Americans at Frenchtown. From Fort Malden, Proctor marched an army of almost 600 regulars and about 800 Indians led by Chief Tecumseh and two chiefs of the Wyandot nation, Chief Roundhead and Chief Walk-in-the-Water. They also had six small cannons. Proctor was relentless, pushing his men across snow and ice, and through bitter cold, day and night, in order to catch the Americans unprepared. It worked.

On the night of January 21, Proctor's army made camp just five miles north of Frenchtown. He was within striking distance. He was joined by the British and Canadians that had fled the village when the Americans arrived, putting his army at more than 1,200 men, significantly larger than the force Winchester commanded in Frenchtown. Moreover, Proctor had the element of surprise and had far more experienced and better trained troops than Winchester. Proctor also had Tecumseh.

Under cover of darkness, Proctor's men dragged their small cannons into position. The attack began before sunrise on January 22. It caught the Americans utterly unprepared. Artillery fire rained down on the sleeping Americans. No sentries guarded the road to the north, from which the

British poured into the village. Because the cannon fire scattered the groggy Americans, Tecumseh's braves were able to perform a flanking move. While Tecumseh hit the Americans from the side, Canadian militiamen poured musket fire from the perimeter of the battlefield. Only minutes into the battle, the Americans were in disarray and on the run. Many raced back toward the River Raisin.

The Kentucky volunteers rushed forward in an attempt to hold the line but were unable to do so and had to pull back. Wells ordered the Kentucky volunteers and his regulars to regroup. They put up a stingy defense behind a picket fence and nearly saved the battle. For a while, the Americans held their line, repelling three successive British assaults and inflicting heavy casualties. The Americans on the line were inspired by an enlisted man named William O. Butler. Upon seeing the British marching toward a farmhouse roughly 150 yards away, which would likely be used as a staging ground for the next assault, Butler raced with a firebrand to the farmhouse. Shots whizzed by him as he zigzagged to the farmhouse and piled straw in and around the structure. After setting the property on fire, Butler ran back to the American line. The British continued to fire at him while the Americans cheered him on. Amazingly, Butler made it back among the ranks. His comrades observed that he had a bullet hole through his shirt but was unharmed!

## ROUT

Outside of town in his farmhouse, General Winchester was awakened by artillery fire. Without putting on his full uniform or ascertaining the nature of the threat, the general and his aides rushed to the site of the battle. They arrived at the scene to observe the Americans being beaten back toward the River. General Winchester and his party also found themselves surrounded by Indians, who had encircled the village. Winchester surrendered. He was taken prisoner and marched to Colonel Proctor.

The fighting continued to favor the British. Many of the American troops fled in a full panic after seeing widespread Indian atrocities committed on their brothers in arms. One American officer, Captain James Price, rounded up fifty men to try and move the wounded off the battlefield before they would be scalped by Indians. But he and his men were attacked by a war party of braves. Nearby, Lieutenant Ashton Garrett, in command of twenty men, laid down their guns to surrender. But Tecumseh's warriors swooped down on them and, as the Americans turned to run, they were killed. Only Lieutenant Garrett survived the ordeal.

The fighting had turned into a chaotic rout and a killing zone. Through the battlefield and in the wooded areas surrounding it, fleeing Americans were caught and put to the tomahawk as they attempted to surrender. A quick-thinking captain by the name of Richard Matson ordered thirty of his men to abandon their boots. They left only footprints as they ran through the snow, fooling their Indian pursuers into thinking they were tracking fellow warriors. Matson and his men survived the battle.

Back at the American line, the Kentucky volunteers were still fighting when they saw a white flag of truce emerge in front of them. Some thought the British were surrendering. But, it turned out to be Major James Overton, one of General Winchester's aides, coming to inform them to surrender. Colonel Proctor had told General Winchester that he should send the aide with an order to surrender. If he complied, Proctor would assure the Americans' safety. If not, then the Indians would kill the American prisoners and wounded. The Kentuckians and others on the American line were reluctant to surrender, boasting that they "would rather die on the field" than surrender. Their officer, Major George Madison, a relative of the President, demanded to see Colonel Proctor. Madison attempted to threaten Proctor, claiming his men would fight to the death. Scowled Proctor, "Sir, do you mean to dictate to me?" Madison's ruse did not work. Winchester surrendered. Madison would not have been able to continue fighting. The Americans were running low on ammunition. It could have been worse— Wincehster's folly could have resulted in more Americans being killed.[6]

## THE RIVER RAISIN MASSACRE

An agreement was reached between Proctor and Winchester, and the remaining American troops and Kentucky volunteers surrendered. The battle on January 22, 1813, ended as a decisive victory for the British. Nearly 400 Americans were killed or wounded, and 500 were taken as prisoners. The British lost only twenty-four men with another 158 wounded, nearly all of them while attempting to assault the Kentucky line. There were also likely a few dozen Indian casualties.

Despite the resounding victory, Colonel Proctor hurried the surrender proceedings. It was a bitterly cold day and Proctor worried that General William Henry Harrison might march in relief of General Winchester.

Sure enough, Harrison was en route with 900 troops. But he was slowed because the road was covered in mud and ice.

On the afternoon of January 22, Proctor ordered an immediate march back to Fort Malden, taking the American prisoners with him. Some of the wounded were loaded onto sleds that were otherwise used for carrying supplies across the snow. But the British did not have enough sleds for all the wounded, so over sixty of the severely wounded Americans were left behind at Frenchtown. Proctor stated that he would send men back with additional wagons and sleds to bring the remainder of the wounded to Fort Malden. Captain William Elliott volunteered to stay behind with his wounded colleagues. He was joined by a few other soldiers, three Native interpreters, and two U.S. surgeons—Gustave Bower and John Todd.

The Americans soon realized that they were vulnerable at Frenchtown. The Indians along the River Raisin did not honor Proctor's surrender and were seen scouting the American encampment. Allegedly, one of the interpreters offered a thinly veiled threat that the Indians would make excellent physicians for the dying men. Sure enough, at ten o'clock in the morning on January 23, roughly 200 warriors attacked Frenchtown. The war party confronted Dr. Todd and wanted to know why the wounded Americans were not taken to Fort Malden. When the surgeon told them that the British would soon return with sleds, the leader of the warriors responded that the British were "damned rascals" and threatened to kill the Americans. And then the massacre began.

The Indians attacked the Americans and set buildings containing the wounded on fire. Survivors reported hearing the screams of agony and terror inside the burning structures. Those wounded soldiers who crawled out of the fire were scalped and then hacked to death. The entire village was then put to the torch. It is estimated that thirty-five of the Americans were murdered that day. The survivors were then force-marched to Fort Malden. Any wounded solider unable to keep pace was killed by the Indian escorts, leaving one surviving soldier named Elias Darnell to recall that "the road was for miles strewed with the mangled bodies."[7]

When General Harrison learned of the defeat by his advance scouts, he sent 170 men from his army to Frenchtown to aide any American survivors. It was too late. It was yet another defeat. Harrison decided it was futile to continue the offensive or to attempt to liberate Detroit. Dejected, Harrison pulled his troops back to Ohio and established camp for the winter. All hope of liberating Detroit or invading Canada that winter was abandoned.

The Battle of Frenchtown was a decisive victory for the British, but the massacre would come back to haunt them. Once again, the Americans were unable to march into Canada or even attempt to recapture Detroit. The Ohio frontier was still vulnerable to invasion from the British and raids from the Indians. After the terrible setback at Tippecanoe in 1811, many Indian nations once again felt hopeful that they could still retain control of what the Americans called the Northwest Territory. In a larger sense, after successive failures to invade Canada, dispirited American soldiers along the Niagara frontier and Great Lakes, and from the Northwest Territory to New York hunkered down for a long, cold, and bitter winter. Commanders on both sides of the fighting used the winter to reassess the war effort, but for entirely different reasons and from entirely different vantage points. Many of the American volunteers deserted that winter, while militiamen were allowed to return home. Questions remained as to whether enough of them would return in spring for the war to go on.

## THE RAID AT OGDENSBURG

Both the main British and American armies set up camp for the winter. The Canadian border returned to quiet during the rest of the winter and the war looked all but lost for the United States. There were only a few minor raids and skirmishes that winter, most of them resulting in losses for the Americans. One unforeseen result of the failed U.S. invasion of Canada was that the British, with their Canadian militiamen and Indian allies, felt emboldened to attack American towns on the border. The British sought revenge for the American invasion and atrocities against civilians by responding in kind. Many communities on the U.S. northern border that had been at peace with Britain, traded regularly with Canadians despite the war's embargo, and even opposed war were now thrust into war.

One such example was a raid on Ogdensburg in New York. The British commander, Sir George Prevost, who also served as the Crown's governor, was a defensive-minded and excessively cautious man. While his armies and officers were camped for winter, Prevost departed from Quebec on February 13, 1813, to inspect fortifications in Upper Canada. His travels took him to Fort Wellington in the village of Prescott. While there, Prevost met with officers such as Lieutenant Colonel Thomas Pearson and the commander of the Glengarry Light Infantry, Lieutenant Colonel George MacDonnell, a tough-as-nails Scot known affectionately to his men as

"Red George." Red George informed the governor that a group of about 200 American marauders led by Major Benjamin Forsyth had been raiding villages along the border.

Forsyth had arrived on the New York–Canadian border in October of 1812 and was assigned the task of ending the illegal trade that northern merchants were undertaking with the British, Canadians, and Indians. The Major ruthlessly attacked Canadian villages and civilian populations thought to be trading with New York merchants. He and his band harassed villages, unnerved the local population, stole muskets and supplies, and liberated Americans from Canadian prisons. Two of Forsyth's raids occurred in early February just prior to Governor Prevost's arrival on the border. Right under British noses, Forsyth attacked the village of Brockville on the St. Lawrence River, confiscating weapons and supplies, and then liberated recently captured American prisoners from Elizabethtown. The raider even had the audacity to then take about fifty of his own prisoners back to New York.

These raids infuriated Red George and the Scot complained to Governor Prevost that Forsyth and like-minded raiders had to be taught a lesson. The feisty officer even suggested his men be allowed to raid American towns and offered the border community of Ogdensburg in New York as a potential target because it was the headquarters of Forsyth. Prevost, who was always worried about provoking the Americans and overextending his inadequate forces on offensive missions, ordered Red George not to attempt any offensive or retaliatory action against any of the raiders. In fact, the governor felt so strongly about it that he wrote to Red George MacDonnell that same month with his final word: "You will not undertake any offensive operations against Ogdensburg without previous communication with Major General de Rottenburg," his superior officer.

But, Red George was intent on revenge. He thus noted that the wording in Governor Prevost's letter prohibited action ". . . unless the imbecile conduct of the enemy should offer you an opportunity for his destruction and that of the shipping, batteries and public stores, which does not admit of delay in availing yourself of it."[8] Red George took the letter as a green light and, in the predawn hours of February 22, decided to teach the Americans a lesson.

The day was a bitter cold one and the weather should have deterred nearly any military action. But, Red George's Glengarries crossed the icy river in a snowstorm and headed to Ogdensburg, where Forsyth was camped. It was a treacherous march, as men slipped and fell repeatedly on the ice and many solders suffered frostbite on their exposed faces and hands.

Arriving at the defenses on the outskirts of Ogdensburg, Red George ordered his army of roughly 300 Glengarries and an equal number of militia into formation. They attacked. However, there was no fire from the American positions. Rather, the Americans wisely waited until the Scotsmen were close, then they opened up with their cannons and muskets. The Glengarries fell from the barrage but their commander willed them on, charging directly into the American position. Seeing Red George and his men undeterred from the cannon fire, the American defenders panicked and fled. Major Forsyth escaped, high-tailing it to Sackets Harbor.

The defeat hurt Forsyth's ability to harass border villages. Moreover, the schooners in dock at Ogdensburg used for crossing the St. Lawrence were burned along with the barracks and other buildings. Twenty of Forsyth's men were killed, with another seventy taken prisoner. Red George seized Forsyth's supplies, ammunition and powder stores, and eleven of his cannons, proudly dragging them back across the frozen St. Lawrence despite the loss of seven of his own men with another forty-eight wounded. He even ordered that private buildings be looted.

Despite yet another defeat, the direction of the war was about to change. Word spread about the atrocities on the banks of the River Raisin—that Americans attempting to surrender were slaughtered by the Indian allies of the British. One report described the massacre as follows: "The savages were suffered to commit every depredation upon our wounded. Many were tomahawked, and many were burned alive in the houses."[9] As a result of what became known as the "River Raisin Massacre," many Americans renewed their commitment to the war and many American soldiers finally began to fight with a sense of purpose. Over two decades before Americans would "Remember the Alamo," a rallying cry emerged that helped spark a change in the tide of the War of 1812—"Remember the Raisin!"[10]

# 1813

*"The Noble Lads of Canada"*

*Oh! Now the time has come, my boys, to cross the Yankee line,*
*We remember they were rebels once, and conquered John Burgoyne;*
*We'll subdue those mighty Democrats, and pull their dwellings down,*
*And we'll have the States inhabited with subjects to the crown.*

—Popular Canadian song during the War of 1812

"Col. Winfield Scott leading the attack/Capture of Fort George." Acknowledgment: By Alonzo Chappel, 1857; U.S. Library of Congress, Washington, DC (USZ62-48156)

# 13

# THE SACKING OF YORK

## DESPERATION

On February 10, 1813, Secretary of War Armstrong ordered General Dearborn to attack the town of Kingston as well as the surrounding forts on the Canadian side of the vitally important Niagara River. The War Department had waited long enough and was desperate to reverse the disasters of 1812. The plan was to organize 4,000 troops at nearby Sackets Harbor and another 3,000 men at Buffalo.[1] Once again, however, rather than launch an offensive into Canada, General Dearborn worried that the Canadians and British might be amassing an army at Kingston. He thus prepared defensive positions. The President and War Department were getting used to frustration and inaction.[2]

War planners ultimately proposed attacking the capital of York, which sat on the Canadian shores of Lake Ontario at present-day Toronto and was less well defended than Kingston. This would mark the beginning of a larger invasion of Canada in the year 1813. From there, the Americans could destroy the British fleet in port, control Lake Ontario, and then push through Canada. The general leading the invasion was Henry Dearborn, whose inaction delayed the invasion last summer and fall. But the naval operation was led by Isaac Chauncey who had recently been appointed to lead the American navy on Lake Ontario. Chauncey amassed an impressive fighting force and was thought to be a worthy commander. Sure enough, Chauncey's initial disembarkment of troops and naval bombardment of the city were well organized and efficient.

On April 22, the American army was ready, but poor weather once again delayed the invasion by a few more days. A flotilla of fourteen American ships and transport craft finally ferried over 1,500 infantrymen from Sackets Harbor to the Canadian shoreline, arriving at York on April 26.

They were supported by a few hundred naval personnel. York was a community of just over 600 people on the northwestern bank of Lake Ontario and was sparsely defended even though it served as the capital of Upper Canada. A victory was badly needed for American morale and York was a symbolically important prize [see Map 2 in Appendix].

Fortunately, General Dearborn picked Brigadier General Zebulon Pike to lead the attack at York. Pike, who was born in Trenton in 1779, was an adventurous fellow. As a young lieutenant, he was assigned to chart the Mississippi River to its source, which he traced all the way to Minnesota's Leech Lake, a point very close to the real source. In 1806, Pike had led a small unit from St. Louis west to the Rocky Mountains to chart rivers and trails in the region and to find the source for the Red River. Unfortunately, the young lieutenant and his party never discovered the Red River's origin, as they were captured by Spanish soldiers who took Pike's maps. Pike's only other blemish was that he worked for General James Wilkinson, whose scheming and treason on the western frontier nearly cost America the Louisiana Territory. In fact, it is highly possible that Wilkinson sent Pike on these missions not for the stated purpose but in order to assist him with his plans—and those of his accomplice, Aaron Burr—to seize a western empire. It is doubtful Pike was aware of any ulterior motives. Rather, he was likely just a pawn for Wilkinson and Burr. Today, a high mountain peak in Colorado that he climbed is named in his honor.

The night prior to Pike's invasion of York, he wrote a letter to his father. In it he wrote:

> I embark to-morrow in the fleet, at Sackets Harbor, at the head of a column of 1500 choice troops, on a secret expedition. Should I be the happy mortal destined to turn the scale of war, will you not rejoice, oh my father? May heaven be propitious, and smile on the cause of my country. But if we are destined to fall, may my fall be like Wolde's to sleep in the arms of victory.[3]

Pike would succeed in seizing York and had the good sense to order his soldiers to refrain from plundering during the mission. He even threatened them with imprisonment and death if his orders were not followed. The general was determined, unlike his predecessors, to invade Canada and, also unlike his predecessors, to conduct the campaign without looting and harassing civilians. However, Pike's passage to his father proved prophetic. He would not survive the battle.

# EXPLOSION

The landing began at 8:00 on the morning of April 27. With three full regiments ashore, General Pike gave the command to attack the fort and city. The British general Roger Sheaffe, who had reinforced Queenston Heights and assumed command on the death of General Brock, was in command at York. But, Sheaffe had been ill all winter and consequently had done little to plan the defense of York. He had only about 700 men and 100 Indian allies to defend the capital city. The American invaders thus had a three-to-one advantage.

In support of General Pike's troops, who were fighting their way ashore and to the fort, Commodore Chauncey ordered his flagship, the USS *Madison*, to bombard the fort and city. Three batteries had been set up on the shoreline to repel any invasion, but their construction was incomplete. The earthworks around the city and fort were also sparse and still under construction at the time of the invasion, and the fort's cannons were old. General Sheaffe decided to keep the majority of his small force inside the fort, thus allowing the Americans to control the shoreline and establish a beachhead.

The full force of 1,700 American troops came ashore. But strong winds and musket shots from Indians gathered on the shoreline forced some of Pike's boats off the course and away from the intended landing zone. However, naval artillery returned fire and drove the Indians off the shoreline. In an effort to prevent the Americans from landing, units of Grenadiers and Glengarry Light Infantrymen fixed bayonets and charged the beachhead. However, they should have been waiting for the Americans rather than be sent in after the fact. The Grenadiers and Glengarry units took the wrong path through the woods to the beach and arrived at the site where General Pike already had a few companies ashore. The British defenders put up a good effort, but were overwhelmed by sheer numbers. They suffered many casualties. Before long, Pike landed another company on the Canadian shoreline.

The naval gunfire from Chauncey's warships not only provided cover for the invading force by pinning the British down inside the fort, but it was deadly accurate. The artillery barrage blew apart much of the fort, destroyed the few defensive batteries that were operational, and took a toll on the city. The bombardment also panicked General Sheaffe's local militiamen, who fled from the fort into the woods. In short order, Sheaffe found himself losing control of the battle.

As the outcome of the battle seemed inevitable, Sheaffe ordered a quick retreat, affirming the suspicions of many back in Britain who considered him a coward. Also, Sheaffe had been born of American parents in Boston. So, his loyalty to Britain was frequently questioned. Sheaffe's retreat ended up being less a military maneuver than a disorderly panic. The British commander fled with his regulars to Kingston in such a hurry that the Union Jack still flew over the fort. Sheaffe left behind a few local militia commanders with instructions to surrender and seek good terms from the Americans. Sheaffe was certainly no Brock and the Canadian militia offered only token resistance.[4]

The Americans easily fought their way into the city and to the walls of the fort while the shelling from Chauncey's naval guns continued to inflict massive damage. However, just when the battle seemed over, one of the cannonballs hit and ignited the main ammunition depot in the fort. The resulting explosion was so powerful that it was heard at Fort George across the river and was said to have lifted the entire fort off the ground. Soldiers of both sides and the local townspeople were knocked to the ground and temporarily lost their hearing. Trees were knocked flat and wood, rock, and other debris rained down throughout the town.

A gaping hole was blown out of the fort. Twenty militiamen in the fort were killed immediately in the explosion along with several dozen invaders. The Americans were victims of their success. They had managed to enter the fort and had greater numbers inside the fort than the British defenders when the depot blew. Many of them were killed or wounded in the explosion. With General Sheaffe already on the run, the few remaining militiamen, disoriented from the explosion, either surrendered or melted away into the woods.

General Pike had been sitting on a tree stump outside the fort with his officers at the time of the explosion. He was unaware that General Sheaffe had fled the fort. His troops were continuing their advance into town and fort when the ammunition depot was ignited. Just moments before, however, some of the American soldiers brought a prisoner to Pike for interrogation. The prisoner, a sergeant, was seated across from Pike when the depot exploded. A massive boulder was sent hurtling upward from the explosion. It landed directly on top of General Pike and his prisoner, killing them both instantly. Pike was one of roughly thirty Americans killed by the explosion. About 200 others were wounded by it.

It was a victory of sorts, but more American casualties were sustained by the explosion than by the fighting. The impact of the explosion was apparent throughout the fort, town, and surrounding countryside. One surgeon, who tended to the men inside the fort at the time of the detonation of the depot, said he "waded in blood, cutting off arms, legs, and trepanning heads. . . ." The carnage was such that the surgeon "cut and slashed for 48 hours without food or sleep."[5]

## PUT TO THE TORCH

The loss of Zebulon Pike, one of the few experienced, competent generals in the American army, hurt. Operational command went back to General "Granny" Dearborn. Dearborn finally came ashore when the fighting ended, but his terms of surrender were far less honorable than what Pike would have offered. The British suffered the humiliating loss of their capital city in Upper Canada, 150 casualties, and 300 militiamen were taken prisoner. Dearborn could have let the British down lightly or capitalized on the victory by helping the townspeople or marching quickly to the next fort. He did none of the above.

With so many wounded among their own ranks and with a large cadre of British prisoners, the U.S. army camped in York that night. General Dearborn then decided to extend their stay for five days. However, with Pike dead and Dearborn in charge, nothing prevented the American soldiers from looting or taking their frustrations out on the people of York. Against the late general's express orders, the U.S. army pillaged private property, looted public buildings, and harassed the town's remaining residents. Then they put the capital city to the torch.

The burning started when a group of soldiers set the parliament building on fire. History is not certain exactly who it was that started the first fire, but one story that has been passed down suggests that U.S. soldiers saw scalps hanging on a door in the building in place of the speaker's powdered wig. Displaying the spoils of Indian raids on American settlers was highly inappropriate. It is said to have ignited the rampage.[6] The American troops needed little excuse to pillage. After taking for himself General Sheaffe's personal belongings and parliamentary mace, General Dearborn ordered that General Sheaffe's residence and the military and government buildings be burned. The looting was justified on grounds that it was payback for the British raid on Ogdensburg that winter, which itself was a response to the looting that occurred by Major Forsyth's raiding parties.

The victory at York was marred by the death of Pike and the accidental explosion that destroyed the fort. Commodore Chauncey had hoped to seize several new warships that American intelligence suggested would be in port at York. But, there was only one ship, the newest in the navy, HMS *Sir Isaac Brock*. But it was burned by the British before evacuating the fort. Now the victory was completely undermined by the savage behavior of the American troops.

## A BLEMISHED VICTORY

With General Dearborn dallying at York and word of the American atrocities spreading through Canada, the British planned to avenge the attack by striking Sackets Harbor in New York. The War of 1812 had transformed Sackets Harbor from a sleepy fishing village into a bustling military base, port, and shipyard. It was also a primary forward staging ground for the American offensive into Canada. The population ballooned to the point where it was New York's third largest city at the time, behind only New York City and Albany. It was a tempting target that Dearborn failed to secure.

On the morning of May 29, the assault began against the harbor. A force of 750 British soldiers and militia sailed on six ships and were supported by two gunboats. They transported a few dozen cannons for the purpose of leveling American towns, forts, and shipyards, including the shipyards at Sackets Harbor and nearby Fort Tompkins. The British were confident, knowing that Dearborn was preoccupied at York. However, just as the Americans had lost one decent general in Zebulon Pike, they were about to discover another one.

Brigadier General Jacob Brown of the New York militia learned of the attack. Moving with much haste, he ordered 400 regulars to disperse widely through the forests rimming the shores of Lake Ontario. These troops were supplemented by 500 militiamen that General Brown managed to wrangle up on a moment's notice. Any British landing party would now come under fire from the forests as they tried to establish a beachhead. Brown hoped that this would either turn back the attack or delay it.

Sure enough, the British arrived near the shipyard and port. Believing their arrival went undetected by the Americans, the British began disembarking at a leisurely rate. However, once they were in the open on the shoreline with boats anchored, they came under an intense barrage. From the cover of the forests, the Americans fired from either side of beach. One British soldier recalled of the attempted landing: "I do not exaggerate when I tell you that shot, both grape and musket, flew like hail."[7]

The British were forced to fall back amid the bewildering fire from the tree line. The British tried again and again to establish a beachhead, and were eventually successful. But they suffered casualties and the attack was now delayed. The outnumbered Americans pulled back from the shoreline. Unlike other American units, they did not panic or run. Brown moved his men back in an organized manner, fighting a gradual withdrawal. General Brown then reorganized his men and counterattacked the British, who were forced back onto their ships. The British had had enough and sailed back across the lake. The defenders had prevailed.

Unfortunately, yet another stroke of incompetence and cowardice would blemish the victory. The American harbor and shipyards were defended by Fort Volunteer and Fort Tompkins. Brown won at the shoreline and then pushed the British from the town. However, his forts fell to the British after vicious hand-to-hand fighting. As the few American defenders fled into the town, which was now secured by Brown, one of the officers at Fort Tompkins decided to deny the British the spoils of battle by blowing up the ammunition and powder. Unaware that his comrades had successfully defended the harbor and town, he also set the nearby shipyards ablaze. In so doing, he did the job for the British. General Brown was livid, declaring the act to be "infamous," and one of the worst in American military history![8] For his conduct in battle, Brown would be awarded a commission in the regular army and rose to the rank of general.

While the American press and political supporters of the War Hawks viewed the conquest of York as a grand victory, members of James Madison's administration fumed in private. They were furious with Dearborn's mishandling of the victory, the looting and burning of York, and allowing General Sheaffe to escape. Roared Armstrong, the new secretary of war, how could the remainder of Sheaffe's army be "permitted to escape to-day that it may fight us to-morrow?" Surprisingly, General Dearborn was allowed to stay in command after a minor reprimand. Much as the cry "Remember the Raisin!" emboldened American soldiers on the battlefield, the British and Canadians would not forget the burning of York. They would soon put American villages and forts to the torch . . . including America's own capital city.[9]

# 14

# VICTORIES AT LAST

## FORTIFICATIONS

The bitter defeat of General James Winchester's army at Frenchtown in the winter of 1813 dashed America's hopes of a winter invasion of Canada. After news of the loss and of the massacre of wounded American troops at River Raisin, a frustrated William Henry Harrison marched his army through the cold and back to his headquarters in northwest Ohio. Harrison picked a site during the winter of 1812/1813 not far from the famous Battle of Fallen Timbers where, in 1794, the Americans had defeated an Indian coalition.

A first order of business was to contend with the fortifications in the Northwest Territory, which could barely be called forts. Most were badly in need of repairs or stronger defenses. So, General Harrison ordered his men to reinforce the small outposts and build new forts along the Ohio frontier at key settlements and near rivers. Two of the main forts built that winter were Fort Stephenson on the Sandusky River and Fort Meigs, named for the governor of Ohio and erected on the south bank of the Maumee River near the rapids. While his men built forts, Harrison departed on a tour of the territory to recruit additional troops and secure needed supplies. Unfortunately for Harrison, he was not well connected in Washington and the secretary of war was not a fan. Harrison was therefore often wanting for supplies and troops, and was typically relegated to mostly defensive campaigns.[1] Harrison also sent a small detachment of men to Fort Meigs on the Maumee River. The fort was still under construction, but the concern about Indian raids and a British offensive in the region that winter or spring prompted Harrison's men to rush to complete the fort.[2] It was a good thing they did.

After the boondoggle by General Hull, General Dearborn's refusal to attack Kingston and his mixed success at York, and the disastrous River Raisin affair, Harrison was feeling pressure from all corners to secure a victory. He was eager to retake Detroit and gain control of Lake Erie. He received the go-ahead from the secretary of war, John Armstrong, who instructed Harrison to attack Fort Malden, which sat on the shores of the western edge of Lake Erie, near the Detroit River, which separated Canada from the United States. Harrison decided against attacking from Cleveland using the mouth of the Cuyahoga River and Lake Erie because the United States did not have control of the lake or the naval resources for such an invasion. Instead, Harrison planned to attack Fort Malden and the town of Amherstburg by land [see Map 2 in Appendix].

After securing a sizeable army of volunteers that winter, mostly from militia units, Harrison began his push to Fort Malden and Amherstburg. In February, they marched to Lake Erie. From there, he could cross and strike the British stronghold at Fort Malden in Amherstburg. However, when Harrison's army arrived, they discovered the ice was breaking apart and a crossing would be impossible. A dejected Harrison was forced to march back to Fort Meigs. When it must have seemed that his winter could not get any worse, General Harrison returned to his fort to discover that the officer in charge, Brigadier General Joel Leftwich of Virginia, along with most of the his army, had abandoned the half-finished fort. Leftwich and the militiamen were serving a six-month tour of duty, which had expired. They simply walked out of the fort. The grounds of the fort were in disarray, the fort utterly undefended, and the wood for the completion of the fort long ago burned for firewood.

Harrison placed Major Eleazer Wood, an engineer by training, in charge of the completion of the fort and gave him orders to rush the completion on account of the imminent threat of Indian attack and likelihood of a British offensive in spring. Wood commanded only a few hundred regulars and some militiamen from Pennsylvania and Virginia, but he tasked them to work around the clock on the fort and took care to organize defenses.

The Americans enjoyed a bit of long overdue good luck when the recently promoted general, Henry Proctor, the British commander in the region who replaced the deceased Isaac Brock, decided not to attack the demoralized American units along the Maumee River and at Fort Meigs. A winter assault by the British would likely have succeeded. However, Proctor delayed the offensive until April, which gave Major Wood time to make progress on the construction of the small fort.

## THE SIEGE OF FORT MEIGS

In very little time Major Wood built one of the largest forts on the continent, measuring over eight acres with a 12-to-15-foot-high picket fence running 2,500 yards around the perimeter of the grounds. Fort Meigs was now a first-rate fort, with eight large blockhouses, artillery batteries, and the natural defense of the banks of the Maumee River along one side. It could now function as a safe, forward staging ground for the coming assault on Detroit and Lake Erie. However, it would first have to serve another purpose.[3] As soon as the weather warmed that April, the British commander, General Proctor, began his attack on American ports, shipyards, and forts along the border. His invasion of America began at Fort Meigs.

Proctor, who was born in Ireland in 1763 and the son of an army surgeon, came to Canada in 1802 with Isaac Brock. But he was no Brock. Proctor survived the war, but his reputation as a military commander fared far less well, in part from the brutality of the River Raisin massacre. The incident would come back to haunt Proctor in other ways as well, when "Remember the Raisin!" was used as the rallying cry for Kentucky volunteers who would soon destroy Proctor's army at the Battle of Moraviantown.

With an army of over 400 regulars and about 500 Canadian militiamen, supported by an artillery unit with two powerful cannons and many smaller ones, Proctor sailed from Fort Malden toward Fort Meigs in April of 1813. Proctor's army landed at the mouth of the Maumee River and marched along the banks toward the new fort. Joining Proctor for the siege was Chief Tecumseh, with over 1,000 warriors. The new fort's defenses would be put to the test.

Fortunately for the defenders in the fort, General Harrison arrived from his recruiting effort just prior to Proctor's attack. Wood's meager forces were thus supplemented by Harrison's new volunteers. The fort's defense was also aided by a downpour. Heavy rain delayed the British from attacking and limited their ability to dig artillery batteries on the banks of the opposite shore that would be needed to bombard Fort Meigs. On April 30, the defenders inside Fort Meigs opened fire on the British positions along the river. The British responded. When the rain stopped on May 1,

Tecumseh had his warriors surrounded the fort, cutting off routes for escape or reinforcement. When Harrison sent men out from the fort on reconnaissance missions, they were killed by Tecumseh's warriors. Fort Meigs was cut off. Undermanned and surrounded, Harrison offered encouragement to his army, telling them never to surrender:

> Can the citizens of a free country think of submitting to an army composed of mercenary soldiers, reluctant Canadians, goaded to the field by the bayonet, and of wretched naked savages? Can the breast of an American soldier, when he casts his eyes to the opposite shore [the site of the famous Battle of Fallen Timbers], the scene of his countrymen's triumphs over the same foe, be influenced by any other feelings than hope and glory? To your posts then fellow citizens, and remember that the eyes of your country are upon you.[4]

The American general, however, had a few cards up his sleeve and was aided by the weather. The rains not only delayed the siege but provided the fort with ample water in the event of a long siege. The weather also limited visibility. During the deluge, Harrison had his men put up large tents along the perimeter of the fort. Behind the tents, Major Wood's engineers worked miracles establishing a perimeter of earth walls and trenches. When it stopped raining and the tents were taken down, the British were shocked to discover an additional layer of defenses in place. The siege continued with barrages of cannon fire from both sides. Thanks to the deluge, British cannonballs simply sunk into the fresh mud and earthen walls, doing virtually no damage.[5]

Harrison had very little ammunition, so he ordered his men to hold most of their fire until the British or Indians attempted to charge the fort. He also had only 360 cannonballs for his 18-pounder and roughly the same amount for his smaller 12-pounders. By luck, the British were shooting from the same type of cannons. Harrison thus ordered his men to dig the unexploded cannonballs out of the mud. They were cleaned, loaded, and fired back at the British. Harrison even offered an award of a "gill" (a large shot of whiskey) to any man salvaging a cannonball. In all, nearly 1,000 gills were given out to the fort's defenders after the siege, such a volume that the fort ran low on its supply of spirits! The British eventually realized that their artillery barrage was useless and that their own cannonballs were being fired back at them. They therefore changed tactics and began using shots fused so that they exploded over the fort, raining down shrapnel on the defenders. It was a full-scale siege.

## DUDLEY'S MASSACRE

The other card up Harrison's sleeve was that, while seeking recruits, the general had convinced the governor of Kentucky to provide him with 1,200 militiamen. The Kentuckians, under General Green Clay, were at that moment marching to Fort Meigs. On May 2, Harrison dispatched a rider to find General Clay and his Kentuckians. By luck, the rider managed to slip by Tecumseh's warriors and find General Clay to deliver an urgent request to rush to the besieged fort. Harrison ordered General Clay to strike the British battery on the north bank of the Maumee and then come into the fort to assist in its defense. Meanwhile, Harrison coordinated a simultaneous strike on the battery on the south bank of the river, sending men from the fort to silence those cannons.

On the morning of May 5, General Clay arrived at the battle. He immediately sent Colonel William Dudley across the river to its north bank to disable the British battery. Dudley led over 800 Kentucky militiamen and a few regulars. Fortunately for them, the Indians on the banks of the river seemed unwilling to assist in the defense of the battery. The Kentuckians successfully stormed the minimally defended battery. However, two things happened. The Kentuckians failed to spike the cannons with handspikes, which would permanently disable them. Rather, they used ramrods. The cannons could thus be un-spiked and fired again. Second, Tecumseh's warriors had moved back into the woods as part of a trap laid by the great chief for the Kentuckians.

Believing the Indians were retreating rather than defending the artillery battery, the undisciplined Kentucky militiamen excitedly gave chase. Taking the bait, they ignored the pleas of their commanding officer, Colonel Dudley. General Harrison is said to have observed the drama unfolding from the high walls of the fort and attempted to motion for Dudley's troops to stop their attack and come to the fort. Tecumseh only led the militiamen deeper and deeper into the woods. Watching the trap play out from the fort, a frustrated Harrison complained, "They are lost! They are lost! Can I never get my men to obey orders?"[6]

Colonel Dudley abandoned the artillery post he seized and chased after the Kentucky militiamen in an attempt to bring them back to the battlefield. He took with him a few men and left Major James Shelby behind to guard the artillery battery. It was a double disaster for the Americans.

When the British noticed the sparsely defended battery, they quickly organized a counterattack. Major Adam Muir, with three companies of regulars and one company of Canadian militiamen, stormed the battery, killing or wounding all of Shelby's men and easily retaking the post. The recaptured cannons were repaired and reengaged in the bombardment of Fort Meigs. Meanwhile in the woods, Tecumseh sprang the trap and the Kentuckians ran right into it. In the chaos that followed, Tecumseh's 1,000 warriors surrounded the disorganized militiamen and made quick work of them. Of the over 800 Americans that ran into the woods after the Indians, only 150 came out. The fighting in the woods became known as "Dudley's Massacre" or "Dudley's Disaster."

Over 150 Kentuckians were killed and another 500 were taken prisoner by Tecumseh. The chief took his prize to General Proctor, who later marched them to be held at the ruins of an old British fort in Miami Indian country. There, while in the custody of the warriors and Proctor, at least one dozen of the American prisoners were murdered. It was the second time Proctor had failed to protect prisoners in his charge or control his Indian allies. Proctor was later confronted by Tecumseh, who was not at the fort when the prisoners were murdered. The great chief demanded to know why the British colonel had not stopped the massacre. Proctor is said to have responded that it was the fault of the warriors and that Indians cannot be controlled, whereupon the great chief cursed the British general: "Be gone! You are unfit to command." Tecumseh then ordered the warriors to stop the slaughter. They did as commanded. Tecumseh took his warriors and abandoned Proctor, saying "I conquer to save; you to kill."[7]

## ANOTHER SUCCESSFUL DEFENSE

The battle was turning in favor of the British, who had regained control of the key artillery and whose Indian allies slaughtered Dudley's militiamen and the Kentucky volunteers. General Harrison needed a victory and was about to get it. He sent a force of 350 regulars and militiamen under Colonel John Miller to hit the other British battery on the south bank of the Maumee. Colonel Miller's men overran the British defenders at the artillery post, killing and wounding several and taking forty-one prisoners.

They properly put the cannons out of commission—permanently. However, while Miller's men were spiking the cannons, they came under fire by a British counterattack organized by Captain Richard Bullock. Bullock had three companies of British soldiers and roughly 300 Indians in his command. The Americans put up a good defense but were suffering heavy casualties. Colonel Miller ordered his men to retreat back into the fort. However, they accomplished their mission. The British cannons at the second battery were no longer a threat to the fort.

The British siege continued for five more days, but the fort held. Proctor and his men began to lose their enthusiasm for the protracted fight. On May 7, an agreement was reached for a prisoner swap. Roughly forty British soldiers had been captured and well over 600 Americans, mostly from the Kentucky militia, were being held at an old British fort. Proctor continued firing on the fort with the cannons repaired from the first battery for two more days. They had little impact on the fort. Most of Tecumseh's Indians, preferring action to watching an artillery barrage, tired of the drawn-out siege. They wanted to rush the fort but Proctor ordered them to wait. Instead, they disappeared into the wilderness in the middle of the night.

Proctor's Canadian militiamen were also growing restless. It was planting season and they too tired of what appeared to them to be a futile siege and an inspired defense. On May 9, Proctor finally abandoned the siege of Fort Meigs and returned to Amherstburg. He was surprised that the Americans had not surrendered, as had happened earlier in the war. He had not counted on Harrison's strength. Known to history as the Battle of the Miami, both commanders claimed victory. The British correctly noted that they had inflicted massive casualties on the Americans, while suffering only about fifteen dead and forty-seven wounded, with a reported nineteen casualties among their Indian allies. Proctor informed Sir George Prevost that the Americans sustained well over 1,000 casualties. The exaggerations continued to grow. Governor Prevost announced another "brilliant" victory "which terminated in the complete defeat of the Enemy and the capture, dispersion or destruction of 1,300 men by the gallant division of the Army under the command of Brigadier General Proctor."[8]

General Harrison had eighty dead and 190 wounded among the defenders in the fort, while the Kentuckians under General Clay suffered worse numbers, with many missing in action and hundreds captured. Harrison informed the War Department that the Kentucky militia had only fifty killed and claimed the remainder escaped on the river. Like his foe, General

Proctor, Harrison reported a resounding victory, saying "congratulations" were in order to the troops "having completely foiled their foes and put a stop to their career of victory which has hitherto attended their Arms." The Americans suffered higher casualties but the day belonged to them.[9]

Chief Tecumseh, disgusted by General Proctor's leadership, abandoned both the siege and the general. However, he later returned and coerced the British commander into a second attempt on Fort Meigs. Proctor's army and Tecumseh's warriors returned to the Ohio frontier and commenced a second siege from July 21 to July 29, 1813. Proctor and Tecumseh led a combined army of at least 2,500 regulars, militiamen, and warriors, but Proctor failed to bring along the large artillery he would need to bombard the fort. Nevertheless, Proctor and Tecumseh felt confident because General Harrison was no longer at the fort, having marched his army to Camp Seneca on the Sandusky River to begin planning for the liberation of Detroit and an offensive into Canada. General Green Clay of Kentucky was in command of Fort Meigs and had only about 100 men to defend the massive fort.

During the second siege, Tecumseh knew his warriors would not wait for another long engagement. They wanted blood immediately. So, he organized a mock attack in the woods in an attempt to draw General Clay out of the fort and into the open, much as he had successfully done in other engagements and against the Kentucky militia before. However, unbeknownst to the British and their Indian allies, Clay was so short on men that he was forced to remain inside the fort. After shooting muskets wildly at the fort and wasting too much ammunition, Tecumseh's warriors tired of the siege and Proctor again showed that he had little stomach for battle. The British general called off the siege and the Americans again held Fort Meigs. The fort was so lightly garrisoned that it could have easily been overrun had Proctor organized a full assault and bombardment. Eventually, Harrison ordered the fort be destroyed so the British could not take it.

## TAKING FORT GEORGE

Fort Niagara was one of the most important American fortifications on the Great Lakes. It had been turned over by the British to the Americans in 1796 according to an agreement in the Jay Treaty. The British therefore needed a countermeasure, so they built Fort George on the other side of Lake Ontario by the mouth of the important Niagara River.[10] Fort George became the main British fortification on the Niagara River. It was near the town of Newark (aka "Niagara-on-the-Lake") and was defended by just over 1,000 regulars, 350 militiamen, and a few Indian allies under Major General John Vincent. Roughly 750 British soldiers and Canadian militia were not far away at Fort Erie, and could be called to reinforce Fort George if necessary. The strong fort was protected by a half-dozen large earthworks, enough barracks for a large army, high wooden walls, and several artillery batteries. Ever since the beginning of the War of 1812, men from both forts engaged in very small skirmishes against one another, and their cannons occasionally exchanged fire. But, there had been no direct assault on either stronghold. Until May of 1813.

May was a full month for both armies and a good month for the Americans. To the east of Fort Meigs and Fort Stephenson, an American force of in excess of 5,000 regulars, militia, and naval personnel was en route to Fort George, traveling aboard a flotilla of large ships. The American attack was commanded by General Henry "Granny" Dearborn, whose hesitancy and softness had already cost America multiple opportunities in Canada. Fortunately, Dearborn was not leading the charge. Rather, he turned operational command of the fighting over to Commodore Isaac Chauncey and Colonel Winfield Scott.

Scott had been captured by the British during the disastrous battle at Queenston Heights but was now out of the Canadian prison. Scott was lucky that the gentlemanly norms of the times were such that the British and Americans often either exchanged prisoners or released them on their word of honor, providing they agree not to pick up arms again during the war. While Scott was a proud man, he was, first and foremost, eager to fight and apparently ignored any oath the British made him swear regarding his continued service in the war. If such paroled soldiers were captured a second time, however, it usually resulted in them being put to death. Scott was willing to risk death.

Inside Fort George, General Vincent did not have enough troops to hold the fort against such a massive invasion supported by artillery from Chauncey's armada. He also did not know exactly where the Americans would land. So Vincent gambled and divided his army into three brigades. The general stayed in the fort with one unit; Lieutenant Colonel Harvey led one team of men to the edge of the river to a spot where the Americans might land. A third force was commanded by Lieutenant Colonel Myers and supported by Captain Robert Raunchy. They were charged with preventing an American landing on the lakeshore. General Vincent's plan depended on his men harassing the landing craft from a tree line behind the river banks and lakeshore. He hoped this would prevent the Americans from securing the beach and discourage them from landing their invading force. He guessed wrong.

## SURPRISE AT DAWN

The first wave of the attack began at dawn on May 27, 1813, after a brutal bombardment of the fort by Chauncey's naval artillery. Colonel Scott landed 400 men on the shoreline of Lake Ontario at Newark. Scott was assisted by Benjamin Forsyth, the notorious marauder that had harassed border towns during the prior winter. The landing was near the mouth of the Niagara River and very close to Fort George. The plan was for Scott to secure a beachhead; that done, a few thousand troops on board the ships would come ashore the following day. Scott had also put in play a contingency plan calling for Colonel James Burn to lead another advance force across the Niagara to nearby Queenston. Establishing a position there would block the British force inside Fort George from escaping down the river. It would also cut off a possible route for reinforcements. General Dearborn remained behind on his flagship, the USS *Madison*, which was a good thing for the invasion because it prevented him from harming the American effort.

From his position in the fort, General Vincent saw the large American flotilla approaching on the morning of May 27. Under cover of fog, he discovered too late that the Americans were already unloading troops on the lakeshore. Vincent had guessed wrong and had to rush Lieutenant Colonel Myers to another point on the lakeshore where the Americans were already establishing themselves. Captain Raunchy's men arrived first and fired on the Americans. But, as soon as Raunchy's men opened fire, American artillery from Commodore Chauncey's warships and cannons from Fort Niagara across the river were able to spot them. The Americans let loose a massive artillery barrage, which overwhelmed the exposed defenders, driving them off the landing site.

Commodore Chauncey also inflicted serious damage on the fort, using heated shot to set off fires. The Americans were ashore and marching on the fort, while artillery blasted the fort and pinned down the defenders. The battle was turning into a quick rout. As a last ditch effort, Vincent sent two smaller units—the Glengarry Light Infantry and Royal Newfoundland Infantry—to attack Scott's advance force on the shoreline. The British and Canadian infantrymen fixed bayonets and charged. Scott was nearly run through during the hand-to-hand fighting. But, the British and Canadian infantrymen were greatly outnumbered and were easily defeated. British soldiers manning the fort's outer defenses began retreating for the cover of the fort.

Heavy fog rolled in across the lake and river, and the winds calmed. This hampered the landing effort later that day and the next to the extent that the bulk of American forces were stuck on Commodore Chauncey's transport ships. Colonel Scott's small advance force was on its own. But they carried the day without the main army. Seeing the British retreating, Colonel Scott rushed forward in an attempt to cut off their escape. From within the fort, General Vincent ordered a full retreat. He fled so quickly that women and children from the village were left behind at the fort. Scott was unable to catch Vincent and the bulk of the army. Only a few of the last soldiers had yet to leave the fort. During the quick interrogation, Scott learned that the fort was set to be blown up in order to deny the Americans the rich stores of ammunition and powder. A fuse had already been lit. It was a risky move to rush into a fort about to be detonated, but that is what Scott did in an attempt to salvage weapons and supplies.

Just as Colonel Scott arrived at the fort one of the magazines exploded, knocking him off his horse. He broke his collar bone in the fall, but remounted and continued into the fort to attempt to stop further detonations. Several of his men were also knocked flat to the ground from the force of the blast. The brave commander succeeded in cutting the remaining fuses, thus saving the fort and securing a cache of weapons and supplies. Fort George was in American hands. Roughly 350 British soldiers were either killed or wounded and another 250 captured in the assault. Colonel Scott proved himself a worthy commander and the Americans suffered few casualties. It was a momentous victory, perhaps the best of the war to date.

Sure enough, General Vincent led his army along the Niagara River, but his escape was blocked by the second American advance force, led by Colonel Burn. General Vincent was forced to find another escape route. He also ordered the British garrison at Fort Erie to abandon the fort in advance of the Americans. The British were defeated and on the run, and the Americans now controlled two key forts along the Niagara.[11]

## THE DEFENSE OF FORT STEPHENSON

After abandoning the second attempt for Fort Meigs on July 28, Tecumseh's warriors departed and General Proctor moved his army up the Sandusky River to Lake Erie. A large supply depot holding much of General Harrison's provisions for his forts in the region was Proctor's next target, but it was defended by Fort Stephenson. The fort was far less impressive than Fort Meigs. It was garrisoned by only a light detachment of roughly 160 men and had just one small 6-pound cannon. Proctor planned for an easy and quick siege of the small fort. He would then destroy Harrison's large cache of supplies.[12]

Fort Stephenson was commanded by a 21-year-old major named George Croghan. However, Croghan was a courageous and determined young man, inspired by his uncle, the great hero George Rogers Clark. Upon hearing that Proctor's large army was descending on the small fort, General Harrison sent an order to Major Croghan to burn Fort Stephenson and then retreat along the Sandusky River. Croghan opposed the plan and sent a courier to inform the general that "We have determined to maintain this place, and by heavens we can."[13]

Harrison was furious and wanted Croghan tried for insubordination, despite the fact that the young officer had served bravely under him at the Battle of Tippecanoe. Croghan was thus summoned to Harrison's headquarters. There, Croghan soothed the irate general by saying that his earlier terse reply was but a ploy because he suspected the large force of Indians and British soldiers in the area would capture the courier and his dispatch. Harrison reluctantly decided to let Croghan defend the fort. Major Croghan rushed back to the fort and Harrison prepared his army to march in support of Fort Stephenson.

General Proctor's army arrived at the fort on August 1, 1813. When he observed that the fort was still defended, he correctly suspected that Harrison would attempt to reinforce the small post. Proctor therefore decided to rush the siege. However, as was customary in such engagements, Proctor first offered Croghan terms for surrender, but the major rejected them. General Proctor threatened his stubborn opponent that he could not and would not even attempt to restrain the warriors in his army, who wanted blood. Proctor promised Croghan a brutal massacre. This threat had worked well against other American commanders. But not against Croghan. The brave major responded that he would fight to the last man. If the fort was taken, he informed Proctor, it would mean that all his men were dead and there would be no massacre.

Proctor had ships nearby in support of his army, so he ordered them to begin the bombardment of Fort Stephenson. However, the ships carried only 6-pounders aboard which did very little damage to the small fort. Inside the fort, Major Croghan ordered his men to hold firm and not to surrender. He also had them rush their single, small cannon from one wall of the fort to another, firing wildly so as to give the British the impression that they had several cannons. The British continued shelling the small fort all night long. In the morning, they were shocked to see that the fort held.

At sunrise on August 2, General Proctor ordered a frontal attack. His regulars, Canadian militia, and Indian allies charged the walls of the fort. Inside, Major Croghan, who had disciplined his men, ordered them to hold all fire until his command. Croghan let the attackers get within fifty yards of the fort and then he ordered his men to let loose. A volley of musket fire poured out from the small fort. An entire line of attackers fell. This initial carnage persuaded Proctor's Indian allies, who rarely ever agreed to attack an entrenched position, to abandon the charge. Most of the warriors simply walked off the battlefield. Proctor's men fell back and regrouped.[14]

But the British and Canadians continued their assault, making it to the wall of the fort this time. However, Stephenson's walls were rimmed by an eight-foot-wide and eight-foot-deep moat. Proctor had failed to bring along siege ladders to scale the walls of the fort, so the British and Canadians found themselves stuck at the base of the fort's walls. It was then that Major Croghan ordered his small cannon fired. It had been placed by the main entrance and loaded with grapeshot, which tore into the attackers. The Americans reloaded as fast as they could and fired repeatedly down at the attackers.

Bodies piled up at the walls of the small fort. Sixty-seven British and Canadians were either dead or wounded, mingled with the bodies of several dead warriors. Proctor called off the assault. Before Harrison could arrive to reinforce the fort, Proctor loaded his men on the waiting ships and departed the battlefield for his headquarters at Fort Malden. The British had sustained roughly 100 casualties. Major Croghan lost only a single soldier and had only seven wounded in the short siege.

Croghan showed his mettle, but General Harrison was rightly criticized in the War Department for not hurrying to the small fort's defense. Harrison had reversed his earlier decision—apparently without informing Major Croghan—and decided to stay at Fort Seneca. Harrison never marched to Fort Stephenson, thereby missing an opportunity to possibly catch Proctor's army and destroy them. It seems Harrison's anger at Major Croghan's insubordination was such that he was willing to let the young officer, his men, and the fort fall to Proctor.

Proctor's incompetence had cost the British yet another battle and the Americans rejoiced at the news of another victory. Tecumseh, who had greatly admired General Brock, viewed General Proctor as a coward and dismissed him as weak and unfit to command his warriors. "Go and put on your petticoats," he mocked the British in Proctor's command.[15] The important Indian alliance with the British was, along with Tecumseh's patience, beginning to fray.

# 15

# THE BATTLES OF STONEY CREEK AND BEAVER DAMS

## THE BATTLE OF STONEY CREEK

The Americans repaired Fort George and garrisoned it. Their new possession offered a perfect staging ground for the invasion of Canada and gave the Americans control of much of the border by the Niagara. The only facet of the battle that failed was that the Americans were not able to catch and destroy Vincent's army. General Vincent managed to escape westward, making it to Decew Falls on May 28 and then to Burlington around June 1.

Claiming illness, General "Granny" Dearborn, who commanded American forces during the battle for Fort George, remained behind but sent Brigadier General William Winder and Brigadier General John Chandler to pursue Vincent's army and destroy it. Vincent's army was all that was standing between the Americans and the Niagara River and the two eastern Great Lakes. Reports suggested that General Henry Proctor might be marching east from America's Northwest Territory, possibly to reinforce Vincent's army. Therefore, Generals Winder and Chandler took off immediately from Fort George with a force of 3,000 infantrymen, 150 cavalry, and four cannons. It was enough to do the job. However, both generals were political appointees who lacked experience in battle. It would prove to be their undoing.

The Americans pursued General Vincent but were unable to catch him. Vincent's successful retreat was made possible by a mix of luck, his outright cowardice in abandoning the fort so hastily, and the heroic efforts of a group of dragoons led by William Hamilton Merritt, who harassed the Americans from the rear of Vincent's army. Merritt's men put up fights at creek crossings, destroyed bridges, and blocked roads and trails, all the while conducting quick hit-and-run attacks on the pursuing American troops. While the general fled to safety, Merritt's dragoons assured the army's survival. They bought Vincent enough time that he was able to then locate the companies of men who had abandoned Fort Erie.

The main problem for Vincent's retreating army was that they were cut off from supplies. He therefore attempted to meet up with Captain Sir James Yeo, whose navy was based out of Kingston and who set sail on June 3 for the rendezvous. The plan was to obtain enough supplies to dig in on the hilltop overlooking Burlington Bay, supported by Yeo's navy. Vincent rendezvoused with Yeo and began constructing defenses at Burlington Heights (present-day Hamilton in Ontario).[1] He would make his stand there [see Map 2 in Appendix].

General Vincent was offered an unexpected opportunity, one that would stop the American advance into Canada. On June 5, the Americans arrived at Stoney Creek, about six miles from Vincent's army at Burlington, and established camp at Gage Farm. They were within striking distance of Vincent's army and planned to attack him the following day. The American army was exhausted from the long march and constant harassment from Merritt's dragoons along the way. As had happened with other American commanders, Generals Winder and Chandler foolishly made camp without establishing adequate defenses. Only a few sentries were posted at the American camp and they did not change their password—"Wil-hen-harr," which was an abbreviation of William Henry Harrison—at checkpoints around the camp. This would prove to be their undoing.

The American generals also seemed to have had conflicting intelligence reports and different perspectives on the status of Vincent's army. General Winder seems to have believed Vincent had restocked his army and that it was equal or superior to the American forces, while General Chandler appears to have assumed Vincent's fleeing army was beaten and would be equally exhausted. Both were partially correct. Vincent's army had marched vigorously to flee the Americans but, along the way, he mustered men from outposts and other forts the British had abandoned. Even though Vincent dismissed his militiamen, he had built his army to 1,600 strong and most were regulars.

While preparing to make camp, the Americans came upon local residents who were obviously curious about the invading army. One of them was a young man named Isaac Corman, who was detained by the American scouts. After interrogating Corman, an officer made the young Canadian promise on his honor not to reveal anything he had seen or heard in the camp. Corman agreed and was released. However, he immediately informed his 19-year-old brother-in-law, Billy Green, that the password the Americans used in camp was "Wil-hen-harr." Billy borrowed Corman's horse and rode as fast as possible to tell the British. He rode to meet Lieutenant James Fitzgibbon, a dashing, young officer who conducted hit-and-run raids on the Americans and, earlier, had barely managed to elude capture by two Americans by fighting them off with his sword. Lieutenant Fitzgibbon quickly passed the information up the chain of command. For his service to the war effort, Billy was given a sword.[2] His intelligence report was worth far more.

## "WILL-HEN-HARR"

The British now knew precisely where the American camp was located and the password for the camp. General Vincent ordered his number two, Lieutenant Colonel John Harvey, to reconnoiter the camp. To his surprise and excitement, Harvey found the camp unprepared. He reported back to Vincent: "The enemy's guards were few and negligent; his line of encampment was long and broken; his artillery was feebly supported; several of his corps were placed too far to the rear to aid in repelling a blow which might be rapidly struck in front."[3] Harvey recommended an immediate nighttime attack on the much-larger army.

Young Billy Green and Lieutenant Colonel Harvey hurriedly led a detachment of 700 British regulars through the woods to the American position. The attack was organized into three columns, led by Lieutenant Colonel Harvey, Major Charles Plenderleath, and Major James Ogilvie, with General Vincent following safely from the rear. They departed shortly before midnight and arrived in the predawn hours of June 6 at the American camp at Stoney Creek. It was King George III's birthday and the British intended a very special present for their sovereign.

The British managed to make it to the perimeter of the American defenses undetected, taking advantage of the very dark night. Their advance scouts used the not-so-secret password, "will-hen-harr" to gain access to the American sentries and kill them. However, as the British were fixing bayonets to storm the American camp, a few undisciplined soldiers started yelling and screaming. Rather than unnerve the Americans, the foolish bravado only served to alert the camp. Also, as they rushed forward they discovered that part of the camp was deserted and the fires unattended. By dumb luck, several American units had moved to higher ground earlier in the evening. Musket balls began flying down on the attackers. The British had to turn and charge up the hill.

The Americans, with the high ground and superior numbers, managed to organize counterattacks and beat back the attackers. The Americans also wisely loaded cannon with grapeshot and fired at the British. The tide of the battle was turning in favor of the defenders. However, General Winder worried about being surrounded and ordered an infantry unit to redeploy to guard the camp's left flank. The problem was that the unit in question was holding the center of the American line and supporting the artillery batteries. At the same time, General Chandler rode to the opposite flank to inspect it. Chandler's horse was either spooked or shot and the general thrown to the ground and knocked unconscious.

With the American line now exposed and their artillery undefended, Major Charles Plenderleath and his British regulars charged the batteries. Even though the cannons were not supported by infantry, it would be a risky charge. Plenderleath told his men to wait until the cannons fired and then rush them before the artillerymen had time to reload. If the cannons managed to prepare a round of grapeshot before the attackers made it to them, it would be a suicide mission. About twenty-five men volunteered for the mission, fixed bayonets, and, after the cannons fired, they charged the line using the black of night as cover. One of the British soldiers who volunteered for the charge was a brave, young sergeant named Alexander Fraser.

As fate would have it, at that very moment an American commander gave the order to cease firing. Captain Nathaniel Towson ordered his four batteries silenced. It was a costly mistake. The British were upon them, bayoneting the defenseless artillerymen and even killing the horses used to pull the cannons. It was a quick and decisive victory for the British. Major Plenderleath then turned the cannons and fired on the American camp.

Meanwhile, General Chandler had regained his sense and limped back into camp in the direction of the artillery fire. But, when he walked up to the batteries, to his surprise, he now found them controlled by the British. While protesting and claiming to still be disoriented from his fall, Chandler was captured by the British and held at bayonet point by young Sergeant Fraser. Said Fraser to the American general: "If you stir, sir; you die."[4]

## GENERAL-LESS

The generals on both sides of the battle were of little use to their armies. Not long after General Chandler was taken prisoner, General Winder was also captured. The British commander, General Vincent, was not seen during the battle. He too claimed to have fallen off his horse and was dazed by the fall. He was later found wandering in the woods seven miles from the battle and escorted back to his headquarters at Burlington on June 7. It is possible the general was dazed by cowardice as much as a fall.

Although the British were outnumbered, they took advantage of the confusion of fighting at night and the poorly prepared American camp. With no word from either American general, Colonel James Burn took charge of the battle and ordered a cavalry charge directly into the British line. However, in the black night, the cavalry mistakenly charged an American line, who fired on their own men. After roughly one hour of fighting, Lieutenant Colonel Harvey ordered his men to spike the cannons he had seized from the Americans and then retreated from the battlefield. He had accomplished his mission. At daylight, the Americans surveyed the damage. Seventeen of their men were dead, thirty-eight wounded, and nearly 100 were missing and presumed captured. Although the numbers were not overwhelming, the Americans lost both of their generals, a major, and three captains. All were captured, depleting the command structure. The Americans were also exhausted and shocked by the nighttime raid. Citing limited ammunition, Colonel Burn decided to abandon both the camp and the plan to attack General Vincent's headquarters at Burlington Bay.

The commander of the invasion, General Dearborn, who had botched earlier attempted invasions, had not even accompanied his army into Canada. Even if he had, it may not have mattered. The Americans deserted the camp and marched back to Forty Mile Creek and eventually all the way to the border. Obviously unnerved by the nighttime assault, they were in such a rush that they did not even properly bury their dead.

Arriving at the mouth of the Niagara River on Lake Ontario, the Americans expected support from Commodore Chauncey's navy. Winfield Scott had sent twenty boats from Chauncey's navy with supplies to reinforce the army. They were not to be found. It turned out that the British commander of the lakes, Captain Sir Yeo, had intercepted the American flotilla. Without ships or supplies, the Americans abandoned the invasion of Canada and returned to Fort George. However, on the way back to Fort George, they vented their frustration by burning a nearby village.

The British suffered over twenty dead, 136 wounded, and over fifty captured in the daring nighttime attack on the American camp at Stoney Creek. The Battle of Stoney Creek was, technically, a military draw. But, in reality it was a huge success for the British. This was likely the closest the Americans would come to successfully invading Canada. If they had sent a better general and more troops, the Americans would likely have crushed the last remaining British-Canadian army in the entire region. Given the fact the Vincent's army was all that opposed the American invaders, the battle might have saved Canada.

## THE BATTLE OF BEAVER DAMS

Later that same month, the Americans suffered another setback that undid the impressive victories they had enjoyed in spring and summer. The American victories certainly changed the tide of the war, but disastrous campaigns such as the Battle of Beaver Dams demonstrated that the American commanders still had many lessons to learn and that the war was turning out to be an evenly matched stalemate.[5]

After the American defeat at Stoney Creek, General Dearborn's army holed up at Fort George on the border, a fort they had seized in late May. The swashbuckling British officer, Lieutenant James Fitzgibbon, who had served under the legendary General Brock, continued to keep the Americans on edge by conducting quick raids against American forts, supply lines, and scouting parties. Fitzgibbon had recruited the equivalent of today's "special forces" to conduct his successful hit-and-run raids. These raids went unpunished and the War Department and Congress expressed impatience that General Dearborn controlled an important British fort, large American armies on the border, and yet nothing was happening! Finally, General John Boyd, the commanding officer of Fort George at the time, had quite enough of the pesky Fitzgibbon and ordered a campaign to capture or kill the Lieutenant and wipe out his raiders.

With a force of almost 600 regulars and a light artillery detachment, the Americans marched in pursuit of Fitzgibbon in late June of 1813. They were led by recently promoted Colonel Charles Boerstler, who ordered roughly forty mounted New York militiamen to proceed in advance of his army to scout a path through Canada. After a few days, Boerstler camped on the west bank of the Niagara River by Queenston, site of an earlier defeat of the American army. His plan was to attack a large stone house that quartered British soldiers—and possibly Lieutenant Fitzgibbon—in the town of Thorold in Ontario and then strike the British outpost at Beaver Dams. Both places were known to be used by Fitzgibbon's raiders.[6]

## CANADA'S HEROINE OF THE WAR

Some of the American officers including Colonel Boerstler billeted themselves in the home of a Canadian militia officer named James Secord, who had been wounded at the Battle of Queenston Heights fighting for General Brock. In order to prevent word of their attack from leaking, the Americans prohibited anyone from the village from leaving and detained a few men. However, Captain Secord's wife, Laura, a 38-year-old mother of five, overheard talk of the American plans at her home. She also observed the size of the American force occupying her town. Mrs. Secord had been nursing her wounded husband back to health and he was not yet fully recovered from his wounds. But she felt compelled to help stop the American invasion. Laura Secord bravely set out by foot after darkness on a difficult journey through the wilderness to alert the British. It is estimated that she traveled between twelve and seventeen miles through swamps, woods, and Indian country on June 22.[7] At Twelve Mile Creek, she was captured by a Caughnawaga war party who, luckily for Mrs. Secord and Canada, turned out to be allied with the British.

After alerting the warriors to the pending American attack, Mrs. Secord was taken to meet Lieutenant Fitzgibbon. Fitzgibbon was initially suspect of the story and wondered how a middle-aged mother could travel so far so quickly at night. But he too suspected an American attack and decided to act on her report. Mrs. Secord provided him with details of the American army's whereabouts and plan of attack.[8] Fitzgibbon posted scouts along the likely route the Americans would take, but the initial report was that no Americans had been sighted. As such, Mrs. Secord's loyalties were questioned by some of the British soldiers. However, a French ally and his Indian loyalists also happened into the British camp around the same time with reports that corroborated Mrs. Secord's story.

The Americans headed out to pursue Fitzgibbon unaware that he was hunting them. The path the Americans traveled to get to Thorold and Beaver Dams was through a wooded area. As they climbed a hill by St. David's on their way to the Beaver Dams settlement, the soldiers observed a small Indian war party shadowing them in the woods. Foolishly, Colonel Boerstler ignored the war party and continued the march on its present route. The war party alerted the British army that the Americans were coming on the exact path predicted by Laura Secord. An ambush was organized roughly one mile east of the village of Beaver Dams. As the Americans walked into the trap they were attacked by 400 Mohawk, Iroquois, and Caughnawaga warriors, the latter being Christian converts from the Mohawk nation who came from Quebec to fight against the Americans.

Musket balls poured down on the Americans from the woods on either side of the trail. One of the first Americans hit was their commander, Colonel Boerstler, who was carried to a wagon. The Americans tried to move to an open field in order to draw the Indians out from the cover of the forest and to put their two cannons to use. However, the battle collapsed into disorder. The American army broke and tried to run, but their escape was blocked by the warriors. Several soldiers foolishly took cover in a gully only to find themselves easy targets for braves who circled them and fired down into the killing pit.

At the rear of the American column were wagons and artillery that blocked a retreat back down the trail. The artillery detachment managed to fire one round of grapeshot at the Indians who were now charging forth from the woods. It killed five warriors, one of them a chief, and wounded an Indian boy. However, before they could reload, the artillerymen were overrun and either killed or wounded. As a last-ditch effort, Colonel Boerstler tried to organize a countercharge into the woods, but the Indians overwhelmed his men as he was giving them orders. Only moments later, Lieutenant Fitzgibbon emerged from the woods flying the flag of truce. He met with the junior officers in the American force to offer them terms, claiming falsely that the Americans were outnumbered and surrounded, and warning them of the Indian atrocities that would follow. Word was relayed to Colonel Boerstler who surrendered the entire army, claiming to be low on ammunition. It is likely he was simply afraid of being scalped.

The terms arranged by Fitzgibbon were not honored. Even though the British officers allegedly tried to prevent it, the Mohawks scalped and killed some of the Americans. It was another humiliating and unnecessary defeat for the Americans and another example of poor planning and cowardice. The Americans lost twenty-five men and had fifty wounded in the quick battle. Over 500 men were taken prisoner. The British suffered no casualties but their Indian allies lost fifteen warriors, with another twenty-five wounded.

Of the battle, it has been said amusingly and not inaccurately, "The Caughnawage got the victory, the Mohawks got the plunder and Fitzgibbon got the credit."[9] Laura Secord has also been credited for the victory and, over the years, she has become an iconic figure in Canada. Several versions of her night walk and bravery exist, including one that suggests that she took a cow with her to give the appearance that she was not spying but simply going to the market early![10]

Word of another loss made its way back to Fort George and further demoralized the troops. Soldiers no longer wanted to volunteer for scouting missions and officers were reluctant to lead them for fear of being massacred by Indians. On December 10, the Americans abandoned the important fort that they had recently won and pulled back across the border. They also evacuated Fort Erie and Fort Chippewa. Yet another American invasion of Canada—and the only one that appeared to be succeeding—had been stopped.

# 16

# THE BATTLE OF THAMES

## THE FORT MIMS MASSACRE

As if the problem of having the British arm and incite Indian nations in the north and west was not enough, it was discovered that the Spanish government was doing the same along the Gulf Coast. Spanish officials in Pensacola in Spanish West Florida were providing arms to Creek warriors, including the notorious Red Sticks, so-called because of the color of their battle clubs. Under their leader, Peter McQueen, who was of mixed Indian and white blood, the warriors began conducting bloody raids against American settlements. The Red Sticks were among the most fearsome of all warriors and had joined Tecumseh in battles against the Americans, including at the massacre at River Raisin.

The War of 1812 provided the Red Sticks and other Indian nations the opportunity to attack American villages in hopes of limiting or stopping white settlement on their ancestral lands. During his vast travels, Tecumseh had visited the Creeks in present-day Alabama near the Coosa and Tallapoosa Rivers and encouraged them to join him in attacking the Americans. Although some Creek communities in the southern part of the state and along the Georgia border by the Chattahootchee River chose not to fight, many other warriors answered Tecumseh's call to arms. As a result, white settlers in the south clamored for protection. But it was not forthcoming. The federal government had committed most of the army along the Canadian border. As such, residents of the Gulf Coast took matters into their own hands by organizing a 180-man militia under Colonel James Caller and a tough frontiersman named Sam Dale. The hunt for the Creek war parties began.

The showdown occurred in July of 1813 after McQueen, the half-Creek chief, led 300 warriors to Pensacola where he obtained an arsenal of weapons from the Spanish. On July 27, the militia units attacked McQueen's raiders at an Indian village north of Pensacola in what became known as the Battle of Burnt Corn.[1] After the attack, Colonel Caller discovered a cache of weapons at the village. News of the find alarmed Americans and opened a new front in the ongoing violence between whites and Native Americans. It also sparked a struggle between Creeks loyal to the Red Sticks and those opposed to their ways. The wrath of the War of 1812 was visited upon the Gulf Coast when both white militia units and hostile Creeks began conducting brutal raids on innocent villages with increased frequency. The situation spiraled out of control.

The administration of James Madison finally responded by erecting forts along the Gulf and throughout the South, while local communities organized additional militia operations against Indians. One of the forts built was Fort Mims. It was located a few miles north of Mobile along the Alabama River in the southern part of the state. The high walls of the fort offered settlers living in the surrounding small villages safe haven during Indian raids. Roughly 350 people and militiamen lived in and around the fort, which was commanded by Major Daniel Beasley. However, Beasley ignored the ongoing tensions and occasional Indian raids, doing little to prepare the fort, his small garrison, or the people of southwestern Alabama for an attack.

## RED STICKS

In August, some former slaves arrived at Fort Mims in a panic with news that a Creek war party was headed toward the fort. Major Beasley sent out scouts to look for the Creeks but they found no evidence of any imminent attack. As such, Beasley ordered that the slaves, whom he believed were falsely alarming the villages, be whipped. But tensions remained high among the settlements, as additional rumors of war parties circulated. Major Beasley seems to have been the only one unconcerned by the reports. He failed to put the fort on high alert. In fact, when a Red Stick Creek war party finally stormed the town at noon on August 30, the front gates of the fort were wide open and the soldiers inside were eating lunch!

The massive Red Stick war party numbering roughly 1,000 braves was led by Chief Red Eagle, also known as William Weatherford. He was born around 1780 to a white frontiersman, Scott Weatherford, and a Creek mother. Weatherford was educated and spoke fluent English, and was also widely feared as a brutal leader despite his constant claims that he regretted the conflict with whites. When Weatherford and his warriors burst through the open gate of the fort one of the first soldiers to meet them was Major Beasley, who was running to try and close the gate. Consequently, the major was one of the first men killed in the raid.

Settlers, along with slaves and Indians opposed to the Red Sticks, had rushed to the fort for protection. They now found themselves under attack. And it was a deadly attack. The warriors overwhelmed the fort and moved through the nearby village killing anyone they encountered in hand-to-hand combat. The raid lasted four hours and when it was over, nearly every militiaman and villager was dead. However, despite being caught utterly unprepared, the militiamen put up a good fight and inflicted many Red Stick casualties.

Weatherford claimed to have attempted to stop his warriors from killing women and children. It is uncertain whether he really did, but it did not matter. The fort was set on fire, the town looted, anyone caught was scalped, and slaves were taken to serve their new Creek masters. When American soldiers arrived ten days later, they found a ghastly sight: mutilated bodies in large piles throughout the fort and town.[2] Said Weatherford: "My warriors were like famished wolves and the first taste of blood made their appetites insatiable."[3] The brutal attack came to be known as the Fort Mims Massacre.

## ABANDONING THE NORTHWEST TERRITORY

The massacre at Fort Mims was but one of many tragic raids on innocent civilians by Indians and white soldiers in the region. The Indian attacks were futile, as they only served to bring the full force of the American military to bear on peaceful villages. Moreover, bickering and warring among the many native nations across the continent continually undermined any prospect of a unified resistance to the white settlers or the American government. The defeat of Tecumseh's army at the Battle of Tippecanoe in 1811 on account of The Prophet's foolish attack proved to be a turning point for the American Indian in North America. It dashed any hope of forging a grand Indian confederation to oppose the expansionistic Americans.

In the post-Tippecanoe era, many Indian leaders felt their only hope was to throw their lot in with the British, who were the lesser of two evils. Among them was the great chief, Tecumseh, who joined the British in

Canada. A British victory, reasoned Tecumseh and others, would slow the American conquest of the continent and thereby allow Indians to retain their lands. With Tecumseh's support, in 1812 the British enjoyed many successes against the Americans, including in the western Great Lakes and American Northwest Territory. However, in 1813 the British navy suffered defeat on Lake Erie at the hands of Oliver Hazard Perry. This left the forts the British had conquered and their troops in the American Northwest without supplies, reinforcements, and vulnerable to attack. As a result, the British commander, General Proctor, ordered the forts abandoned. The British pulled out of Fort Detroit, Fort Malden, and the entire region and began their march across the Detroit River into Canada on September 27, 1813. General Proctor even abandoned Amherstburg and other towns and forts on the Canadian side of the river, and continued his retreat to the northeast.

Tecumseh, who always considered Proctor to be a coward and not half the man General Brock had been, was furious. The Shawnee chief wanted to keep the forts and use them as a forward staging area for additional attacks on the American frontier. But Proctor's mind was made up. Tecumseh pleaded with the British general: "Father, listen! We are very much astonished to see our father preparing to run away. We wish to remain here and fight our enemy."[4] Promises had been made to the Indian allies that the British would provide them land in the region in return for their support in battle. With the British now abandoning Indian territory, the warriors were disillusioned and angry. Like the British troops in Proctor's command, their will to fight was gone. Many quit the war and returned home. The Indians had tired of fighting *with* white men to fight *against* white men. The Indian cause would be dealt another terrible blow when two bitter adversaries—Tecumseh and William Henry Harrison—met yet again on the field of battle at Thames.

## TECUMSEH AND HARRISON AGAIN

Alas, without the British army, Tecumseh's small, dispirited war parties stood no chance against the American military. Despite his disagreement with Proctor and the many defections suffered among his warriors, Tecumseh continued to fight with the British. The great chief was joined by his own faithful Shawnee braves, and small bands of warriors from the Sioux, Chippewa, and other nations, and William Caldwell, a hero of the American Revolution. Caldwell was a fighter and he and Tecumseh respected one another. Caldwell's Rangers, as his small band of men were known, fixed themselves to Tecumseh's force of Indians, which now numbered only 500 to 750 loyal warriors.

Making matters worse for Proctor and Tecumseh, their retreat to Canada was slowed by a lack of supplies, overloaded wagons, sagging morale, and the many women, children, aged, and wounded who sought protection in the British army. The slow pace of retreat would prove deadly, as Tecumseh's old nemesis, General William Henry Harrison, was marching his army of several thousand men to catch Proctor. With each passing day, Harrison's army continued to close the gap with the fleeing British.

General Proctor had, by this time, essentially abandoned his command. He was spending all of his time with his family and had turned the daily leadership of the army over to Lieutenant Colonel Augustus Warburton. Both Proctor and Warburton, in their rush to retreat deep into Canada, failed to destroy bridges they crossed or burn food and supplies, which would have slowed Harrison's pursuit. Nor did they deploy a rear guard to harass and slow the Americans. This incompetence further enraged Tecumseh, who began taking it on himself to destroy bridges the British army crossed.

One such rear-guard mission occurred at a site called McGregor's Creek. Just as Tecumseh's Shawnee braves were about to destroy the bridge over the creek, an American advance unit arrived. Hiding in the woods nearby, the chief organized a surprise attack on the American cavalry and beat them back across the river. The Americans fled, leaving their dead and wounded behind, but soon returned with the main army and Tecumseh was forced to flee. The effort only temporarily slowed the American advance. Tecumseh now knew General Harrison would eventually catch the British army and his own braves.

In late September, Harrison's army crossed into Canada hot on the trail of Proctor. Harrison's army was supplemented by a very large militia from Kentucky, raised by the state's governor, Isaac Shelby, a hero of the American Revolution. Harrison and Shelby were friends and the general greatly admired the governor, even requesting he come to Canada to lead his Kentuckians in battle. Governor Shelby agreed, announcing "I will lead you to the field of battle and share with you the dangers and honors of the campaign."[5]

Harrison's massive army was further supplemented by Richard Mentor Johnson, another Kentucky politician who would go on to serve in the U.S. Senate and as vice president in Martin Van Buren's administration. Johnson would end up becoming a national embarrassment and was dropped from the ticket by Van Buren during his reelection campaign in 1840. Ironically, in that campaign, President Van Buren would be defeated by none other than William Henry Harrison. However, Johnson and Harrison were still on good terms in 1813, and Johnson led a force of 1,200 mounted Kentucky volunteers to join General Harrison and Governor Shelby. Johnson's volunteer cavalry passed River Raisin on their way to join Harrison's main army. The stories of the massacre of their countrymen by Indians and the site of decomposed bodies whipped the Kentuckians into a frenzy. Harrison now commanded 5,500 men and they were all itching to fight.[6]

## A FINAL STAND

Tecumseh knew the British army would be caught by the Americans. He thus counseled General Proctor to stand and fight. The general had no choice but to fight or be slaughtered while on the run. The chief selected the site of their stand—the Thames River near Moraviantown, roughly 50 miles east of Detroit [see Map 2 in Appendix]. The Thames flowed between Lakes Erie and Huron and was surrounded by woods and swamps. It was as good a site as any. And the British and their Indian allies were out of time. The date was October 5 and while they were still discussing their decision to face the Americans, Tecumseh spotted General Harrison's army advancing on the road in front of them at roughly 8:00 in the morning.

There was no time for the British army to build a fort or even to prepare defenses. Tecumseh chose a swampy, wooded area by the Thames for his warriors. The natural cover would diminish Harrison's advantage. The British army included roughly 800 regulars and militia. Proctor arranged them in a long, thin line with Tecumseh's braves hiding in the forest on the army's flank. On the battlefield in front of them were roughly 5,500 U.S. infantry, cavalry, and militia. Proctor and Harrison had faced one another before, and Tecumseh and Harrison had squared off against one another many times. This would be their last.

The battle was over as soon as it started. There would be no terms, no negotiations, no exchange of volleys. General Harrison immediately ordered a cavalry charge by Richard Johnson's mounted Kentuckians directly into the center of the thin, British line. It was obvious to him that the British line was too overextended to hold. The Kentuckians rode wildly and broke through the center of the line, sending the British fleeing. The British line managed just one or two volleys and were now running in full panic. Indeed, the sight of over 1,000 horses charging at a narrow spot with their riders screaming "Remember the Raisin!" would be enough to unnerve even the most resolute soldier. Said General Harrison: "The American backwoodsman rides better in the woods than any other people. I was persuaded too that the enemy would be quite unprepared for the shock and that they could not resist it."[7] He was right.

From behind the broken British line, General Proctor turned and ran too, leaving his men to their fate. The American army poured into the British line, which immediately surrendered. General Harrison had arranged Governor Shelby's Kentucky volunteers on the flank to fire at Tecumseh's warriors in the forest in order to prevent them from trying to counterattack on the American flank.

After dispatching the British line, General Harrison turned his attention to Tecumseh's braves in the forest, ordering another cavalry charge. Richard Johnson's mounted Kentuckians raced into the woods shouting "Remember the Raisin!" However, Tecumseh ordered his men to stand their ground. They were protected by the marsh and cover of trees, poor terrain for the cavalry. Johnson's Kentuckians dismounted and the fight continued hand-to-hand. The great chief's last words were said to be addressed to his braves, "Our lives are in the hands of the Great Spirit. We are determined to defend our lands, and if it is his will, we wish to leave our bones upon them."[8] They did not have a chance.

Through the fighting, it was said that Tecumseh screamed with anger, rallying his braves to keep fighting. It is unknown who it was that killed Tecumseh, but his death ended the Indian resistance. With Tecumseh gone, many braves turned and fled. Caldwell's Rangers, however, loyal to the great chief, stayed and fought. Caldwell himself ran out of ammunition and threw his musket at a Kentucky attacker, hitting the man in the face before he was killed. Soon after, Governor Shelby's army followed and quickly overwhelmed the few remaining braves. The Kentuckians, motivated by the River Raisin massacre, set about hacking to death wounded Indians. They also mutilated the bodies of the dead, so much so that it was difficult to attempt to identify Tecumseh's body. Richard Johnson was shot in the hip and thigh during the battle. He would later claim that it was he who killed

Tecumseh, which is highly doubtful despite the famous frontier chant he inspired: "Rumpsey, dumpsey, Colonel Johnson killed Tecumseh!"

Tecumseh's body was never found. It is believed that his braves quickly hid the body or carried their dead leader from the field as they fled. The warriors claimed that Tecumseh was immediately "carried up into the sky."[9]

Even though it was an important battle, there were not a lot of casualties. Only about three dozen British were killed. Most of the army—about 600—surrendered immediately. The remainder ran. There is no firm count, but there were also many Indian casualties. General Proctor managed to escape with about 250 men to Moraviantown. Even though he blamed his men for the loss, Proctor was later court-martialed for his conduct. But this penalty was reduced to a public reprimand and he was docked both pay and rank. The British continued to miss General Brock and they would come to miss Tecumseh too. Because of the Battle of Thames, the British were no longer able to organize a strong force in that region. They no longer dominated the Great Lakes and, with Tecumseh dead, the inevitable happened—the Indian alliance with the British ended. The victorious Harrison commented on his longtime foe: "Tecumseh was one of those uncommon geniuses, which spring up occasionally to produce revolutions and overturn the established order of things."[10] The great chief's life was captured in a poem titled "Death of Tecumseh," popular during the war:

> The moment was fearful; a mightier foe
> Had ne'er swung his battle-axe o'er him;
> But hope nerved his arm for a desperate blow,
> And Tecumseh fell prostrate before him.
> He fought in defence of his kindred and king,
> With a spirit most loving and loyal,
> And long shall the Indian warrior sing
> The deeds of Tecumseh the royal.[11]

# THE HIGH SEAS

*"The Impressed Seaman's Appeal"*

*Shall that arm which haughty Britain*
*In its gristle found too strong—*
*That by which her foes were smitten—*
*Shall that arm be praised long?*
*See our sons of ocean kneeling*
*To a tyrant's stripes and chains!*
*Partisan! Hast thou no feeling*
*When the hardy tar complains?*
*See the British press-gang seize him,*
*Victim of relentless power!*
*Stout his heart is, but must fail him*
*In the evil, trying hour.*

—American song from the War of 1812

"Capture of the Guerriere by the Constitution." Acknowledgment: By Samuel Walker, 1834; U.S. Library of Congress, Washington, DC (USZ62-10752)

# 17

# THE MAKING OF A NAVY

## NAVAL OPERATIONS IN THE WAR

At the beginning of the war, both sides largely ignored the naval theater of operations and what little action occurred was not well planned. This is surprising, given Britain's naval superiority around the world. Had the Royal Navy made it a priority, they could have blockaded the Great Lakes and major rivers on the border such as the Saint Lawrence, Niagara, and Detroit, which would have prevented the Americans from transporting troops and supplies for the invasion.[1] But Britain was otherwise focused on the more pressing conflict against Napoleon in Europe and needed all available ships for that war. So too did the British underestimate the Americans, believing the War of 1812 would end quickly and that no one could challenge them on the seas.

At the same time, the American navy consisted of only sixteen warships when the fighting broke out. Of them, only seven large frigates were seaworthy in 1812. Some American military planners believed it would be futile to even attempt to challenge the Royal Navy, which had more than 100 large frigates, hundreds of other large warships, and hundreds of smaller vessels on the seas. War planners therefore essentially ignored naval operations altogether.[2]

The American navy included three classes of warships in 1812: ships of the line or "man-of-war" ships; frigates and brigs; and smaller vessels such as sloops and schooners. These smaller ships were light, fast, and usually had only one deck and one main mast. Frigates had three masts and two decks, while brigs had two masts and a single, large deck. The man-of-war was a powerful vessel with multiple decks and multiple masts. Warships were also rated by how many guns they carried. For instance, the man-of-war often bristled with fifty, sixty, or over seventy naval guns, making them the most formidable vessels on the seas. Frigates were armed with thirty or forty guns, and sloops, brigs, and other smaller ships typically carried around twenty guns.

These guns included a variety of smooth-bore, cast-iron cannons, both long- and short-range, as well as carronades, which were short-barreled, short-range, light cannons named for Carron, the site in Scotland where they were manufactured. Naval artillery shot a variety of devices, including large balls (or rounds), bar shot, chains designed to tear holes in sails, grapeshot (nails and metal), and other armaments, depending on whether the objective was to scatter shot into sailors attempting to board your ship, rip a mast apart, or punch holes in the ship's water line. The larger ships sported long, thickly barreled cannons that were capable of firing 18-pound or 24-pound rounds for long distances. The drawback was that they were less effective in close combat and such cannons needed to be pulled back into the ship in order to be reloaded and then "run" back out of the gunports to be fired.

A common tactic in naval warfare at the time was the "broadside," whereby ships aligned sideways and unloaded their cannons in a massive wave of fire. In such cases, a different type of shot and short-range cannons were used.[3] Broadsides were often followed by grappling hooks, which were hurled onto the enemy ship so that the two ships could be tied together. Boarding parties then clamored across the railings and onto the enemy ship. When boarding another ship, the fighting was often very bloody and relied on cutlasses, axes, pikes, pistols, and an early type of shotgun called a blunderbuss. Many warships also carried small swivel-guns designed to repel boarding parties.[4]

The three largest ships in the young American navy were the USS *United States*, USS *Constitution*, and USS *President*. If there was a bright spot at the beginning of the war it was that these ships proved to be among the fastest, strongest, and most durable vessels afloat. They shocked the world by besting several British warships. The British mistakenly decided that large flotillas were not needed to dispatch the pesky American navy. They sent only a few inadequately supplied ships to battle the Americans. As a result, the British failed to implement a serious blockade of American ports or organize a massive naval offensive at the outset of the war.[5] The British admiralty's overconfidence cost them dearly, as British commanders and ships were on the receiving end of these three great American ships.[6]

The Royal Navy was also plagued by shortages of seamen, which was the reason for the policy of impressment, which in turn ignited the war.

By conscripting sailors, including Americans, into service, all the British did was assure themselves morale and desertion problems; and many of the impressed sailors ended up being landlubbers who lacked both the will to fight and sea legs. Even British sailors often deserted, preferring the liberty and opportunity of the United States to the harsh life aboard a British warship. The Royal admiralty did not know how to respond to reports of so many British citizens deserting to the United States and aboard American ships. One admiral thundered, "We must on no account shrink from the duty of putting to death every British subject caught fighting against his country."[7] British newspapers stoked the passions, by condemning the defectors and the Royal Navy's failure to prevent and punish desertions. In London, the *Times* wrote, "The Americans cannot, by any verbal process whatever, rob England of her right to the services of English-born subjects. They cannot naturalize against nature."[8] Of course, all this only made matters worse. British doctrine refused to recognize the notion that any of His Majesty's subjects could change his or her citizenship. In fact, it decreed of loyal subjects to the Crown that "it began with their birth, and can only terminate with their existence [death]."[9]

An American naval prisoner serving in Dartmoor penned a line that perfectly described the situation and would become famous during the War of 1812: "An American, in England, pines to get home; while an Englishman and an Irishman longs to become an American citizen."[10]

## MASTERS OF THE SEAS

The British navy was the undisputed master of the seas. No naval force—not the French, not the Spanish, and certainly not the Americans—could rival them. The Royal Navy had roughly 1,000 ships operating throughout the world and they had the best trained commanders and crews. As such, it would stand to reason that the United States, with only a handful of ships and inexperienced crews, stood little chance of success on the seas. However, the Americans shocked the British. Even though attempt after attempt to invade Canada ended in disaster during the first year of the war, it was an entirely different matter on the seas, where the Americans performed surprisingly well.

These successes were, however, *in spite* of the naval command rather than *because* of it. For instance, Paul Hamilton, the former governor of South Carolina, was the secretary of the navy but knew nothing about naval warfare, and President Madison's cabinet could not agree on a unified strategy. While James Monroe, the secretary of state, wanted the small navy kept safely in ports only to be used in emergencies, Albert Gallatin, the treasury secretary, preferred the navy be used to escort and protect American commercial shipping. Ultimately, Commodore John Rogers decided, and President Madison agreed, that two squadrons would be organized and their primary mission would be to protect commercial shipping. But events occurred that would change the mission.

Britain eventually decided to have its navy blockade American ports, effectively strangling the American economy. Also, several young, gifted American commanders such as William Bainbridge, Stephen Decatur, and Isaac Hull proposed taking the fight directly to the British navy through guerilla tactics and hunting the Royal Navy on oceans around the world. And they did. And they succeeded. These daring attacks forced the British to add to their blockade the need to defend commercial shipping on the open seas. This had the effect of thinning any concentration of British naval power toward any single mission, which made the otherwise invincible Royal Navy vulnerable.

Several dashing and daring American naval commanders emerged as heroes. They outmaneuvered, outwitted, and outfought their vastly more powerful foes. American sailors, although poorly trained, turned out to be adept at ship-building and converting merchant ships to military vessels. They also knew their coastline, harbors, and currents better than the British and benefited by the enlistment of New England whalers, fishermen, and traders, who ably crewed the new American warships. The young, brash American commanders also employed asymmetrical warfare, often surprising the British with sudden attacks, taking advantage of lightly patrolled trade routes rather than engaging heavily armed British convoys, frequently fleeing the larger, heavier British ships, or relying on cunning privateers to harass British ships.

Making matters worse for the British, when the war broke out, Britain had only about three dozen ships patrolling North American waters. This small squadron was based in Halifax, Nova Scotia and was commanded by Vice Admiral Sir Herbert Sawyer, who was an unimpressive figure at best and would make many costly mistakes during the war.[11] His fleet consisted of eight ships with roughly thirty guns each, a few small craft, and one massive warship, the HMS *Africa*, with sixty-two guns. The small American force was concentrated in New York's harbor but, while the over-confident Vice Admiral Sawyer dallied, the American commander, John

Rodgers, quickly recruited and empowered his young, daring commanders and ordered the American fleet out to sea immediately.

## THE *PRESIDENT* DEFEATS THE *BELVIDERA*

One of the first naval engagements of the war occurred soon after its declaration. A merchant ship had tipped off the British frigate, HMS *Belvidera*, of the whereabouts of an American naval squadron patrolling waters off the coast. The *Belvidera* set sail to investigate the report and shortly after six o'clock on the morning of June 23, 1812, it spotted three frigates. Because the American ships were larger than the *Belvidera* had expected, the British warship opened her sails and made a run for it.

The commander of the American squadron was Commodore John Rodgers of Maryland, whose small squadron had set sail on June 21. His flagship, the USS *President*, was armed with forty-four guns. It was accompanied by the USS *United States*, which was of similar size, the USS *Congress* with thirty-eight guns, the USS *Hornet* with eighteen guns, and the USS *Argus* with sixteen guns. At the time of the sailing, Rodgers's squadron was one of the most powerful ever put to sea by the young nation.

Rodgers, who joined the U.S. navy when it was established in 1798, would emerge as the first of many heroic commanders. He brought the necessary experience to his command, having served on the storied USS *Constellation* and commanded the USS *John Adams*. Rodgers earned a reputation as a brave and skilled commander during the Barbary Pirate wars of the early 1800s and, as a result, was given command of the Mediterranean squadron in 1805. With tensions rising between the British navy and American merchant ships, Rodgers was given command of the USS *President* in 1811 and assigned the dual objectives of protecting merchant ships and keeping watch on British warships in U.S. waters. However, with the Royal Navy repeatedly boarding American ships, pressing sailors into serving the Crown, and harassing American shipping, Rodgers took the bold step of going after large British warships rather than simply reporting British aggression.

Rodgers pursued the *Belvidera* and other warships rumored to be in the area but, while searching for it, managed to catch a smaller sloop, HMS *Little Belt*, and proceeded to blow it to pieces. The *Belvidera* was wise to run rather than engage Rodgers. From his flagship, the USS *President*, Rodgers gave the order to continue the hunt for the *Belvidera*, taking advantage of the fact that the *President* was made for speed. She thus closed the distance quickly. Following not far behind was the USS *Congress*, another fast craft. Captain Byron, the commander of the *Belvidera*, realized he could not outrun the American ships so he sounded the alarm for battle stations.

Rodgers ordered the *President's* gun ports opened and the cannons were brought to bear on the enemy. From the bow of his ship, Commodore Rodgers fired the first shot himself. At least three shots scored direct hits on the *Belvidera*, causing damage to her decks and casualties among the crew. However, as the *President* was preparing to fire again at the damaged ship one of her cannons on the main deck blew up. Shrapnel flew across the deck, killing and wounding sixteen, including the Commodore whose leg was shattered in the explosion. This gave the *Belvidera* an opportunity. The British warship turned and set sail, returning fire with her stern guns as she pulled away. Amid the chaos caused by the explosion aboard the *President*, the *Belvidera's* cannons scored their own hits and six more American sailors fell.

Despite his serious wounds, Commodore Rodgers ordered the *President* to continue the pursuit. The faster American warship again caught her prey, while the other ships in the squadron gave chase from behind Rodgers's flagship. Rodgers ordered the *President* to pass by his prey and a full broadside of cannons damaged the *Belvidera's* rigging. Rodgers pulled his ship around for another volley, which destroyed the *Belvidera's* main topmast and cross-jack yard. Unfortunately, the *President* had sustained enough damage to limit her maneuverability. Rodgers was unable to continue to pursue his foe. So, the *Belvidera* was able to limp away with severe damage and many casualties, but not before Rodgers ordered the *President's* forward bow-chasers to fire. They scored additional hits. The *Belvidera* escaped to Halifax harbor, a severely disabled ship.[12]

Although the British warship managed to escape, it was nonetheless a symbolic American victory against the world's premier navy. Had the *President's* cannon not exploded, seriously wounding her officer, it is likely the *Belvidera* would have been sunk or captured. American pride swelled and the British navy was put on alert. As for Rodgers, he went on to capture twenty-three ships during the war and, after the war, was put in charge of the Board of Navy Commissioners. He also had two warships named for him and was the father, grandfather, and great-grandfather of noted naval officers who served the country from the Civil War through World War I. Equally important, Rodgers motivated a new generation of bold naval commanders eager for engagement and who would soon distinguish themselves during the war.

## THE *WASP* DEFEATS THE *FROLIC*

A few months after the USS *President* bested the HMS *Belvidera*, the USS *Wasp* sailed from Delaware. She was commanded by Jacob Jones and crewed by over 150 men. The small sloop was overloaded with two long cannons and several short-range carronades, which reduced her speed and maneuverability. In mid-October of 1812, she encountered a bad storm off the American coast and lost her jib-boom and two men. However, rather than return to port, Jones continued the mission and the next day, October 17, he spotted sails on the horizon. It turned out to be a fourteen-ship merchant convoy sailing for Britain. The lucrative commercial fleet was returning from British Honduras and was escorted by the British warship, HMS *Frolic* with eighteen guns.

The *Frolic* had been operating in the Caribbean for several years and had battled French raiders during that long war. As a result, many of her crew members had been killed by the French or lost to malaria, and the small warship was not at full strength. The British convoy she escorted had encountered the hurricane in the Caribbean that damaged the *Wasp* and also sustained considerable damage. The *Frolic* lost both her main sails. As a result, the convoy was moving slowly and repairing the ships while under sail.

On October 18, the *Wasp* closed the distance and prepared to engage the *Frolic*. However, the *Frolic* hoisted Spanish colors in an effort to delay the engagement long enough for the merchantmen to escape. Commander Jones closed the distance to just 100 yards to determine whether it was a British or Spanish convoy and, at 11:30 a.m., the *Frolic* suddenly raised British colors and opened fire. The *Wasp* returned fire. Thanks to superior training of her sailors, the *Frolic* managed to fire roughly three broadsides to every two fired by the Americans. However, this advantage was mitigated by the rough seas which produced high waves. With both ships being tossed in the high waves, it was hard to land direct hits. The Americans were lucky, as the *Frolic*'s broadsides went high or fell short into the water. Finally, the *Frolic*'s commander made the necessary adjustments to account for the rise and fall of the sea, and timed his broadside perfectly. Just prior to noon, a cannonball tore down the *Wasp*'s main top-mast.

Even though her decks were littered with debris, the *Wasp* kept fighting. Making his own adjustments, Commander Jones ordered his men to fire during the low crest of the waves. Several critical hits penetrated the *Frolic*'s hull. Other cannons poured shot into the *Frolic*'s deck. Wood and shrapnel exploded on the ship, the sails were torn away, and water rushed into the hull below decks. Men fell bleeding and the *Frolic*'s guns fell silent. The British warship was now dead in the water.

The *Wasp* came alongside and attempted to board her enemy, but the rough seas slowed the operation. Eventually, the Americans managed to charge the *Frolic*'s main deck but encountered no opposition. A man at the wheel was shell-shocked from the explosions and, as Jones's boarding party made their way below decks, they found the crew unable and unwilling to fight. Half the ship's crew was either dead or wounded and the commander, Captain Thomas Whinyates, and his senior officer were unable to stand. Standing only because he was being held up by crew members, Captain Whinyates surrendered his sword. It had been a quick and decisive battle. Shortly after the noon hour, the *Frolic*'s colors were lowered. The *Wasp* suffered only five dead and another five wounded. It was another American victory against the powerful British navy. With so few American victories to celebrate, the heroics of the *Wasp* and the *President* were celebrated far and wide.

But the *Wasp*'s celebration did not last long. Commander Jones was unable to seize the British merchant convoy. Later that same day, the British warship HMS *Poictiers* arrived. With the *Wasp* tied to the *Frolic* and with her own masts and rigging damaged, the American warship was unable to either pursue the fourteen-ship merchant convoy or escape. As such, she was captured by the Royal Navy and renamed the HMS *Loup-Cervier*. In 1815, the ship was lost at sea with all hands. However, mindful of the importance of this early naval victory, the U.S. War Department launched another ship carrying the name *Wasp*.[13]

## THE *ENTERPRISE* DEFEATS THE *BOXER*

On the morning of September 5, 1813, the American ship USS *Enterprise*, commanded by 28-year-old Lieutenant William Burrows, sailed past Monhegan Island in the Gulf of Maine. There she encountered the British brig, HMS *Boxer*. It was an even contest. The *Boxer*, commanded by Captain Samuel Blythe, carried a dozen carronades and two cannons, and was sailed by a crew of sixty-six. The *Enterprise* had fourteen carronades and two cannons, with a crew of roughly 100.

Lieutenant Burrows spotted the British ship first, roughly four miles away, and closed in for battle. However, the winds calmed and neither ship could close the distance. Around noon the winds picked up and both ships were under full sail. By three o'clock that afternoon they were ready to engage. Captain Blythe commanded his crew to raise their colors and instructed them to nail the flags to the mast because he would never lower his flag! And the broadsides began.

Captain Blythe never did surrender because he was killed immediately when an 18-pound cannonball tore through him. His First Lieutenant, David McCreery, took command. Both ships exchanged volleys at close quarters and then sailed into position for another broadside. The American commander, Lieutenant Burrows, was critically wounded but refused to abandon the fight. Nor would he allow his men to carry him below deck for medical treatment.

The young lieutenant brought the *Enterprise* around for another broadside around 3:30 and it was deadly accurate, bringing the *Boxer*'s main mast and top-sail yard crashing down on deck. The British warship was now idle in the water with crew members buried under the wreckage. Burrows ordered the *Enterprise* to come alongside and hit the wounded ship with two additional broadsides, reducing the top deck to splinters and inflicting serious casualties among the crew. After forty-five minutes, the battle ended when the *Boxer*'s lieutenant surrendered. The successive waves of broadsides from the American carronades drove several of the sailors aboard the *Boxer* to hide below decks. Four of them were later court-martialed for cowardice by a British tribunal. The British reported that three men were killed and another two dozen wounded in the battle, but the numbers appear to have been far worse and were likely fabricated by the Royal Navy because of the embarrassing string of defeats. The Americans lost only two men.[14]

Lieutenant Burrows was mortally wounded. He had to be carried by his men so that he could accept the sword of the fallen British commander, who was the second in command. After the surrender, the young lieutenant's last words were, "I am satisfied. I die contented." Both commanders were buried side-by-side in Portland, Maine. The nation mourned their lost commander in an elaborate and highly public funeral, while newspapers and political leaders celebrated yet "another brilliant naval victory." Henry Wadsworth Longfellow was so moved by the terrible but heroic battle that he referenced the battle in his poem "My Lost Youth," writing:

> I remember the sea-fight far away,
> How it thundered o'er the tide!
> And the dead captains,
> As they lay in their graves,

O'erlooking the tranquil bay
Where they in battle died.
And the sound of that mournful song
Goes through me with a thrill
A boy's will is the wind's will,
And the thoughts of youth are long, long thoughts.[15]

## ON THE SEVEN SEAS

Surprisingly, even though the United States was severely outgunned and outmanned in her territorial waters, the American navy did not restrict its efforts to defending her coasts and ports. Several daring commanders took the fight to the British. From the Mediterranean to the Pacific, from South America to Europe, American warships prowled the world's oceans and engaged surprised British merchant ships and warships alike, often with much success.

A case in point was the voyage of the USS *Hornet*, an 18-gun sloop under the command of Captain James Lawrence. The *Hornet* sailed for Central and South America in the winter of 1813, harassing British merchant ships. On February 24, she encountered the HMS *Peacock* off the coast of Guyana. Both ships exchanged broadsides, but Captain Lawrence maneuvered the *Hornet* to put the wind at his back and, as the *Peacock* attempted to do the same, the *Hornet* bested her foe. In only a matter of minutes, the *Peacock*'s rigging and decks were blown apart. The British warship suffered eight dead and thirty wounded before surrendering. The *Hornet* lost only one man.

Another one of the dashing American naval commanders was Captain David Porter. His ship, the USS *Essex*, had a reputation as one of the worst ships in the U.S. fleet. In fact, Porter repeatedly requested to command another ship but ended up going to sea with what he had. The *Essex* was a 32-gun frigate, measuring some 140 feet in length. As such, it was a mid-sized warship. However, Porter had it loaded with forty-six guns, making the already unwieldy ship even less seaworthy. Porter's other concern was that all but six of the guns he was given were carronades, which were effective only in short-range combat. The captain summed up his frustration and his situation, saying "My insufferable dislike to Carronades and the bad sailing of the Essex render her in my opinion the worst frigate in the service."[16]

But the condition of the ship did not stop Porter. In October of 1812, the *Essex* had sailed from Delaware to rendezvous with the USS *Constitution* and USS *Hornet* at the Cape Verde Islands. However, the ships were late and Captain Porter assumed the worst. He was also eager to attack the British. So, he set sail for the Pacific and, in March of 1813, Porter sailed the *Essex* past Cape Horn and into the Pacific Ocean to harass British whaling ships. The *Essex* now had the distinction of being the first American warship to sail in those waters. En route he resupplied in Chile. By the spring and summer of 1813, the *Essex* had sailed to the Galapagos Islands and had captured or destroyed a dozen British whalers. While there, Porter also symbolically established Fort Madison as an American outpost, even though there was no way of garrisoning or resupplying the remote location, and his crew dined on the islands' famous tortoises.

The British were not amused by Porter's attacks and dispatched three warships to hunt him in the Pacific. In January of 1814, Porter arrived in Valparaiso to resupply. In tow was a captured ship he renamed the *Essex Junior*. It was then that the British finally caught him. The 36-gun frigate HMS *Phoebe* sailed into Chile's main port on February 8, 1814. Because the port was neutral and both ships were anchored, the two command-ers met. However, when Porter challenged his counterpart, Captain James Hillyar, to battle, the Briton declined, citing the neutrality of the host country. While the *Phoebe* had more long-range cannons, the *Essex*'s many short-range carronades provided Porter with a clear advantage if the two ships pulled anchor and fought. It is also possible that, in the face of the brave American commander, Hillyar lost his nerve.

Instead, the *Phoebe* set sail. At sea the ship rendezvoused with the 18-gun sloop, HMS *Cherub*. Together the two ships returned and block-aded the Chilean port, which they thought would prevent the *Essex* from leaving. They even fired a warning shot into the harbor, apparently forget-ting previous concerns about it being a neutral port. Despite his precarious position, Porter gave the order to sail anyway. His boldness again unnerved the British who retreated rather than face the *Essex*.

Out in the open ocean, Porter ordered his crew to chase the British warships. But, while doing so the *Essex* was caught in a sudden and severe storm. She sustained considerable damage. Her main top-mast was unusable and the ship had trouble sailing. Porter thus tried to take shelter in a nearby harbor to begin repairs on his ship. It was then when the two British ships attacked after observing the extensive damage to the *Essex*. Hillyar used his advantage—long-range cannons—and kept a safe distance from the *Essex*.

He bombarded the wounded American ship and, every time Porter tried to sail closer to engage both ships, they simply sailed away and hit him with long-range shot. The *Essex* was too damaged to sail at the speed needed to catch her foes and was soon reduced to a hulk.

Porter even tried to sail her onto the rocks in order to scuttle the ship rather than allow it to fall into British hands. But, the ship was so unseaworthy that he was unable to do so. With two British warships threatening to annihilate his remaining crew, Porter was forced to surrender. He was furious that the British claimed neutrality but then attacked and cursed the fact that he was unable to engage them in a fair ship-to-ship battle. Still, Porter's accomplishments in the Pacific were notable and inspired additional American naval exploits.

# 18

# A NEW GENERATION
# OF HEROES

## ISAAC HULL AND THE
## HUNT FOR THE *GUERRIERE*

Isaac Hull was born into a military family on March 9, 1773 in Derby, Connecticut. Derby was a small village on the Housatonic River, not far from Long Island Sound. Given its location, residents of Derby often found themselves making a living on the water. Such was the case with Hull, who grew up on the water and whose father was a veteran of several Revolutionary War naval battles, where he managed in one instance to capture a British schooner. Sadly, Isaac's father died while a prisoner onboard the HMS *Jersey*. The boy was adopted by his uncle, General William Hull. Young Isaac disappointed his family by abandoning his studies for a career on the sea, working as a cabin boy on a merchant ship at age fourteen. When he was sixteen, his ship sank and the teen saved the injured captain's life by supporting him in the water and swimming him to shore.[1]

On March 13, 1798, Hull was commissioned a fourth lieutenant in the new American navy and served on the USS *Constitution*. The ship was new, having just been built in Boston's shipyards, and was untested. It was, however, a site to behold. At 204 feet in length, with a beam of forty-three feet, the *Constitution* brimmed with over seventy different sails, including a main mast that soared 233 feet into the air! It was perhaps the most expensive ship in the American fleet to date and sported forty-four guns and a whopping 400 crew members. The warship was capable of sailing at twelve knots, a speed unheard of at the time. This behemoth was the third of three large frigates put into service by the new navy. All three would distinguish themselves during the war.[2]

Hull was captaining his own ship at age twenty-eight. In addition to the *Constitution*, he served on the USS *Adams*, the USS *Enterprise*, and the USS *Argus*, fighting against the Barbary pirates off Africa and in the Mediterranean. Hull thus understood ships and was a veteran of many battles. With a growing reputation in the navy, he was one of the officers asked to serve on the military court that reprimanded Commander James Barron for losing the USS *Chesapeake* to the HMS *Leopard* before the war without a shot fired. One of the new breed of younger, daring naval commanders to emerge before and during the War of 1812, Hull was put in command of his old ship, the *Constitution*, on June 17, 1810. It was in that command that he scored one of the most celebrated naval victories of the war and helped redeem the family name—his uncle was General William Hull, whose failures on the Canadian border undermined the nation's invasion of Canada during the war.

When the war broke out, the *Constitution* sailed from Annapolis in July of 1812 after organizing a crew and taking on supplies. With Hull in command, she sailed through the Chesapeake Bay and along the east coast in order to begin patrolling the Atlantic. Hull sailed the *Constitution* a few hundred miles from the coast of Massachusetts looking for British warships that might be headed to the United States.

The HMS *Guerriere* was commanded by Captain James Richard Dacres and was leading a flotilla between Halifax and New York that included the 64-gun HMS *Africa*, the 38-gun HMS *Shannon*, the 36-gun HMS *Belvidera*, and the 32-gun HMS *Aeolus*. The squadron had been dispatched by British vice admiral, Herbert Sawyer. Their mission was to attack the upstart American navy and Captain Dacres was so confident that he mockingly flew a sail with the words "Guerriere, not the Little Belt," a reference to the smaller ship the Americans attacked after mistaking it for the larger frigate.[3]

Captain Hull spotted the squadron of ships at a great distance. He knew that Captain Rodgers had been dispatched with a squadron of American warships, so he tried signaling the closest ship at night with lights to determine if it was Rodgers or a British convoy. There was no response, so Hull prepared the *Constitution*. At dawn, Hull was able to determine that the closest ship was the *Guerriere* followed by four more British warships, all under the command of Captain Philip Broke. Fortunately for Hull the wind died down in the morning so that the British squadron could not attack him. Hull ordered his rowboats be lowered and his men to row the massive *Constitution*. The British ships did the same, pursuing Hull. In an effort to put distance between his ship and the squadron, Hull lightened his ship by pumping tons of drinking water out of his ship and into the ocean. He also ordered the crew to try "kedging," whereby the anchor was rowed ahead and dropped, then the ship winched forward. The maneuver was tried again and again, thanks to the fact that the ocean was only about twenty-two fathoms (130 feet) deep.[4]

The wind did not materialize for three days. All the while, the warships rowed frantically for position. Then, finally, a breeze picked up, filling the *Constitution*'s sails first and then those of its British pursuers. The *Constitution*'s impressive speed allowed it to easily put space between itself and the British. Hull sailed back to Boston and Captain Broke was livid that his ships could not catch her. After quickly resupplying, Hull again set sail on August 2, eager to do battle. He sailed the *Constitution* along the Canadian coast and off the Gulf of St. Lawrence, where there was sure to be British commercial shipping. Sure enough, Hull captured and sank a few British merchant ships. He then set sail for Bermuda but en route passed Captain Stephen Decatur who informed Hull that they had just outrun large British warships. This was all Hull needed to hear. He ordered his men to hunt the British. On August 19, they found their target, the powerful HMS *Guerriere*.

## "OLD IRONSIDES"

Aboard the *Guerriere*, Captain Dacres is said to have announced that the Yankee ship "is certainly ours." He even challenged the crew that if they destroyed the Americans in fifteen minutes "I promise you four months' pay."[5] It was Dacres that fired first. In the late afternoon the *Guerriere* began firing from long distance but the shots fell harmlessly into the water well shy of the *Constitution*. It was likely meant to scare off the American ship. Dacres was eager to scare off or destroy the Americans and demanded that his crew continue to fire and fire. Hull did not panic. He calmly ordered the *Constitution* to sail to engage the British warship and for his crew to load cannons but hold their fire. Despite protests from his officers, Hull kept his cannons silent as British shot began striking his ship. Amazingly, the cannonballs bounced off the ship causing one excited crew member to holler, "Hurrah, her sides are made of iron!" And the *Constitution* earned her famous nickname, one that would become legendary: "Old Ironsides."[6]

At the site of her cannonballs bouncing off the sides of the formidable American ship, which was approaching at an alarming speed, the *Guerriere* attempted to flee. However, the *Constitution*, like her sister ships, was built much faster than the large ships of the Royal Navy. It did not take long for Hull to catch his foe. Still, he did not fire. Pulling alongside the British ship at a distance of only twenty-five yards and amid loud taunts and jeers from the British crew, Hull unloaded his first broadside.

It was a mixture of cannonballs and grapeshot, and the impact was immediate and devastating. The British crew fell silent, as bodies, wood, sails, and debris littered the deck. Hull ordered his crew to fire again and again. Then he quickly crossed in front of his opponent's bow and employed the guns on his starboard. The maneuverable *Constitution* repositioned herself at will for broadside after broadside, blowing the helpless *Guerriere* to pieces. The *Guerriere* never had time to recover from the mayhem. Her sails were ripped apart, the hull damaged, and the masts shattered. At one point, the ships collided and the *Guerriere*'s front rigging became entangled on the *Constitution*. Both crews attempted to board, and small arms fire poured across the decks. Hull's lieutenant fell dead and, on the *Guerriere*, Captain Dacres was shot while encouraging his men to board the American ship. The grapeshot and musket fire was so severe that neither crew was able to board its opponent. Rather, Hull ordered his cannons to fire at point-blank range. It blew the ships apart and with her remaining rigging and masts now crashing into the water the *Guerriere* was completely out of commission.

Rather than board the British warship, Hull backed away around 6:30 p.m. but remained close by while ordering repairs to his ship. Thirty minutes later, the *Constitution* returned but a now-humbled and wounded Captain Dacres struck his colors. The battle had lasted thirty minutes. It was a masterful display of power and sailing. Hull, who was a thickly built man, was so excited he jumped with joy, screaming that they had beaten the massive man-of-war and "We've made a brig of her!" Hull celebrated so much that he split his pants wide open![7]

Hull sent Lieutenant George Read and some marines to bring Captain Dacres to him. They found the British captain in his cabin bleeding profusely. As per the custom, Read announced: "Captain Hull presents his compliments, sir, and wishes to know if you have struck your flag?"[8] Dacres and his men were taken aboard the *Constitution*, whereupon the British captain was ordered to present his sword to Hull. However, Hull permitted his foe to keep his sword, allegedly on account of his bravery. Dacres requested to have his mother's Bible spared, so Hull sent men to fetch it.[9]

The *Guerriere* was so badly damaged that it could not even be towed back as a prize. It was burned at sea and sunk, and her crew taken prisoner. Hull lost his lieutenant and six men, with seven wounded, all from the close-range musket fire. Aboard the *Guerriere*, Captain Dacres was wounded along with several dozen of his sailors and another twenty-three were dead. The *Constitution* proved to be not only exceptionally fast and maneuverable, but "Old Ironsides'" strong wooden hull seemed impervious to cannonballs.[10]

Hull sailed back to Boston a hero. This important victory shocked the Royal Navy and emboldened the Americans. British newspapers cried out that the captain should have gone down with his ship and that "Never before, in the history of the world, did an English frigate strike to an American."[11] Of course, such reports were untrue. John Paul Jones had famously captured the HMS *Serapis* during the Revolutionary War. Dacres would later blame his defeat on the fact that the *Guerriere* was a French ship captured by the British in 1806; He also blamed his crew, which he suggested were impressed Americans (when only ten of them were). Boasted the defeated captain:

> I am so well aware that the success of my opponent was owing to fortune that it is my earnest wish to be once more opposed to the Constitution, with the same officers and crew under my command, in a frigate of similar force to the Guerriere.[12]

News of the victory also prompted Congress to finally allocate funds for the navy. Even the obstructionist southern and frontier members agreed to a 2.5 million dollar budget for the construction of four large man-of-wars and six frigates.[13]

## STEPHEN DECATUR AND THE BARBARY PIRATES

During the early 1800s, merchant ships from the United States and Europe were harassed in the shores off the northern African coast by Barbary pirates, who imprisoned the crews, stole the merchandise, and demanded payment from Western governments. The Barbary States of northern Africa had long harassed Western merchants, sailors, and explorers, dating to the early crusades in the eleventh and twelfth centuries. The first American ship captured by the Barbary pirates occurred in 1784 and the United States government began paying "tributes" to appease the pirates. But such payments did not guarantee that all American ships would be safe and Thomas Jefferson, upon taking office in 1801, decided to forego the bribes and build a navy to deal with the situation. As a result, under Presidents Jefferson and James Madison, the United States engaged in an ongoing, small war against the pirates. One of the heroes of that conflict was Stephen Decatur, who led successful raids against the Barbary pirates, defeating and capturing their ships.

But it was the burning of the frigate USS *Philadelphia* on February 16, 1804 that assured Decatur's status as one of the most courageous American fighters in history. The *Philadelphia* was a massive warship that had been sent to the African coast to protect American shipping. However, because accurate naval charts of the waters of the Tripolian coast were unavailable, the ship became grounded on rocks and was captured by the Barbary pirates in October of 1803. It was a painful loss, as it both depleted American sea power in the region and embarrassed the U.S. Navy. Consequently, back in the United States, Commodore Edward Preble began planning to recapture or destroy the *Philadelphia*. However, Tripoli's harbor, where the ship was being held, was well-fortified. Some worried that it would be a suicide mission.[14]

Impressively, many young American naval officers volunteered for the daring mission and Lieutenant Stephen Decatur, who commanded the schooner USS *Enterprise*, was selected. Using a small ship that had been recently captured from the Barbary pirates and renamed *Intrepid*, Decatur sailed from Greece in February of 1804 with hand-picked members of his own crew and a few sailors from the USS *Constitution*, all disguised as pirates. They were piloted to Tripoli by a Sicilian sailor familiar with the coastal waters and language. The *Intrepid* almost never arrived in Tripoli because of strong storms. But, the small, dingy ship eventually sailed into Tripoli harbor on February 16 at night and requested permission to tie up near the *Philadelphia*, claiming they had lost their anchor at sea.

However, just as they were about to dock, the Americans were discovered by two guards in the port. Decatur ordered his men to rush to the *Philadelphia* and enact the plan. His crew dove overboard and began to swim to shore. Making it to the *Philadelphia*, Decatur set the ship ablaze and ordered the few men with him to push off in rowboats, which they did while under fire from the harbor guards. Decatur waited until he was certain the fire could not be put out, leaving the ship last.

The *Philadelphia* was destroyed and only one member of Decatur's crew was wounded. It was a dashing success, described by the great British admiral, Horatio Nelson, as "the most bold and daring act of the age."[15] For his bravery, Decatur was promoted to captain and, at the age of twenty-five, became the youngest naval captain in American history.

## CAPTURING THE *MACEDONIAN*

Stephen Decatur was born in Sinnepuzent, Maryland on January 5 1779, and spent much of his life on the sea. It was said that Decatur fell in love with the sea when, at age eight, his father took him to Europe to recover from a severe case of whooping cough.[16] As a cabin boy, he crossed the Atlantic and later received his commission in the navy as a midshipman on April 30, 1798. Decatur served aboard such legendary ships as the USS *United States*, a 44-gun frigate, the similarly-sized USS *President* and USS *Constitution*, and as an officer under the famed William Bainbridge aboard the USS *Essex*.

It was while commanding the *United States* that Bainbridge led another one of the most famous naval battles in American history. This time he squared off against the British frigate, HMS *Macedonian* near the Azores on October 25, 1812. Earlier that month, Commodore John Rodgers sailed from Boston in pursuit of British ships. With his flagship, the *President*, Rodgers commanded a squadron of ships including the *United States*, captained by Decatur. During the voyage, the *United States* and the USS *Argus*, with sixteen guns, separated from the squadron in order to better their chances of finding British ships. They sailed across the Atlantic to the Canary Islands, where they spotted the 50-gun *Macedonian*, one of Britain's most celebrated warships.

The *Macedonian* had the advantage of having the wind at her back. Early that morning, her captain, John Carden, used the wind to race toward the *United States*. He fired three cannons but the shots fell short into the ocean. This fact alerted Decatur that he had the advantage of longer range cannons. So, he maneuvered away from the *Macedonian*, keeping his distance. The fast, powerful American warship was able to fire long-range hits with her massive 24-pounders, picking apart her pursuing enemy. Decatur launched a constant fifteen-minute barrage from his powerful cannons. In an act of desperation, Captain Carden ordered the *Macedonian* to sail as fast as possible. They had to catch the *United States* or be slowly blown to pieces. It did not work. The superior speed of the *United States* and Decatur's excellent seamanship prevailed. The guns of the *United States* shattered their opponent's main masts, tore apart her sails and rigging, and blew the mizzenmast, main yard, and top-sails down in a great crash. Any cannon shot that reached the *United States* did little damage thanks to the strong wood that lined her hulls.[17]

With the *Macedonian* barely able to sail, Decatur closed the distance and finished off the British warship, speeding around behind her where she had little firepower. The *United States* unloaded into the *Macedonian*'s stern, then closed ranks and spewed grapeshot and canisters of metal into the sails and crew. Over 100 cannonballs were punched through the *Macedonian*'s hull and on deck forty-three sailors were dead and over seventy wounded. The British commander had no option but to surrender. Decatur lost only seven men, with another five wounded. The world now knew that the *United States*, like her sister ship, the *Constitution*, was one of the fastest and most powerful vessels afloat! Decatur repaired and crewed the *Macedonian*, bringing his prize back to port. It was another resounding morale booster for the Americans and another devastating psychological blow to the British.

The upstart American navy was proving itself against the greatest naval power in history. During their long confrontation, the French had managed only one decisive victory over the British on the seas. It occurred in 1807, when the *Milan* defeated the outgunned HMS *Cleopatra*. The Americans had bested the French record in a matter of months.[18]

Decatur continued to harass British shipping during the war, capturing merchant ships and defeating warships until he was taken prisoner at the end of the conflict while commanding the *President* against a superior British squadron. Freed after the war, Decatur returned to naval service, including a particularly sensitive assignment. Both young naval heroes—Stephen Decatur and Isaac Hull—were asked to serve on the court of inquiry charged with ruling on Commodore James Barron's disastrous handling of the "*Chesapeake* affair" that sparked the war. The cowardly Barron responded by challenging Decatur to a duel, during which the dashing, young naval officer was killed. Public backlash ruined what little remained of Barron's reputation, while Decatur was buried on March 22, 1820, by a mourning nation.

## WILLIAM BAINBRIDGE

The Naval Act of 1794 funded the construction of several large warships, including the USS *Constitution*, which was launched by 1797 and named by President George Washington. The shipyard used wood from dense coastal oaks in its design, which later proved invaluable when British cannonballs simply bounced harmlessly off her sides, leading to her famous nickname and the expression "She has sides of iron."[19] "Old Ironsides" ended up being one of the fastest, strongest, and most successful naval ships in history, fighting in the Barbary Pirate wars of the early nineteenth century, capturing many merchant ships, and sinking warships during the War of 1812.

On December 29, 1812, she engaged in one of the most vicious and famous battles of the war against the HMS *Java*. But this time, the *Constitution* had a different captain. After defeating the HMS *Guerriere*, Captain Hull took a short leave of duty because his brother had died. In the interim, the *Constitution* was sent back out to sea under the command of Captain William Bainbridge, who was thirty-eight at the time.

Bainbridge was a successful commander but had tasted defeat, which had hardened him for battle against the *Java*. As a young lieutenant, for example, Bainbridge had commanded a small schooner, USS *Retaliation*, but was forced to surrender to two larger French warships. Later, in command of the USS *Philadelphia*, his ship was lost to the Barbary pirates after it ran aground in uncharted waters. Bainbridge was captured but managed to survive a brutal sentence in a Tripoli dungeon. Bainbridge was born in Princeton, New Jersey in 1774 and, as a naval officer later in life, enjoyed much success and cut a striking and imposing figure.

In command of the *Constitution*, Bainbridge also led a small squadron out of Boston harbor on October 26, 1812. They sailed to the Cape Verde Islands and then to Brazil, eventually making port in present-day Salvador. There, the American fleet spotted the HMS *Bonne Citoyenne*, an 18-gun sloop commanded by Captain Pitt Barnaby Greene. Greene wisely refused to engage the American ships, despite Bainbridge's invitation to do so. The *Bonne Citoyenne*'s hull was filled with silver to fund Britain's wars. Bainbridge ordered the 18-gun USS *Hornet* commanded by James Lawrence to blockade the British warship. He then set sail when he heard reports that British warships were in the area.

About thirty miles off the Brazilian coast on the morning of December 29, Bainbridge spotted two ships. One was the HMS *Java*, sailing for Britain. She was escorting the captured American merchant ship, *William*, and was transporting the royal governor of India, Lieutenant General Thomas Hislop, and his staff. The *Java* carried thirty-eight guns and was originally a French ship named *Renommee* that had been captured in 1811 near Madagascar and retrofitted as a British warship. Even though the *Java* carried political leaders and was responsible for the captured American ship, her captain, Henry Lambert, decided to attack the USS *Constitution* rather than flee. The *Java* was known to be a very fast ship and word had traveled about the Royal Navy's defeats at the hands of the Americans. It is thus likely that Captain Lambert wanted to avenge the painful losses.

Aboard the *Constitution*, Bainbridge ordered his ship to keep a safe distance from the *Java* in order to take measure of the situation. The *Java* tried to close the distance and cross in front of the larger American ship, but Bainbridge outmaneuvered his foe. Eventually, one of the shots from the *Java* struck the *Constitution*'s wheel, which allowed the British warship to approach for broadsides. At close range, both ships unloaded wave after wave of broadsides. The *Constitution* was larger and her crew more accurate, so the *Java* took the worst of the exchanges. Her main mast and mizzenmast came crashing down onto the deck, rendering the *Java* dead in the water.

Bainbridge ordered his ship in even closer. Its heavy wood sides easily withstood the British broadsides and the *Constitution*'s marines fired muskets at the British crew with deadly accuracy. Amid the attack, Bainbridge ordered his cannons to fire grapeshot, which cleared the *Java*'s decks and tore away her sails. Captain Lambert was among the casualties. With all of the officers dead or wounded, and roughly half the crew dead or dying on deck, the *Java* surrendered after a deadly three-hour battle. Governor Hislop acted as the commanding officer, presenting Lambert's sword to Bainbridge. The *Java* was repaired and towed. But, she was taking on water so badly that Bainbridge sank her on New Year's Eve amid cheers from his crew.

The British were again beaten at sea. The *British Naval Chronicle* described the loss as "too painful for us to dwell upon."[20] The American navy continued to outdo all expectations, while the *Constitution* went on to defeat the HMS *Levant*, HMS *Pictou*, HMS *Cyane*, and other British ships. "Old Ironsides" remained a part of the U.S. Navy for two centuries of duty, making her the oldest commissioned warship in the world. She serves as a museum ship today.[21]

# 19

# BLOCKADE

## STRANGLEHOLD

Even though the Americans enjoyed a surprising degree of success on the high seas, and despite the heroics of the likes of William Bainbridge, Stephen Decatur, Isaac Hull, John Rodgers, David Porter, and others, the sheer advantage in ships and firepower allowed the British to control most of America's eastern seaboard. Britain thus adopted a strategy of blockading coastal cities and key ports. Not only did the blockade prevent American warships from leaving ports, but trade with the outside world was cut off. American exports dropped precipitously. By the end of the war, America was exporting only roughly one-tenth of the pre-war volume. Moreover, because of primitive transportation systems on land, even trade among the states was dependent on shipping. The British blockade was therefore devastating and there was little the Americans could do about it.[1]

Moreover, with the nation still feeling the effects of the ill-conceived embargo of 1807, the additional restrictions on trade in 1812 wreaked havoc on the already fragile economy. Not surprisingly, there was widespread public and political support for the decision by President Madison in March of 1814 to lift the embargo. The President hoped that neutral nations would increase trade. However, it was little more than a symbolic effort because the British naval blockade was still in effect.

The blockade began a few months after the commencement of the war and, by November of 1812, the Royal Navy had blockaded the important southern ports of Charleston, South Carolina and Savannah, Georgia. Then, on the day after Christmas, they succeeded in blockading key waterways throughout the Chesapeake and along the Delaware coast. With the American economy and military effort reeling from the loss of their main ports, at the end of the year, Paul Hamilton, the secretary of the navy, resigned under pressure.

Leading the Royal Navy's efforts in America was Vice Admiral Sir Alexander Cochrane. Born in Scotland in 1758 as the ninth son of Thomas, eighth Earl of Dundonald, Cochrane was an aristocrat and career naval officer who both sailed and fought in nearly every ocean and sea on the planet. He also served for several years in Parliament and as the Royal Governor of Guadeloupe in the period leading up to the War of 1812.

The admiral, however, had never gotten over Britain's devastating loss to the upstart Americans during the Revolutionary War and he had lost a cousin during in the conflict. As such, the War of 1812 was personal to him and he viewed both the blockade and any naval engagement as personal retribution for the earlier defeats. Obsessed with victory in the war, Cochrane was brutal in implementing the blockade, which he wanted to stretch from the New England coast south and into the Gulf of Mexico. He also ordered the Royal Navy to "destroy and lay waste to such towns and districts upon the coast as you may find assailable."[2]

In Cochrane's "total war," civilians were targeted, merchant ships and fishing vessels were harassed, and coastal communities looted and burned in "hit-and-run" raids. It was a frontrunner to psychological ops of modern times. With their fishing fleets destroyed and ports blockaded, towns up and down the American seaboard were ordered to declare neutrality or loyalty to the King, or suffer starvation and continued raids. Cochrane's navy even sailed far up rivers to harass populations farther inland, such as when a British squadron sailed up the Connecticut River to burn boats and ports. When the Americans foolishly burned the capital city of York, Cochrane was furious and urged his sailors to remember the atrocity committed by "the American army toward his majesty's unoffending Canadian subjects." He then ordered raids to be increased with orders to "spare merely the lives of the unarmed inhabitants."[3]

## AWAKENING A GIANT

Americans were more successful on the seas than on land in 1812, but British naval superiority was never in doubt. The American victories were, nevertheless, symbolically important for the young nation and its new navy. Even though, in the larger sense, they did not reduce the power or presence of the British navy or pry open a blockaded port, they were confidence boosters and also helped in recruiting soldiers and sailors for the war. But the American successes also had another effect. They caught Britain's attention. Shocked by the success of the American navy in 1812, the Royal Navy responded by sending more warships and stepping up the effort to blockade American ports.

By March of 1813, the British admiralty had a formidable force of ten large warships, thirty-eight frigates, and fifty-two small schooners and gunboats prowling American coastal waters.[4] This constituted a huge increase over the skeleton fleet in North America when the war began. With the arrival of these additional ships, the British had a seven-to-one advantage on the water. In 1813, the British admiralty also decided that they would destroy the pesky American navy once and for all. Sir John B. Warren, the British commander of the Royal Navy's North American forces, declared that it was of the "highest importance to the Character and interests of the Country that the naval Force of the Enemy should be quickly and completely disposed. . . ." Admiral Warren and Admiral Cochrane gave the order to blockade the entire American coastline and destroy all American ships.[5] The small American navy would be put to the test.

As a result, by the end of March of 1813, the Royal Navy had successfully blockaded important commercial ports in the northeast. Two months later, they succeeded in blockading much of the southeast. It continued. The British soon controlled the waters off Georgia, then the Carolinas, followed by Maryland and Delaware, then Massachusetts and New York. By November of 1813, nearly the entire eastern seaboard of the United States was closed off. Larger ports had forts and cannons to slow the British blockade, but smaller ports and rivers had no defenses and fell immediately. American merchant ships were seized, their crews pressed into service or imprisoned, warships were sunk, and coastal communities were bombed. A few coastal communities in New England managed to avoid blockades but British warships were prowling just offshore, awaiting any ships that managed to "run" the blockade. Food shortages triggered alarm across the country and prices soared for such staples as sugar, tea, and farm equipment. With the navy blockaded in port, the naval theater of the war took a turn for the worst for the Americans. The British however, were able to land supplies and troops at will and wherever they wanted.

## A SCRAPPY DEFENSE

The Americans put up a resistance. Coastal communities scrambled to organize their defenses. But even America's dashing naval commanders and most storied ships fared poorly. After defeating the HMS *Java*, the USS *Constitution* was stuck in port for much of the year. The USS *Constellation* found herself stuck in Norfolk, Virginia. Commodore Stephen Decatur managed to sneak the USS *President* past a British blockade in New York in May, but after entering port in New London, Connecticut, was also unable to return to sea for several months. The USS *Wasp* broke a blockade at Portsmouth and the *President* eventually made it out to sea where she joined the USS *Congress* and a few other ships but they were forced to remain at sea for extended periods of time. This caused shortages of supplies and took their toll on the crews and badly needed repairs.

Rear Admiral Sir George Cockburn was a ruthless commander. Like his fellow commander, Admiral Cochrane, he began his career on the seas at a tender age. Cockburn served on numerous ships all around the world and distinguished himself in battle after battle. He was even a personal friend of the legendary Lord Nelson. In fact, after the famous British victory at Waterloo, it was Admiral Cockburn's ship that transported the most notorious prisoner of the war—Emperor Napoleon—to his exile at St. Helena. The admiral even served as the island's governor for a time.[6]

When the War of 1812 was declared, Cockburn was assigned to serve in the command of Sir John Warren, who dispatched him to take the vitally important Chesapeake Bay. In early April of 1813, Cockburn sailed into the bay, destroying or seizing ships and supplies, burning warehouses, and harassing local residents. Aboard his flagship, the powerful HMS *Marlborough*, Cockburn initiated a reign of terror in the region. Like Admiral Cochrane, he did not distinguish between public and private property and attacked both military and civilian populations without differentiation. With few military installations and no navy in the area, American towns fell to Cockburn's squadron—Frenchtown, Havre de Grace, Georgetown, and Fredericktown were either seized or burned. U.S. newspapers decried his attacks on civilian populations, to which Cockburn claimed he would have spared private property had the Americans not resisted. There were even claims that the Admiral permitted, if not encouraged, his sailors to loot villages, likening the Americans to the privateers and pirates he fought during his lengthy service in the Mediterranean.[7]

However, when Cockburn's flotilla sailed to the far northern end of the Chesapeake, near the mouth of the Susquehanna River, which flowed through Pennsylvania, the local residents fought back. Small batteries set up by militia units on the banks of Concord Point near Havre de Grace surprised the British with a blistering artillery barrage. These "potato batteries" poured potato-sized iron shot from small cannons. Shocked and angered by the aggressive resistance, Cockburn set ashore roughly 150 Royal Marines on the night of May 1, 1813. Their orders were to destroy the batteries and punish the town.

Although the militiamen and townsfolk put up a strong defense, they were gradually overcome by the invaders. Most of those fighting back were killed and the small potato batteries were knocked out. Still, the overmatched Americans fought to the last man. When all but one gun had been silenced, the British stormed the final battery to find only one man still alive—a local resident named John O'Neil, who tried to fire one more time. The British captured him and planned to hang him, but later released him because of his extraordinary bravery. Accounts of such bravery inspired other coastal communities to resist the invaders.

The blockade and raids continued through the summer. Admiral Cockburn again returned to the Chesapeake later that summer with plans to invade Baltimore and Washington. However, he first set about raiding and burning small communities along the Chesapeake that had escaped his wrath earlier that year. On the morning of August 10, his squadron of warships appeared off the coast of St. Michael's in Maryland. Cockburn gave the order to bombard the town. But, unbeknownst to him, his naval cannons overshot the village and did little damage. In preparation for the bombardment, St. Michael's residents had cleverly placed lanterns on trees far behind the town, giving the appearance at night that the town was father back from the bay than it actually was. Two nights later while sailing past the town, the British were treated to a surprise. The town's batteries opened up with gusto, striking the British ships. Cockburn decided to sail away and the town was saved.

Earlier that summer, George Cockburn's armada of four massive warships with roughly sixty to seventy guns apiece, four frigates, two sloops, and three transport ships sailed to the Virginia coast and dropped anchor near Craney Island. The plan was to destroy the important port and naval yards at Norfolk as well as the USS *Constellation*, one of America's most successful and powerful warships. Admiral Cockburn was joined by Admiral Sir John Warren, the head of British naval operations, which indicated the importance of the mission.

Craney Island was a key defensive post in the protection of Norfolk. It was close to shore, well-fortified, and connected by a bridge to mainland Virginia. The northwest end of the island held a battery of 18-pound cannons manned by roughly 100 sailors from the *Constellation*. Fifty marines were also dispatched to the island, standing ready to secure any corner of the small island. It was a small but determined force.

Admirals Cockburn and Warren argued over the plans for attacking the island and sacking Norfolk. Their delay only allowed the small American force to ready themselves. Finally, Warren decided to send the ship HMS *San Domingo* under Captain Pechell to attack Craney Island. On June 22, the warship arrived and unloaded fifteen smaller boats that rowed toward the island carrying roughly 700 regulars and a few sailors. Warren reasoned it would be a quick and easy victory. However, the Americans held their fire until the British were landing, then let loose with everything they had. Three small boats were sunk immediately, another forced onto a rocky shoal, and over ninety British soldiers fell in the water and on the shoreline.

Captain Pechell called off the attack and the British hurried back to the armada. The vigorous defense persuaded Admirals Cockburn and Warren to call off the raid. Because it was low tide, the sailors who defended Craney Island waded into the water and captured a few small boats left behind by the British. An important American city and port was saved. Such scrappy resistance in coastal towns and guerilla tactics by citizen's groups proved successful. The Americans realized they could stand against the British. It helped give birth to the privateers.

## OLD SALTS AND SEA DOGS

The Americans had other types of naval heroes during the war besides those in uniform. Because of the overwhelming advantage the British had on the seas and the extensiveness of their blockade of the American east coast, fishermen, private citizens, and various unsavory personalities conducted hit-and-run attacks on British shipping. Either for patriotism or in order to make money, an abundance of sailors risked their lives in the capacity of privateers. Part pirate, part businessman, and part mercenary, these colorful characters harassed British shipping enough that the British ended up diverting precious resources to deal with them.

The federal government recognized their effectiveness and began licensing privateers when President James Madison issued the "Letters of Marquee and Reprisal" to shipowners around the country. It permitted them to arm themselves and function as legal pirates. The American navy had only about twenty-three ships operating during the height of the British blockade, but there were over 500 privateers that participated in the war. As such, the navy's 556 total cannons were supplemented by 2,893 more guns aboard the privateers.[8] These sea dogs were assigned the task of harassing British ships and taking as many supplies as they could manage. And they did!

Some of the privateers became very wealthy. It is estimated that the British lost upward of $45 million in cargo and supplies to American privateers.[9] In total, the American navy sank or captured an impressive 254 British ships during the war, a number far beyond what anyone would have hoped for when the war started. Yet, it is a number that pales in comparison to the estimated 2,893 British ships taken by American privateers![10]

A popular story told during the War of 1812 celebrated the antics of privateers. The story tells of the British warship, HMS *Dublin*, which was dispatched for the express purpose of catching American privateers, including one notoriously bothersome pirate. The captain of the *Dublin* told of being in Valparaiso at a drinking establishment when he met an American sailor who said he liked the story of the privateer and asked the captain to tell him more. The captain complied, remembering, "I was once almost within gun-shot of that infernal Yankee skimming-dish, just as night came on. By daylight she had out-sailed the *Dublin* so devilish fast that she was no more than a speck on the horizon." The American astonished the British captain and those around them by saying that he knew about the story and knew the American ship. The British captain then asked, "By the way, I wonder if you happen to know the name of the beggar that was master of her." The American confessed that it was he. They drank a toast to one another![11]

## "THE NEST OF PIRATES"

The Chesapeake Bay has always been one of America's most important commercial waterways. Not surprisingly, Baltimore had more than its fair share of privateers. It is estimated that as many as 100 privateer ships were in operation against the British from Baltimore alone. In fact, the constant harassment from the city's privateers was a main reason it was so aggressively blockaded and the reason why the Royal Navy sent several raiding parties to destroy "the nest of pirates" there. But, as soon as one privateer was sunk, two others appeared along the coast.[12]

One of Baltimore's most legendary privateers was Thomas Boyle. With his 16-gun *Chasseur*, nicknamed "The Pride of Baltimore," and another fast ship aptly named the *Comet*, Boyle captured a remarkable fifty-three British ships, earning for himself and his crew millions of dollars during the war. Boyle, who was born in 1775 in Marblehead, Massachusetts, took to the sea at around age ten and spent his life on the water until his death in 1825. By sixteen he was captaining his own ship out of Baltimore.

In July of 1812 at the outset of the war, Boyle sailed for the West Indies and captured four British merchant ships valued at over $400,000. He did not come back to port until October. In late November of 1812, he set out again, this time for Brazil, capturing another five ships. However, at the end of his raid, his ship was captured by a British warship that seized his prize but, remarkably, did not put Boyle and his crew to death. When the Chesapeake was blockaded in 1813, Boyle was one of the very few captains that managed to sneak out of port, using bad weather to cover his movements.

Boyle captured over twenty ships during the winter of 1813/1814. The privateer also managed to elude four British warships that hunted him during that voyage. This would become commonplace for the swashbuckling Boyle who, during one week of operations, claimed to have been chased unsuccessfully by one dozen different British warships. Boyle managed to elude his enemies by pushing his cannons overboard to lighten the load and outrun the larger warships. He also ingeniously put two guns in the stern, cut off the railing, and swiveled the cannons to fire at his pursuers. On his fourth cruise of the war, which occurred on the *Chasseur* during the summer and fall of 1814, he captured another eighteen ships. On his return to port, he boasted that he was single-handedly blockading the British isle! Even after the war, the British continued to hunt the notorious privateer. Boyle not only harassed British ships and made himself a rich man, but he also spied for the U.S. navy and army, reporting on the whereabouts of British warships and inspiring a generation of privateers to fight the British.[13]

Another skilled naval commander and part-time privateer operating out of the Chesapeake was Joshua Barney. Barney knew combat. He had served in the French navy, fought in the Revolutionary War, had been under fire in nearly three dozen naval battles, and was even imprisoned three times. He somehow managed to escape his captors, once by wearing a disguise. From his ship, *Rossie*, he harassed British warships on the Chesapeake and merchant ships on the Atlantic, and was perhaps the first privateer to fly the American flag on his ship and use the symbol of the flag to recruit fellow privateers. Barney would later play a decisive role in defending Baltimore and the Chesapeake from the planned British invasion of 1814, when he assembled a ragtag band of sailor and barges, dubbed the Chesapeake Bay Flotilla, to defend the vital port.[14]

The Chesapeake was not the only base of operation for pirates and privateers. One of the more notorious of these sea dogs was Otway Burns. Born around 1775 in Swansboro near the banks of the White Oak River in North Carolina, Burns would go on to become the state's first hero of the War of 1812. At an early age, the frail but scrappy Burns developed a passion for the sea and spent his youth sailing, later earning a living as the captain of a merchant vessel. When the war broke out, Burns and his business partners purchased a light, fast clipper in Baltimore and named her the *Snap Dragon*. The ship was just over eighty-five feet in length and Burns fitted the ship with eight cannons. He received permission in the way of a license from the federal government to plunder British ships as a privateer . . . and did he ever!

Burns used the speed of his ship and his skills as a sailor to attack British warships and merchant ships as well as anyone loyal to or trading with the English. He plundered from Newfoundland to South America. In all, Burns commandeered forty British ships and millions of dollars in cargo, while inspiring other seamen to become privateers. After burying his third wife, Burns died on October 25, 1850. He was buried in Beaufort, a cannon from the *Snap Dragon* marking his grave.[15]

Boyle, Barney, and Burns were among the 500 licensed privateers authorized by the U.S. government to supplement the meager navy. They came from every state, even New York and New England where many residents were opposed to the war and militia units were unwilling to cross into Canada to fight.[16]

## THE HUNT

Even through 1814, much of the American seaboard was blockaded. And then the British decided to inflict a fatal blow to the American navy by going after America's largest warships, those that had proven so elusive and deadly in battle and were captained by the nation's younger officers. It was decided to embarrass the Americans while also demonstrating to the bewildered British people that the Royal Navy was still "mistress of the seas." As such, in the words of the one of Britain's most celebrated officers, Captain Broke, "We must catch one of these great American ships with our squadron, to send her home for a show, that people may see what a great creature it is, and that our frigates have fought very well, though unlucky."[17] And so the hunt was on.

In the waning days of the war, the Royal Navy blockaded New York harbor, where the USS *President* and other powerful ships often docked, and other home ports for America's most successful warships. Outside of New York harbor waited four massive warships: The 56-gun HMS *Majestic*; the frigate HMS *Endymion*; the HMS *Pomone*; and the HMS *Tenedos*. Even though the war had officially ended just days prior, the news had not reached America. So, in January of 1815, the USS *President* under the command of the able Stephen Decatur set sail in a snowstorm to rendezvous with other American ships in the south Atlantic. The small squadron was then ordered to sail to the East Indies to raid British merchant ships. In anticipation of a long voyage and tour, the *President* was overloaded with supplies, which slowed her progress considerably and undercut her natural speed. Not long after passing out of New York she struck an unmapped sandbar and was stuck for about ninety minutes. Even though the ship was freed, there was damage to the hull.

Commodore Decatur wanted to return to port but was prevented from doing so by a strong westerly gale, so he sailed to Long Island and then south. Unbeknown to him, he was being hunted by a British squadron. But they too were blown off course. On the morning of January 15, the *President* sailed right into four British warships led by Captain Hayes of the *Majestic*. Realizing his predicament, Decatur ordered spare equipment and supplies to be thrown overboard to lighten the damaged ship. The *Majestic* and *Endymion* closed the distance and by noon were close to striking distance. In desperation, the *President* even dropped her lifeboats and anchors. At 2:30 p.m., the British squadron opened fire with bow chasers. The *President* continued to run while returning fire with her stern guns.

Later that afternoon, the *Endymion* was able to sail beside the *President* on her starboard and began a series of broadsides. The battle was ferocious and for three hours cannon volleys were exchanged. All the while the *President* continued to run. Decatur used "star and chain" shot which spewed chunks of steel designed to cut a ship's rigging and tear sails. It worked . . . temporarily. The *Endymion*'s rigging and sails took damage and the *President* pulled away from her foes. But the *President* had taken many hits. The once invincible ship was now running low on shot and her maneuverability was cut to a minimum. Late that day the *Pomone* and *Tenedos* caught the large frigate and pounded her with broadsides. With the *President* nearly dead in the water, the British squadron surrounded the ship for musket volleys. The proud Decatur realized he had lost and surrendered late in the day. It had been a long and frustrating day for the dashing commander and he had lost not only one of the crown jewels of the navy but twenty-four men, with another fifty-five wounded. The British suffered about half the casualties.

The *President* was taken back to Britain as a prize of the war. But, on the way across the Atlantic, the squadron ran into a strong gale that further damaged the pride of the American navy. When they finally arrived, the *President* was a shell of her former majesty but the British people and politicians celebrated the victory despite the fact that the war had officially ended.

# 20

# THE CURSED *CHESAPEAKE*

## CAPTAIN JAMES LAWRENCE

The USS *Chesapeake* was, to say the least, an unlucky ship. It was the attack on the *Chesapeake* in 1807, after all, that was partly responsible for the rise of Anglo-American hostilities. It occurred when the ship's inept commander, Commodore James Barron, still sailing with gun ports shut, inexplicably failed to ready his crew or defenses despite direct threats from a British warship. Barron then allowed his ship to be boarded and beaten without firing a shot. It was a bitter defeat that the *Chesapeake* would never avenge. Rather, the ship endured a series of stinging losses and unproductive missions.

Even though the *Chesapeake* was considered one of the worst ships in the American fleet (and her crews considered her to be cursed), she was not taken out of service. This time she eventually sailed under a far better commander named James Lawrence. Lawrence had commanded smaller warships in locations around the world, all the while longing to command a larger warship in the main theater of battle. Earlier in the war, he led the USS *Hornet*, which was sent to South American to hunt British merchant and warships. As a commander, he enjoyed a few victories and few disappointments. While in Brazil in the winter of 1812–1813, Lawrence pursued the HMS *Bonne Citoyenne*. When the British warship took cover in a harbor, Lawrence blockaded the port. The *Bonne Citoyenne* refused to attempt to break the blockade, instead waiting in port for the arrival of another British warship. Lawrence patiently waited most of January and February. The standoff was broken when the HMS *Montagu*, a man-of-war with seventy-four guns arrived. The *Hornet* had only eighteen guns so Lawrence had little choice but to escape north along the Brazilian coast.

On February 24, 1813, Lawrence caught the 18-gun HMS *Espiegle* off the coast of Guyana. But, just as the *Hornet* prepared to do battle, another British warship, the HMS *Peacock*, appeared near the shoreline. The *Peacock*, commanded by Captain William Peake, set sail to engage the *Hornet* and Lawrence boldly prepared his ship to do battle against both warships. The *Peacock* came at an angle to cross the *Hornet* in order to fire a broadside. Lawrence sailed his ship to do the same. The two warships exchanged broadsides, then turned for another run past one another. During the second broadside, the *Hornet* scored numerous direct hits and inflicted serious damage on the *Peacock*. Captain Peake had enough and surrendered. Fortunately for Lawrence, the *Espiegle* sailed a safe distance away from the battle where it appeared to observe the fight from afar. The ship's captain would later claim that he did not know his fellow commander had engaged the *Hornet*, despite the cannon fire!

After the surrender, Lawrence sent part of his crew over to determine whether the *Peacock* could be towed or sailed to port. They discovered that the *Peacock* was too badly damaged and was taking on water. Lawrence took the crew as prisoners of war and, as the *Peacock* sank below the waves, sailed home. Interestingly, the Americans and their British captives became fast friends on the sail back to port in New York, reminding everyone that the war was fought between people that used to be countrymen.[1]

Born in Burlington, New Jersey near the Delaware River, Lawrence was thirty when the war broke out. He had been considering a career in the law, but opted to serve in uniform. Training came courtesy of one of the best, as Lawrence was second in command to Stephen Decatur on the USS *Enterprise*. In his own command, Lawrence would attempt to replicate the bold and courageous decisions of Decatur. His leadership was recognized by President Madison, who promoted Lawrence. On May 20, 1813, he finally achieved his goal of commanding a frigate. The bad news for Lawrence was that the ship was the *Chesapeake*. The problems began immediately. Believing the ship to be cursed, crew members refused to reenlist if it meant sailing aboard the *Chesapeake*!

## THE *SHANNON* DEFEATS THE *CHESAPEAKE*

Lawrence was given orders to attack British convoys, merchant ships, and troop ships. The *Chesapeake* was outfitted with fifty guns, including long-range cannons, and had a crew of 379. However, most of them were new recruits and were poorly trained. With so few ships in service, the *Chesapeake* was rushed back to sea without readying the crew.

Around noon on June 1, 1813, the *Chesapeake* sailed out of Boston harbor only to find a British frigate—the HMS *Shannon*—waiting for her. The *Shannon* was considered one of the best ships on the ocean. She was strong, fast, carried fifty-two guns, and had a seasoned and disciplined crew. It was said of the *Shannon* that she was "as pleasant to command as it was dangerous to meet."[2] The *Shannon* had been given orders to wait outside Boston harbor to intercept American merchant ships. But, it was a bigger prize her captain, Phillip Bowes Vere Broke, had in mind.

The 37-year-old commander was the consummate British officer—well-trained, well-educated, utterly dedicated to the Royal Navy, and a fearless fighter. He was so eager to engage the Americans and so supremely confident that he had a messenger deliver a note to Lawrence in port. It read, "Do me the favor to meet the *Shannon* [with the *Chesapeake*], ship to ship, to try the fortunes of our respective flags." Lawrence recognized the message. It was the same one he had delivered to the captain of the *Bonne Citoyenne* in port in Brazil. Captain Broke had been hell-bent on destroying the celebrated American frigates. He had earlier hunted the USS *Constitution* with no success, even ordering his men into rowboats to pull the *Shannon* in an effort to catch the *Constitution* when there was no wind. He was still sore from not being able to bag the *Constitution* or her sister ships.

Broke had commanded the *Shannon* since 1806 and enjoyed many notable successes. His crew had been with him all those years, making the *Shannon* an efficient weapon of war with a cohesive, experienced crew. Upon receiving the "invitation" from Broke, Captain Lawrence, unlike his predecessor, Commodore Barron, accepted the challenge. He pledged to engage any and all ships, and never to surrender the *Chesapeake*. And so Lawrence sailed out of port with his ill-prepared crew.[3]

## THE *CHESAPEAKE'S* LAST BATTLE

Broke saw the American frigate leaving port, so he set sail to engage her. Around five o'clock that afternoon, both ships aligned to run parallel to one another, preparing for broadsides. Holding their fire until the last minute, the *Chesapeake* and *Shannon* fired as they ran side-by-side. The *Shannon's* gunners were far more accurate. Their broadsides hit the mark. Aboard the *Chesapeake*, the jib sheet and foretop sail were torn away, riggings were destroyed, and the deck was awash in blood and wreckage. The helmsman fell and shortly thereafter, his replacement did as well. Lawrence was now commanding an unwieldy ship without an experienced helmsman.

As the *Shannon* turned to prepare for another pass and broadside, she fired her aft guns, preventing the Americans on deck from readying their ship for another broadside. As the *Shannon* again sailed past the *Chesapeake*, she hit her with another powerful broadside. The British were getting the better of the Americans. The *Shannon* passed for another broadside but the damaged and unwieldy *Chesapeake* ran too close and the British warship's anchor became entangled on the wreckage of the American frigate. At six o'clock, the ships were lashed together and boarding parties charged over the railings. Broke and Lawrence were the type of commanders who led from the front and they both were in the lead as fighting broke out on the decks. As the hand-to-hand fighting was beginning, Captain Lawrence, who was on deck giving orders, was shot by a musketball. He had to be carried below deck by his sailors for treatment. But the wound was mortal. Aware of his ship's reputation, Lawrence's famous final order was "Don't give up the ship. Fight her till she sinks."[4]

Broke was the first to step foot onto the American deck, and he was followed by twenty marines. Pistols, swords, and even fists were brandied about and, after only a few minutes, most of the American sailors ran. With Lawrence below deck dying and his second in command killed, the *Chesapeake's* other officers were unready and unwilling to assume command. Chaos reigned on the American warship. A young lieutenant on the *Chesapeake* tried to get her sails in position to break free and run, but while doing so was shot and his crew abandoned the effort, running for cover. With the crew in a panic and without orders from the officers, the American bugler blew the signal to return to stations.

Only a few Americans attempted to fight. As Broke led his men to sweep the Americans from the deck, a small counterattack came from a handful of marines. Most of their fellow marines had been killed or wounded, so there were not enough men to stop Broke's boarding party. Below deck, Lieutenant George Budd tried to rally the cowering sailors, rushing up onto the deck to face the British boarding party. However, only a handful of sailors followed Budd up the ladder and they were quickly overcome. One other courageous American was the ship's chaplain, Reverend Livermore, who stood his ground on deck. The chaplain fired at the boarding party and at Captain Broke, but the shot missed and Broke brought his sword down on Livermore's arm, nearly severing it from the body. The chaplain died soon after of his wound.

The chaos was such that the *Chesapeake* never struck colors and no officer either ordered the surrender or presented himself to offer his sword. Most of the American officers had been killed and the crew simply stopped fighting. Broke took over the ship, ordering the *Chesapeake*'s colors to be hauled down. In the bloody exchange, the *Shannon* had lost thirty-three men and sustained fifty wounded. But the *Chesapeake* had sixty-one killed and eighty-five wounded. Broke later described the resistance by saying "The enemy fought desperately, but in disorder."[5]

Back in Britain, they were eager for a naval victory. Accordingly, the news of the defeat and capture of this most symbolic ship was met with much celebration. Captain Phillip Broke returned to Britain a hero, was given the key to the city of London, and even given the title of baron. The *Chesapeake* was sailed to Halifax where she was repaired and sailed to Britain, arriving to a huge celebration. The British had been humiliated by the upstart American navy. Some of the most powerful and celebrated ships in the Royal Navy—the *Guerriere*, *Java*, and *Macedonian*, to name a few—had been lost. This victory over the *Chesapeake* was a much-needed morale booster for the Royal Navy.

Captain James Lawrence and his fellow officers were given a military burial in Halifax, Nova Scotia. In the United States, Lawrence was hailed as a hero and his final words, "Don't give up the ship," joined "Remember the Raisin" as a rallying cry for American soldiers and sailors.

# THE GREAT LAKES THEATER

*"The Battle of Lake Erie"*

*September the tenth, full well I ween,*
*In eighteen hundred and thirteen,*
*The weather mild, the sky serene,*
*Commanded by bold Perry,*
*Our saucy fleet at anchor lay*
*In safety, moor'd at Put-in-Bay;*
*'Twixt sunrise and the break of day,*
*The British fleet*
*We chanced meet;*
*Our admiral thought he would them greet*
*With a welcome on Lake Erie.*

—American song from the War of 1812

"Oliver Hazard Perry at the Battle of Lake Erie." Acknowledgment: By W. H. Powell, 1877; U.S. Library of Congress, Washington, DC (USZ62-3484)

# 21

# "WE HAVE MET THE ENEMY AND THEY ARE OURS"

## PRESQUE ISLE SHIPYARDS

It is hard to overstate the strategic importance of Lake Erie and Lake Ontario during the War of 1812. These two smaller lakes and their adjoining rivers—the Niagara and Saint Lawrence—constituted not only the physical border between the two warring countries, but the waterways were critical sources for trade and supplying armies. The lakes also linked east with west and large civilian populations hugged the shorelines of the lakes and rivers. Thus, both the United States and British militaries made it a priority to control these two lakes [see Map 2 in Appendix].

Arguably, however, the lakes were even more vital for the British. While the Americans could resupply some of their forts by land, the British had trouble traversing the dense forests, steep valleys, and numerous creeks and rivers of southern Canada. This inaccessible wilderness was also controlled by Indians, some of whom were anything but friendly to white inhabitants. As such, food, ammunition, cannons, and soldiers had to be transported on the lakes. This advantaged the British, who enjoyed naval superiority in every theater of the war. The United States had no large warship on the lakes and no serious ship-building effort when the conflict began. However, one of the most remarkable stories of the war was that the Americans ended up prevailing on the Great Lakes.

The Americans struck early, capturing British schooners on Lake Erie on October 9, 1812. Exactly two months later, Lieutenant Jesse Elliot was sent to capture two British warships, the HMS *Caledonia* and the HMS *Detroit*, which were anchored near Fort Erie. The problem for the Americans was that the fort's guns were formidable. So, rather than attempt a

199

direct assault on the ships anchored at the fort, Elliot recruited about 100 sailors and soldiers who attempted to sneak aboard the ships, overpower the skeleton crews, and make off with their prizes.

The plan worked . . . sort of. As the Americans were boarding the ships, they were discovered and came under fire from the British fort. Elliot and his men managed to subdue the sailors on both ships and hurriedly cast off while musket and cannon fire rained down on them. The *Detroit* was hit multiple times and Elliot had not planned for the swift current where the Niagara River joined Lake Erie. The battered ship became difficult to sail and succumbed to the current, running aground on Squaw Island. Before abandoning ship and joining his men aboard the *Caledonia*, however, the young lieutenant ordered the *Detroit* set ablaze so the British would not recapture her. Elliot returned triumphal with the *Caledonia*, which was made a part of the small American squadron. The effort constituted a rare victory for the Americans. It also helped sooth the bitterness Americans had harbored ever since the attack on the *Chesapeake* before the war started.

The Americans also rushed to build ships. One of the ironic but unsung heroes of the war was a sailing master named Daniel Dobbins who was selected to build a navy. Dobbins convinced the navy to choose a peninsula by Erie, Pennsylvania, named Presque Isle, for the undertaking.[1] The location offered easy access to the lake and nearby rivers, a protected harbor, and an abundance of hardwood forests. However, Dobbins also picked the site because it was near his home and he knew he stood to benefit financially from the shipyards. The drawback of Presque Isle was that its waters were not deep enough to build large warships. Nonetheless, by the end of 1812, Dobbins was hiring craftsman and building ships. One of the missed opportunities for the British at the outset of the war was not attacking Presque Isle when it was vulnerable. General Proctor considered an attack, but then unwisely called it off, thereby changing the outcome of that theater of the war. The Americans proceeded to build ships at a furious pace.

## A HERO EMERGES

Another turning point in the lakes campaign was the appointment on March 27, 1813, of Oliver Hazard Perry to command Presque Isle. As was abundantly clear with the disastrous invasions of Canada by such inept generals as Hull, Dearborn, Smyth, Van Rensselaer, and Wilkinson, leadership—or lack thereof—mattered. Commodore Perry was the right man for the job. Born in Rhode Island in 1785, Perry grew up around the sea and in a family of sailors. At age fourteen, he was appointed a midshipman and gained skills in boat building and all facets of naval warfare, having served in the West Indies and in the Mediterranean during the Barbary pirate conflicts. Only twenty-seven at the time he assumed command of Presque Isle, Perry had also served with the late Commander James Lawrence and was eager to exact revenge for the attack on the *Chesapeake*. The losses touched him so personally that he ordered flags to be flown at half-mast and took to wearing a black mourning band in honor of his former commander. Later, Perry would order a special sail for his flagship that featured the words "Don't give up the ship!" The white letters on a dark blue banner, a reference to his vow to not repeat Lawrence's decision, would soon become famous at the Battle of Lake Erie.[2]

Like the Americans, the British understood the vital importance of both lakes, but focused their efforts on Lake Ontario. Therefore, when Robert Heriot Barclay assumed command of British naval forces on Lake Erie, he had only three junior lieutenants, a surgeon, and roughly twenty sailors. Period. Compounding his difficulties, Barclay had run afoul of Sir James Yeo, the officer commanding Britain's naval forces on the lakes. Accordingly, Yeo ignored most of Barclay's requests for men, supplies, and ships.

As a commander, Barclay was competent, brave, and experienced. He had fought at Trafalgar and lost an arm while aboard the HMS *Diana*. Like Perry, Barclay was only in his twenties and was ambitious, but was eternally frustrated by his unappreciated and understaffed command on Lake Erie. The loss of the *Caledonia* and *Detroit* to the American raiding party led by Lieutenant Elliot hurt the strength of the lakes' squadron. But Barclay was committed to rebuilding the *Detroit*, which was named in honor of General Brock's victory at the outset of the war and would soon become the most powerful ship on the lakes. Until then, however, Barclay wanted to avoid engagement. He knew about the growing strength of the American fleet under Perry because newspapers in New York foolishly printed the status of ship construction!

Commodore Perry pursued an ambitious, multifaceted agenda on Lake Erie. He sought to supply and support General William Henry Harrison's Canadian invasion, destroy British trade and supply efforts on Lake Erie, and defeat the British naval presence on the lake. But, to accomplish all this he needed at least 740 sailors and many more ships. A lesser leader might not have been able to build so many warships or train such skilled sailors. But Perry worked doggedly.

Perry, as an officer on the USS *Constitution*, had not only gained experience commanding men but he took it upon himself to train his sailors, including the least experienced among them. He began training everyone in his command at Presque Isle. Commodore Chauncey, who commanded the American naval forces on Lake Ontario, assisted Perry by sending him roughly 100 of his sailors. Ultimately, Perry was able to put nine ships into the water with a total force of 532 sailors. Chauncey also sent Lieutenant Jesse Duncan Elliott, who had conducted the earlier raid on British ships, to assist Perry. Perry assigned his young officer to command the USS *Niagara*, the second most powerful ship in his flotilla behind the USS *Lawrence*, which served as Perry's flagship. It was time to engage the British.

## THE BATTLE OF LAKE ERIE

Perry's first test came quickly. In July of 1813, British warships blockaded the waters off Presque Isle, preventing the American fleet from leaving the harbor. The shallow water and large sandbar running some distance out from the peninsula and shipyards ended up being a blessing in disguise. It prevented Barclay from sailing all the way into Presque Isle to hit the shipyards and the vulnerable American fleet. It also presented problems for Perry. The depth of the water was only six feet at the entrance to the harbor. But due to poor planning by the British command, the flotilla ran short on supplies and had to abandon the blockade. It was also rumored that the young British commander had his eye on a widow who lived across the lake at Port Dover and felt the need to pay her a visit. Whatever the reason, on July 31, 1813, Barclay's small fleet abandoned the blockade and returned to port at Amherstburg. This allowed Perry to continue both his aggressive ship-building schedule and visit his lady friend.[3]

Perry suspected that Barclay may not have abandoned the blockade but only pulled back as a ploy to lure the Americans out into the lake. So he sent his smaller gunboats out to reconnoiter the area. He also used them in the event the British blockade had only pulled back to lure him out on the lake or if a warship happened by the harbor while he struggled to sail his larger ships out of the shallows. While his small gunboats made a show of force near the harbor, Perry ordered that the *Lawrence* and *Niagara* be lightened and their guns removed in order to sail over the sandbar and shallows. Even without guns and supplies, the *Lawrence* repeatedly became stuck on the sandbar. So logs were placed under the hull in order to push the large warship up and over the sandbar.[4]

While the *Niagara*, without her guns, was being hoisted over the sandbar some of Barclay's smaller gunboats appeared off shore and opened fire on the stranded warship. Perry had the *Lawrence* stand to as if she were ready for combat. Fortunately, the presence of such a large warship intimidated the smaller gunboats, who quickly dispersed without realizing the *Lawrence* was unable to sail. After a few days—during which time the two large warships were completely vulnerable to attack—both ships managed to make it to open waters, the *Lawrence* first and then, on August 4, the *Niagara*.

Across the lake the British encountered problems. A strike over poor pay by the shipbuilders caused a long delay in the completion of the powerful *Detroit*. Neither navy was fully ready. Perry was still short on sailors and Barclay was impatiently waiting for the *Detroit* to be completed. Barclay also lacked enough cannons and those he had were old and mismatched for his ships. But by the end of August, Perry was able to build and launch more warships and gunboats than the British on any lake! He also converted captured British merchant ships into gunboats. His flotilla included two large warships, the *Lawrence* and *Niagara*, each with eighteen guns; four mid-sized warships, the *Ariel*, *Caledonia*, *Scorpion*, and *Porcupine*; and three small, single-cannon gunboats, the *Somers*, *Tigress*, and *Trippe*.

On August 12, the American flotilla set sail. After delivering supplies to General William Henry Harrison's army, Perry ordered his fleet to drop anchor about thirty miles from the British port at Amherstburg. The *Detroit* was completed on August 17. However, any advantage the British may have had with the powerful *Detroit* was mitigated by the fact that its cannons included old Revolutionary War guns confiscated from the Americans, and other misfit weapons collected from old ships and various forts. The old guns fired slowly and required a flintlock, like a musket, at times forcing the ship's sailors to fire pistols across the vents to get them to fire! Said the famed naval historian, Alfred Thayer Mahan of Barclay's fleet, "A more curiously composite battery probably never was mounted"[5]

From his flagship, the *Detroit*, Barclay commanded three other large warships, the 17-gun *Queen Charlotte*, the 8-gun *General Hunter*, and the 13-gun *Lady Prevost*. He also had a small, 3-gun sloop named *Little Bell* and a 1-gun schooner, the *Chippewa*. Perry's nine ships prepared to meet Barclay's larger, but poorly armed, six ships. The commanders went to battle with what they had available. Still, the British were confident. The

Royal Navy remained the envy of the world and Sir Yeo had recently captured two U.S. schooners from Commodore Chauncey on Lake Ontario.
The British wrongly believed that all American naval commanders on the
lakes were weak and untrained. With that in mind, on the afternoon of
September 9, Commander Barclay ordered his six ships out of the harbor
at Amherstburg.

## "DON'T GIVE UP THE SHIP!"

At dawn the next morning, the cry "Sails ho!" was heard from the lookout
on the *Lawrence*, Perry's flagship, with its flag "Don't give up the Ship"
flying high above the deck. Initially, the wind was at Barclay's back, giving him the advantage. Barclay's fleet approached cautiously. At 10:00 that
morning, only three miles separated the two squadrons. However, the wind
suddenly died and both navies sat motionless, tension mounting on the
decks of the warships. Barclay, with long-range guns, hoped to close the
distance in order to bombard the Americans from afar. But sails and flags
stood motionless the remainder of the day and night, as both navies waited
for wind. It was a sleepless night on the lake.

Perry's luck held on September 10 when the winds shifted and blew
from the back of the American fleet. The *Lawrence* and her sister ships,
rushed in to engage the British. They closed the distance so quickly that
they neutralized the advantage of Barclay's long-range cannons. At about
one mile's distance, Barclay fired a "ranging" shot from the *Detroit's* long
24-pounder. It splashed harmlessly in the water in front of the American
squadron. Perry continued rushing forward. Adjusting the range, the British
opened up as the Americans tried to close the gap. A shot hit the *Lawrence*
on the forward bulwark, sending splinters and shrapnel across the deck.
Perry had powerful, short-range cannons and, thanks to the wind pattern,
he was able to close ranks on the British and hit them with volleys of
broadsides from very close quarters.

With great difficulty on account of the direction of the winds, the
British attempted to organize their warships in a line from the *Chippewa*,
*Detroit*, *Hunter*, *Queen Charlotte*, *Lady Prevost*, to the *Little Belt*. With the
wind still at his back, Perry engaged the British at good speed in his own
line of the *Scorpion*, *Ariel*, *Lawrence*, *Caledonia*, and *Niagara*, followed by
the four small gunboats *Somers*, *Porcupine*, *Tigress*, and *Trippe*. He ordered
his flagship, the *Lawrence*, to sail directly for the *Detroit*.

The *Detroit* and *Chippewa* unloaded their guns on the approaching warship. Perry wisely placed the *Scorpion* and *Ariel* in front of him so that the *Detroit* or another ship could not cut him off or cross his bow. Meanwhile, he sent the *Niagara* to engage the *Queen Charlotte*. The close range favored the Americans who could reload their newer cannons faster and whose ships contained more carronades, ideal for close combat. The fighting began in earnest at 11:45 a.m. and to the horror of the British, Perry's ships maintained their tight, disciplined line. His officer's and crew were well trained. On his signal, they poured accurate broadsides in rapid succession on the British fleet. A blast from the *Caledonia* rang out during the fight, hitting the *Queen Charlotte* amidships, killing her captain. For over one hour, the two long lines of ships exchanged blows.

Another officer assumed command on the *Queen Charlotte* and, in an effort to assist the British flagship, the *Detroit*, turned his ship to engage the *Lawrence*. With two warships firing on the *Lawrence*, Perry's flagship sustained considerable damage. Barclay had made the destruction of the American flagship a priority. He nearly succeeded. On the receiving end of concentrated fire, four of every five crew members aboard the *Lawrence* were now dead or wounded. Shockingly, Perry's officer, Lieutenant Elliott, in command of the *Niagara*, did not maneuver to aid his commander. Speculation began immediately after the battle as to whether the ambitious young officer may have wanted Perry out of the way and for his ship to steal glory in the fight. But the Americans continued to fire back. The *Queen Charlotte*'s next in command was also hit, and control fell to a very junior officer. With the *Queen Charlotte* in disarray, Perry was able to maneuver the damaged *Lawrence* in for a full broadside against the *Detroit*. Perry ordered every cannon available to be loaded and fired. The broadside scored a direct hit. The *Detroit* had her sails and rigging blown to pieces. The British flagship was now dead in the water and, for the seventh time in his career, the one-armed Barclay was hit by shrapnel. But the *Lawrence* was also nearly out of commission. Both ships attempted with great difficulty to fire their cannons.

Finally, Lieutenant Elliott pulled the *Niagara* alongside its sister ship and engaged the *Detroit* and *Queen Charlotte*. To prevent other British ships from rescuing the *Detroit*, the two small gunboats, *Scorpion* and *Ariel*, came to the aid of Perry and kept the larger British warships at a distance. Perry then ordered the *Niagara* and *Caledonia* to turn their guns on the next largest of the British flotilla, the *Queen Charlotte*. Because the wind was at the backs of the Americans, the *Queen Charlotte* had trouble turning to confront her attackers and was quickly knocked out of commission. Through the day of fighting, one by one, Barclay's senior officers fell in the line of duty. The tide of the battle had definitely turned to favor the Americans.

## THE DECOY

It was then that Perry undertook his famous trick. Around 2:30 in the afternoon the *Lawrence* was dead in the water. But Perry ordered the ship to keep fighting. After taking down his famous banner "Don't give up the ship!" Perry ordered a small boat lowered and he and four crewmen rowed it to the *Niagara*. But to give the impression that the *Lawrence* was still in the fight, Perry ordered the ship to continue to fly the American flag and for his second-in-command, Lieutenant James Yarnell, to continue firing the flagship's cannons. Despite being wounded three times, Yarnell courageously kept up the ploy. It worked. The British thought Perry was still aboard his ship and they concentrated their attention and fire on the *Lawrence*.

With Perry safely off the ship, the *Lawrence* finally struck its colors. Seeing the American flagship surrender, the British let loose a roar believing they had won. Cannon fire momentarily stopped and a brief lull in the battle ensued. But, while the British were distracted by the *Lawrence*, Perry had rowed to the *Niagara* to assume command from Lieutenant Elliott. Perry's famous banner was raised above the *Niagara* and cheers erupted from American sailors on every ship. The commodore sent Elliott and other junior officers by rowboat to deliver new plans to the other American ships. He then proceeded to sail the *Niagara* at full mast directly to the *Detroit*.

With the British caught unprepared, Perry released a devastating, close-quarters broadside on the sitting target. Perry's fast-firing, short-range carronades hit the British flagship again and again. From the deck, Barclay was hit yet again, this time by grapeshot in his one functioning shoulder. Command passed to Barclay's second, Lieutenant George Inglis. Yet, even as Barclay was carried below deck he was ordering his men to find and attack Perry. Inglis tried to swing the broken ship around to fire with the starboard guns. However, in the chaos of battle and under the command of a young officer, the damage to the unwieldy ship was such that it crashed into the *Queen Charlotte*. With their rigging entangled, both British ships became sitting ducks. Perry swung the *Niagara* around again, crossed the bows of both ships, and raked them with another volley. Both large British warships were utterly destroyed by the broadsides and taking on a lot of water. One observer noted the extent of damage to Barclay's flagship, saying "It would be impossible to place a hand upon that side which had been exposed to the enemy's fire without covering some portion of a wound, either from grape, round, canister, or chain shot."[6]

There was to be no rescue for the *Detroit* and *Queen Charlotte*. Perry immediately attacked the other ships in the British fleet. His squadron unloaded on the *Lady Prevost*, blowing her deck apart. Her commander, Lieutenant Edward Buchan, lay screaming in agony in the wreckage. One by one, the British ships began hoisting the flag of surrender, believing the order had been given by Barclay. By 3:00 p.m., all six British ships were destroyed and had struck colors. Seeing the carnage, Perry ordered the battle stopped. As was custom, Barclay offered Perry his sword in surrender, but Perry refused, saying his opponent and his men had fought so gallantly that they deserved to keep their swords. It was a devastating battle. Perry's squadron suffered twenty-seven killed and nearly 100 wounded, but the British had vastly higher casualty counts and their entire navy had been destroyed.

## THE IRONIES AND INJUSTICES OF HISTORY

Shockingly, the brave Barclay was court-martialed by the Royal Navy, forced to endure the humiliation with his one arm still in a sling and eight wounds covering his body. Fortunately, the stoic, young British commander was eventually acquitted but still reprimanded for not attacking Perry at Presque Isle before he had time to build a navy.

It was one of the most important victories of the war. With this victory, the Americans controlled Lake Erie and British forces in the region were cut off from supplies and reinforcements. It also made Oliver Hazard Perry a hero. So too, the words from a letter he dispatched to General Harrison about the battle have become immortalized as part of American history. Writing on the back of the envelope, Perry said simply: "We have met the enemy and they are ours."[7] Perry also tallied the victory count for Harrison: "Two Ships, two Brigs, one Schooner, and one Sloop."

But it also came to Harrison's attention that during the battle Lieutenant Elliott was slow to support Perry's flagship. Elliott's hesitancy may have changed the outcome of the battle. Consequently, there was a growing call for Elliott to be court-martialed. But Perry let his junior officer off the hook.

Perry was even magnanimous when Elliott publicly claimed credit for the victory. Mused Harrison, "Commodore Perry has saved [Elliott's] character for which he will never forgive him."[8] The General's prediction proved prophetic. Perry and Elliott would go on to become rivals in the navy. Elliott continued to complain that he was deprived the glory that should have been his, but it is Perry who has been remembered by history. Elliott foolishly aligned himself with James Barron and other officers involved in efforts to undermine fellow naval commanders and whose conduct was, at best, suspect. Ultimately, his actions only served to ruin his reputation.

Perry eventually came to regret that he did not condemn Elliott when the battle was over, ultimately responding to Elliott's constant complaints by saying: "The reputation you lost . . . was tarnished by your own behavior on Lake Erie and has constantly been rendered more desperate by your subsequent folly. . . ."[9] Elliott was less discrete. He challenged Perry to a duel over the letter. Perry refused. He had fought a similar duel years before with a disgruntled captain, courageously holding his fire while his foe fired but missed the mark. Ironically, this duel occurred on the same spot—Weehawken, New Jersey—where Aaron Burr killed Alexander Hamilton in 1804 in the nation's most famous duel. Perry's "second" during that duel (a "second" was required by the etiquette governing dueling) was none other than Stephen Decatur, fellow naval hero during the Barbary Pirate campaigns and War of 1812.

Elliott belatedly faced court martial four years after the War of 1812 concluded. The charge was "Conduct unbecoming an officer by entering upon and pursuing a series of intrigues, designed to repair his own reputation at the expense and sacrifice of his . . . commanding officer." Such a court martial required the word of the commanding officer. Although Perry had finally confirmed that, during the Battle of Lake Erie, Elliott did not come to aid of the *Lawrence*, he was unable to be at the proceedings. Duty intervened and Perry was dispatched to South America to rescue American ships. While on the mission, he died of yellow fever in the port of Trinidad. It was August 23, 1819, the day of his thirty-fourth birthday.[10]

The court-martial proceedings were then passed to Perry's friend, Stephen Decatur. But, before the trial began, Decatur was challenged to a duel by James Barron, one of Elliott's accomplices and one of the officers at fault on the doomed *Chesapeake*. Decatur accepted the challenge and, on March 22, 1820, was killed in the duel. Barron's "second" during the duel was Elliott. The court martial would likely have happened had Perry and Decatur not died. Elliott would go on to live a long and prosperous life;

and Barron, despite his record, was given command of the main naval yards in Philadelphia. Still, history remembers Elliott and Barron as miscreants, while Perry and Decatur are celebrated as America's greatest naval heroes.

As for the Presque Isle shipyard, where the preparation of the Battle of Lake Erie began, it was the site of great tragedy. The winter after the great naval victory was one of the coldest on record. Many of the sailors stationed there—including those who had served so ably under Perry—died from the weather and a disease that tore through the region. The proud peninsula and harbor were nicknamed "Misery Bay" from then on.[11]

# 22

# THE BATTLE OF
# THE CARPENTERS

## STALEMATE ON LAKE ONTARIO

Lake Ontario was unique from the other Great Lakes in that it had a
direct waterway to the Atlantic Ocean via the St. Lawrence River, making
it invaluable to both the American and British efforts to resupply their
armies in the region [see Map 2 in Appendix]. However, it was far more
important to the British, who otherwise lacked a convenient means of
bringing food, weapons, and troops to the lakes. Navigating the St. Lawrence, however, was a challenge because stretches of the river are narrow
and the current is rough. Historically, large ships could not traverse the full
length of the waterway, forcing them to stop at Montreal. Consequently, the
larger warships used on Lake Erie during the War of 1812 had to be built
at shipyards on the lake. Given its importance, the fight for Lake Ontario
turned into a ship-building race fought more by carpenters than by sailors.

Lake Ontario was also a key staging area for the American invasion
of Canada. Here, American efforts were less disastrous on the water than
on land, but equally ineffective with the exception of Commodore Perry's
decisive victory on nearby Lake Erie on September 9, 1813. However, this
only heightened the stakes on Lake Ontario. Both the Americans and British understood that Ontario might be the key to that theater of the war.
They also believed that one major battle might swing the outcome of the
war in the Ontario region. As a result, both naval commanders grew excessively cautious and avoided an all-out fight by never committing all their
ships to battle. In doing so, both commanders missed several opportunities.

At the beginning of the conflict, the Americans had only one warship
on Lake Ontario, the 18-gun brig USS *Oneida*, launched in 1809. Three

other problems presented themselves. One was that they had only a single deep-water harbor on their side of the lake at Sackets Harbor. The second problem was that Sackets Harbor, on the eastern shore of the lake, was in a remote and nearly inaccessible part of New York. The third problem was that the British recognized its strategic importance and attacked Sackets Harbor time and again. As such, the *Oneida* and Sackets Harbor were involved in one of the first naval battles of the war on July 19, 1812, when several small British vessels sailed across Lake Ontario.

One of the objectives in attacking Sackets Harbor was to destroy or take the American brig, *Oneida*, which was commanded by Lieutenant Melancthon Taylor Woolsey. The plan nearly worked when the British trapped the *Oneida* in the harbor. However, the British ships were carrying short-range cannons, which allowed the more powerful guns of the American fort that protected Sackets Harbor to easily push the enemy back. This was the first of many assaults on Sackets Harbor and the shipyard would figure prominently in nearly every decision and battle on and around the lake.[1]

## CHAUNCEY

Not long afterward, on September 3, Isaac Chauncey was appointed to command U.S. naval forces on the Great Lakes. Chauncey focused his efforts on Ontario, leaving Erie and other lakes to his commanders. Commodore Chauncey immediately put forth an effort to commandeer commercial and fishing craft along the lakes and fit them with cannons. He also captured small Canadian and British ships. However, his main effort was to hire shipbuilders and carpenters in an effort to make Sackets Harbor a major shipyard. Workers came in droves for opportunities and Sackets Harbor was soon a bustling port. The result was that Chauncey would build seven ships on the lake.

Isaac Chauncey was born in 1772 in Fairfield County, Connecticut. Although he prepared for a career in the law, his passion was the sea. At age nineteen he was commanding merchant ships and was commissioned a lieutenant in the newly formed navy in 1799. The navy was so impressed with Chauncey that, in 1807, they offered him command of the vital New York shipyards. It was there where he oversaw the building of the USS *President*. He later served on that storied ship and other legendary warships such as the USS *Constitution*, USS *John Adams*, and the infamous USS

*Chesapeake.* Chauncey's impressive military record also included service in the Mediterranean and against the Barbary Pirates off the coast of Tripoli.[2]

Chauncey gained fame not only for his service in these conflicts, but for his courage when at the helm of the *Beaver*, a merchant ship, that was threatened by the 64-gun HMS *Lion*. Unlike the international incident in 1807 when the commander of the USS *Chesapeake* permitted the British to board the American vessel without a shot, Chauncey refused to allow the British warship to board his merchant vessel or press his sailors into serving the Crown. Chauncey even informed the British commander to fire or do what he needed to do, but he would not be permitted to board the *Beaver*! The British backed down.

## A WOODEN ARMS RACE

Throughout the war, both sides attempted to undermine their opponents' ship construction at Sackets Harbor and Kingston. They were assisted by Mother Nature. The bone-chilling winters essentially stopped all construction. During his first winter in command, Chauncey suspected the British would send infantry across the ice to attack his shipyards. As such, he ordered the ice around the *Oneida* to be cut so the ship could be maneuvered to fire at any enemy. But the attack never came. The British were also hindered in their plans to build a navy by feuds among the Canadian shipbuilders and carpenters in Kingston harbor. Master shipbuilders were fired and disagreements led to work-stoppages. Although behind schedule, the British did manage to build several ships in Kingston thanks largely to the protection of Fort Frederick, which stood strategically at the intersection of Lake Ontario and the Saint Lawrence River. From that spot, it could not only protect Kingston's vital shipyards but harass any ship traveling the route from the Atlantic down the St. Lawrence and into Lake Ontario.[3]

The British naval commander, John Steele, was in his late seventies and did little to prepare for the war. But in 1813 he was replaced by Sir James Yeo, who used Kingston harbor as both his headquarters and main shipyards. Like his American counterpart, Commodore Chauncey, Yeo sought to build a large navy at Kingston. And the ship-building race was on.

The British had naval superiority at the outset of the war. Over the next two years, the edge in the number of ships launched see-sawed back and forth. The war ended with the Americans holding an advantage. In what became known as "The Battle of the Carpenters," both commanders prioritized ship building and something of a wooden arms race occurred on the lake. Ultimately, the British constructed a total of thirteen ships on the lake, including one major warship, two frigates, six brigs and sloops, and four small schooners and gunboats. The Americans amassed two frigates, six brigs and sloops, and twelve smaller schooners and gunboats for a flotilla of twenty ships on Lake Ontario. The fight for Lake Ontario began in 1812 and lasted the duration of the war, but was marked by very few naval battles, few casualties, and no battle with conclusive results. Rather, both Chauncey and Yeo adopted such a cautious and defensive posture that the fighting on Lake Ontario ended with the British losing only two brigs and one sloop. Another brig was captured by the Americans. The Americans lost a brig, had two of their schooners sunk, and two smaller ships were captured.

## HALF MEASURES

Once he had constructed or equipped a few ships, Chauncey attacked the British shipyard at Kingston across the lake. On November 6, 1812, he sailed out of Sackets Harbor aboard the *Oneida*, supported by four smaller ships—the *Conquest, Growler, Julia,* and *Pert*. Chauncey also had his eyes on the 21-gun sloop, the HMS *Royal George*, which was in port. On November 8, Chauncey's small squadron encountered the *Royal George* just outside Kingston harbor but the outgunned warship quickly sailed back into the protected harbor. Chauncey pursued his adversary to the harbor's entrance and both sides opened fire. The Americans fought through the day but the British shore batteries from nearby Fort Frederick proved to be too powerful. Chauncey ordered his squadron to pull back away from the batteries' range and drop anchor. Unfortunately, the winds never picked back up and the Americans were forced to abandon the mission.

Yeo retaliated a few days after Chauncey attempted to hit Kingston Harbor. With the American fleet occupied on the western end of the lake supporting an attack on Fort George, the British seized the opportunity and attacked Sackets Harbor again on May 29, 1813. Yeo landed nearly 1,000 troops on American soil and, while they advanced on the shipyards and fort, he attacked by sea. The goal was to destroy this important American installation. If Yeo succeeded, the Americans would have little ability to wage war on Lake Ontario.

The Americans had minimal defenses under militia general Jacob Brown. However, after a short but bloody battle and just when the British were poised to destroy the important American harbor and shipyards, their commander panicked. Like so many of his American counterparts he was cautious to the point of timidity. Brown's ferocious defense of the harbor intimidated Yeo, who worried that the Americans might have superior forces on reserve and called off what could easily have been a major British victory.

It was nevertheless a victory for the British, not because of Yeo but in spite of him. A junior American officer panicked, believing the fort and harbor were about to be overrun. He ordered the recently captured *Duke of Gloucester* and other ships burned, lest they fall into British hands. During the confusion, the American ammunition depot caught fire and blew up. Parts of the fort burned, along with surrounding structures and the newest ship in the fleet. Chauncey had to rebuild the harbor and fort, and repair the USS *General Pike*. It was a costly defense.[4]

In July of 1813, Commodore Chauncey received a dispatch informing him that he should attack the British supply depot at Burlington Heights on Lake Ontario. On July 21, Chauncey sailed to Burlington Heights on the western end of the lake. On the evening of July 29, the Americans attacked with a flotilla of thirteen ships.

Chauncey aided Colonel Winfield Scott in landing a few hundred soldiers and sailors, but the British were in strong defensive positions and easily repelled the assault. A quick reconnaissance of Burlington Heights revealed to Scott and Chauncey that they lacked the equipment and cannon necessary to take the depot. Unceremoniously, the Americans returned to their ships with a few cows they had confiscated. The Americans then sailed to York (modern-day Toronto) where they re-attacked the city they had sacked not long before. It was a symbolic victory with little to show. However, unlike the previous raid, which resulted in private homes being looted and the town burned, Chauncey ordered his men to act with honor.

And thus the battle for Lake Ontario continued for the duration of the war, marked by a few tit-for-tat exchanges, cautious commanders, and aggressive ship building. Both navies built what they could during the winter months and the U.S. War Department anticipated a huge battle on Lake Ontario during the spring and summer of 1813. But it never happened. There were skirmishes, however.

In late July, the British fleet under Sir Yeo sailed with six ships—the *Beresford, Earl of Moira, Lord Melville, Royal George, Sir Sidney Smith,* and the *Wolfe*. The Americans met them with eleven ships. It resulted in one of the few direct engagements of both navies on Lake Ontario. Commodore Chauncey sailed his flotilla to attack Yeo near the mouth of the Niagara River. Yeo's ships had long-range guns so he preferred to fire from afar, whereas Chauncey was in possession of more carronades, which were effective in close combat. As a result, both navies maneuvered in order to obtain an advantage, with Chauncey trying to close the distance but Yeo trying to open up space between his ships and the Americans. Little else happened, until a strong gale kicked up on the lake just prior to midnight on August 7. Amid high winds and rough waves, two American schooners, rigged as warships, sank on account of the weather and not the British. The *Scourge* had begun to list far to one side, which caused her cannons to break loose and roll across the deck. The ship capsized. Nearby the *Hamilton* also sank. Many sailors were trapped while others did not know how to swim. The rough seas claimed nearly eighty lives. The weather deterred both timid commanders and the engagement ended.[5]

Finally, on the night of August 10, the long-awaited battle commenced.

## AT LONG LAST

They met in open water. Chauncey sailed his fleet to within twenty miles of the British flotilla and formed two columns, one led by the USS *Julia* and containing the *Growler*, *Asp*, *Pert*, *Ontario*, and the *Fair American*. The other column, a bit farther behind the first line, had the USS *Pike* in the lead along with the *Oneida*, *Madison*, *Governor Tompkins*, and the *Conquest* arrayed behind it. But, as the Americans closed to within four miles the winds shifted at around eleven o'clock that morning and began blowing at the backs of the British.

Seizing the opportunity, the HMS *Wolfe* sailed directly for the *Ontario* and *Fair American*. The Americans fired on the approaching warship but, firing from short-range cannons, the shots fell into the ocean shy of the target. The *Wolfe* closed the distance and, at 11:30, fired on the American ships. However, Commodore Chauncey had planned a trap. He ordered his lines of ships to turn to give the impression they were fleeing, but the idea was to have the British follow and then catch them out of formation and in between his two columns.

Chauncey gave the order and the *Ontario* and *Fair American* sailed away from the engagement. The *Pert* and *Asp* turned and joined them. But the plan failed. The *Julia* and the *Growler* missed the maneuver and sailed too close to shore where they were cut off from the main American squadron. Nor did Yeo take the bait. Rather than pursue the more important "fleeing" ships, he focused his attention on the two, small schooners, each armed with only two guns. The British cut off their escape and opened fire, easily subduing the *Julia* and *Growler*. Minutes later, British marines boarded and seized both ships, taking the crews prisoner.

On September 28, 1813, both navies met again, this time at York Bay. Yeo was there to resupply British troops fighting at Niagara while Commodore Chauncey was nearby supporting the American army in the region. Yeo had set sail from Burlington Bay on the afternoon of September 26, while Chauncey's flotilla sailed the following evening. Chauncey spotted the British squadron of six ships in the morning and ordered his 10-ship flotilla to set a northerly course to engage the enemy. Shortly past the noon hour, Yeo's ships changed course and prepared for the American broadside. Both lines exchanged broadsides and the American cannons were particularly effective. They targeted the British flagship, the HMS *Wolfe*. Realizing this, Yeo quickly turned his flagship to escape, but Chauncey ordered the USS *Pike* to pursue the large warship.

Chauncey caught the *Wolfe*, maneuvered his ship alongside and, around one o'clock in the afternoon, fired a broadside with fourteen large cannons. In the fight that ensued, the Americans concentrated their fire on the *Wolfe*, while the British hit the *Pike*. Both ships were damaged. The *Wolfe* took several direct hits and the sails on the 23-gun sloop came crashing down, but the British flagship continued to return fire. Chauncey ordered the *Pike* to close in and finish off the *Wolfe*. However, Commander William Mulcaster, aboard the *Royal George*, rushed his ship to intercept the *Pike*, bringing the craft in between the two warships. While the *Royal George* poured shot into the *Pike*, the *Melville* and *Moira* also directed fire at the *Pike*. Now taking considerable damage and caught in a brutal crossfire, the *Pike* was forced to sail away.

The organized lines broke and the battle fell into chaos. All the ships maneuvered for position, firing on one another. Then an opportunity presented itself. During the confusion, two British ships, the HMS *Beresford* and the 14-gun HMS *Lord Melville*, became separated from the squadron. Chauncey had a chance to either destroy of capture them, as had been the case a month earlier when the British captured the two American schooners after they were separated from the main flotilla. At the same time, Yeo had had enough fighting for the day. He ordered his fleet to set sail, abandoning the two ships to their fate. The damaged *Wolfe* trailed the departing ships, moving slowly without its main mast.

But, rather than attack the easy prey, Chauncey appears to have been enticed by the shift in the battle. He ordered "all or none" and his ships set sail in pursuit of Yeo, allowing the *Beresford* and *Melville* to escape. Chauncey chased the four main British warships, but the winds were strong and the waters choppy. Chauncey's fastest ships—the *Pike*, *Sylph*, and the newest ship, the USS *Madison*, bristling with twenty-eight guns, were among the best on the lakes, but all three warships were towing lightly armed schooners (the *Asp*, *Ontario*, and *Fair American*). Chauncey should have either cut loose the schooners being towed in order to lighten his load and catch the British ships; or he should have simply settled for capturing the two easy targets. But he did neither.

Three hours later and thanks both to the winds and Chauncey's mistake, Yeo's ships managed to escape to Burlington Bay. Even the *Wolfe* managed to limp back to safety. Chauncey called off the pursuit, which became known as the "Burlington Races." He again came up empty-handed and no decisive blow was dealt. Moreover, one of his largest warships, the 28-gun sloop, USS *Pike*, was damaged after taking several hits and having one of her cannons blow up. Chauncey reported twenty-seven casualties, while the British lost similar numbers.[6]

Chauncey did not have to wait long to avenge his mistake. A few days later on October 5, he caught a small flotilla of British schooners and gunboats in support of troop carriers. The Americans attacked and captured all five of the small ships, including, ironically enough, his former ships, the schooners *Growler* and *Julia*. Throughout the war, as both sides captured one another's ships, the vessels were retrofitted, renamed, and put back into service.

## THE BATTLE OF FORT ONTARIO

For the most part, Commodore Chauncey avoided attacking Fort Frederick and the Kingston shipyards. He consequently missed opportunities to deliver a knockout blow. Both Chauncey and Yeo put their navies to use moving men and supplies around the densely forested lake. However, there was an attempt on a fort near the Oswego River on the shores of Lake Ontario that had operated from the time of the French and Indian War in the 1750s. It was Fort Ontario, also known as Fort Oswego.[7]

Sir Yeo wanted to attack Fort Ontario in the spring of 1813 but did not have enough men. However, Yeo had built the best and biggest ships of the lakes theater, including the 21-gun sloop HMS *Sir George Prevost*, the 42-gun frigate HMS *Princess Charlotte*, and two 58-gun frigates, the HMS *Prince Regent* and HMS *Psyche*. His new navy was ready in late spring of 1814 to sack the key American fort.

About two hours before sunrise on May 4, 1814, Yeo set sail from Kingston harbor for Fort Ontario. Yeo commanded roughly 900 sailors, 550 infantry, and 400 marines, all of whom were crammed into a few ships. His flotilla consisted of two large brigs and two smaller schooners. The ships also towed smaller gunboats. The next day, in the morning, a lookout at Fort Ontario spotted the flotilla.

The small fort on the eastern shore of the bay was vulnerable to attack, especially from such a relatively large force supported by two large brigs. It sat atop a hill overlooking the bay and lake and included a few low barracks and buildings and five old cannons. The fort stored supplies for Sackets Harbor, protected the shipyards there, and was defended by Colonel George Mitchell and only 290 soldiers. Yeo nearly caught the fort undefended. Many of the defenders that had been sent by General Brown with orders to protect the fort at all costs had arrived only days before on April 30.

Colonel Mitchell was an enterprising officer, determined to hold the fort with his small garrison. He built pickets and other defenses, and constructed small platforms around the fort for three of his cannons, all with views of the lake. The other two guns were placed to face the possible landing zone on the shoreline. Mitchell then ordered his men to hide out of sight. They were also commanded not to surrender.

It took the British ships until May 5 to sail to the fort because of a paucity of good winds. The next morning the winds picked up, so they approached slowly, apparently looking for signs of resistance, and stopped just out of range of the fort's guns. From inside the fort, Colonel Mitchell ordered his men not to fire and to remain hidden. The chop on the lake built to the point where a landing would be a risky endeavor. But Yeo was emboldened by no sign of resistance. Around 6:00 a.m., the landing craft were readied and filled, and the ships opened fire on the fort in order to provide cover for the landing. One of them, the HMS *Niagara*, sailed close to the fort and anchored in the bay. From there she shelled the fort with nine long-range cannons, one large cannon, and two mid-sized guns. The bombardment rocked the small fort. But Mitchell's men held and waited.

As the British landing craft were approaching, the Americans appeared from the cover of the woods and opened fire. Under fire from the Americans and amidst rough waters, the British struggled to make land. Two boats managed to make it to shore that afternoon around two o'clock. Out of the boats came the Royal Marines and the famed Glengarry Light Infantry. Although few in number, it was a worthy force. However, the difficult and soggy landing had ruined the gun powder and the British force had to fix bayonets. From the fort, Colonel Mitchell rushed men not busy manning the fort's five cannons to the beachhead to help repel the invaders. From the cover of trees, the Americans fired into the landing craft and the bayonet charge. Mitchell also redirected the fort's cannons to the beach. The British landing party stood little chance. Their captain and six marines were killed as soon as they landed. Another thirty-three marines fell wounded. Few men made it to the edge of the woods in the bayonet charge.

Mitchell then ordered his few artillery batteries to heat the shot. Red-hot cannon shot did the trick, igniting several fires on the British ships and killing or wounding many sailors. The artillery exchange continued throughout the day, making the assault on Fort Ontario one of the main battles on the lake. Meanwhile, the British landed additional troops, led by Captain Mulcaster, on the other side of the fort. Armed with pikes and swords, they made their way to the two batteries defending the landing zone and caught the American artillery units by surprise and unsupported. However, the Americans picked up muskets and fought back. Captain Mulcaster was shot through the leg and dropped to the ground. Surprised by the Americans' resolve, his men retreated. But the overwhelming advantage in numbers by the British began to pay dividends by the afternoon. The artillery barrage from the ships was inflicting damage on the fort and the American defenders at the beachhead had held as long as they could with such limited numbers. Landing craft continued to come ashore and by mid-afternoon over 1,000 British troops were marching to the fort.

The Americans put up a gallant defense, but Colonel Mitchell was forced to abandon the fort. Before doing so, however, he put supplies to the torch and scuttled the few small boats stationed there. The British eventually entered the fort and tore down the American flag flying above it. They found an officer and twenty-five dead defenders inside and burned the bodies. Approximately twenty-five additional American troops were taken prisoner. It was a hard-fought victory for the British and they had little to show for it except that they recaptured the USS *Growler*, a 5-gun schooner that had been captured and recaptured multiple times.

The Americans lost the fort but inflicted casualties and fought bravely. They were also lucky. Several large naval guns were scheduled to be delivered to Fort Oswego, but were late arriving. When the attack occurred, the ships carrying the guns were still a few miles up the Oswego River. The guns and supply ships thus managed to avoid destruction or capture.

## THE BATTLE OF SANDY CREEK

Sometimes referred to as the Battle of Big Sandy Creek, the effort was one of the last conflicts on Lake Ontario and happened on May 29 and 30 in 1814 on the New York side of the lake. The battle occurred after the successful British offensive against Fort Ontario earlier that month.

After his hard-fought victory at Fort Ontario, Sir Yeo pulled back to the Galloo Islands which dotted the northern edge of Lake Ontario. From there, he established a blockade near Oswego, using four warships to patrol the waters in hopes of intercepting American supplies and ships heading in and out of Sackets Harbor. By May 20, 1814, Commodore Chauncey was growing impatient, writing to the War Department that the British warships "were now anchored between Point Peninsula and Stoney Island, about ten miles from the harbor, and two brigs between Stoney Island and Stoney Point, completely blocking both passes . . . this is the first time I have experienced the mortification of being blockaded on the lakes."[8]

Chauncey was eager to avenge the defeat at Fort Ontario and launch his three new warships. But he was blockaded. He also needed additional armaments and rigging for his two new brigs, the USS *Jefferson* and USS *Jones*, and the frigate USS *Superior*. However, it took months to transport the materials from the Brooklyn shipyards. Once they arrived on the Oswego River, care was taken not to alert the British of the precious cargo. Chauncey dispatched Lieutenant Melancthon Taylor Woolsey, who had escaped the attack on Fort Ontario, to proceed to Oswego to pick up the armaments and rigging, and to escort them safely back to the rebuilt shipyards. Woolsey, with a small force of five officers and twenty-five sailors, set out on the USS *Lady of the Lake*, taking care to avoid Yeo's navy.

Woolsey secured the supplies and headedback to Sackets Harbor. But in the middle of a driving rain storm on the evening of May 28 one of the boats carrying the precious cargo was lost. Soon after, it was captured by the British who easily outgunned the small boat. During the interrogation by the British, the American crew talked openly and gave up the details of Lieutenant Woolsey's mission. Now alerted to the American effort to transport important guns and materials, the British gave chase. They were led by Commander Stephen Popham who had two gunboats and three cutters. Because of the importance of Woolsey's cargo, four additional gunboats under Commander Francis Spilsbury were ordered to join Popham in the hunt for Woolsey.

Lieutenant Woolsey took evasive measures, traveling close to the shoreline while en route to Sackets Harbor. Woolsey's mission was likely saved the next morning when roughly 125 Indians from the Oneida nation joined him near the Big Salmon River and Major Daniel Appling arrived with 130 riflemen to escort the ships. Woolsey had nineteen small boats transporting long- and short-range cannons, riggings for the new warships, and supplies. But he also now had a small force to defend them. With the Indians on the shoreline and Woolsey's boats hugging it, they moved cautiously back to Sackets Harbor.

On the afternoon of May 29, one of Woolsey's scouts observed three British troop carriers and small gunboats approaching their position. Woolsey was only about eight miles from Sackets Harbor, but decided to fight rather than make a run for the fort. He alerted his riflemen, Indian allies, and crew to prepare for battle. The British arrived early the next morning and began a carronade bombardment from their gunboats. Woolsey ordered his small force to hide in the tree line, while he pulled his boats and troops back from the shoreline to Big Sandy Creek. The British would now have to engage him on a small tributary rather than in the open waters, and they would have to pass through a thick forest where Woolsey's Oneida allies were hiding.

On the morning of May 30, the British pursued Woolsey up the creek, not realizing that the Americans were retreating farther and farther up the tributary. At around 10:00 a.m., Lieutenant Woolsey gave the order and the Oneida braves appeared from the woods and attacked the surprised British. They were joined by militia units who had miraculously arrived on the scene only one hour earlier. The New York militia also brought artillery, which Woolsey ordered used against the British. From both sides of the creek fire poured down on the British, who were stuck in the middle of a trap. Woolsey then ordered his men to charge the British. The battle lasted but ten minutes. Realizing his men were completely overwhelmed, and wounded himself, the British commander quickly surrendered.

The British suffered around fifteen dead and thirty wounded, including two officers. Popham, along with perhaps 150 of his troops and their gunboats, were captured. Only one American soldier was wounded, along with one of the Oneida allies. The Oneida braves were not easily pacified, however. They wanted blood, but Woolsey managed after considerable struggle to stop the warriors from executing the British. Woolsey took his prize and prisoners back to Sackets Harbor along with the supplies for the three new American warships. Upset by the defeat, Yeo abandoned his blockade of the region and sailed back to Kingston harbor on June 6. Chauncey was finally able to finish and launch his new ships.[9]

## THE END OF THE ARMS RACE

The enormous HMS *Saint Lawrence* was completed in the fall of 1814, near the end of the conflict. It was launched on September 10, 1814 and, with 112 guns and at nearly 200 feet in length, the *Saint Lawrence* was the largest warship on the Great Lakes. It was even larger and more powerful than the HMS *Victory*, the flagship used by the legendary Admiral Horatio Nelson during the Battle of Trafalgar. It was crewed by nearly 700 sailors. With such an impressive armada, the British could have destroyed any American naval or military presence on or around Lake Ontario, but the *Saint Lawrence* never saw action. Yeo failed to order a decisive strike on Lake Ontario.

Rather than engage the *Saint Lawrence*, Chauncey ordered his ships to remain in and near the protected waters of the port. Commodore Chauncey managed to construct two powerful frigates, the 58-gun USS *Superior* and 42-gun USS *Mohawk*. By July of 1814, Chauncey was once again in possession of more ships, although the British still had the better and more powerful warships. It did not matter. That month, the Americans were planning another naval engagement, but Chauncey delayed the attack because of his illness. Rather than allow a subordinate to assume command, Chauncey waited until he was recovered. But, once again, when he sailed onto the lake, Sir Yeo simply retreated to the protected harbor at Kingston.

By the end of the war, Chauncey was building his most powerful warship, the 110-gun USS *New Orleans*. However, the war ended before its launch and neither the *New Orleans* nor the massive *Saint Lawrence* saw action or met in battle.[10] Lake Ontario never experienced a massive, major naval battle. Both hesitant commanders fought to a stalemate at this strategic lake that could well have altered the outcome of the war.[11]

# 23

# SAVING CANADA

## A TWO-PRONGED ATTACK

During the autumn of 1813, the Americans changed tactics. They continued to pursue the objective of conquering the Great Lakes, but shifted the focus of their invasion of Canada from the western to the eastern end of Lake Ontario. General Henry Dearborn, who had presided over the disastrous first attempt on Canada, had effectively retired in early July, removing one of the major impediments to a successful invasion. However, there remained both concern and debate over the objective. The concern was that the cowardly Dearborn was replaced by the incompetent and corrupt General James Wilkinson, who had both spied for the Spanish and schemed in Louisiana to create a western empire. Wilkinson's career was undeservedly saved time and again by the fact that he had served in the Revolutionary War with the secretary of the army, John Armstrong. It was Armstrong who, above the chorus of complaints about Wilkinson, gave the general command of the important port and fort at Sackets Harbor. Among those most pleased with the appointment were the citizens of Louisiana, who were finally rid of Wilkinson![1]

General Wilkinson wanted to take Montreal and the St. Lawrence, whereas the secretary of war had his eyes on Kingston and Lake Ontario. Ultimately, Secretary Armstrong paid a visit to his general at his headquarters at Sackets Harbor, where he foolishly deferred to Wilkinson's plan. Secretary Armstrong and General Wilkinson then devised a two-pronged plan. Wilkinson would lead one army to strike the western entrance to Montreal. General Wade Hampton would lead a second army north from Vermont, where he was defending Lake Champlain, to strike from the other direction [see Map 2 in Appendix]. Although he had served with Francis Marion, the famous "swamp fox," in the American Revolution,

Hampton was a dubious pick to lead the army. He was well known to be a heavy drinker.[2]

There were other problems. General Hampton's junior officers and troops were inexperienced, inadequately trained, and when the army arrived at the forward staging ground it had very few provisions. The British had controlled Lake Ontario since early June, which made resupplying the American units operating in the area nearly impossible. British raids around Lake Champlain and Lake Ontario further hampered the operation. The invasion was probably doomed from the get-go. Moreover, General Hampton, like so many other American commanders, had a history with Wilkinson. He not only distrusted the corrupt general but was refusing to serve with him. Secretary Armstrong was forced to personally visit with Hampton to assure him that all orders would come directly from the War Department and not Wilkinson. Hampton eventually agreed to the joint operation, which by then had been delayed. The invasion was shaping up like every attempt before it.

On September 19, Hampton's army of over 4,000 regulars and militia units, supported by ten cannons, boarded boats and sailed from Burlington to Plattsburgh. But they were again delayed and diverted. Hampton's scouts discovered British ships throughout Lake Ontario and soldiers at Kingston, preventing any American landing there. So Hampton was forced to find a new landing site. The American army finally established camp at Four Corners where they were forced to wait until mid-October on account of Wilkinson. Despite Hampton's own delays, General Wilkinson's army was still not yet ready!

Even though he had received his orders in May, Wilkinson did not arrive in Washington until July 31. After meeting with Secretary Armstrong, Wilkinson again dallied, traveling at a leisurely pace. It took him several more weeks to prepare his army. When Wilkinson finally took command of Sackets Harbor on August 20, 1813, he had 3,483 men but only 2,000 were ready for duty. The general was never one to prioritize training or preparation, so the army remained unprepared when the fighting started. Yet another setback occurred when army cooks mistakenly mixed contaminated water from a latrine with their flour. Much of the army fell ill. Wilkinson needed more men so he sailed to Fort George and commandeered Colonel John Boyd and 1,000 of Fort George's soldiers, leaving the key fort vulnerable to attack. During the travels, the general came down with an illness, which further slowed the already delayed invasion.

Most officers in the army were now refusing to serve with him. One of them was the celebrated Winfield Scott. As a result, Wilkinson ordered Scott to remain at the fort rather than be a part of the invasion and put him in command of the worst soldiers in the army. Wilkinson later reversed his decision when he realized he might need more troops. He sent for Scott and put him far in advance with the front guard, perhaps as a way of silencing one of his loudest critics.[3]

## MARCHING INTO A TRAP

Meanwhile, General Hampton and his army waited impatiently on the border. The weather had slowed both American armies. The entire area had been hit by a drought that dried up streams and wells, thus leaving the armies without adequate water supplies. At the same time, the repeated American delays gave the British more time to muster troops in the region.

Finally, on October 18, Hampton received word that General Wilkinson's army was *nearly* ready. That was good enough for Hampton, who was tired of waiting and knew the longer he waited the more prepared the British would be for his arrival. He ordered his army to break camp. Once again, the same problem plagued the Americans. The militia units from New York refused to go deep into Canada and simply disobeyed Hampton's direct command. With 1,400 militiamen refusing to fight, Hampton's army was down to 2,600 soldiers. As the New York militia units marched back home, Hampton pushed on without them. His army headed along the Chateauguay River on their way to Montreal, but made little headway. The British had ordered bridges destroyed and trees to be felled across the roads. The evidence was obvious: The enemy was ready for Hampton. His army would never make it to Montreal.

The Americans marched into a village known as Spears or Ormstown and attacked the few local militiamen defending the town. It was a quick success, with General Izard executing a quick outflanking maneuver. However, many of the Canadian defenders managed to slip away, racing back toward Montreal to warn Lieutenant Colonel Charles de Salaberry, who was in charge of preparing the city's defenses. Hampton not only allowed the Canadians to escape but he did not take advantage of his success by advancing immediately on Montreal. Rather, he ordered his men to make camp. They were only six miles from where de Salaberry was preparing a trap for them. The cunning French-Canadian, de Salaberry, had scouts monitor every move the Americans had been making since crossing the border into Canada.

The Canadians were thus waiting by the banks of the Chateauguay, which flowed into the St. Lawrence near Montreal. They established their defenses on the outskirts of Montreal at a point on the river roughly fifteen miles north of the St. Lawrence. This time they had sufficient numbers. The governor of Canada, Sir George Prevost, had ordered Lieutenant Colonel George MacDonnell to march his army from Kingston on the shore of Lake Ontario to block the entrance to Montreal. MacDonnell's army was backing de Salaberry's line. The new commander of the garrisons in Montreal, Major General Louis de Watteville, had also mustered militia units and requested two battalions of regulars for the city's defense. He and Governor Prevost were marching these reinforcements to Montreal.

Colonel de Salaberry picked a site where the river made a sharp bend, integrating this and other natural features, such as a large ravine into his defensive plan. His men would be protected on one side of the river by swamps and, on the other by forests, in which he placed his Mohawk warriors with instructions to make noise in order to give the impression that they had larger numbers. Trees were placed across the road as obstacles. Small earth works were erected on either side of the river and de Salaberry placed Captain George Ferguson and his irregulars, known as "fencibles," a term for Scottish volunteers, behind them. The land in front of his defenses was cleared to allow for a field of fire and, should the Americans try to cross farther down the river in the swampy terrain, a small militia unit under Captain Charles Daly was posted there to slow the Americans and prevent the larger British-Canadian army from being outflanked.

The French-Canadian colonel viewed the Americans as invading his home and was prepared to defend it at all costs. De Salaberry placed roughly 200 regulars and 100 Canadian militiamen on the front where he assumed the main attack would occur and had them dig in. Behind him were over 1,000 soldiers and 180 Mohawks under Lieutenant Colonel George "Red" MacDonnell, a tough and able Scot, ready to reinforce de Salaberry's line or any other point of attack. Red MacDonnell's men dug earthworks behind the front line, with one roughly every 300 yards. Even if the larger American army managed to break the front line and natural defenses, they would face one obstacle after another. It proved to be a sound plan. The only advantage the Americans had was that the main British and

Canadian forces under de Watteville and Prevost had not yet arrived. The Americans still had numerical superiority.

Scouts warned General Hampton that de Salaberry's men were waiting down the road. Late in the day on October 25, 1813, Hampton ordered over 1,000 men from the 1ˢᵗ Brigade commanded by Colonel Robert Purdy to cross the south bank of the Chateauguay River and try to outflank the British position the next morning. Purdy's force moved farther up river and crossed, but became lost in the marshy woods and tangled in the thick underbrush. A scout was blamed for the mistake, and it took Purdy's men an entire night to make it through the marshlands. Purdy's advance force was supposed to outflank the Canadian defenses and strike at sunrise. But, it was after noon when the Americans finally trudged out of the swamp in the wrong location and they were in no condition to fight when they finally emerged on the 26ᵗʰ tired, cut, bitten, and frustrated. Purdy's men discovered that they had not found the Canadians; the Canadians had found them. Captain Daly, guarding the flank with 160 men from Colonel MacDonnell's larger force, ordered his men to open fire on the soldiers stuck in the swamp. It was a rout. Purdy's large army retreated.

Another 1,000 men of the American 2ⁿᵈ Brigade attacked along the main road, striking the center of the British line. They were led by Brigadier General George Izard. Fatefully, a messenger arrived from Secretary Armstrong, just as Izard was about to attack, with a bizarre order. The War Department was placing General Wilkinson in command of all American troops in the region and General Hampton, on account of the multiple delays in the invasion, was to return immediately and establish a winter camp capable of housing the entire American army in the region. There would be no invasion of Canada that fall and the message implied that Hampton should abandon Montreal and march back across the border.[4]

## THE DEFENSE OF MONTREAL

It was too late for General Hampton to call back General Izard's charge. Izard's men moved down through a ravine on their way to the main British line, but were easy targets as they struggled up and out of the hole. Izard foolishly rode out of the ravine to offer the British a chance to surrender. However, he had no flag of truce and was shot. Accounts suggest it was Colonel de Salaberry who shot his opponent. Both armies exchanged volleys, but the British were behind trees and defenses, while the Americans were stuck in a ravine. Few casualties were inflicted because the Americans simply hunkered down in their unfortunate position. Units that did not follow Izard into the ravine, attempted to outflank the British on their right, but just as they were about to do so, the reinforcements Colonel de Salaberry had organized rushed to hold the line. The crafty colonel also sent buglers into the woods to sound the charge, making the Americans believe they were surrounded and facing bayonet or cavalry charges. From the other direction, de Salaberry's Indian allies made a great commotion, suggesting another charge. Without General Izard, the Americans panicked, fled the ravine, and pulled back three miles.

It took Colonel Purdy an entire day and night to fight and find his way back out of the marshes and back across the Chateauguay. A company under Captain Daly harassed them the whole way. When Purdy rendez-voused with the larger army neither column was in the mood to fight. General Hampton met his dejected army and proposed a council of war. The vote was unanimous to retreat. Hampton attributed the decision to a lack of supplies and ammunition rather than cowardice and incompetence. The army withdrew all the way to a town known as Four Corners.

Colonel de Salaberry did not purse the fleeing Americans. He did not have enough troops, but sent Mohawk scouts to follow and report on the American's retreat. After the fighting, Major General de Watteville and Sir George Prevost finally arrived with their armies. Colonel de Salaberry was furious that the generals took so long to arrive. Had they been at the battle, he could have followed and annihilated General Hampton's army before it retreated back to the border. The only thing Prevost and de Watteville did was take credit for the victory and exaggerate the scope of the battle on both sides. They reported that 300 Canadians defeated 7,500 Americans.[5]

Nonetheless, it was a great victory for the outnumbered Canadians. Just over 1,300 Canadians and Mohawks held their line against 2,600 Americans. The Canadians lost just two men, with about sixteen wounded and a handful missing in action. The Americans sustained fifty-five dead and wounded, sixteen captured, and another thirty missing.

The British reinforcements were not the only ones late. General Wilkinson's army had made little progress. He had barely made it to the St. Lawrence River by the day of the battle. When he received news of the defeat from Hampton's courier, Wilkinson in turn sent word for Hampton to stay and fight. Hampton refused the order and marched his army back to Plattsburgh where he tendered his resignation. By the time General

Wilkinson was notified that his second would not comply, his own army was under attack at the Battle of Crysler's Farm.

## THE BATTLE OF CRYSLER'S FARM

The other wing of the St. Lawrence campaign, designed to capture Montreal in a pincer move, never materialized because it was led by one of the war's most notorious scoundrels, General James Wilkinson. Wilkinson's massive army never joined General Hampton's army to assault Montreal. Wilkinson set sail on 150 ships along the St. Lawrence River but, because of numerous delays, ice and snow on the river, and the general's own illness, the army did not embark until October 17, well behind the planned timeline for the invasion.

Things did not get easier. A few of the boats sank and, at Grenadier Island on the St. Lawrence, some of the boats were damaged by ice. The repairs necessitated further delays. Wilkinson's army was making little headway and morale was becoming a problem. While hunkered down by the river, some of the soldiers approached a local farmer who grew potatoes. The American soldiers offered him fifty cents per bushel. After the farmer informed them that the British army paid him twice that, the Americans simply took all his potatoes. Wilkinson was losing control of this army too.[6] On another occasion, while the American army was camped on the banks of the St. Lawrence, a British transport flotilla sailed by at night. It carried supplies and was commanded by William Mulcaster. Seeing the American camp, Mulcaster ordered the gunboats escorting his supply ships to open fire on the camp. In the morning, the Americans were able to force Mulcaster's small flotilla to retreat, thanks to Lieutenant Colonel Moses Porter's artillery, which fired heated shot to burn the British transport ships. Although it was a victory, the fighting further delayed Wilkinson and the all-night shelling while in camp unnerved the American army.

Throughout their advance, General Wilkinson's army was harassed by Indians and local citizens. As the army marched by villages, farmers took pot-shots at them from barns and behind trees. To deal with the constant harassment from the wooded shoreline, the Americans frequently had to stop and disembark small scouting parties to clear the area of the enemy before advancing. Wilkinson finally tired of the skirmishes and sent 1,200 soldiers in advance to destroy farms and villages. Major Benjamin Forsyth, the infamous leader of raids on border villages, was one of the men leading these missions. The problem was that Wilkinson and Forsyth handled the matter in a way that, just like the potato incident, only incited more resistance and caused additional damage to the American army's tarnished image.[7]

The Americans finally disembarked the army on November 9 and 10, with General Jacob Brown leading the advance guard ashore. The main army behind them was led by General Wilkinson and the rear guard by Brigadier General John Boyd from Fort George. However, before they marched toward Montreal, Wilkinson convened a council of war to discuss the campaign. Even though they were running well behind schedule and had encountered so many problems, the officers decided to march on Montreal. But, they proceeded very cautiously on account of inaccurate reports suggesting the British had a massive army in the vicinity. The cautious and still-ill Wilkinson ordered his men to set up camp, even though they had just disembarked. They camped near a farm owned by a man named John Crysler.

There was no massive British army marching to intercept the Americans. Rather, the British had assumed Wilkinson would strike at Kingston on Lake Ontario. British troops had been rushed to the harbor's defense. When the British learned otherwise, the lieutenant governor of Upper Canada, Major General Francis de Rottenburg, dispatched a force of 650 men and some warriors from the Iroquois and Mohawk nations commanded by Lieutenant Colonel Joseph Wanton Morrison to rush to find the Americans. On November 7 they sailed from Kingston on schooners commanded by William Mulcaster, who had earlier harassed General Winchester's army while they camped at water's edge. Reaching their landing site at Prescott two days later, the small army was joined by 240 men from a nearby post. Colonel Morrison then ordered his army of nearly 900 to double-time it to the American camp.

## FIX BAYONETS!

On November 11, the British arrived near the Americans in camp at Crysler's farm in Morrisburg, Ontario. The next morning, a Mohawk warrior encountered an American scouting party and shots were exchanged. Nearby, both armies were roused from breakfast by the shots and poured onto the farm fields. The terrain was open but the fields were muddy. It was a rainy, cold day when the soldiers gathered in lines. The day started well for General Wilkinson when he received reports that General Jacob Brown's advance scouts had just defeated a small British force at Hoople's Creek nearby. It appeared that the road to Montreal was cleared of enemy combatants. But rather than follow Brown and march on Montreal that morning, Wilkinson decided to stand and fight the smaller British force awaiting his men on the farm fields.

Wilkinson was under the weather from a lingering fever and from consuming too much laudanum, an opiate that seems to have impacted his already suspect judgment. His men reported observing him having severe mood swings; one minute, the general could be "very merry" singing songs, but the next minute he could be paranoid. Wilkinson was also known to repeat everything he said.[8] So the general passed his command to his second, Major General Morgan Lewis. But Lewis also complained of illness. So, command fell to General Boyd. Despite their incapacitated generals, the Americans had a decisive advantage. Over 2,500 men marched onto the cold, wet farm fields.

The British awaited the larger army in three small detachments, each one taking advantage of the fencing throughout the farm and some natural cover. On one wing was Major Frederick Heriot with his Canadian voltigeurs and a few Mohawk warriors. They occupied a ravine and the woods that lined the farm. On the opposite wing was Lieutenant Colonel Thomas Pearson, commanding a group of Canadian fencibles and light artillery. They were protected by a small gully. The main army under Lieutenant Colonel Charles Plenderleath and Colonel Morrison was in the center, with some regulars in reserve for the purpose of reinforcing any of the three lines. Each of the three detachments had a 6-pound cannon.

But the American attack did not come. The men simply held their ground, which only served to exhaust the army. After many long and tense hours in a light rain, the attack finally came in the middle of the afternoon. On one flank, an American infantry unit under Colonel Eleazer Ripley marched on the British skirmish line by the ravine and woods. In the fighting that ensued, the British pulled back into the woods. As the Americans advanced into the woods they were suddenly met by British regulars who had reinforced the line. From their positions behind trees, the British fired into the American columns, pinning them down in the woods. It had the desired effect, and Colonel Ripley ordered his men to retreat.

The Americans also attacked the opposite flank. Led by Brigadier General Leonard Covington, the American army climbed down into and then up the gully. There they encountered the British line wearing grey greatcoats. Mistaking them for militiamen, General Covington shouted to his men, "Come on, my lads! Let us see how you will deal with these militiamen!" But they were Canadian fencibles reinforced by the battle-hardened 49th Regiment. The defenders poured musket volleys into the Americans. One of the first hit was General Covington, who later died from his wounds. His second-in-command was killed also. Amid the barrage, another American unit turned and retreated.[9]

The main disaster for the American army occurred on the center line. At the start of the fighting, the Americans hollered and fired a few shots expecting what they thought were untrained Canadian militia units to turn and run. They did not. The Americans advanced and were brimming with confidence, but the British held their line. When the Americans were close, the outmanned British commander screamed, "Make ready. Present. Fire!" After a volley from their muskets, the disciplined British soldiers then received a very bold order from Colonel Morrison—fix bayonets and charge the much larger enemy. This shocked the American troops and broke their lines. The Americans, including officers, ran chaotically from the battlefield. In fact, the British pushed them all the way off the farm fields.[10]

## RETREAT (IN ANOTHER DIRECTION)

The American army was now in retreat and the British saw an opportunity to capture the American artillery on the field. Colonel Morrison ordered the 49th Regiment under Captain Ellis to charge the batteries. However, the British came under intense cannon fire and were forced to abandon the charge. At that moment, the U.S. Dragoons, a cavalry unit under Colonel John Walbach, charged into the flank of the retreating 49th. Any unit of soldiers, much less those retreating, had trouble standing their ground in the face of charging horses. But, Captain Ellis ordered his men to stand firm, then they executed a wheeling maneuver: "Halt . . . Front, pivot . . . Left wheel into line. . . ." In an amazing reversal of fortunes, the 49th repelled the American cavalry attack, which regrouped and charged two more times. The British prevailed and even went on the offensive, beating back the cavalry and taking one of the artillery batteries stuck in the mud.

Although greatly outnumbered, the British continued to attack and by late afternoon the Americans were in full retreat. The weather again turned stormy, and amidst the rain that evening, the Americans abandoned the battlefield, boarded boats, and crossed the St. Lawrence River into New York. The British did not have enough soldiers to give chase. Rather, they held the ground in the event the Americans returned. They never did. One British soldier described the battlefield as "covered with Americans killed and wounded."[11] It was an accurate assessment. The Americans suffered over 100 killed and 237 wounded in the battle. A few officers and over 100 soldiers were captured by the British. The British also suffered many casualties, but nowhere near the American count. They reported thirty-one dead, 148 wounded, and a few missing.

With Wilkinson and Brown now back across the river with their depleted army, word arrived that General Hampton was neither marching on Montreal nor joining them. He too had been defeated. Hampton returned to Plattsburgh and resigned his command, likely before he was stripped of it. Using Hampton as an excuse, Wilkinson reconvened his war council and decided to abandon the campaign for Lake Ontario and the St. Lawrence altogether. They marched to Cornwall and then to the border town of French Mills, a few miles from the St. Lawrence, to establish their winter camp. All the while, Wilkinson maintained he was not retreating but simply advancing in another direction![12] Because of illness and supply shortages, Wilkinson ultimately moved his whole army to Plattsburgh.

Canada was again saved at Chateauguay and Crysler's Farm. The latter battle is considered by some historians as the most important in Canadian history.[13] Another massive American army was defeated in consecutive upsets and the invasion of the critical St. Lawrence-Montreal-Lake Ontario region was stopped. Yet another inept American commander cost his nation a disastrous defeat. Wilkinson's biographer even admits: "Never have so many Americans been beaten by such inferior numbers on foreign soil."[14] However, General Wilkinson never admitted defeat or accepted responsibility for this or his many other defeats. Rather, he criticized everyone around him for undermining his efforts and put the blame for the St. Lawrence River campaign on General Hampton. The *New York Gazette* immortalized the cowardly scoundrel with a poem:

> What fear we, the Canadians cry
> What dread have we from these alarms?
> For sure, no danger now is night,
> 'Tis only Wilkinson in arms.[15]

## A REPEAT OF 1812

General James Wilkinson and the entire U.S. army needed to redeem themselves for the string of disasters in Canada, including the recent embarrassment at Crysler's Farm. After a long and bitter winter in camp in Plattsburgh, New York, Wilkinson marched his army yet again into Canada in another effort to sack Montreal.

This time the army traveled north along Lake Champlain and the Richelieu River, arriving in the Canadian village of Lacolle Mill, the site of an earlier defeat when, in 1812, General Henry Dearborn had organized an army of 5,000 regulars and New York militia to march on Canada. But, while attacking a small detachment of British soldiers at Lacolle Mills, reinforcements from Colonel Charles de Salaberry counterattacked the Americans and drove them off. It was enough to unnerve General Dearborn who marched the massive army all the way back to Plattsburgh for the winter. The earlier embarrassment was surely not lost on General Wilkinson and the Americans as they again arrived in Lacolle Mill, this time around eight o'clock on the morning of March 30, 1814. The general commanded roughly 4,000 troops, including eleven infantry regiments, the First U.S. Rifle, a cavalry regiment, and eleven cannons. Wilkinson was under pressure to produce a victory, and the small mill seemed a likely place to both avenge the earlier defeat and launch the last-ditch effort to invade Canada.

The village was garrisoned by only 180 regulars and some Canadian voltigeurs under Major Richard Handcock. As the Americans marched on the village, Major Handcock placed his men in defenses around the three-story mill on the south side of the Lacolle River and at wood barracks on the other side of the river. Despite being severely shorthanded, the major ordered the defense of the village knowing another 550 Royal Marines and regular infantry were only a few miles away at L'Ile-aux-Noix. He sent a rider for reinforcements as soon as the Americans were spotted.

General Wilkinson again delayed the battle. Rather than strike immediately, he waited until mid-afternoon before sending roughly 1,200 men to the north and west in an effort to outflank the British. The maneuver was slowed because of snow and mud, and only two cannons could be dragged into position. By the time Wilkinson was ready to attack, British reinforcements had arrived. Others were on their way. When the two cannons—a 12-pounder and 5-inch mortar—opened up on the mill they discovered that they were too close to the target. As the Americans were preparing to pull their artillery back, the British and Canadian defenders opened fire on them with muskets and Congreve rockets. It drove the American artillery back. But, unlike earlier campaigns, the other American units did not retreat. Fierce fighting followed. The American numbers were too great and the British and Canadians were pushed back.

However, units of Canadian fencibles and voltigeurs arrived on the battlefield with Native warriors, just as the Americans were gaining the upper hand. They caught the Americans by surprise and charged. The bold maneuver succeeded briefly. But, an American counterattack drove them back again. The reinforcements also managed to bring a cannon from a nearby naval ship. The fighting continued late into the day, with both sides advancing and retreating several times while exchanging artillery fire. By nightfall, both armies were exhausted and the weather turned harsh. Finally, Wilkinson called off the invasion and pulled his large army all the way back across the border to Lake Champlain. The British and Canadians suffered eleven dead, forty-six wounded, and four missing. The Americans lost only thirteen but suffered well over 100 wounded or missing. This battle at Lacolle Mill ended the American campaign to invade Lower Canada and sack Montreal, which began in 1812.

Wilkinson's pathetic career in the military was over. He was finally stripped of his command and faced court martial. One year later, a military tribunal in Washington acquitted Wilkinson of the charges of misconduct; but he had been utterly discredited and never again wore the uniform. Unfortunately for the Americans, Major General George Izard replaced Wilkinson.

## 24

# TURNING THE TABLES ON THE INVADERS

## THE BURNING OF NEWARK

Yet another American invasion of the Great Lakes and Canada came to an embarrassing end in late 1813. However, some American war planners pointed to General William Henry Harrison's decisive victory at Thames, where he defeated Britain's Indian allies and killed the great Tecumseh, as evidence that the war was not lost. Moreover, Sir George Prevost ordered an evacuation of Upper Canada all the way west to Kingston. There were simply not enough British troops or Canadian militia to secure the region. As such, even though the British victories at Chateauguay and Crysler's farm stopped the American invasion of Quebec and Montreal, the Niagara region remained vulnerable to another American attack.

The war in Upper Canada was in flux. With the British evacuation, the Americans quickly reoccupied parts of the Niagara region, including Queenston and Chippewa [see Map 2 in Appendix]. However, frustrated politicians and a weary public had long since tired of the failures. Occupying a few communities along the border did not substitute for a successful invasion. One individual upset with the failures was an American expatriate named Joseph Willocks, an American living in Upper Canada who claimed he was treated poorly by his neighbors. Willocks grew so impatient with the inability of the American military to invade Canada that he organized a group of American expats, militiamen, and Canadian volunteers loyal to America and made plans to sack villages along the Niagara. Willocks claimed that it would slow any British forces advancing to the border, but it appears the attacks were motivated more by resentment of his neighbors and anger over the failed invasion.[1]

December 10, 1813 was a bitterly cold and snowy day. Willocks and his men entered the town of Newark (present-day Niagara-on-the-Lake) near the border in Ontario and announced that they would put the entire village to the torch beginning at sunset. The residents were ordered to take their belongings and abandon the town. As night fell and amidst a snow storm, Willocks and his marauders looted homes and farms, then proceeded to burn the town.

One of the homes they raided was the Dickson house. Willocks himself entered the building with two of his men, all carrying fire brands. There he found a woman confined to her bed with an illness and ordered her carried from the home. She was placed outside the home in the snow. The owner of the home, William Dickson, was taken prisoner and marched to the United States were he and several other villagers, including an 80-year-old alderman named Peter McMicking, were jailed on charges of disloyalty. Nearly 100 homes and farms were burned that evening. In total, roughly 400 people were left homeless, including many women and children.

Major General John Vincent commanded the few British forces remaining in Upper Canada. He was alerted to the senseless attack at Newark and similar raids. One of his officers, Colonel John Murray, was so angered by the reports of violence against civilians that he requested to go after the American raiders. General Vincent dispatched Murray and a force of 400 regulars and Canadian volunteers to the Niagara to protect the residents from American raids. The small force rushed to Newark, stopping briefly at Forty Mile Creek where they established camp. One of the residents of Newark who was arrested by Willocks during his nighttime raid was Thomas Merritt. It turned out that Merritt's son, William Hamilton Merritt, was a captain in the Canadian militia who was leading a small group of Canadian dragoons assigned to Colonel Murray's army. While Captain Merritt was in camp at Forty Mile Creek, he saw in the distance the eerie image of the sky set aglow from a massive fire. It came from the direction of Newark. Merritt and his volunteers ran through the woods to catch and punish the Americans.

The village they entered was completely burned to the ground. Merritt and his men reported being horrified by what they saw. Furniture and possessions were scatted among the barren streets. Several of the village's residents, including women and children, were dead in the snow, frozen stiff from the cold. Only a few people had survived and they were freezing and hungry. Captain Merritt vowed vengeance. The Americans had also burned parts of Queenston, but were about to pay for their repeated attempts to sack Canada and the atrocities directed at civilian populations during the war. As Merritt described, it was "many a long and weary ride, in the lonely hours of the night, in hope of catching Willocks and making an example of him and all traitors."[2]

## THE LOSS OF FORT GEORGE

Captain Merritt finally caught the retreating American raiders and militiamen at Twenty Mile Creek. On a tip from Indian allies, he knew which road his enemy was using for their retreat. Merritt caught the retreating raiders and struck the American rear guard, charging ferociously into the back of the line. Though greatly outnumbered, the Canadian dragoons fought with a vengeance. With two Americans killed immediately and many wounded, the soldiers in the rear guard surrendered and were taken prisoner by Merritt. The main American force fled down the road. Having dispatched the rear guard, Merritt's small force pursued the American army all the way to Fort George, which the Americans had recently captured from the British.

Back at Fort George, a flustered General George McClure contemplated whether to hold or abandon the fort. The problem was that most of the fort's garrison had earlier marched to join General Wilkinson on his invasion of Canada, thus leaving him with only 250 men from the New York militia to defend Fort George. Making matters worse, the general complained that perhaps only sixty of them were ready and willing to fight![3] General Wilkinson and other commanders had neglected to adequately garrison or provision the fort. As reports of a pending attack poured into Fort George, General McClure watched with frustration as his militia units simply walked out of the fort and returned home. In the wake of failures at Chateauguay, Crysler's Farm, Stoney Creek, and Beaver Dams, American morale was sagging. The militiamen's resolve was further dampened by the bitterly cold winter and the fact that their terms of enlistment had expired. McClure now faced the prospect of trying to defend Fort George with a handful of men, so he frantically and unsuccessfully tried to recruit additional militiamen from New York. Most militia units in New York now opposed both the invasion of Canada and the war itself.

A panicked McClure dispatched scouting parties to attempt to locate the British and Canadian armies in the area. He had heard reports that

Colonel Murray and Captain Merritt were marching to Fort George. What McClure did not know was that they had only a small force of men. But, the scouts dispatched from Fort George were attacked by Indian war parties and locals still fuming over the American raids by Willocks and others. When a handful of McClure's scouts managed to make it back to the fort with news that a British and Canadian force was on their way, the general decided it was time to abandon the hard-won fort.

McClure retreated across the Niagara River and to what he thought was the safety of Fort Niagara on the American side of the border. On December 12, the British and Canadian forces arrived to re-occupy Fort George. But, the British were not content with simply retaking their fort. The burning of Newark inspired them to seek revenge. Even General McClure noted later that, "The enemy is much exasperated."[4] This would turn out to be an understatement.

McClure would later be dismissed from service for doing nothing while Willocks and others looted and burned Canadian villages in the region. The general did not even offer shelter, warm clothing, and food to the displaced civilians. However, McClure may have been a scapegoat, as evidence suggests the order to burn the town came from the secretary of war, John Armstrong.[5]

## FORT NIAGARA, FALLS

Fort Niagara sat majestically guarding the mouth of the Niagara River at Youngstown in New York. Built by the French in the late 1600s, the grand structure consisted of two stories of ramparts and large stone walls. To the French it was "the house of peace," while Indians in the area referred to it as "The French Castle." During the French and Indian War, the British managed to take it from the French during a tough nineteen-day siege. They controlled the fort through the duration of the Revolutionary War, but finally relinquished control to the Americans under the Jay Treaty of 1796. Fort Niagara was not only one of the strongest fortifications in the entire Great Lakes region, but a strategically important staging ground during the War of 1812 for conducting operations against Queenston Heights, Fort George, and other sites on Lake Erie and Lake Ontario.[6]

Remarkably, the Americans failed to prepare the fort for attack, despite the numerous American losses just across the Canadian border in the preceding months and even in the wake of their recent abandonment of

Fort George. The fort had not been resupplied and was in need of repairs. Even with General McClure's small detachment from Fort George, Fort Niagara was still severely undermanned. Only about 400 men guarded the vital fortress. As had been the case at Fort George, most of Fort Niagara's garrison had been sent to support General James Wilkinson's recently failed invasion of Canada. It was about to go from bad to worse. Observing a hopeless situation, the cowardly McClure decided to leave Fort Niagara, fleeing to the safety of Buffalo.

McClure left the important fort in the hands of an incompetent, junior officer named Nathaniel Leonard. Captain Leonard, an artillery officer, was a drunk and the source of several negative reports from the War Department. After McClure's departure, Captain Leonard rode out of the fort to visit his family, who lived a few miles away. It remains uncertain whether Leonard was a coward, doubted the British would attack the impregnable stone fort, or was simply grossly incompetent. Neither McClure nor Leonard prepared the defenses at the fort before abandoning it. The only preparations were to warn settlers in the region of the possibility of British attack.[7]

While American commanders did nothing, an important development advantaged the British. General Proctor, whose weakness had cost the British victory on the battlefield, had finally been relieved of his command. In his place, Lieutenant General Sir Gordon Drummond was appointed commander of all British forces in Upper Canada on December 13. Drummond, the son of a Scottish military paymaster, was born in Quebec in 1772 and became the first Canadian-born officer to command both the Crown's military and government in Canada. He took the American raids on civilians personally and wanted revenge for the atrocities at Newark. Unfortunately for the Americans, Drummond was a worthy commander, having joined the British army in 1789, serving with distinction from the Netherlands to the Caribbean to Egypt, and rising quickly through the command. He planned for an immediate, surprise attack on Fort Niagara in order to catch the Americans unprepared and hunkered down for the winter.

On December 17, he selected Colonel Murray to lead the attack. Commandeering all available troops in the region, General Drummond ordered the army to rendezvous with General Vincent's army that same day. Captain Merritt and his Canadian volunteers were charged with gathering every available boat from miles around. In a matter of days they managed to transport a sufficient number of craft overland on sleds to the staging ground at St. David's. The armies boarded boats and sailed under cover of darkness for the American border.

On the night of December 18, an advance party under Colonel Murray landed two miles from Fort Niagara near Youngstown, New York. Roughly 550 men from the Royal Scots, British regulars, and Canadian militia snuck undetected during the night to the first of the American outposts. There they ambushed the sentries who, embarrassingly, had abandoned their guard post to play cards at a nearby tavern! At bayonet point, the British enticed the Americans to reveal the password for gaining access to the fort's perimeter. Armed with the password and motivated by vengeance, the British advance unit gained access to the other American guard posts and killed all the sentries. Arriving at the drawbridge of the massive stone fort on the cold snowy night, the British were amazed to find that it had been let down over night. The gates remained wide open. Furthermore, sections of the fort that had been damaged by artillery fire earlier in the war had not been repaired, no defensive perimeter existed around the compound, and the soldiers inside were all asleep.

Colonel Murray attacked at roughly four o'clock in the morning. Several companies of regulars charged through the wide open front gate, while other units attacked the sides of the fort and established diversions nearby in the event the fort was prepared for attack. Facing no resistance, Murray's men simply used bayonets and knives to quietly kill the few men on guard duty (who were sleeping) as they entered the fort. From the sides of the fort, the attackers used ladders to scale the high stone walls. The garrison remained asleep in their barracks and many sick soldiers filled cots in the infirmary. Without firing a musket, the British and Canadians simply bayoneted the Americans as they slept.

The only real resistance to the attack was in one of the barracks at the southern blockhouse where American soldiers barricaded themselves in the stone building and refused to surrender. Several attempts by the British to breach the blockhouse failed. Colonel Murray announced that he would offer them no quarter if they did not surrender. When they did not, Murray dragged a cannon to the front of the massive structure and blew the door down. Murray hollered "Bayonet the whole!" and the British and Canadians killed everyone inside.[8]

The remainder of the American garrison quickly surrendered. In total, sixty-five defenders were killed, including many men in the infirmary and those barricaded in the blockhouse. Many more were wounded. The British had only eleven casualties—six dead and five wounded. It was an important victory. As December 1813 closed, both major installations in the Niagara region—Fort George and Fort Niagara—were in British hands. Colonel Murray confiscated nearly thirty cannons, thousands of muskets, and stores of ammunition and supplies. The fort also housed the Canadian prisoners taken by the despised raider Willocks. These men were freed and the American garrison at the fort was jailed in their place. The American flag on the famous fort was hauled down and later shipped to London as a prize.

Captain Leonard was later captured at his home and imprisoned. He was allegedly drunk when the British found him. Ultimately, General McClure blamed Captain Leonard for the embarrassing defeat, however, both men were guilty. Both would suffer the same fate. They were discharged after nearly being court-martialed. As one scholar observed, Captain Leonard proved to be "either a traitor or a derelict."9 The same could be said for General McClure. The British held the fort for the remainder of the war.

## LIGHTING THE SKIES ON FIRE

Nevertheless, the British and Canadians proved to be no better than the American army. Without an American military presence in the area, the British along with angry Canadian militiamen and Indian allies exacted a bloody revenge. For three days beginning on December 19, the invaders looted and burned homes and farms for miles in every direction. Civilians, including women and children, were murdered and scalped. Villages in the area were destroyed. The entire region was about to be put to the torch.

The same day that Fort Niagara was taken, British reinforcements arrived under Major General Phineas Riall. Riall ordered additional raids and had Youngstown burned. The carnage continued as the British then marched to the village of Tuscarora and set it on fire too. Roughly 500 warriors had joined Riall's small army, and the scalping and murders continued. When the British army descended on Lewiston, the American defenders fled so quickly that they left behind hundreds of barrels of flour and supplies as well as a cache of cannons, muskets, and ammunition.

The swath of terror continued, as General Riall marched to Manchester (present-day Niagara Falls) and put it to the torch too. Riall's final prize was Buffalo. About the only opposition the invaders encountered was that some thoughtful and brave Americans destroyed the bridge over the Tonawanda Creek. As a result, Riall had to march his army back to Lewiston to a harbor on the riverbank and await boats to take him down the

Niagara River. The delay allowed many civilians in Buffalo to escape. Nevertheless, the entire region had fallen to the British. Panic spread throughout the Niagara region, as one American unit after another fled and towns and forts fell. Much of the region was now evacuated and witnesses describe seeing the night skies glow from so many villages being burned.[10]

Traveling on the river, General Riall proceeded to Buffalo, the largest town in the area. En route, he marched to Fort Schlosser, which guarded the entrance to the portage around Niagara Falls and sat on the site of an old French fortification. During the French and Indian War, France burned their fort rather than allow the British to take it, but the British had rebuilt the fort prior to the American Revolution and named it for the outpost's first commander. The fort, which was nicknamed Fort Little Niagara Falls, had been sacked before. Back on July 5, 1813, while conducting raids in the area, a small detachment from the 49th Regiment and a Canadian militia unit surprised the Americans, who quickly surrendered. The British confiscated a few small boats, supplies, and a cannon during that raid.[11]

Despite being sacked before, the Americans failed to fortify the site. The fort had only eight men in it when General Riall's army arrived on December 22. The British imprisoned the defenders without firing a shot and burned the small fort. Riall then marched to Buffalo and Black Rock which, like Niagara Falls, were strategically located in the strip of land separating Lake Erie and Lake Ontario. The British were close to their goal of controlling access to both lakes and the important harbors and coastal communities throughout the Niagara region. General Riall knew that many ships would be docked in Buffalo for the winter and that the supply depot at Black Rock would house soldiers, ammunition, powder, and supplies for a springtime offensive. To destroy the ships and depot would undermine America's ability to fight in the region.

American commanders at Buffalo and nearby Black Rock were alerted to the approaching British army and rushed to try to recruit militiamen from New York to stop the invasion. However, they were able to muster only a few units. The British began their three-day siege of Buffalo and Black Rock on December 29. The Americans put up only a meager defense. With thirty soldiers dead and another forty wounded, the army abandoned the town. In their panic, they neglected to destroy the fort or evacuate civilians. Many of the fleeing soldiers were captured. Three warships in the American fleet that protected the lakes were still sitting in dock and were destroyed by the British. Supplies and weapons were confiscated, adding to the immense yield the British had seized throughout the region.

After the three-day siege and artillery bombardment ended, only three buildings in Buffalo remained standing, one of them a stone jail. Over 330 buildings, homes, and farms were burned. Although British commanders ordered their men not to loot and attack civilians like the Americans had done, the opposite occurred. Canadian militiamen and Native warriors, filled with alcohol and vengeance, scalped, looted, and burned their way through Buffalo. No reliable numbers exist for civilian casualties, but it is likely it was in the hundreds. Another American city had been obliterated, leading Lewis Cass, a soldier who had fought in the Detroit campaign, to describe it as "a scene of distress and destruction such as I have never before witnessed."[12]

The American border was in flames and was now entirely controlled by the British. General Riall suffered only 100 casualties in the campaign, but his army proved themselves no better than the Americans when it came to war-related atrocities. The British command excused the behavior, suggesting that the atrocities committed by the Americans earlier in the war gave the British no choice. Sir George Prevost even dismissed the barbarity as a minor anomaly "so little congenial to the British character."[13]

America was now being invaded. The warmongering from southern and frontier Hawks throughout 1811 and 1812 now seemed especially ironic. The glorious triumphs the Americans enjoyed earlier that year were undone. The American military needed better trained soldiers, not unreliable militia units, and with the British threatening to push southward from New York, it needed them right away. The War Department also needed better commanders. The likes of Generals Dearborn, Hampton, Hull, Smyth, Van Rensselaer, Wilkinson, and others were costing America thousands of lives and the war. It now appeared as though they would cost America its very existence as a nation.

The *New York Gazette* summed up the invasions of Canada with a poem referencing the failures and the irony of General "Granny" Dearborn asking to be present at General Hull's court-martial:

> Pray, General Dearborn, be impartial
> When president of a court-martial;
> Since Canada has not been taken,
> Say General Hull was much mistaken.
> Dearborn himself, as records say,
> Mistaken was, the self-same way.
> And Wilkinson, and Hampton, too,

And Harrison, and all the crew.
Strange to relate, the self-same way
Have all mist-taken Canada.[14]

It remained to be seen whether quality leaders would emerge in 1814 and whether the young Republic would long endure.

# 1814

*"The Burning of Washington"*

*A veteran host, by veterans led,*
*With Ross and Cockburn at their head,*
*They came—they saw—they burned—and fled!*
*They left our Congress naked walls—*
*Farewell to towers and capitols!*
*To lofty roofs and splendid halls!*
*To conquer armies in the field*
*Was, once, the surest method held*
*To make a hostile country yield.*
*The warfare now the invaders make*
*Must surely keep us all awake,*
*Or life is lost for freedom's sake.*

—A popular poem from the war

"Capture and burning of Washington by the British, in 1814." Acknowledgment: By Richard Miller Devens, 1876; U.S. Library of Congress, Washington, DC (USZ62-117176)

# 25

# CANADA'S BLOODIEST BATTLE

## A TURN OF EVENTS

America's three-pronged invasion of Canada—in the northwest from Detroit, across the Niagara River in the center, and to Montreal via the St. Lawrence in the east—had failed miserably. After two years of fighting in which both sides took their lumps, the war returned to a status quo. The Americans had benefited greatly from the fact that the British had been preoccupied with war in Europe. With the pressing threat from Napoleon, few troops and ships—and even less attention—had been devoted to defending Canada.

The Napoleonic war raged through 1813. After numerous successes, it seemed as if the French emperor was unstoppable. However, in the spring of 1813, the combined armies of Russia, Prussia, and Austria marched on France from the east, while Wellington's army on the Iberian Peninsula dealt France a stinging defeat. The British were thus able to pivot and advance on France from the south. Faced with a massive invasion from several sides, Napoleon was finally captured and exiled to Elba.[1]

With Napoleon beaten, opponents of the War of 1812 in America hoped the British would make peace on the continent. Not so. The British were able to turn their full attention to the pesky Americans who had made little progress in two years. But rather than simply mobilize to defend their Canadian holdings, Britain planned to invade the United States. In a cruel twist, the British prepared a three-pronged invasion of their own—a northern campaign on the Canadian border at Plattsburg and Lake Champlain, a central prong on the Chesapeake, and a southern campaign at New Orleans. America was about to find herself facing invasion, destruction, or re-colonization. It would be a fight for survival!

America was also facing internal political divisions and economic collapse. Banks were forced to suspend payments, public credit collapsed, and the war had devastated merchants and shippers, while communities on the border and coast suffered repeated British and Canadian raids and plundering. This emboldened a growing "peace hawk" movement. Federalists in New England and New York had never supported the war, but there was now even talk among the region's radical Federalists of leaving the Union. As a result, a strong movement to seek an end to the war began in 1814. Massachusetts and other states in the northeast began planning their own peace negotiations and Connecticut, Massachusetts, New Hampshire, Rhode Island, and Vermont sent delegates to Hartford to begin talks.[2]

Public sentiment in Britain had also soured on both the War of 1812 and the practice of impressment, which had served to ignite the war. The British people had endured bloody wars for two decades and their campaigns against Napoleon had sapped both the national treasury and will. However, a string of embarrassing defeats of the Royal Navy at the hands of the small, upstart American fleet along with the continued effort to invade Canada strained British sensibilities. Many in Britain, although tired of war, wanted to punish the Americans or, as the *London Times* advocated: "Chastise the savages for such they are, in a much truer sense, than the followers of Tecumseh or the Prophet."[3] British reinforcements sailed with vengeance to America, remembering border raids and the burning of the capital of York.

However, at that same time a change was occurring across the Atlantic. For most of the war, the American military had fought reluctantly under inept commanders and often refused to cross into Canada. But they now had found their motivation. It came from a series of corresponding British atrocities directed at civilian populations on the border and throughout the Chesapeake as well as Indian attacks on the Gulf Coast. Joseph Nicholson, who was the brother-in-law of Treasury Secretary Albert Gallatin, summed up the quandary in a letter to the secretary of the navy, William Jones: "We should have to fight hereafter not for 'Free Trade and sailor's rights,' not for the Conquest of the Canadas, but for our national Existence."[4] Facing the darkest hours of the war, some of America's finest hours were about to occur in 1814.

## A SURPRISING VICTORY

The American army was desperate for new leaders. It found several, prompting new optimism late in the war for the invasion of Canada and defense of the homeland. A new commander, Major General Jacob Brown, a 39-year-old Pennsylvanian, was put in charge of the Great Lakes campaign by Secretary of War Armstrong. One of the new breed of military leaders, Brown was a lawyer in New York City who had once served as military secretary to Alexander Hamilton. Brown proved to be highly capable during the defense of Sackets Harbor in 1813 and was still bitter about serving under the incompetent Wilkinson during the disastrous campaign along the St. Lawrence River. Secretary Armstrong also promoted Peter Porter, Winfield Scott, and other younger commanders. The newly promoted Scott, only twenty-seven at the time and a favorite of President Madison, was well over six feet tall, ambitious, charismatic, and a favorite of the soldiers. He was named as Brown's top officer.

Although the army still suffered from illness, desertion, and inadequate supplies, they were now led by competent generals who prioritized training, paid attention to provisions and logistics, and were eager to turn the tide of the invasion. They vowed that this march on Canada would be different. Boasted Scott: "The men are healthy, sober, cheerful, and docile. If, of such materials, I do not make the best army now in service, by the 1st of June, I will agree to be dismissed from the service."[5] With the Napoleonic war ending, American war planners made one last-ditch effort to invade Canada. It occurred along the Niagara River.

Early on the morning of July 3, 1814, in the midst of a downpour and under cover of darkness, General Scott snuck his troops across the Niagara in small boats and into Canada. Scott, who always led from the front, was in the first boat where he even reached over the bow and used his sword to measure the depth of the shallow water on the banks of the river. Once the boats reached the shoreline, Scott jumped overboard but stepped into a deep hole near the banks of the river and disappeared momentarily under the water. Although he reemerged soaking wet and angry, the incident alarmed his troops who saw it as a bad omen for the start of the campaign. Scott dismissed it and pushed his soldiers forward.

Joined by General Peter Porter, Scott marched to Fort Erie, which was defended by only 170 men. After surrounding the fort, Scott ordered the siege to start. Fort George was not far away and from its walls the British heard the bombardment of Fort Erie [see Map 3 in Appendix]. The commander in Fort George was Major General Phineas Riall, who had earlier raided the American border with savage efficiency. Riall scrambled his men to march in support of the beleaguered soldiers inside Fort Erie. He never arrived in time. Fort Erie fell to General Scott. However, General Riall formed a defensive line not far away along the Chippewa River in order to stop the American advance [see Map 3 in Appendix].

Based on earlier campaigns, Riall assumed the Americans would be unprepared so he decided to hit them quickly in hopes of surprising the larger force. He therefore sent an advance guard ahead of his main army of 2,100. It was led by Lieutenant Colonel Thomas Pearson, who, as fate would have it, had captured Winfield Scott early in the war at the Battle of Queenstown Heights. Riall and Pearson hoped to catch the American army as it marched out of Fort Erie. They nearly did.

On July 4, 1814, General Brown ordered General Scott to move part of the American army forward in response to intelligence reports that Riall's forces were nearby. But as the American march was getting under way the next day, the British charged across the Chippewa Creek on the north side of the American camp. They also hit the camp with artillery fire, certain it would scatter the Americans as it did earlier in the war. However, General Scott was not one to run. A veteran of several battles and a stickler for training, Scott had disciplined his army and forbidden them from surrendering. Scott responded by charging his men over a small bridge to counterattack the British. From their lines, Scott's men delivered disciplined musket and cannon volleys into the British. This is not what Riall anticipated. Moreover, when he saw the unusual gray uniforms worn by Scott's brigade rather than their usual blue, he assumed the Americans were militiamen. The British continued their charge, confident that the untrained American militia units would soon wilt. However, the gray Riall saw were the heavy coats of Scott's regulars, not the uniforms of militia units. The Americans continued to fight and did not give ground. When the British sent units to outflank the lines, Scott simply adjusted his flanks and poured fire into the advancing soldiers. Realizing the Americans were regulars and were undeterred by the charge, Riall is alleged to have gasped, "Those are regulars, by God!"[6] The Americans held.

Both armies continued to fight and advance. However, toward the end of the battle, Scott saw an opening on Riall's far right flank and rushed Major Thomas Jesup and an infantry unit to attack the spot. Scott also divided his army into two wings, giving the impression to the British that his center was folding. Riall took the bait. The British made one final attempt to charge the middle of the American line, but found themselves caught in a trap. From both sides, Scott's army closed in, while Jesup outflanked the British in reserve. As British soldiers dropped on the field, Riall retreated.

The fighting took most of the day. But, after underestimating the Americans, General Riall ordered his army to retreat back across the Chippewa. Scott advanced but did not engage the British, wisely waiting until General Porter's army joined him. With more American troops arriving, Riall decided to march his army the entire way back to Fort George. Scott and Porter thus made camp. The British suffered roughly 400 casualties, with another few dozen taken prisoner. The Americans endured 300 casualties. It was a great victory for the Americans. Finally, after two years of boondoggles in Canada, they had defeated a large British army in Canada. Of the battle, Scott would later record in his memoirs: "History has recorded many victories on a much larger scale than that of Chippewa; but only a few have wrought a greater change in the feelings of a nation."[7] Americans had heroes on the water, but it needed a success in Canada and Scott both looked and acted the part.

## LOST OPPORTUNITY

General Jacob Brown wanted to go deeper into Canada and capture additional forts. However, the problem was not incompetence or cowardice as with earlier campaigns. Rather, Brown's army was running low on supplies and ammunition, and needed the additional stores planned for the invasion. Brown had momentum after Chippewa and knew Sir Yeo, the British commander on the lake, was reluctant to fight. The time to strike was now. But Commodore Isaac Chauncey refused Brown's request to resupply him and transport his reinforcements. Brown desperately wanted Chauncey to join him, writing:

> I do not doubt my ability to meet the enemy in the field and to march in any direction over his country, your fleet carrying for me the necessary supplies. We can threaten Forts George and Niagara, and carry Burlington Heights and York, and proceed direct to Kingston and carry that place. For God's sake let me see you: Sir James [Yeo] will not fight!"[8]

But Chauncey declined, writing that his navy was preparing to "fight the enemy's fleet, and I shall not be diverted in my efforts to effectuate it by any sinister attempt to render us subordinate to, or an appendage of, the army."[9] Even though he lacked the men and supplies necessary to sack a large fort or continue his raids along the border, Brown was not ready to abandon the invasion.

Another opportunity slipped by further west. Emboldened by the news of Scott's victory, General William Henry Harrison launched an offensive that same month farther west in northern Michigan designed to control the upper Great Lakes. Harrison teamed with Colonel George Croghan, who had commanded forts in the region, to begin planning an attack on Fort Mackinac and St. Joseph Island. On July 20, American forces arrived on the island and, meeting little resistance, burned the small fort there. However, unlike earlier attacks, Colonel Croghan did not burn homes or harass the civilian population. The army of 700 then set out on five ships to retake Fort Mackinac, which had fallen to the British at the start of the war.

Arriving on July 26, the Americans began the assault on the fort, which was commanded by Colonel Robert McDouall. Naval cannons shelled the high walls of the fort for two days. However, the fort still stood and a dense fog drifted across the lake, making it hard to see the fort. Satisfied that the fort's defenses were sufficiently softened, the Americans set ashore a landing party under Major Andrew Holmes. As Holmes led his unit through thick woods and over a ridge, he arrived at a clearing near Dousman's farm. Not far away were the earthworks and perimeter defenses of the fort.

The fort looked vulnerable so Croghan ordered Holmes to cross the clearing separating them from the fort. But as soon as the Americans marched out from their cover they came under severe fire. Colonel McDouall had sent men out to scout for the Americans and they were waiting. Thirteen Americans fell dead, including Major Holmes and his officers, and another fifty-one were hit. Without another effort, Croghan ordered his advance force to pull back to the boats. Despite having a numerical advantage, the Colonel decided to abandon the effort. Fort Mackinac remained in British hands.

Another prong of General Harrison's western offensive also failed to capitalize on a good opportunity. This time it was at Prairie du Chien. The Americans hoped to solidify their control of rivers and lakes in the region and disrupt an important trade route for the British and Canadians with area tribes such as the Fox, Kickapoo, Ojibwa, Sioux, and Winnebago. To that end, Harrison dispatched another army supplemented by a smaller force of regulars and militia units led by the famed explorer William Clark, who was serving as governor of the Missouri Territory. In May and June of 1814, Clark traveled up the Mississippi River and defeated an army of Sac warriors aligned with the British before heading to Prairie du Chien.[10]

Prairie du Chien was a small outpost defended by Captain Francis Michael Dease and a handful of men. When Dease learned an American army was headed his way, he abandoned the outpost. Clark took the outpost without a shot. Afterward, he put Lieutenant Joseph Perkins and a small force of sixty-five men in charge of expanding the fort's defenses. The new fort was renamed for Isaac Shelby, the governor of Kentucky who supported the war by sending thousands of Kentuckians to the Canadian border. Once the fort's defenses were strengthened, the Americans could use it as a staging ground for a large advance into Canada. Everything was going as planned. So Clark returned to the Missouri Territory.

The British, however, learned that the Americans had taken the outpost at Prairie du Chien so Colonel Robert McDouall, who had successfully defended Fort Mackinac just days prior, sent a scouting party to determine what it was the Americans were up to. The small force, led by the recently promoted lieutenant colonel, William McKay, took with them one small cannon and traveled fast. Along the way, the small British scouting party was joined by 600 Indians.

Arriving at the outpost on July 17, they caught the Americans by surprise. Fort Shelby was still under construction and the small garrison of Americans was forced to quickly take shelter inside. The British asked for an unconditional surrender, but Lieutenant Perkins refused and the siege began. However, the British cannon was so small that it had little impact on the fort. The Americans held out for a few days, but even though the shelling had little effect the defenders were running low on ammunition and water. When the British lined up to storm the fort, the Americans surrendered. The British held the small fort through the end of the war, burning it when they departed after the war concluded.[11]

## LUNDY'S LANE

As the American armies abandoned Fort Mackinac and Prairie du Chien, farther to the east, General Brown was wrestling with the shortage of supplies and lack of reinforcements on account of the reluctance of Commodore Isaac Chauncey's navy to assist him. The timing could not have been worse, as Brown was about to run into a massive British army. The final major battle of the Canadian theater of operations occurred on July 25, 1814, at Lundy's Lane, just across from the border by Niagara Falls [see Map 4 in Appendix]. It would be one of the bloodiest battles of the war and most ferocious ever fought on Canadian soil. It would end in a draw . . . and it almost didn't happen.

Had Brown had other armies supporting his or had Commodore Chauncey cooperated in supporting Brown's invasion, this final campaign might have ended very differently. But, Brown forged ahead alone. His army was in the vicinity of Queenston Heights, the site of previous engagements. However, he received word that General Riall was on the march and that additional armies were en route to support him, including Colonel Joseph Morrison's regiment, fresh off their victory at the Battle of Crysler's Farm. Lieutenant General Gordon Drummond, the British commander of Upper Canada, was determined to stop another invasion. He thus marched every available unit to intercept Brown and personally took command of the army. Because of Commodore Chauncey's mismanagement of Lake Ontario, Drummond sailed troops and supplies across the lake without problem. Running low on supplies and ammunition, and without reinforcements, the Americans would have a fight on their hands.

While marching from the Chippewa toward Queenston, Brown sent General Winfield Scott in advance of the main force to be on the lookout for the British armies marching to engage them. On the way, Scott passed a tavern on Portage Road near Horseshoe Falls Overlook on the afternoon of July 25. As he was approaching, his scouts saw British officers rushing out of the tavern and fleeing on horseback. The last one to depart taunted the Americans by saluting them. Scott hurried into the tavern to question the owner, a widow named Deborah Willson who informed the Americans that "If you had only been here sooner you would have captured the British officers."[12] Scott was unsure whether or not to believe Mrs. Willson. He was right to worry. She appears to have tricked her interrogators by telling them the nearby British force was much smaller than it really was. But, she directed Scott to Lundy's Lane, a dirt trail named for a Quaker settler named William Lundy that ran west from Portage Road. Scott set off in that direction with his advance force, doubting the British would really be there.[13]

The British were there . . . waiting with 1,700 soldiers. Scott's men had marched into the trap and were exposed in an open field when they realized their error. Despite the mistake, Scott rushed his 1,500 men forward to battle. He also sent riders to inform General Brown to bring his brigades forward to the fight.[14]

The British were in position on a hill with seven artillery batteries near a church and cemetery atop the hill. They were in command of good ground—artillery dug in on the high ground, superior numbers, cover in the form of forests at their backs, and the Americans marching through open fields in front of them. But the British delayed their attack. As Scott would later note, "by standing fast, the salutary impression was made upon the enemy that the whole American reserve was at hand and would soon assault his flanks."[15] Scott's apparent confidence gave Generals Drummond and Riall pause as they waited to see if the main American army was being held in reserve. This only gave the main American army time to arrive at the battle.

Never one to shy away from fight, at 6:00 p.m. Scott ordered his men to charge. The Americans tried to storm the hill but were beaten back by a blistering barrage of muskets and cannon fire. Scott was wounded and ordered his men to pull back and regroup. He planned another assault. However, British reinforcements had rushed to the scene of the fighting. Though greatly outnumbered and outpositioned on the high ground, Scott did not retreat. Fortunately for him, General Brown also arrived at the battle with American reinforcements. What started as a large battle now turned into a bloodbath between two massive armies who fought well into the night.

Scott's brigade was taking heavy losses, but he held. Brown was in support of Scott, but he did not bring his entire army. Worried that the British might also be marching across the Niagara and into America, he kept General Porter's brigade there to guard the border. The immediate problem, however, for Scott's embattled brigade was the cannons on the high ground. At 10:00 that evening General Brown used Scott's forces as a sacrificial ploy. They stood their ground in the center, absorbing the attention of the British army while Colonel James Miller was sent around behind the hill to attempt to capture and silence the artillery fire. With 300 men from the 21st Infantry, perhaps the most seasoned unit in the American army, having fought with Harrison at Tippecanoe, Hull at Detroit, and Wilkinson along the St. Lawrence, Miller snuck under cover of darkness around the British lines. Undetected, he managed to climb the hillside cemetery where the artillery batteries had been organized. When his men were within only twenty yards of the cannons, he ordered them to charge the rest of the distance up the hill.

With fixed bayonets, Miller's 21st boys overwhelmed the British gunners. One of the British gunners who survived the fight, recalled that Miller "charged to the very muzzles of our cannon and actually bayoneted the artillery-men who were at their guns."[16] Unfortunately for Miller, General Drummond was alerted to what was happening on the hilltop and ordered the 89th Foot, which was nearby, to counterattack from the church cemetery. Under cover of heavy fire from the main British army, the 89th charged up the hill to attack Miller. Colonel Miller was a physically big man who led his troops in the fighting, inspiring them to hold the artillery batteries at all costs. When ordered to take the hill, Colonel Miller had responded, "I'll try, Sir!" Throughout the battle, his men emboldened themselves by crying out "I'll try, Sir!" and "We'll try, Sir!" Their motto worked. Miller's brave men beat back three separate attacks from the 89th, all the while enduring musket and cannon fire raining down upon them. The cannons remained in the hands of the Americans on top of the hill. Miller described the fight as "one of the most desperately fought actions ever experienced in America."[17]

## INTO THE NIGHT

The fighting was so intense that smoke billowed across the battlefield, further cutting visibility during the night battle. During the chaos, soldiers on both sides were mistakenly shot by their own men. The sway of the battle favored one side and then the other. While the main British line was strengthened when General Phineas Riall arrived with additional reinforcements, under the constant attack from Scott's men, it was forced to pull back. The Americans soon surrounded Riall's army and, during the fighting that ensued, Riall was shot in the arm, which he later lost on account of the severity of the wound. In an effort to save their commander, Riall's aides escorted the general back through a wooded patch and out of the line of fire. While doing so they encountered soldiers in the dark woods and announced to them: "Make way for General Riall!" To their horror, the response from the dark was: "We are Americans and now you are our prisoners."[18] Riall countered, demanding "What is the meaning of this?" Captain Daniel Ketchum, who was leading a small infantry unit up the hill, responded simply, "You are our prisoner, sir."[19] Riall would be the highest ranking British officer captured during the war.[20]

The American commander nearly met the same fate. General Brown rode forward to congratulate Colonel Miller and his battle-worn men. While en route, he noticed that the British had pulled back, but suspected they did so only to lure the Americans forward. To warn his men of a possible trap or counterattack, Brown quickly rode to Lundy's Lane to gather intelligence on the British movements. But in the dark, he mistakenly rode up on a British unit. His aide, 19-year-old Captain Ambrose Spencer, bravely rushed ahead and yelled out, "What regiment is that?" When he heard the reply: "The Royal Scots, Sir," he quickly thought to impersonate a British accent, ordering "Stand you fast, Scotch Royals!" Captain Spencer then sped back to General Brown and escorted him to safety.[21]

By 11:00 p.m., both armies were exhausted from the hand-to-hand combat. They had sustained major casualties and most of the generals and senior officers were dead, wounded, or captured. General Brown suffered a bullet shot in his thigh and had to be carried off the field. His trusted aide, Captain Spencer, who had just saved his life, was killed and his best officer—General Scott—was also wounded. Scott was still fighting when he took another bullet to the shoulder and had to be carried to the rear. Command was passed to Captain Abraham Hull, the son of the disgraced general whose hesitancy and cowardice undermined the initial invasion of Canada. In an effort to redeem his family name, the young Hull ordered another charge. But he was shot and killed. Even the British commander, General Drummond, was wounded.

General Brown was losing blood from two bullet wounds and thought he was dying. As such, he gave the order to find General Scott in order to hand over command. But the wounded Scott was also thought to be dying so Brown desperately asked an aide named Captain Loring Austin to find General Ripley and hand over the army to him. Unfortunately, with the senior command structure incapacitated, Ripley decided in the predawn hours of July 26 to withdraw.

Unbeknownst to him, the Americans were in control of the battle. The army fell back to Chippewa. From the cemetery hill, Colonel Miller and his brave men protested and were reluctant to leave the hard-fought high ground. Miller wanted to take the cannons with him as a prize from the battle, but did not have enough horses still alive. He reluctantly abandoned the hill and joined the retreating American army. As the American army retreated, General Brown ordered that all bridges be destroyed to prevent the British from following them. The Americans need not have bothered. The British were beaten and were in no mood for more fighting. The exhausted American army made it to Chippewa, where they finally ate and slept, then withdrew all the way to Fort Erie.[22]

In the first light of morning, General Drummond's staff observed that the American army was gone and they promptly declared victory.

The casualty counts were staggering. The British lost nearly ninety men dead, 559 wounded, and almost 200 missing, with dozens taken prisoner. The Americans suffered 173 dead, hundreds wounded, and dozens missing and taken prisoner. As dawn gave way to day and the British army slowly walked across the battlefield, they observed a ghastly site. Dead and wounded bodies and the corpses of countless horses were strewn across the open field and hill. Too tired to dig graves, the British uncharacteristically piled the dead together and burned them. Both sides claimed victory. However the British colonel, Hercules Scott, observed "we boast of a 'Great Victory' but in my opinion it was nearly equal on both sides." Indeed, it was a costly tie and a battle rightly celebrated by many Canadians as their Gettysburg.[23]

## OUT IN DISGRACE AND WITH A WHIMPER

There would be no further attempt to invade Canada. After the failed summer campaigns, the Canadian theater of operations fizzled to a series of small raids and skirmishes. One of the raiders throughout 1814 in the western reaches of Upper Canada was Colonel John Campbell, who sacked small Canadian villages such as Charlottesville (also known as Turkey Point), Long Point, Patterson's Creek, Port Dover, and Port Talbot. His disgraceful actions resulted in the destruction of houses and plundering of farms and mills, the killing of livestock and burning of crops, and the harassment of civilians. One eyewitness account described the barbarous raids as follows.

> On the 16th of August, a party of about 100 Americans and Indians landed at Port Talbot on that lake (Lake Erie); and robbed 50 heads of families of all their horses, and every article of household furniture, and wearing apparel, belonging to them. The number of individuals who were thus thrown naked and destitute upon the world, amounted to 49 men, 37 women— three of the latter, and two of the former, nearly 70 years of age—and 148 children. A great many of the more respectable inhabitants were not only robbed, but carried off as prisoners: among them, a member of the House of Assembly, Mr. Barnwell, though ill of fever and ague.[24]

Campbell's behavior so embarrassed the Americans that General Brown brought him before a court of inquiry and nearly had him court-martialed. While this was one of Campbell's last raids, it was certainly not the only such action by American forces. In July of 1814, American forces laid waste to the town of St. David's. Nor were the British through with their own attacks on civilian populations. Indeed, Vice Admiral Alexander Cochrane delivered direct orders to forces under his command to "Destroy and lay waste such towns and districts as you may find assailable."[25]

The effort to invade Canada ended in disgrace. The last skirmish on Canadian soil occurred on October 20, 1814, near Cook's Mills at Lyons Creek. It was led by Major General George Izard in command of a massive army of 8,000. They were met by Lieutenant General Sir Gordon Drummond, who was greatly outnumbered. The Americans tried unsuccessfully to outflank their opponents but were driven off by Congreve rockets and a stingy defense. Had Izard pressed forward he could have easily overrun the outgunned British. But he did not. He had suffered sixty-seven dead and inflicted only nineteen casualties on the smaller British army in the brief confrontation. Izard pulled his army back and both commanders claimed victory. There was not much will to fight by either army, and the last engagement of the war ended in a whimper.

# 26

# VICTORY ON LAKE CHAMPLAIN

## THE ARMADA ARRIVES

After Napoleon's abdication in 1814, the British were finally in a position to send extra ships and troops to North America. An impatient Earl of Bathurst, the government minister in charge of the Crown's North American colony and war, informed Governor George Prevost that he was sending "twelve of the most effective Regiments of the Army [that served] under the Duke of Wellington together with three Companies of Artillery on the same service."[1] These were not just any troops; they were battle-hardened veterans who had defeated the powerful French army. The Earl's orders arrived on June 3, 1814, and his expectation was that this massive army would end the war. Prevost would soon command a staggering 29,000 men in Canada, enough to destroy Sackets Harbor, control Lakes Erie, Ontario, and Champlain, and march on the Michigan territory. From there, Prevost was instructed to march south and invade the United States.

However, the hesitant Prevost responded that he would move as soon as all the promised force arrived. He also warned that his "defensive measures only will be practicable, until the complete command of Lake Ontario and Champlain shall be obtained, which cannot be expected, before September."[2] Obviously, this was not the response the Earl of the British high command wanted to hear. The Earl shot back, warning Prevost: "If you shall allow the present campaign to close without having undertaken offensive measures, you will very seriously disappoint the expectations of the Prince Regent and the country."[3]

As promised, the powerful British force arrived at the St. Lawrence on an armada of ships. The only problem now facing Prevost, was how to feed, provision, and clothe such a massive force. The answer came from his enemy. American farmers and businesses in New York and New England had been supplying beef to the British army throughout the war and the new temptation of sizeable payments in gold from the Crown overruled any sense of patriotism.

The American general, George Izard, upon learning that his countrymen were supplying the enemy was so irate that he fired off a dispatch to the War Department complaining:

> This confirms a fact not only disgraceful to our countrymen but seriously detrimental to the public interest. From the St. Lawrence to the ocean an open disregard prevails for the laws prohibiting intercourse with the enemy . . . On the eastern side of Lake Champlain the high roads are insufficient for the cattle pouring into Canada. Like herds of buffaloes they press through the forests, making paths for themselves. Were it not for these supplies, the British forces in Canada would soon be suffering from famine.[4]

Governor Prevost even altered the path of his invasion so as to not march through Vermont, which provided much of his supplies, and interfere with the herds of cattle heading north. With reinforcements arriving in North America, the British launched their three-prong invasion of the United States. While the Royal Navy would sail troops to the Chesapeake for the center prong and to the Gulf Coast for the southern prong, a grand army of 11,000 men was organized near the Canadian border for the initial northern prong of the invasion. Led by Prevost, the army marched in late August of 1814 for Plattsburgh, which sat on the western shoreline of Lake Champlain [see Map 2 in Appendix].

Prevost marched along a similar route used by the British general "Gentleman Johnny Burgoyne" during the American Revolution when he attempted to divide New York from New England.[5] Like Burgoyne before him, Prevost intended to strike a decisive blow against his enemy on their soil. He had managed to defend Canada, repelling multiple invasion attempts despite a lack of supplies and troops. It was now time to end the war once and for all!

Any fortification would be vulnerable to a force of this size, but the Americans had mistakenly withdrawn roughly 4,000 men from the garrison at Plattsburgh and sent them under the command of General George Izard to Sackets Harbor. This is where they assumed the northern invasion would strike. Even though he was in command of an army of regulars, Izard had heard reports of the size of the invading British army. He thus predicted the British would control New York and New England in three days.[6]

The general commanding Plattsburgh's defenses, Alexander Macomb, therefore had only 1,500 regulars. When he was given the alarming news that one of the largest armies ever assembled during the war was headed toward Plattsburgh, Macomb rushed to recruit roughly 2,000 militiamen to supplement his meager army. To buy himself time, Macomb wisely sent units in the direction of the British army with orders to burn bridges, cut down trees and place them on the road south, and create other roadblocks to slow the invasion. He also assigned men to strike at the massive army along the trail to Plattsburgh. Because the majority of the militia had been hastily recruited they lacked proper training. Time and again, the New York militia had infamously refused to march into Canada to fight. But this time it would be different. The New York and Vermont volunteers who lived near the lake were now defending their homes.

Governor Prevost's army crossed the border on August 31 and arrived on the outskirts of Plattsburgh on September 6. They were engaged by a small American force making a stand on the south bank of the Saranac River, which ran through the town and into the lake. General Macomb pulled his main army across the Saranac River and to the fort on a bluff overlooking the Plattsburgh Bay. Had Prevost struck the Americans right away, it is likely he would have crushed the small, unprepared force and, in doing so, changed history. But, he delayed.

Over the protests of his commanders, Prevost spent four days camped in Plattsburgh preparing for the conflict. Although Generals Thomas Brisbane, Manley Power, and Frederick Robinson were older and far more experienced than Prevost, and fresh off the war in Europe, the governor of Canada fancied himself the expert on North America. The British generals were outraged with Prevost's delays and war plans, which they believed unmasked him as a bureaucrat and not a general. Grumbled General Robinson after the battle: "It appears to me that the army moved against Plattsburgh without any regularly digested plan by Sir George Prevost."[7] Prevost was hesitant by disposition. But he also waivered because the Americans had sabotaged the main bridge across the Saranac River in order to give Captain George Downie time to sail his flotilla of warships to Plattsburgh to destroy the harbor and American navy there. Prevost planned a simultaneous attack by land and on the lake.

## SHOWDOWN ON THE LAKE

Nestled between New York and Vermont, Lake Champlain runs north-south through the Canadian border but drains northward into the St. Lawrence. It was a key target for the British. The area between New York and Montreal, encompassing Lake Champlain, the Hudson River, and Richelieu River, had long been desired—and fought over—by the Americans, British, and several Indian nations. It was the site of bitter fighting during the French and Indian War and the American Revolution (including by young officers such as Benedict Arnold, Aaron Burr, and James Wilkinson).

America controlled Lake Champlain until the summer of 1813 when British ships defeated two American sloops used to defend the lake, the *Growler* and *Eagle*. The British then began ship building on the lake in earnest. But the Americans had a secret weapon on the lake—Thomas Macdonough.

Commander Macdonough, was born in Delaware in 1783 and enjoyed a successful career in the navy after enlisting at sixteen. For unknown reasons, he changed the spelling of his last name from McDonough to Macdonough. He gained distinction serving in the Mediterranean aboard the USS *Enterprise* under the heroic Stephen Decatur and was even part of the secret mission that burned the USS *Philadelphia* after it was captured off the coast of Tripoli by the Barbary pirates. As a young midshipman, Macdonough served on the USS *Ganges* which captured three French ships in the West Indies in 1800, then as an officer on the famed USS *Constellation*, and was later given command of the USS *Wasp* and charged with enforcing President Jefferson's trade embargo of 1807. Macdonough was a bold leader, fearless warrior, and skilled sailor. The Americans were wise to place him in charge of Lake Champlain in October of 1812.

Like his fellow officer, Oliver Hazard Perry on Lake Erie, Macdonough prioritized the building of ships and training of his sailors. The highlight of his efforts was the launch on April 11, 1814, of the USS *Saratoga*, named to remind the British of the great Revolutionary victory. The *Saratoga* was armed with eight long-range guns, six mid-sized guns, and twelve smaller carronades, and was crewed by 210 sailors. Macdonough also had a new steamship named *Ticonderoga*, sporting a dozen cannons and five carronades, but the new technology on the ship frequently malfunctioned. The American fleet included a smaller ship confiscated from the British and renamed the *Eagle*, carrying eight mid-sized cannons and a dozen carronades, and was captained by Robert Henley, as well as the small sloop, *Preble*, with seven cannons, and ten small gunboats, each armed with a cannon.

Macdonough had beaten his British counterpart, Lieutenant Daniel Pring, and reasserted American control over the vital lake. Even though Pring was a decent officer, he was disliked by Sir James Yeo, who commanded British naval forces on the lakes. Yeo replaced Pring with Captain Peter Fisher, but then tired of his new commander and replaced him with Captain George Downie who, like Macdonough, was in his early thirties at the time of the battle.

Downie was the son of a clergyman, born in Ireland in the village of Ross. He joined the navy at an early age and enjoyed a distinguished career, serving in the West Indies and elsewhere. He assumed command of the HMS *Sea Horse* in 1804 and was later promoted to captain and assigned to Lake Ontario. However, Sir Yeo reassigned Downie to Lake Champlain after firing his two predecessors. Downie was the most—and perhaps only—experienced British sailor on the lake.

In anticipation of a naval engagement on the lake, the British also established aggressive shipbuilding efforts on the 100-mile long lake—from opposite shorelines, the British from the northern reaches of the lake in Canada, and the Americans from the southern half of the lake. The British believed they had naval superiority on the lake, having constructed the 36-gun frigate HMS *Confiance*, which was by far the largest warship on the lake. But thirty of the *Confiance's* cannons were long-range guns, which would later prove to be problematic. The warship was launched on September 2, 1814.

Downie's fleet on the lake also included the HMS *Linnet*, an 85-foot long brig armed with sixteen long-range cannons, two smaller sloops, the *Chub* and *Finch* (which had been the American warships *Eagle* and *Growler* until they were captured and renamed), and a dozen small gunboats, each with one cannon.

The number of ships, guns, and sailors was roughly even on Lake Champlain at the time of the famous battle. While the British had more long-range cannons, the Americans had more carronades which were better in close-range combat. Macdonough also had the advantage of experience on the lake and was fighting from the deeper water at the southern end of the lake by the Plattsburgh Bay. Atop the nearby bluff, his navy was supported by General Macomb's artillery.

## THE WAR'S MOST DECISIVE NAVAL BATTLE

Commander Macdonough selected a bend in the lake for his fleet. It was a wise choice. If the British had favorable winds behind their sails when attacking from the north, Macdonough knew that as soon as they rounded the sharp bend by the mouth of the bay it would become a headwind. The British ships would not be able to maneuver. Moreover, there were several rocky shoals near the bend, the location of which Macdonough and his sailors knew. He was correct in guessing that the British were unaware of this.

On September 11, when the order was given by Governor Prevost for the British to attack, Macdonough anchored his ships just behind the bend, aligning them sideways in order to deliver broadsides. The American ships stretched across the mouth of the bay. He knew that the British, when they veered sharply westward to enter the bay, would be sailing with their bows facing forward. They would therefore have little firepower at the moment they encountered the American fleet. The enterprising commander also built a system of winches connected to his anchors. This would enable the fleet to be quickly turned from side to side without sails or winds. Lastly, Macdonough placed his small ships on either end of the entrance to the bay in order to guard the shallows.

Captain Downie's fleet was not quite ready to fight. But Prevost, under pressure to commence the battle, grew tired of his naval captain's delays. In a dispatch delivered to Downie, Prevost warned: "In consequence of your communication of yesterday I have postponed action until your squadron is prepared to co-operate. I need not dwell with you on the evils resulting to both services from delay." Against his better judgment, Downie ordered his fleet to sail down the lake to Plattsburgh. His flagship, *Confiance*, was not yet completed. This mistake would cost the British dearly, as was observed by the noted naval historian Admiral Alfred Thayer, who commented, "It scarcely needs the habit of a naval seaman to recognize that even three or four days' grace for preparation would immensely increase efficiency."[8] Downie was still gathering crew—who were untrained. The warship lacked adequate guns and cannonballs and her carpenters were still working even as she sailed into combat.

Just before midnight on September 9, the British squadron set sail. The winds on the lake shifted and they now faced headwinds, making it impossible to sail to Plattsburgh. Early in the morning on September 11 the winds filled their sails and Downie was able to continue. There was still no sign of the Americans, but he correctly figured they were behind the bend hidden by the heights at the bend, known as Cumberland Head. The larger British warships were only about seven miles from the Americans.

Downie ordered his ships to pause around 5:00 a.m. in order to give the smaller ships in his squadron time to catch up and form lines beside his flagship. Hoping to both signal Governor Prevost that he was ready to attack and draw the Americans out into the open, Downie ordered his cannons be fired without shot in them. The British captain also smelled a trap. He personally rowed a boat out to the point where the lake bent sharply into the bay to reconnoiter the area. What he saw was bad.

## OUTMANEUVERED

Macdonough had his ships aligned side-by-side, prepared to fire broadsides. To inspire his men, the commander flew a sail with large words reading "Impressed seamen call on every man to do his duty!"[9] Downie was worried but sailed to engage the Americans, lining his ships up in order so that when they turned into the bay the smaller ships would be aligned to fight the smaller American ships and his bigger ships the bigger American ships. Macdonough had a few more ships, so the British commander was forced to use small gunboats against the *Ticonderoga* and *Preble* in hopes of occupying them long enough that they would not be able to engage his larger ships.

At 9:00 that morning, Downie's fleet rounded Cumberland Head and the battle began. Downie led sixteen warships, the massive *Confiance*, three mid-sized ships (*Chub*, *Finch*, and *Linnet*), and a dozen small gunboats. Waiting for him was Captain Macdonough with fourteen ships, including three larger ships (*Eagle*, *Saratoga*, and *Ticonderoga*), one mid-sized ship (*Preble*), and ten small gunboats. Downie had more guns and ships, but his cannons were for long-range strikes. Downie hoped Macdonough would sail out to meet him, thus allowing the powerful long-range British guns to pulverize the American fleet from a safe distance. But Macdonough did not take the bait.

The only advantage Downie had was that he assumed Governor Prevost's grand army would defeat the outmatched Americans in the fort. A quick victory by the huge British army would prevent the American fort from firing artillery down on his fleet and, once the fort was taken, the cannons could be trained on Macdonough's squadron. However, when

Downie turned the bend in the lake to attack, Prevost's army was idle. The simultaneous naval and land invasion never occurred.

As soon as Downie's ships sailed around the sharp bend, their sails fell flat. There was no wind as Macdonough had predicted. In close quarters, the short-range American guns proved far more effective. Unable to sail or turn, the British gunners were forced to try and adjust their unwieldy cannons. It did not work. Macdonough's ships simply winched into position to strike their opponents. The HMS *Linnet* fired first but missed. The British fired desperately, knowing their ships were sitting ducks. A cannonball struck the USS *Saratoga* but destroyed only the chicken crates and some food rations. One rooster lived through the explosion, flapping about in shock on the deck, leading the American sailors to let out a loud cheer. One of them yelled that it was a tough bird. And the Americans let loose with broadsides from the entire squadron.

The British ships sustained major damage, especially the HMS *Chub*, whose masts and sails came crashing down on the deck. But Downie ordered his ships to reload and fire. The British had heavier guns and they hit their mark. One of Macdonough's ships, the *Saratoga*, burst into flames from two heated shots from Downie's large flagship, the *Confiance*. But the Americans quickly put out the fire and the *Saratoga* maneuvered to hit the *Confiance* with broadside after broadside.

The wind and Macdonough's ingenious winches allowed the American ships to gain the upper hand against the idle British flotilla. After his fleet fired broadsides into the British, Macdonough ordered the ships to use the winches to spin around 180 degrees and hit the British with broadsides from their unscathed sides. The USS *Eagle* was also hit hard and damaged by the larger British cannons. But her captain cut loose the anchor and sailed around the *Saratoga* and next to the *Confiance* with one working topsail. From the other side of the *Confiance*, the *Eagle* joined in the bombardment of the pride of the British on Lake Champlain.

On board the *Confiance*, wood and metal flew about, sails and masts fell heavily to the deck, and a large cannon was blown completely off its mounting. The massive gun landed on Captain Downie and killed him instantly. One sailor recalled the tragic loss of their brave commander, noting that "His skin was not broken, a black mark about the size of a small plate was the only visible injury. His watch was found flattened, with its hands pointing to the very second at which he received the fatal blow."[10]

The *Confiance* was in trouble. Downie's second-in-command, Lieutenant Henry Robinson, attempted to sail the big ship away from its attackers but without a winch or sufficient wind, the damaged hulk only turned far enough that her front and back faced the Americans. She was unable to fire broadsides. The *Saratoga* and *Eagle* fired another round of deadly broadsides into the wreck. Water was now pouring into the large ship, which began to list heavily to one side. The crew scrambled to try and move cannons from the listing side of the ship in order to balance her. It did not work. The ship was sinking.

With over 100 cannonball holes in her, the *Confiance* struck her colors after one hour of the lop-sided battle. A few minutes later the *Linnet* followed suit, followed quickly by the small British ships and gunboats. The surviving British officers were brought to the Saratoga to present their swords to Captain Macdonough. After greeting his vanquished foes with the customary bows, Macdonough announced, "Gentlemen, return your swords into your scabbards and wear them. You are worthy of them."[11]

In one of the most decisive naval battles of the war, the British fleet and its powerful flagship were in flames, sinking, or wrecked. It was also a particularly bloody naval battle. The Americans suffered roughly fifty dead and fifty wounded, while the British sustained hundreds of casualties and about 300 British sailors were taken prisoner.[12]

## THE BATTLE OF PLATTSBURGH

Governor Prevost ordered the massive naval and land attack on Plattsburgh to begin on September 11. His army would strike the American fort atop an overlook by the lake while Captain Downie would hit the harbor. With a simultaneous attack, the fort could not support the ships and harbor, while the ships could not fire on the invading army.

Major General Frederick Robinson was sent by Prevost to perform a flanking attack on the fort at Plattsburgh, while British artillery units were placed on the other side of the fort. A third, smaller force was assigned the task of performing a fake assault at the sabotaged bridge in hopes of either distracting American firepower or drawing the defenders out of the fort to strike at the unit pretending to be repairing the bridge. Prevost would attack with the main army, numbering into the thousands.

However, nothing went as planned. Prevost never moved his army into position. His commanders had been waiting since well before dawn for the order to attack the fort. All the while, they listened to the cannon blasts from the lake, indicating that Downie was attacking the American flotilla in the bay. But, no signal to attack ever came. Frustrated, General Robinson finally rode to Prevost's headquarters to demand an answer. Prevost delayed until 10:00 that morning and when he gave the command to attack, his orders were unclear. It took another hour for the invasion of the fort to begin. By then, it was too late to save Downie's navy. During the wait, the British army heard the cheers from the victorious Americans.

The three strike forces failed to coordinate the timing of their attacks. As the British marched to hit the fort's flank, they had to cross a small creek. After becoming momentarily lost, when they attempted to forge the creek they came under intense fire. Macomb had anticipated their very move and had stationed a small unit on his flank at the edge of the creek. They were dug in waiting for the British and succeeded in repelling the assault. On the other side of the fort, the Royal Artillery commenced their bombardment. But Macomb's gunners inside the fort responded with deadly accuracy, knocking out the artillery. And, the decoy force at the bridge was met by an inspired American unit who made quick work of them as well.

For some inexplicable reason, while the three advance wings of the attack were taking their lumps and the massive main force was sitting idle waiting for the order to attack the fort, Prevost sent a dispatch for all his commanders to return to headquarters. He called off the attack. The largest British force ever assembled on American soil was ordered by the governor to begin what would be a long march back to Canada. From inside the fort, General Macomb and his troops could not believe what they were seeing. It was as if Prevost was channeling Dearborn, Hull, Smyth, Van Rensselaer, Wilkinson, and other disastrous American commanders. Macomb did not have the numbers to pursue Prevost's army. But, he held out. It was a great victory for the Americans. The British had lost their entire navy on the lake as well as their naval commander, and had sustained roughly 700 casualties on land and on the lake. The Americans had less than 200 casualties.

After news of the embarrassing campaign reached Britain, Sir Prevost was called home where he endured savage criticism from his fellow commanders, politicians, and the press. Sir Yeo, the naval commander, who deserved his own tongue-lashing, blamed Prevost for the failure of the British to invade America from the north. All the way down to Lieutenant Pring, who earlier had lost control of Lake Champlain to Captain Thomas Macdonough, heads would roll. Pring was nearly court-martialed and he and other commanders were forced to either resign or had their reputations destroyed. Amazingly, Prevost escaped court martial thanks to two unusual events. One of them was the word of the highly respected Duke of Wellington, who wrote:

> Whether Sir George Prevost was right or wrong in his decision at Lake Champlain is more than I can tell . . . I have told the ministers repeatedly that a naval superiority on the lakes is a *sine qua non* of success in war on the frontier of Canada, even if our object should be solely defensive.[13]

There was even a call in Britain for the respected hero of the Napoleonic war to replace Prevost and lead the war in North America. The Americans, however, were fortunate that the Duke of Wellington declined. It was he who would destroy Napoleon at Waterloo. The other event that spared Prevost from court martial was that he died the night before his trial.

As for Captain Macdonough, he became the latest of several American naval heroes. The humble hero remarked, "In one month, from a poor lieutenant I became a rich man."[14] The great American president and naval historian, Teddy Roosevelt, was less subdued, saying of Macdonough: "Down to the time of the Civil War, he is the greatest figure in our naval history." Roosevelt even maintained that Lake Champlain was "The greatest naval battle of the war."[15] Indeed, Macdonough's tactics and Prevost's incompetence likely saved New England and New York from complete destruction.

# 27

# "THE BLADENSBURG RACES"

## THE CHESAPEAKE THEATER

With a shift in war sentiments on both sides of the Atlantic, peace negotiations began on August 8, 1814, in Ghent, a scenic city located in the Flemish region of Belgium. The very next day, the United States signed the Treaty of Fort Jackson with the Creek nation, officially ending what had been a long and violent conflict, and one that was unwinnable for the Creeks. Of course, none of this brought an end to hostilities in the War of 1812. While many Americans hoped for peace, the fighting continued unabated. Only one month after delegates arrived in Ghent, Governor Prevost marched the largest British army ever to step foot on North American soil to invade Lake Champlain. It was the initial salvo in Britain's three-pronged invasion of America. And it failed miserably.

All the while, President James Madison understood that, with most of his army along the Canadian border, the nation's capital and critical Chesapeake Bay region were vulnerable. Because of the size of the bay, the fact that the Potomac River that ran up to the nation's capital, and the extensive system of waterways in the area, it would be nearly impossible to defend the city by water under the best of circumstances. But the American navy was virtually nonexistent on the Chesapeake. The British had destroyed most American warships operating on the bay and now controlled the vital waterway. The city's defenses amounted to a few coastal batteries and privateers who occasionally harassed the Royal Navy. It was no better on land. Only a small "army" of 500 poorly trained regulars were garrisoned near the capital.

It was during this critical hour that an old Revolutionary War hero stepped forward. His name was Joshua Barney. Through the war, the aged hero functioned as a privateer, wreaking havoc on British commercial ships and making an enormous amount of money doing so. Realizing the futility of trying to build and launch warships on the Chesapeake, Barney proposed dispatching a fleet of shallow barges mounted with oars, sails, and a cannon on both the bow and stern. In the confined shallows of the Chesapeake system, they could create problems for the large British warships. He likened the situation to a swarm of angry hornets assaulting a large bear.

During the spring and summer of 1814, a few dozen of Barney's barges were launched. In the shallows they gave the British headaches, but on open, choppy waters they handled poorly. Still, they delayed and distracted the British until June 1, which was a fateful day in the war. Barney's barges engaged Admiral George Cockburn's fleet, one that included the massive, seventy-four-gun HMS *Dragon*. The Americans were beaten so soundly and quickly that they were forced to flee up the Patuxent River. At low tide the river was too shallow for such large warships to follow, but the battle occurred at high tide. When Cockburn's fleet sailed up the small river in pursuit of Barney, he observed to his astonishment that the region around the capital city was unprotected by forts. The British decided at that moment to change strategies and march by land on the capital and important port of Baltimore.[1]

While Cockburn blockaded the Patuxent, Potomac, and Chesapeake, a large armada arrived off the coast in the middle of August under the command of Admiral Alexander Cochrane. They transported 5,000 of Britain's most experienced troops under one of Britain's most celebrated commanders, Major General Robert Ross.

Born in Ireland in 1766, Ross enjoyed a long, successful military career. A veteran of wars in Europe and Africa, he was tough and was known to be a demanding leader who prioritized the training of his troops. The general was at the side of the famed Duke of Wellington during Britain's Napoleonic campaign in Spain, where he had two horses shot out from under him while fighting in the Pyrenees. With Ross and Cochrane in charge, the central prong of the invasion had begun. The U.S. War Department had not even prepared for the defense of the capital city. Suddenly, the country was fighting for its very existence.

## A CITY UNDEFENDED

A month prior, on July 14, President Madison had warned his generals of attack and asked them to prepare for the worst. However, Secretary of War

John Armstrong naively maintained that the British would not attack the capital city, but would target the far larger, strategic port of Baltimore. He was only half right. The fact that Armstrong and others failed to see the symbolic importance of losing the nation's capital reflected the prevailing notion at the time that the United States was more a collection of states than a true nation. Americans lacked the attachment to their capital than, say, the French or British had to Paris or London. Most Americans were loyal to their home states and state capitals. It is also possible that Armstrong, who desired the presidency and had proved himself an unfit war leader, was positioning Madison to fail. For instance, the secretary also demonstrated resentment to James Monroe, the secretary of state who was Armstrong's chief cabinet rival to succeed Madison.[2]

While Armstrong was making contingency plans to take refuge in Pennsylvania, President Madison hastily ordered that the War Department organize the capital city as a military district. Even the disgraced general, James Wilkinson, realized Washington was in trouble. The conniving Wilkinson stepped forward with an offer to defend the city, but he was angling only to overturn his court martial and repair his reputation. The president wisely turned him down. But the president and his war secretary could not agree on the city's defense. Armstrong favored giving command to Brigadier General Moses Porter, an able fighter and Revolutionary War hero who commanded the nearby military district of Norfolk. However, Madison had grown weary of Armstrong and overruled him, selecting a 39-year-old attorney from Baltimore named William Winder.

Brigadier General Winder was well connected politically—his uncle, Levin Winder, was the governor of Maryland—but lacked an understanding of military tactics. The lawyer-turned-general's resume included participating in the disastrous Niagara campaign where he lost the Battle of Stoney Creek and was captured. But the younger Winder had assisted Madison during the war by helping to negotiate prisoner swaps with the British. Otherwise, he would prove to be a terrible choice. The only hope was that Winder's uncle would mobilize his militia to defend the most important city in his state. To that end, Governor Winder did order that 6,000 Maryland militiamen be called to service. However, once again incompetence carried the day. When General Ross began the invasion of the Chesapeake, the governor had raised only 250 volunteers! In desperation, realizing his city and state would be attacked, the governor begged Secretary Armstrong for troops. Armstrong ignored the request, still bitter that the president had overruled his choice to lead the defense of the capital city.[3]

On August 15, nearly 5,000 soldiers under Cochrane, Cockburn, and Ross sailed up the Chesapeake. All three commanders were known to advocate vicious raids on civilian populations and were driven by a simmering, personal need to destroy the Americans. The enormous British convoy of dozens of ships sailed to the upper Patuxent. On August 19, they disembarked at Benedict, Maryland, only twenty-four miles from the nation's capital [see Map 6 in Appendix].

Ross marched his army to Washington destroying homes, burning buildings, ransoming property, and taking prisoners on his path of destruction. He was surprised to discover that no American force opposed him. The only shots or even sounds of shots the British encountered were the distant explosions from Commodore Barney, who ordered that his barges be blown up, lest they be captured. Marching beside the Patuxent while their warships sailed in escort alongside, the only thing that slowed the British army was the humidity of a Washington summer. It was a particularly broiling August. One British infantryman, George Robert Gleig, described the situation as follows: "A greater number of soldiers dropped out of the ranks, and fell behind from fatigue, than I recollect to have seen in any march in the Peninsula [Spain] of thrice its duration."[4]

It is probable that Ross would have entered the American capital city without encountering a single soldier to oppose him if only he had proceeded straight to Washington after disembarking. However, the British assumed that bridges along the way would be destroyed, trees would be felled and placed across the road, and that scouting parties would attack them at key points on the road to Washington. Indeed, while marching by Upper Marlborough, the Washington naval yards, and along the Potomac at Anacostia, General Ross and Admiral Cockburn became alarmed that none of the bridges were defended or destroyed. They suspected a trap. As such, they decided to detour roughly eight miles out of their way. The maneuver was designed to throw off the Americans who might be monitoring their movements and planning a major counteroffensive.

The British need not have bothered. Unbeknownst to them, the Americans had no idea where they were and had not planned any defenses. American commanders had forgotten the guerilla tactics used by George Washington a little over three decades earlier. As a result, the British ended up circling the city and entering from the northeast.[5]

The British were also delayed by a curious message received late at night on August 23 from Admiral Cochrane. Inexplicably, the letter indicated that Cochrane had turned around and sailed back down the Patuxent and dropped anchor. General Ross did not know what to make of the message and assumed that he was to halt his advance. Admiral Cockburn, however, argued that they had gone too far to stop. He wanted to attack Washington. The bizarre message was par for the course in the War of 1812, a war defined by miscommunications, primitive transportation systems and mapping, and ineptness by commanders. Ross and Cockburn decided to camp for the night. The result was that the Americans, who were far too slow to act, had time to finally blow up two bridges across the Potomac and organize a defense of the city. In the morning, for unknown reasons the British army turned north and marched to Bladensburg rather than directly to the capital.

Meanwhile, William Winder, the general in charge of the defending the city, was rushing his army of 120 dragoons, 300 regulars, and 1,500 militiamen frantically around the Chesapeake looking for the invading British force. However, all this activity simply exhausted his untrained army. At the same time, President Madison and James Monroe were out on horseback scouting for the British. Madison, a scholar who had not served in uniform and suffered from poor health, nonetheless managed to ride twenty miles that day looking for the British. When they learned the British were on their way to Bladensburg, a town just a few miles northeast of Washington in Maryland, the president ordered General Winder's small army to stop the British there. Dashing off on horseback, Monroe joined the army and organized their lines. However, he and General Winder placed the American army in positions that limited their ability to repel the British.[6]

Winder rushed to Bladensburg. On August 24 he made a stand near the town. He was all that stood between the large British army and the capital city [see Map 7 in Appendix].

## LET THE RACES BEGIN

August 24 was a scorcher. Records indicate it was extremely humid and the thermometer reached 100 degrees. Both armies reported feeling the effects of the weather. President Madison rode to Bladensburg shortly before the battle began and nearly encountered the advance British line. It is likely he would have been killed or, at the least, captured, had he not veered off course at the last moment. This is the closest a sitting American president ever came to combat, except when Abraham Lincoln once visited troops on the front line during a Civil War battle. Madison and his aides tried to inspire the nervous and exhausted troops, then quickly moved to the back of the lines as the fighting began.[7]

General Ross reached Bladensburg with his massive army, only to discover that the bridge into town had not been blown up. His troops took the lightly guarded bridge and headed toward town. General Winder was unprepared to defend the road and town in many ways. He did not even give his untrained army a pep talk about saving the capital city. Rather, he instructed them: "When you retreat, take notice that you retreat by the Georgetown road."[8] Not surprisingly, even though the main American line began firing artillery and muskets at the British, as soon as Ross's massive army charged, the Americans dropped their weapons and ran. The British also shot Congreve rockets, which further scattered the American line. Sadly, the first to run were the officers. The retreat was so chaotic that units were running into one another and the president and his aides at the back of the line were nearly overrun by their own men.

The British advance was temporarily slowed, however, when Commodore Joshua Barney, who had been hunting Ross's army, arrived at the battle. Barney rushed his 400 sailors and privateers forward to try and establish a line. The courageous privateer-turned-commander ordered his cannons be placed at the rear of the battle near the road to Washington. As Winder's army ran past him in disarray, Barney ordered his sailors to stand their ground and fire at the British. Sure enough, the artillery fire slowed the British. When British commanders ordered their men to halt, Barney saw an opportunity to save the American retreat. He began screaming orders to the fleeing army to stay put. However, General Winder countered the effort by ordering a full retreat.

Barney's sailors were outnumbered and outgunned, but performed as best as they could under the circumstances. When the British reorganized and charged again, Barney's sailors tried to hold their ground. However, there were simply too many British. Barney, who was seriously wounded, recognized the situation was hopeless and ordered his men to fall back. Several were killed or captured, but not before inflicting damage on the massive army. It is estimated Barney's artillery stand killed sixty-four and wounded 185 more.

General Ross advanced at an aggressive pace, surprised at how cowardly the American army was and how easily they were beaten. In fact, the Americans ran so fast that the battle came to be nicknamed the "Bladensburg Races." After the battle a popular poem ribbed General Winder and his army with the lines:

Nor, Winder, do not fire your guns
Nor let your trumpets play,
Till we are out of sight—forsooth,
My horse will run away.[9]

Under the leadership of General Ross, the British took the town with a disciplined charge.

Unlike his American counterparts, Ross and his officers led their men from the front, urging them forward. One of Commodore Barney's sailors who lived through the battle was a former slave named Charles Ball. Ball described Ross's command in complimentary terms: "I could not but admire the handsome manner in which the British officers led on their fatigued and worn-out soldiers . . . I thought then, and think yet, that General Ross was one of the finest-looking men that I ever saw on horseback."[10] Admiral Cockburn explained why he and Ross did not finish off the Americans at Bladensburg, saying dryly, "The victors were too weary and the vanquished too swift."[11] American newspapers were less charitable, describing the American militia as follows: "They ran like sheep being chased by dogs."[12]

The American army was beaten, despite suffering only ten to thirty dead and a few wounded. The British army was now unstoppable. President Madison, realizing Washington was doomed, had no alternative but to order it vacated. Within just five days of disembarking, General Ross was standing on the wide avenues of Washington, DC.

# THE BURNING OF
# THE WHITE HOUSE

## HEROICS AMID TRAGEDY

America's president, Congress, and senior military command neglected to prepare for an invasion of the nation's capital city despite the fact that the American military had earlier sacked the Canadian capital of York. They also knew that the British hungered for revenge, had looted and burned homes on the Canadian border, and authorized the Royal Navy to engage in a campaign of terror along the Chesapeake. While there is plenty of blame to go around, most of it belongs with the secretary of war, John Armstrong, who repeatedly assured the president that the British would have no reason to attack Washington because it was a small town with little commerce and only a few government buildings and farms. Even when Armstrong was ordered to nonetheless prepare to defend the city, he failed to do so.

With the American army on the run and General Ross's large army on the outskirts of Washington, panic ensued. Residents and government employees began to flee. President Madison ordered as many official papers and documents be removed from the city as possible. This included the Declaration of Independence, Constitution, George Washington's personal papers, and various items of government business such as treaties. The unsung heroes of this tragic chapter in America's history were a few clerks who managed to remove the historic documents. They did so, despite criticism from Armstrong that their actions were unnecessary. Fortunately, they ignored the secretary.[1]

James Monroe, the secretary of state, wanted to turn the Capitol building into a citadel and defend the city. General William Winder, the

commander who presided over the debacle at Bladensburg echoed the secretary's suggestion. But, Winder's sincerity is doubtful given the cowardice
and incompetence he displayed just hours prior. Either way, the American
army had abandoned both Bladensburg and Washington. After the defeat
at Bladensburg, the president was still in the field with his aides and generals. They had frantically but unsuccessfully tried to rally the army and
were now forced to simply secure their own safety and watch helplessly as
the British sacked Washington. Earlier Madison had written to his wife,
Dolley, who was back at the Executive Mansion, trying not to alarm her:

> My dearest, I have passed among the troops who are in high
> spirits and make a good appearance. The reports as to the enemy
> has varied from hour to hour, the last and probably best infor-
> mation is that they are not very strong and are without cavalry
> and artillery and of course they are not in a condition to strike
> at Washington.[2]

Now that the destruction of the city was imminent, Madison had
to contend with the possibility his wife would be captured or killed. The
president rode back to the Executive Mansion around 4:30 p.m. on August
24, just hours before the British army marched into the city. Not finding
his wife there, he gathered a few belongings and fled. The first lady had
vacated the building an hour earlier. But not before she courageously took
the time to preserve priceless artifacts from the nation's founding.

## "QUEEN DOLLEY"

Dolley Madison had heard the dire reports throughout the city and had
observed citizens and soldiers running for their lives. The president and
his cabinet had withdrawn, but the first lady decided to stay. Writing to
her sister, Mrs. Madison calmly described the situation earlier in the day:

> Will you believe it my sister, we have a battle or skirmish near
> the city. I am still within sounds of the cannons, Mr. Madison
> comes not. May god protect us. Two messengers come in and
> asked me to leave the Capitol, I must stay here and wait for
> my husband.[3]

Dolley Madison was perhaps the most beloved first lady in American history. Flirtatious and funny, talkative and opinionated, graceful and smart, fashionable and popular, the first lady was an asset to her husband throughout his career and presidency. The Madisons were, however, an unlikely couple. While Dolley charmed everyone she met, James was notoriously shy, bookish, and aloof. He was an Episcopalian; while she had been raised Quaker, but her warm and fun-loving personality had led her to abandon the strictures of the faith. Dolley was an attractive widow seventeen years his junior when the famous Founder met her. They married in September of 1794 and she immediately made his career hers.[4]

One of her many accomplishments was the Executive Mansion itself. The presidential palace was still being built and its furnishings and social events had been ignored by the widower, Thomas Jefferson, in the years prior to Madison's presidency. As such, Mrs. Madison took it upon herself to decorate the building and host some of the grandest social functions the city has ever witnessed. The popular first lady, nicknamed by the public "Queen Dolley," had invested so much energy into the Executive Mansion that she hated the thought of abandoning it to the British.

In fact, she did not flee until the eleventh hour, but not before rescuing as many priceless artifacts as possible. One of the last to leave the city, the first lady even watched the British army burning public buildings while standing on the roof with a "spyglass." One of the items Mrs. Madison saved was the famous Gilbert Stuart portrait of George Washington hanging on the walls of the mansion. She described the ordeal to save the large painting in a letter to her sister: "The process [getting the painting off the wall] was found too tedious for these perilous moments. I have ordered the frame to be broken and the canvas taken out." After being "assisted by two colored boys . . . we fell into the trail of the army." Having entrusted the objects to Jacob Barker, a fellow Quaker, and Robert G. L. de Peyster, Mrs. Madison raced out of the city in a carriage to elude capture. She would later meet up with her husband at a small inn in Virginia.[5]

## THE NIGHT SKY GLOWS

The large British army led by General Ross and Admiral Cockburn was exhausted from the stifling heat and humidity as much as from their long march and battle at Bladensburg. They rested only momentarily. In advance of the main army, Ross and Cockburn took one of the rear brigades not used in the previous battle and marched into the capital city [see Map 6 in Appendix]. They arrived around 8:00 on the evening of August 24, traveling along Maryland Avenue and Constitution Avenue. The British marched under a flag of truce to demand surrender from the president.

As the army entered the city, shots were fired from a few homes, including the residence of Albert Gallatin, the treasury secretary. Three British soldiers were wounded and one killed. General Ross, whose horse was shot out from under him at Bladensburg, was at the front of the army. When the shots were fired, his horse was hit and Ross was knocked to the ground. Ross ordered the home attacked. After storming the house, the British dragged the defenders out into the street and executed them. The home was later burned to the ground and it remains uncertain as to who fired the shots.[6]

No members of the American government were in the city to meet the conquerors in one capacity or another. Ross and Cockburn rode triumphantly down a deserted Pennsylvania Avenue. After holding a mock vote that poked fun at American democracy, the commanders ordered the city burned. Starting around 10:00 p.m., public buildings including the Capitol, which was still incomplete, were burned to the ground. The British then marched to the Executive Mansion where General Ross noted his surprise at meeting no resistance: "So unexpected was our entry and capture of Washington . . . when our advanced party entered the President's house, they found a table laid with forty covers." The dinner was cold but untouched, so the British sat down and filled their stomachs. After toasting "Jimmy" Madison and their king, they helped themselves to the mansion's wine collection and began their pillaging of the presidential home, taking or destroying furnishings and everything not nailed down, including the president's love letters to his wife which were pocketed by General Ross. Cockburn kept for himself several items, including Madison's sword.[7]

The admiral took delight in the city's destruction, seeing it as revenge for the burning of York. When his men set fire to the offices of the *National Intelligencer*, the city's main newspaper, which had been particularly critical of the admiral, Cockburn bellowed, "Make sure that all the C's are destroyed, so the rascals can have no further means of abusing my name!"[8] Cockburn hoped to find the paper's publisher, Joseph Gales, and wanted him punished. But Gales had fled. However, while looking for Gales, legend suggests that a local resident, observing the newspaper building burning, yelled to the gloating admiral that, had George Washington been alive, he would have killed Cockburn. It is said that Cockburn responded, "No sir, if General Washington had been president we should never have thought of coming here."[9]

One by one, the city's landmarks were burned—the Capitol Building, Executive Mansion, the Treasury Building, Library of Congress, and the naval shipyards, whose defenders had destroyed the ammunition and powder as well as the frigate USS *Columbia* and the sloop *Argus* in order to deny their invaders the spoils of war. The city was on fire. People living miles away in every direction reported seeing the glow in the sky. The president also watched the city burn from a few miles away in Virginia, painfully unable to do anything about it. All the while, he did not know if his wife had made it out of the Executive Mansion alive. Even the whereabouts of his cabinet and so many government employees remained a mystery. The president was not the only American living in the Chesapeake region to endure a long, anxious night.

Late that evening, with the city still in flames, the British set up camp near Capitol Hill and Ross and Cockburn made their headquarters at the home of James Ewell, a physician who lived on First and A Streets in the southeast quadrant of town near the present-day Library of Congress. Only a few citizens remained in the town. One of them, Mary Hunter, described the horror of watching the city burn: "You never saw a drawing room so brilliantly lighted as the whole city was that night. Few thought of going . . . they spent the night in gazing on the fires and lamenting the disgrace of the city."[10]


## PROVIDENCE

The next morning, the British finished destroying the city by burning the war department and state department buildings. When they arrived at the patent office, the director of it, Dr. William Thornton, begged the British to spare the building. Amazingly, they complied. As the British watched the city smolder all around them, they also observed the sky grow dark very quickly. In an instant the winds began blowing with violent force.

Around 2:00 in the afternoon of August 25 all hell broke loose. Gale force winds blew through the capital city, lightning flashed from the sky and touched off more fires, and then the skies opened up in a torrential thunderstorm. Resembling a biblical apocalypse, tornadoes touched down in the heart of the city. British soldiers ran frantically for cover in the burnt-out buildings while others were knocked to the ground from the violent winds. Admiral Cockburn is said to have yelled to a woman who lived in the city, "Great God, madam! Is this the kind of storm to which you are accustomed in this infernal city?" She responded, "No, sir, this is a special interposition of Providence to deny our enemies from our city." While it is unlikely the exchange with Cockburn ever occurred, the storm was one of the worst in Washington's history and inflicted more casualties to the British army than the sacking of the city the day prior.[11]

Many people on both sides of the conflict attributed the freakish storm to the wrath of god. The suddenness and ferocity of the storm unnerved the British army and their commanders vacated the city that night. The storm also put out the fires and saved part of the city. Claiming to be worried about a possible American counterattack, Ross imposed a curfew on the city and rushed his army back along the road to the British ships at port. Before abandoning the city, however, he ordered his men to set campfires around the city in order to give the illusion that British forces were still there and still enforcing the curfew. He hoped it would distract the American counterattack while his forces fled. But the attack never came.

The next day, James and Dolley Madison were reunited. They returned to the site of the tragedy one day later, depressed and frustrated. The city was a ghost town and the few citizens that had returned were in a state of shock. A city that took two decades to build—and was still incomplete— was gone in one evening.

## AFTER EFFECTS

But the Madisons showed great courage and confidence, urging residents to move back to Washington and to continue to fight. The first lady, who was one of the last to leave and one of the first residents to arrive back in Washington, commented that she would have fought the entire British army herself, "if I could have had a cannon through every window . . . but alas! Those who should have placed them there, fled before me, and my whole heart mourned for my country!"[12] Mrs. Madison described the scene that greeted her when she returned to the Executive Mansion. "I remained nearly three days out of town, but I cannot tell you what I felt upon re-entering it—such destruction—such confusion! The fleet in full view and in the act of robbing Alexandria!"[13]

When newspapers began in earnest discussing options for moving the entire capital to Philadelphia or another location, both the president and first lady dismissed the talk. They also assured the country that the city would be rebuilt and that the British would be punished. Madison then ordered the Congress to reconvene and to meet in the only large public building still standing in the city—the post office. On a more practical front, the president accepted the resignations of General Winder and Secretary Armstrong. James Monroe assumed the position of acting secretary of war.

General Ross marched his army back to the Potomac without incident and was glad to find the British armada waiting and providing support with their massive guns. Admiral Cochrane, delighted by the reports of no resistance and a successful mission, quickly dispatched Captain James Gordon in command of the frigate HMS *Sea Horse* with a few smaller warships in support. They sailed to nearby Fort Washington and captured it without a fight. Rather than march immediately to Baltimore or seek and destroy what remained of the American army, however, the British helped themselves to the fort's supplies, which included thousands of hogsheads of tobacco, thousands of barrels of flour, and a bounty of beef, cotton, sugar, and armaments.

On the other side of the Atlantic, the British press and many citizens were appalled by the burning and looting of Washington. Even the *London Statesman* opined: "The Cossacks spared Paris, but we spared not the capitol of America."[14] James Madison echoed these sentiments, rallying his countrymen and the world to America's side, saying in a letter to Admiral Cochrane: "In the course of ten years past, the capitals of the principal powers of the continent of Europe have been conquered, and occupied alternately by the victorious armies of each other; and no instance of such wanton and unjustifiable destruction has been seen."[15]

The British set sail on September 1, confident they would not be opposed when they marched on their next target—the important port of Baltimore. The loss of the capital city was a symbolic blow to America and the manner in which it was lost demonstrated the vulnerability of the nation. However, it also hardened America's resolve. As was the case at Plattsburgh and on Lake Champlain just days prior, the Americans were about to stiffen their defenses and beat back another invasion. Moved by the burning of the nation's capital city, Philip Freneau put pen to paper and composed a poem that perhaps best captures the tragic affair:

"On the Conflagrations at Washington"

A veteran host, by veterans led,
With Ross and Cockburn at their head—
They came—they saw—they burnt—and fled.

They left our congress naked walls—
Farewell to towers and capitols!
To lofty foors and splendid halls!

To courtly domes and glittering things,
To folly, that too near us clings,
To courtiers who—tis well—had wings.

Farewell to all but glorious war,
Which yet shall guard Potomac's shore,
And honor lost, and fame restore.[16]

# TURNING POINTS

*"The Battle of Baltimore"*

*The gen'ral gave orders for the troops to march down,*
*To meet the proud Ross, and to check his ambition;*
*To inform him we have decreed in our town*
*That here he can't enter without our permission.*
*And if life he regards, he will not press too hard,*
*For Baltimore freemen are ever prepared*
*To check the presumptuous, whoever they be,*
*That may rashly attempt to evade our decree.*

—Poem written at the close of the War of 1812

"Gen. Andrew Jackson at the Battle of New Orleans." Acknowledgment: By H.G. Thorp, Boston, 1903; U.S. Library of Congress, Washington, DC (USZ62-7809).

# THE DEFENSE OF BALTIMORE

## ON TO BALTIMORE

The burning of Washington was a decisive and symbolically important victory for the British. But, Baltimore was seen as a far more
important target from a strategic perspective. The city, just forty miles
north of Washington, was the main port for the Chesapeake—and
one of the main commercial ports in the country—and was home to
far more supplies, ships, and people than the capital city. The third
largest city in the United States, Baltimore was also a rabidly pro-war,
anti-British city and was home to some of the most troublesome privateers of the war. Captain Edward Codrington, Admiral Cochrane's
aide, summed it up this way: "I do not like to contemplate scenes
of blood and destruction. But my heart is deeply interested in the
coercion of these Baltimore heroes, who are perhaps the most invet-
erate against us of all the Yankees."[1]

Despite the easy victories in Bladensburg and Washington, the British army was exhausted and unnerved by the freakish storm that hit them
in the capital city. By early September, the unbearable humidity along the
Chesapeake was also taking its toll. Many of the soldiers worried about
reports of malaria and yellow fever in Baltimore and hoped to rest and
wait for reinforcements. Even though Baltimore was close by, the British
command contemplated turning southward to strike at Charleston and
Savannah, then sailing to the Gulf Coast. Another option was simply to
wait. The American military and government were demoralized and in
chaos, and many British soldiers believed the end of the war was near.

Admirals Cochrane and Cockburn debated their options. While
Cochrane wanted Baltimore burned to "ashes" like Washington, General
Ross was hesitant and unenthusiastic about attacking Baltimore. It appears
the general may have had second thoughts about his decision to burn the

capital city, as indicated in one of Cochrane's reports sent back to London where he noted: "Some hint ought to be given to General Ross, as he does not seem inclined to visit the sins committed upon his majesty's Canadian subjects upon the inhabitants of this state."[2]

Nevertheless, three weeks after their victories at Bladensburg and Washington, the British armada set sail for Baltimore . . . with mixed feelings. The plan was to sack and possibly burn the city to the ground. The argument was that taking another city would bring the Americans to their knees and the war would end. The British assumed Baltimore would also be undefended or, if a token American force was encountered, that they would run as had the defenders at Bladensburg. They were wrong [see Map 6 in Appendix].

On September 11, the British arrived near Baltimore. They would later discover that the main British army was beaten at Lake Champlain and Plattsburgh that very day.[3] At three o'clock in the morning of September 12, the army disembarked at North Point, roughly a dozen miles southeast of Baltimore. Around eight o'clock, General Ross organized the army and began the march to Baltimore to invade by land. Admiral Cochrane sailed his large navy to Baltimore to begin the attack by sea.

## THE BATTLE OF NORTH POINT

With cannons from their ships pointed to the shoreline ready to provide cover, the British ferried soldiers in rowboats to the shores of North Point in Dundalk, Maryland. The army was so large that the landing took four hours to complete on the morning of September 12. General Ross organized his army of roughly 4,000 men into two large columns and began the march to Baltimore twelve miles away. He was supported by artillery and British warships that sailed nearby on the Patapsco River. However, the river was too shallow and the warships had to turn around and sail back out. This proved to be fortuitous for the American defenders, but Ross thought little of it. The British were supremely confident. On the way, Ross and his officers even took the time to stop at Gorsuch's farm and enjoy a hearty breakfast. When the reluctant hosts asked the general if he would be back that night for dinner, Ross growled, "I'll sup in Baltimore tonight—or in hell." His only concern was the hot, humid weather that slowed the pace of the army, who were still wearing heavy woolen uniforms.[4]

Simultaneously, Sir Alexander Cochrane sailed to the city's harbor. In all, Cochrane commanded roughly fifty ships. It was more than enough firepower to reduce the fort and city to ruin. Anchored four miles from the mouth of the harbor, the British prepared to bombard Fort McHenry, which stood guard on a hill overlooking the city. Cochrane sent a dispatch to Ross just prior to the start of the invasion, noting the American preparations: "The enemy have been sinking ships across their harbor all day, and in front of the fort. They have a number of men at work to the northeast of town upon the ground which forms a kind of irregular ridge."[5] The British did not know it, but in addition to sinking ships to block the Royal Navy from entering the harbor, the Americans had prepared another welcome.

Brigadier General John Stricker, in command of roughly 3,000 militia volunteers from Maryland, waited on the road into Baltimore. After collecting intelligence on the advancing British army, Stricker ordered his troops to make preparations before camping on the night of September 11. He chose good ground. The Americans lined a narrow spot of land nestled between the Back River on the north and Bear Creek to their south on the outskirts of the city. Artillery was posted along the road, the soldiers were protected by the woods, and they were dug in. Stricker's mission was to try and slow the British advance in order to give Baltimore more time to prepare defenses. The British would have to go directly through him to get to Baltimore.

On September 12, General Ross ordered an advance unit on a reconnaissance mission. They returned with word that many American militiamen were waiting on the road to Baltimore. Ross was confident the Americans would wilt in the face of his massive army, so he ordered them forward straight into the American line, saying, "I don't care if it rains militia!"[6]

Worried that his new volunteers would not stand up to a full charge from British regulars, Stricker ordered his men to attack first. The American's were outnumbered, but they were defending their homes! As the British approached the American position on the road, weary from the heat and long march, the last thing they expected was to be attacked. From Ross's perspective, it rained militia. The Americans opened up with everything they had. Shots came from both sides of the road and from directly in front. The surprise attack cost the British their psychological edge, but they did not retreat. Ross ordered a counterattack but the Americans had strong defensive positions and Stricker had ordered his men to hold their ground.

The British attacked in wave after wave, but the Americans held their line. General Ross, perplexed by the stiff resistance, decided to ride to the front to see what was happening. Observing the Americans dug in, he then proceeded to ride back to bring more reinforcements to the front lines. As he did, an American sniper spotted Ross. The shot rang true, the bullet passing through the general's right arm and into his chest. The wound was fatal. The accounts vary, but some suggest an aide tended to Ross, whose last words were to state his love for his wife. Ross had been seriously wounded during the war against Napoleon and it was his wife, Elizabeth, who traveled to be at her husband's side, nursing him back to health. The general had then made a promise to his beloved wife that the War of 1812 would be his last campaign and then he would return home to retire when it ended. Elizabeth Ross survived her husband by three decades and was said to have never recovered from his death.[7]

Another officer rode to get Admiral Cockburn, who rushed to Ross's side. Although they were opposites in temperament and had disagreed on the planning of the invasion, both men were effective leaders essential to a British victory. Said Cockburn on the death of his fellow officer, "Our country has lost in him one of its best and bravest soldiers and those who knew him, as I did, a friend most honoured and beloved."[8]

Seeing their general killed took the fight out of the British army. One of the infantrymen there that day described the impact of losing their commander: "The death of General Ross seemed to have disorganized the whole plan of proceedings, and the fleet and army rested idle, like a watch without its main spring."[9] The heat and humidity further sapped British resolve. The British reorganized but never recovered from the loss of Ross. Admiral Cockburn rode to the front of the line and urged the army to fight for their beloved general. But the Americans continued to inflict serious casualties on the main British army. Each time the British tried to punch a hole in the American line, they lost men, and Stricker rushed reserves from the rear to quickly fill in the line. From the tree line, American snipers continued shooting officers, which dealt more psychological blows to the British while thinning the officer corps.

Finally, the British were able to outflank the American line, but rather than abandon the field of battle, Stricker ordered his men to fall back fighting. It took until four o'clock that afternoon for the British to push the Americans off the road. However, under the tenacious defense and blistering afternoon sun, the spirit of the British army was broken. Ross's second in command, Colonel Arthur Brooke, lacked the general's resolve and ordered the army to make camp. They were within sight of Baltimore but had suffered hundreds of casualties and were exhausted. Admiral Cockburn abandoned the invasion to join the fleet outside of Baltimore harbor.

## A HERO FROM THE REVOLUTION

Few people—and even fewer soldiers—were pleased with President Madison's decision on July 1, 1814, to put Brigadier General William Winder in charge of the Tenth Military District in northern Virginia and Maryland. His combat record did little to inspire confidence and the disastrous defeats at Bladensburg and Washington utterly discredited the incompetent political appointee. As was the case in Washington, Winder had done little to prepare for the defense of Baltimore. So, even though Winder was the nephew of Maryland's governor he encountered opposition to his command. One of the most vocal critics was a 62-year-old Revolutionary War hero Samuel Smith.[10]

The citizens of Baltimore had heard about the burning of Washington and took it upon themselves to organize a defense of their city. Rather than wait for the War Department, the governor, or General Winder, the mayor of Baltimore, Edward Johnson, established the Committee of Vigilance and Safety. The mayor recommended Samuel Smith be placed in charge of the committee. Winder opposed the appointment and, arriving in the city on the heels of the burning of Washington, announced that he would lead the city against the British. Even though Winder outranked him, Smith simply ignored Winder. The two men argued, but Smith refused to turn over the defense of Baltimore to Winder and dressed down the younger man. The people followed Smith. A hasty defense was organized.

Smith, a general in the Maryland militia and popular U.S. senator, trained the militia and erected defenses throughout the city including earthworks, trenches, and artillery batteries. Knowing Baltimore would face an amphibious assault and bombardment from warships, Smith had ships sunk in the harbor to prevent British warships from sailing into Baltimore. And he ordered the people to have shovels and water ready to put out fires. To implement his plan, Smith urged the mayor to call every able-bodied man for service. Several thousand volunteers answered the call. While Washington ran, Baltimore dug in and fought.

The morning after General Ross was killed, the British broke camp and commenced the short march to Baltimore. They encountered artillery fire, a series of earthworks, and thousands of volunteers determined to defend their city. The British advance came under relentless fire from all parts of the city. From atop earthworks and behind trees, citizens and militiamen fought. It worked. They beat back the British attack and the overly cautious Colonel Brooke called off the engagement and ordered the massive army to fall back. A rag-tag collection of blacksmiths, farmers, and shopkeepers without training had beaten a numerically superior British army, one fresh off victory over Napoleon.[11]

# 30

# "OH SAY CAN YOU SEE"

## FORT McHENRY

After news of the British landing along the Chesapeake, the city of Balti-more scrambled to ready defenses. Fortunately, this was led by the Revolutionary War hero Samuel Smith, who organized a series of earthworks, trenches, and artillery batteries around the city and quickly recruited and trained a few thousand militiamen. Smith was joined by an officer from Virginia in his thirties named George Armistead. Major Armistead came from a long line of military officers and he was about to make his lineage proud. Armistead and Smith came up with the brilliant idea of sinking ships by the entrance to the harbor to block the British from sailing directly into Baltimore. They then convinced reluctant local merchants to allow their ships to be used as an extensive sea wall.

The major, who had served with Winfield Scott during the war, was in charge of Fort McHenry. The five-sided fort, shaped like a star, was built in the 1790s and was named for James McHenry, a signer of the Declaration of Independence and secretary of state for President John Adams. The fort was strategically located on a small bluff overlooking and guarding the city and harbor. Any attack on the city, by land or water, would need to go through McHenry, which was equipped with about two to three dozen strong guns and sturdy walls.[1] It was about to become the focal point of both the city's defense and the wrath of the British army and navy.

The British, now prevented from sailing into the harbor, were forced to bombard the city and fort from sea and attempt an invasion by land. McHenry was a compelling target for several reasons. It was the main fort in the area and it housed roughly 250,000 pounds of powder and an arsenal of weapons, making it the largest ammunition depot in the region. If the fort was lost, Maryland would lose its means to fight back and the front door to Baltimore would be opened. Amazingly, during the bombardment of Fort McHenry that followed, a cannonball made a direct hit on this important powder supply but the fuse did not ignite, thus saving the fort and possibly the city.

The fort and surrounding batteries were garrisoned by 1,000 men. Armistead placed a 3-gun battery on the opposite bank of the Patapsco River, which ran beside the fort, and a 6-gun battery roughly one mile up the river. The defense was further aided by the fact that the river was shallow, thus preventing large warships from striking from close distance. Although the British had a large army and armada of powerful warships, Baltimore was prepared to fight.[2]

A final preparation by Major Armistead was to inspire confidence among both his men and the city. Tradition suggests that he therefore ordered a huge flag to fly atop the fort, one large enough for all the residents, the militiamen stationed on the road into the city and at defenses around Baltimore, and even the British to see. After the battle, a lawyer and part-time poet would also see the flag and be inspired to put pen to paper.

The War Department agreed to the flag request and assigned the task to Mary Pikersgill, the Betsy Ross of this war. Pikersgill was paid a whopping $574.44 for her services. Aided by her 13-year-old daughter, Caroline, she produced two flags. One of them measured an impressive thirty feet in height by forty-two feet in length, making it the largest flag in the country at the time. The flag was so large that it could not be sewn in her home. Pikersgill had to move it to a warehouse. The soon-to-be famous flag featured fifteen stars and fifteen stripes for the original thirteen colonies plus the new states of Kentucky and Vermont. The flag would also be one of the last of its kind ever made. In the year 1818, Congress would designate that the official flag bear only thirteen stripes.[3]

Major Armistead would have his flag. He also motivated the men in his command to hold the fort at all costs. But, all the while, the major was worried about his pregnant wife, who was taken to Gettysburg in order that she could deliver their baby in safety. In private, Armistead must surely have wondered if he would ever see the child.

## DR. BEANES

One week prior to the ground and naval attack on Baltimore, a small American ship, the *Minden*, sailed out of the harbor under a flag of truce.

It headed for the HMS *Tonnant*, the flagship of Admiral Cochrane. The *Minden*'s passengers were seeking an audience with the admiral to discuss a prisoner release or swap. One of the negotiators for the Americans on board the *Minden* was Francis Scott Key, a Georgetown lawyer and avid poet. He joined John Skinner, a Baltimore lawyer who negotiated deals such as prisoner swaps on behalf of President Madison.

The prisoner they sought to release was a 65-year-old physician named William Beanes. Born in Scotland, Beanes had immigrated to America where he amassed considerable land holdings, farmed, and practiced medicine. When the British army under General Ross and Admiral Cockburn marched through Maryland on August 22, Dr. Beanes had opened his home to the commanders. Ross and Cockburn took the doctor up on his offer, dining and lodging at the home. However, Beanes was loyal to America and immediately notified American commanders of the British troop strength and movements.[4]

As the British army marched through Maryland, six of their soldiers fell behind the main army and were captured by the Americans. It was believed that Beanes played a role in tipping off those who caught the British lolly-gaggers. When the British army learned that a half dozen of their men had been captured, they sent a mounted unit back to find them. These soldiers rode back to Beanes's house where they dragged the doctor and two of his guests—Dr. William Hill and Philip Weems—out onto the street. The three men were detained for questioning. Satisfied they had the information they needed, the British then organized a prisoner swap. Beanes's houseguests were released in exchange for the British soldiers. But not Dr. Beanes.

Ross and Cockburn felt betrayed by Beanes and were also likely embarrassed by being duped by the kind, country physician. He was thus arrested for his alleged role in the capture of the six British soldiers and for spying against Britain. In a twist harkening back to the causes of the war, Beanes was accused of treason because he had once been a British citizen, so under the old laws of impressment he was imprisoned on a British warship.

Dr. Beanes was a popular leader in his community. As such, his arrest prompted many neighbors to seek help in obtaining his release. Word of the incident made it all the way to President Madison, who was among the doctor's wide circle of friends and admirers. To assist Beanes, Madison dispatched his negotiator, John Skinner. At the same time, one of Beanes's patients, Richard E. West, a prominent member of Maryland society who had married the older sister of Francis Scott Key, also intervened on the doctor's behalf. Aware of Key's reputation as an outstanding attorney, West rode to Georgetown to request the lawyer's assistance in getting Dr. Beanes freed. Keys agreed to help and immediately thought to obtain letters from former British soldiers whom Beanes had treated. Armed with testimonials to Beanes's Hippocratic charity toward his enemies, Key joined Skinner on board the *Minden*. And the two sailed to the British armada.

The American lawyers arrived at the HMS *Tonnant*, Admiral Cochrane's flagship, where they were treated well and invited to dine with their guest. Aboard the ship for dinner were General Ross (before his doomed assault on North Point) and Admiral Cockburn, who were preparing the land invasion of Baltimore. All was cordial until the lawyers requested the release of Dr. Beanes. At the mention of the alleged traitor, Admiral Cockburn flew into a rage, threatening never to release the physician or even to allow Skinner and Key to present him with as much as soap or fresh underwear.[5] But Key handed General Ross the letters of support for Dr. Beanes. It worked. Upon reading that Beanes treated British prisoners of war with kindness, Ross proposed the doctor be released. However, Cockburn disagreed and the two men locked horns on the matter. Ross eventually carried the argument, reminding the disagreeable admiral that Beanes was the army's prisoner and not the navy's.

Over Cockburn's protest, Ross agreed to release Beanes but only after the siege of Baltimore. Concerned that Skinner and Key now knew details about the planned bombardment and invasion of Baltimore, the two lawyers were ordered to remain on the British warship with Beanes until after Baltimore was destroyed.

## THE BOMBARDMENT

While General Ross marched an army of 4,000 men from North Point to Baltimore, Admiral Cochrane sailed to Baltimore to begin the naval stage of the battle. Although blocked by the sunken ships at the entrance to the harbor, Cochrane was undeterred. He would soon learn that General Ross was killed and the British army's advance was slowed and taking serious casualties. But Cochrane had an armada of powerful warships, whose cannons could fire a distance of three miles with accuracy, whereas many of the guns in Fort McHenry had a range of only roughly half that.

From the deck of his 80-gun flagship, Admiral Cochrane ordered the bombardment to begin just before dawn on September 13. Mortars, rockets, and cannons roared over Baltimore's skies for over twenty-four hours in what was likely the largest artillery attack in the history of the continent at the time. In total, it is likely that thousands of cannonballs and rockets were launched from just outside the harbor, although some of the rockets were fired from close distance when the small warship HMS *Erebus* was able to sail near the fort. Other nearby warships launched short-range mortars set with quick fuses so that they would explode in the air above the fort, raining down deadly shrapnel on Armistead's defenders.[6]

From inside Fort McHenry, Major Armistead kept his men calm amid the destruction and ordered them to continue firing back at the invaders. His gunners used the bright flashes and fireworks that lit the night sky to guide their aim. Throughout the city, candles and lanterns were darkened to limit the warships' ability to find targets at night. For a full day and night the deafening barrage continued, bringing buildings tumbling to the ground, punching massive holes into streets, and even causing the ground to tremble. People scrambled to reinforce shelters and put out fires. They were aided by the fact that September 13 was a dreary, rainy day. However, the massive 24-pound and 32-pound cannonballs failed to bring the walls of Fort McHenry down or subdue the people of Baltimore. The bombardment neither silenced the fort's guns nor beat the city into submission.

At 7:00 in the morning of September 14, Admiral Cochrane observed that the fort held. He called off the assault. The admiral then ordered his ships to hoist anchors and set sails.[7]

Meanwhile, Admiral Cockburn had rejoined Cochrane aboard his flagship outside of Baltimore's harbor, leaving the ground assault to Colonel Brooke. That same morning, Colonel Brooke's exhausted army was beaten by General Stricker's inspired militia units on the road into Baltimore. Unable to either lure Major Armistead's defenders out of the fort and into the open or intimidate the militiamen, and taking excessive casualties, Brooke abandoned the invasion. The army turned and marched back to the rendezvous point to board Admiral Cochrane's ships. A last-ditch effort by Admiral Cockburn, whose men rowed from the ships into the shoreline of Baltimore, was also defeated.[8]

Both the land and sea invasions failed and the British commanders called off the entire Chesapeake campaign. The next day, Admiral Cochrane sailed his fleet to Canada and Admiral Cockburn sailed for Bermuda. From Jamaica, the British army would attempt to regroup and shift their invasion southward to New Orleans for the third and final effort to take America.

Amazingly, Armistead lost only four men with another twenty-four wounded during the massive bombardment. The major, who instantly became an American hero, was also greeted by more good news. Word soon arrived that his wife had delivered a baby girl in Gettysburg. While the commander of Fort McHenry would live for only four more years, his wife and daughter survived him. Major Armistead's large flag also survived the invasion. Interestingly, a half century later, back in Gettysburg, the major's nephew, Lewis Armistead, died during the failed charge by Major General George Pickett on July 3, 1863.

## "BY THE DAWN'S EARLY LIGHT"

From the deck of the British warship where he was being detained, Francis Scott Key watched in horror as the British armada bombed Baltimore on September 13. Nervously pacing the deck throughout the night, Key was shocked by the extensiveness of the bombardment. He understood that, on the heels of the loss of Washington, if Baltimore fell the British would control the entire Chesapeake region. It would be a turning point in the war and likely the end of the United States as he knew it. Key was joined during his night vigil by Skinner and Dr. Beanes. The men strained to hear cannon blasts coming from the fort and looked for signs of life in Baltimore. In particular, they tried in vain to spot the American flag flying above Fort McHenry. Amid the bursts of rockets shot by the HMS *Erebus*, which temporarily lighted the sky above Baltimore, Key finally saw a painful site. The flag had been taken down inside the fort. In a panic, Dr. Beanes asked Key, "Can you see the flag? Is the flag still there?"[9] The men worried that the fort at been destroyed by the naval barrage or had surrendered to the invading army.

In the morning of September 14, the British barrage ended and the American guns fell silent too. An eerie quiet spread across the harbor. From within the fort, Armistead ordered the massive American flag raised. Key observed the flag unfurled above Fort McHenry and heard a great cheer coming from the citizens of Baltimore. Relieved, Key, who opposed the war, took a letter from his coat pocket and began scribbling lines describing what he saw and felt.

> O say, can you see, by the dawn's early light,
> What so proudly we hail'd at the twilight's last gleaming?
> Whose broad stripes and bright stars, thro' the perilous fight,

O'er the ramparts we watch'd, were so gallantly streaming?
And the rocket's red glare, the bombs bursting in air,
Gave proof thro' the night that our flag was still there.

Key, Skinner, and Beanes were released later that morning and the *Minden* made its way back to Baltimore. Two days later, safe in Baltimore, Key was inspired to write out the verses. He completed the poem a few days later. In honor of the victory, the poem was printed on handbills and in newspapers under the title "The Defense of Fort McHenry" and circulated widely throughout the country. It was an instant sensation. Americans were eager for a victory and the words lifted many a sagging spirit.

The newspaper in Frederick, Maryland chose not to publish the poem under the given title. Rather, they ran the words under the heading "The Star-Spangled Banner." So popular were the words, that Americans celebrating victory in pubs began singing them to the popular British drinking song with the impossibly difficult melody and range, "To Anacreon in Heaven." It stuck and in 1931 Congress officially acted to make Key's poem and the British melody America's national anthem.[10]

# 31

# THE SIEGE OF FORT ERIE

## THE SIEGE

The site where Fort Erie stood had been a trading post established by French fur trappers in 1753. After the French and Indian War, the British constructed a fort on the banks of the Niagara River between Lake Ontario and Lake Erie in 1764 [see Map 3 in Appendix]. To some, the fort was unlucky. Men stationed there endured brutally cold winters and the fort was destroyed in March of 1799 by a large sheet of ice driven ashore by a powerful storm. A second fort was built nearby on the river, but it too was wrecked by another severe storm in February of 1803. The next year, it was rebuilt and was still incomplete when the War of 1812 started.[1]

This key fort exchanged hands, sustained damage, and was rebuilt several times during the war. On May 27, 1813, a small British garrison at the fort, about to be overrun by a much larger American force, attempted to blow it up in order to deny their foes the prize. On June 9, after taking the fort the Americans finished the job by burning it to the ground. In December of 1813, the British reoccupied the fort and began rebuilding it. They were still constructing the fort in July of 1814 when the Americans arrived.

A few weeks prior to the British marching on Washington and Baltimore, the American general, Jacob Brown, crossed the Niagara River at Black Rock on July 3 with a force of 4,500 troops and attacked the fort. British outposts were quickly overwhelmed and the American army surrounded the fort. Commanding the high ground at a place called Snake Hill—which would soon be the site of one of the bloodiest fights of the war—Brown dictated terms. He gave the British inside the fort two hours to surrender.

The British had little choice. Major Thomas Buck commanded a garrison of only 137 men in the fort and his perimeter defenses had been destroyed. He surrendered the fort as soon as the American artillery barrage began. The loss of the fort proved costly in another way. Nearby, Lieutenant General Sir Gordon Drummond was trying to reinforce his depleted army and needed more time to do it. His hope was that Buck would hold the fort long enough to slow down the American army and give the British time to recruit Canadian volunteers. It did not happen. The British were so frustrated by the quick surrender that they court-martialed Buck. Drummond's inability to raise additional militia and Indian allies to supplement his ranks would soon cost him dearly when he tried to retake Fort Erie.[2]

Three weeks after General Brown took Fort Erie, the American army fought the British to a bloody draw at Lundy's Lane, which was not far away. Afterward, the army, exhausted, short on horses and supplies, and without several key officers lost in the engagement, pulled back to the safety of Fort Erie. It was a difficult two-day march. On the way to the fort they followed the Niagara River and it proved costly for the Americans, as they came under attack by Indians and local militia units much of the way. The American army was fortunate, however, on one account. Having sustained many casualties and desperately in need of rest and reinforcements, the British army did not initially pursue their foes.

Immediately upon arriving at Fort Erie, the Americans set about preparing to defend it. Time was precious. Lieutenant General Gordon Drummond, the Canadian-born lieutenant governor of Upper Canada, arrived days later on August 1, 1814, and began establishing siege lines and offensive positions. Because he did not have sufficient time to reinforce his numbers or recruit enough volunteers, Drummond's army was not at full strength. But he was determined to destroy the fort. The British siege encountered another setback when the weather turned bad and heavy rains battered the camp day after day. Drummond's camp then came under attack from the guns on American ships on the nearby river. Luckily for the British, their own warships arrived on the river on August 12 and captured the American ships. The siege could continue.

Drummond commenced the siege with an artillery barrage on the fort in order to soften the defenders and defenses in advance of his assault. The British poured shot on the American fort for an entire week. However, they had only four older, small cannons that would prove to be inaccurate and lacking in power. Thinking that the bombardment had damaged the fifteen-acre fort and inflicted both extensive casualties and the necessary psychological effects on the defenders, a confident Drummond ordered the actual invasion to begin on August 15.[3]


## SNAKE HILL

A problem was that both commanding generals—Brigadier General Edmund Pendleton Gaines inside the fort and General Drummond on the siege lines—miscalculated one another's troop strength. But the mistake advantaged the Americans. With the British hiding behind trees, General Gaines assumed Drummond commanded upward of 5,000 men, but he had less than 3,000 in camp. Americans planned for the worst scenario. The British, who were generally superior to the Americans when it came to spying and logistics, believed the fort was defended by only 1,500 men. But twice as many Americans defended Erie and the British had planned for a far lighter defense. Drummond's officers opposed the assault and their commander's plans, believing the fort's defenses were too strong. The British were also concerned because they had planned on Indian support but their allies did not arrive in time. In fact, more than one man in Drummond's army wrote farewell letters to loved ones that night.

While the Americans were ready for battle inside the fort, the British army was wet, cold, and sick. The rain continued for nearly the entire duration of the siege and the area around Fort Erie was reduced to a muddy swamp. Against his officers' advice, Drummond went ahead with the attack, ordering three simultaneous predawn assaults, one at each of the fort's major batteries in front of its walls. Well before sunrise on August 15, the British advanced under the cover of darkness and the dense forest to the perimeter of the American fort. Quietly, three units fixed bayonets and crept forward.[4] The British would also soon learn the hard way that their artillery barrage, despite its length, had resulted in few casualties inside the fort.

General Gaines had prepared his defenders for this exact scenario and even predicted the moment of attack. Moreover, the fort was supported by a system of embankments and trenches on each of its three sides and was protected by the Niagara River on the other. An earthen wall roughly seven feet high and eighteen feet thick protected the batteries, one of which sat atop a thirty-foot high sand cliff known as Snake Hill. All three were thus protected and enjoyed commanding views of the battlefield.

The battery atop Snake Hill was perhaps the most important for the defense of the fort, so Drummond sent a large column of 1,300 men under Lieutenant Colonel Victor Fischer to assault it. On the opposite side, Lieutenant Colonel Hercules Scott attacked the flank battery with nearly 700 men, while the general's nephew, Lieutenant Colonel William Drummond, attacked the center battery with 250 men. Unfortunately for Colonel Fischer and the British, the main unit sent to Snake Hill was the de Watteville regiment.

This Swiss regiment had been beaten so badly in the Peninsula campaign against Napoleon that their numbers were depleted. A decision was made to reinforce the regiment with deserters from the French army as well as Dutch, German, Italian, Polish, and Portuguese soldiers. Other companies in Fischer's assault were so depleted in numbers that they were reinforced with under-age boys. It was a hodge-podge force with little cohesion and less will to fight. One unit was even given the unflattering nickname, the "Rum Regiment"—for good reason. Colonel Fischer had such a problem with morale and desertions that, prior to the assault on Fort Erie, he felt he needed to take roll call. This act delayed the advance enough that the de Watteville's attack was not simultaneous with the other assaults. Hearing the fighting at the other batteries, the Americans on the Snake Hill battery knew they were coming.[5] The de Watteville regiment was about to be further depleted.

The British also failed to reconnoiter Snake Hill. As such, as the de Watteville regiment approached, they encountered an impassable thicket of vines, thorns, and branches. Many of the men became stuck in the thick underbrush. The long artillery barrage that preceded the assault also failed to hit this battery. So rather than face what they hoped would be a demoralized, depleted garrison, the British attacked a battery at full strength.

As the British were trying to hack their way through the thicket at the foot of Snake Hill, they were met by an advance picket of 100 American soldiers. The Americans poured fire into the approaching British, which also served to sound the alarm for the main battery. In an instant, the guns on Snake Hill, commanded by an officer named Townsend, exploded with volleys of shot so ferocious that it was described at lighting up the morning sky. The battery thus earned the clever nickname "Townsend's Lighthouse."[6]

Entangled in the dense thicket and under blistering fire, Fischer's assault force retreated. They tried a second assault designed to outflank the battery. On the way around the battery along the edge of the river, however, men slipped and fell on the smooth, wet rocks. Alerted to the commotion,

Eleazar Wood's regiment rushed to the side walls of the battery and poured musket fire down on the British. Many soldiers were forced into the chilly water, where they struggled to wade or swim back to shore while under fire from above. Others were swept away by the Niagara's swift current. Powder became wet and muskets were rendered useless. Wounded and dead soldiers rolled down the banks onto their comrades and soon the front line of the flanking force panicked. But as they turned to retreat, they were blocked by a larger force sent by Fischer to follow them. Only about 100 men made it to the battery and they were either cut down immediately or captured. The attack was turning into a rout.

## AGAIN AND AGAIN

Colonel Hercules Scott attacked the American battery on the other side of the fort. It was defended by an officer named Douglass. Douglass ordered his artillery to load their cannons with canisters of musketballs and jam them so full that he said he could touch the load with an outstretched arm. They held their fire until the British were at point-blank range below the battery, and then opened fire. The salvo of musketballs and metal was so deadly that British bodies were piled atop one another. The British also came under attack on their right flank from the American 9th Battalion. But the sudden charge on the flank put American soldiers on the receiving end of the canister barrage. Douglass screamed: "Cease fire! You are firing on your own men." The 9th Battalion's bayonet charge had mistakenly crossed in front of the line of fire. Several Americans were killed by "friendly fire."[7]

At the center battery, the attackers discovered that the scaling ladders they brought were too short. The British were unable to make it over the earthworks and walls. As they struggled at the base of the fortification, the American defenders simply rained shot down on them from the ramparts. From below, the British struggled to get their footing to charge, retreat, or even to stand. Days of rain had reduced the ground to an impassable mud pit. Nor could they fire back at the Americans. At the beginning of the assault, General Drummond had foolishly ordered his men to remove the flintlocks from their muskets in order to prevent anyone from firing and alerting the Americans to what was supposed to be a surprise bayonet attack. The result was that the British were unable to fire back when they were stuck at the foot of the batteries.

All appeared lost for the British, but a final attack by Colonel Hercules Scott succeeded in taking the center battery. The British then turned the guns on the fort and managed to destroy the fort's barracks. But the Americans immediately counterattacked. During the hand-to-hand fight that followed, Scott was shot in the head and killed. Without their commander, the British were barely holding the battery when a spark ignited the magazine containing the powder and ammunition under the battery. The resulting explosion rocked the entire fort, knocked both the attackers and defenders to the ground, and sent metal, wood, and bodies flying in every direction. Other British units attacking from the left and right flanks now feared the entire fort would blow up and refused to charge its walls. The British were beaten.

A total of five charges had been ordered on Fort Erie's batteries that morning. All five waves were defeated. General Drummond lost most of his army in the assault. Almost 2,000 men were killed, wounded, or missing in a single day of fighting, making Fort Erie the deadliest battle of the war fought in Canada. So serious was the casualty count that, after the engagement, Drummond's army was not able to piece together a single full battalion. Jarvis Hanks, a British drummer during the battle, described the horrific scene, saying there were huge piles of "legs, arms, and heads separated by the concussion from the trunks to which they had long been attached."[8]

## NAIL IN THE COFFIN

Despite the devastating defeat, General Drummond did not retreat. He slowly pulled his army back to what he thought was a safe distance. Why Drummond did not order a full and expedient retreat is unknown. He would pay for his mistake.

Over the course of several days, his cannons occasionally fired long-range shots at the fort, but they did not inflict damage. What did happen was that the British camp was harassed by small American scouting parties. These hit-and-run skirmishes ran through the remainder of August and into early September. They had the effect of utterly unnerving the British and further thinning the army's numbers. Unknown to the dispirited British army was the fact that, during their siege of Fort Erie, the large British army and navy under Admiral Cochrane in the Chesapeake had just failed to take Baltimore and were beaten on the outskirts of North Point, Mary-land, while the massive northern British army under Sir George Prevost had been beaten at Lake Champlain and Plattsburgh.

Then, on September 17, Major General Jacob Brown led a large strike force out of the fort to finish off the British army. Shockingly, Drummond's camp was unprepared for the counteroffensive. Brown's force attacked and immediately knocked out the small cannons used to shell the fort. It was a quick battle and a crushing defeat, costing the British another 600 men. Drummond and a mere skeletal semblance of his army managed to get away. Decimated, they retreated all the way to Chippawa, burning bridges behind them to prevent the American army from following.

Commodore Isaac Chauncey arrived on Lake Ontario in time to block Drummond's supply lines and reinforcements. There would be no chance to regroup. The British retreated farther into Canada. Major General George Izard pursued the fleeing British army and finally caught them at Cook's Mills in Ontario a month later on October 19. Izard and the New York militia, who had earlier refused to fight in Canada, finally redeemed them-selves by soundly beating Drummond's fleeing army. However, after inflict-ing further damage on the British, Izard failed to finish off Drummond.

An army of nearly 3,000 not only failed to take Fort Erie, they were reduced to a small, beaten force. It was one of the most lopsided and costly defeats of the war in terms of time, troops, and officers lost, including Colonel Hercules Scott. Drummond paid a personal price for his mistakes. His nephew, Lieutenant Colonel William Drummond, was among those killed. Back at Fort Erie, the Americans dug a mass grave for all the fallen British soldiers. There were simply too many bodies to bury. The Americans suffered only about 100 casualties, including General Brown who was injured but was taken to Buffalo and survived his wounds.

Izard ordered Fort Erie set ablaze on November 5, a fitting end to the site of so many battles and so much carnage.[9] More importantly for the Americans, the British had failed to retake important positions at sites of so much conflict along the Canadian border. The northern theater of the war had come to an end that favored the Americans.

# THE BATTLE OF HORSESHOE BEND

## "BRAVE BOY OF THE WAXHAWS"

One of the American heroes of the War of 1812 was born on March 15, 1767, in the Waxhaw region of South Carolina, near the border with North Carolina. The youngest of three sons, Andrew Jackson never knew his father, a poor farmer and immigrant from Ireland, who died just a few days prior to the birth of the third Jackson boy. Andrew's mother, "Betty" Hutchinson Jackson, recognized her youngest son's natural intelligence and consequently prioritized his education above that of her other sons and even hoped he would enter the ministry. But the charismatic young boy would grow up to be a lazy student, poor speller, and a rebellious hellion.[1]

Andrew's oldest brother, Hugh, joined the patriots fighting against the British in the Revolutionary War. Andrew and his middle brother, Robert, wanted to do the same but were too young to enlist. Therefore they ran away, lied about their ages, and fought with local citizens as "irregulars," conducting hit-and-run ambushes against the British. The widow Jackson was devastated by her sons' decisions. Sure enough, Hugh died of a heatstroke in 1779 during the Battle of Stone Ferry. Andrew and Robert were later captured. With their fellow irregulars, the boys were marched roughly forty miles in the heat and without water to a prison. When the news reached Mrs. Jackson she rushed to the camp to beg for the release of her boys.

The widow arrived at a detainment facility to discover that it was infested with disease. Moreover, her son Robert had been struck savagely in the head by a British officer and his health was deteriorating. Andrew, tall, wiry, and full of fire, was also nearly killed by the officer when he refused to shine the man's boots. When the officer swung at the defiant boy with his sword, Jackson deflected the blow with his arm, suffering only minor injuries on his arm and head. It appears the thirteen-year-old boy, brave enough to stand up to an officer, was a handful even for his captors.

Jackson's mother was able to secure her sons' release from the prison, but Robert was so ill that he had to be carried back home on horseback. Andrew, with no shoes, had to walk the distance back home. Robert Jackson would die of his malady, which appears to have been smallpox, but his younger brother survived. Although grieving the loss of another son, Mrs. Jackson returned to the British prison to beg for the lives of other American boys. Tragically, she also succumbed to a fever or disease caught in the prison.

Andrew Jackson was an orphan and not only blamed the British for the loss of his entire family, but developed a powerful vengeance that would fester for his whole life . . . until he was able to satisfy it at the end of the War of 1812. For Jackson, who nearly died of smallpox in prison and at the hands of an angry warden, the coming rematch with the British was deeply personal. He vowed to avenge his family and, while later leading troops against the British, the brave-boy-turned-general was known to bellow, "Those who are not for us, are against us, and will be dealt with accordingly!"[2] The story of the "brave boy of the Waxhaws" was told throughout the Carolinas, making him a minor celebrity. That was only the beginning.

## THE DUELIST

Andrew Jackson was a complicated man, one simultaneously capable of great leadership but also of petty vindictiveness. He had a hair-trigger temper, especially when defending a woman's honor. This is something he would have to do quite regularly as a married man.

Jackson's wife, Rachel Donelson, had married prior to meeting the Tennessee circuit lawyer and judge. At age seventeen, against her mother's wishes Rachel eloped with a miscreant named Lewis Robards, who would later mistreat her. Three years into her turbulent marriage, Rachel could stand it no longer and ran away from Robards. She went back to live with her mother.

The Donelsons were among the first pioneering families to settle Tennessee when Rachel's father, Colonel John Donelson, led a group of 120 settlers from Virginia in 1779 to settle the wilds of Tennessee. However, the settlement came under attack and the colonel was among those killed. Rather than return to Virginia, Rachel and her widowed mother endured the challenges of frontier life. It was in Tennessee in 1788 that they met Jackson, who boarded at their home while traveling in the area. Andrew Jackson and Rachel Donelson Robards instantly developed a strong affection for one another.

Jackson encouraged Rachel to pursue a divorce from her husband but, because women could not legally divorce at the time, Rachel had to request the divorce and wait for Robards to initiate the legal proceedings. At one point, Robards was so outraged by Rachel's abandonment of him that he threatened to come to Tennessee and simply take Rachel back to his home against her wishes. Jackson intervened and escorted Rachel and her mother to Natchez in the Mississippi territory. He continued to monitor the delicate situation until Rachel heard that Robards had finally granted her the divorce. Jackson and Rachel then married in 1791. However, two years later she discovered the shocking news that her divorce was never finalized. She was now married to two men at the same time![3]

When Lewis Robards learned that his wife had married Jackson, he became but the first man to claim Rachel was guilty of adultery. What was an innocent mistake for Jackson's wife soon became a highly public controversy. As news of the marriages spread, Rachel was labeled a "bigamist" throughout Tennessee. Jackson fired off a letter to Robards threatening to cut off both his ears (and perhaps other body parts) unless a legal divorce was immediately initiated. Likely aware of Jackson's violent reputation, Robards promptly and wisely complied. The divorce was settled on January 17, 1794. After proclaiming to Rachel's mother that he would defend his bride with "ten thousand lives . . . if I had them," the Jacksons were married for a second time. This time legally, on January 17, 1794.[4]

Dueling was an alarmingly common custom in the early nineteenth century and Jackson was an avid practitioner. Any man who crossed Jackson or spoke ill of his wife's marriage scandal, was challenged to a duel. Jackson even dueled over minor disagreements, once after exchanging words with the Benton brothers, Jesse and Thomas, on the streets of Nashville. Their long-simmering feud ended not in a duel on a designated "field of honor," but in a melee of flying bullets in town. Jackson, who had threatened to "horsewhip" one of the Benton's, was shot and nearly lost an arm in the brawl. He carried the bullet in his shoulder for the rest of his life.[5] He came closer to being killed in other duels.

As a Tennessee judge, Jackson was once presiding over a case involving Russell Bean, a mountain of a man who routinely terrorized the town. Bean was accused of cutting off the ears of a child during a drunken rampage. The shocking facts of the case resulted in much interest in the trial. While in court, however, Bean simply stood up and walked out of the proceedings, knowing no one would dare stop him. Jackson ordered the sheriff to arrest Bean, but the sheriff declined to face the behemoth. So Jackson empowered the sheriff to "summon a posse, then, and bring him before me," but the posse also cowered and failed to do so. Apparently no one had the courage to stand up to the giant. Losing his patience, Jackson shed his robe, grabbed a pistol, and walked out of the courthouse to personally bring Bean back to stand trial. A showdown loomed in the streets of the town when the judge confronted the town menace, threatening "Surrender, you infernal villain, this very instant, or I'll blow you through!" Bean wisely backed down and Jackson brought him to justice.[6]

Perhaps Jackson's most famous duel was against a fellow Tennessean named Charles Dickinson, a popular and powerful figure known to be a crack shot. After arguing about a horse-racing debt that escalated into Dickinson speaking ill of Mrs. Jackson's chastity, Jackson demanded the "satisfaction" of a duel. Jackson could not have picked a more worthy opponent. Dickinson carried on his person a piece of cord that he allegedly split with a pistol at twenty-four feet—the distance in which duels were fought. Accepting Jackson's impulsive challenge, Dickinson boasted to a crowd while holding aloft the evidence of his marksmanship that, "If General Jackson comes along this road, show him that!"[7]

The duel took place in 1806 in Logan County, Kentucky, near the Tennessee border. In their quick-draw duel, Jackson knew he was at a competitive disadvantage because Dickinson was a better shot. Stoically, Jackson decided to hold his fire rather than risk missing in the quick draw. Rather, Jackson simply stood his ground while his opponent drew and fired. Dickinson did and hit Jackson in the chest. But, Jackson remained standing, leading Dickinson to blurt out in disbelief, "Great God! Have I missed him?" With the crowd looking on, Jackson then carefully took aim and pulled the trigger. He now had the luxury of taking his time and aiming. But the hammer stuck. Dickinson began to panic, babbling illegibly that Jackson should be dead. While efforts were made to calm Dickinson, Jackson pulled a second pistol and fired. The shot was true and Dickinson bled to death. To the astonished audience at the duel, Jackson boasted that he would have lived to kill his foe even if he had been "shot through the brain."[8]

It was said of Jackson that when he walked, "he rattled like a jar of marbles" on account of the many bullets that filled his body.[9] Not surprisingly, Jackson earned the nickname "Old Hickory" because he was a strong as the tree. As president, Jackson even survived an attempted assassination when a deranged British expatriate named Robert Lawrence, claiming to be King Richard III, fired two pistols at the president outside the U.S. Capitol. Miraculously, both pistols misfired. Jackson then sprang on his would-be assassin and beat the man with his cane.

## THE SOUTHERN INDIANS

Jackson had made a name for himself not only as a duelist but as a judge and possible political leader. When the War of 1812 broke out, Jackson was made a general in the Tennessee militia. He was eager to get into the fight, having spent his entire life waiting to exact revenge for what the British did to his family. Writing to General William Henry Harrison after the Battle of Tippecanoe, Jackson asked to join the fight. He also spent the first year of the war making requests of Tennessee's governor, Willie Blount, and the secretary of war to permit him to raise a militia of 4,000 men for the invasion of Canada. Jackson boasted he would be ready to march in ten days.[10] To his dismay, Jackson was passed over in each instance. As such, Jackson grew impatient during the first year of the war, champing at the bit to see action.

Congress ultimately authorized Tennessee to raise volunteers for the war effort and Jackson made it known throughout Tennessee that he would lead his state to glory in Canada. He wrote:

> How pleasing the prospect that would open to the young vol-
> unteer, while performing a military promenade into a distant
> country . . . To view the stupendous works of nature, exempli-
> fied in the falls of Niagara . . . would of themselves repay the
> young soldier for a march across the continent.[11]

Jackson never was sent to Canada, but his dance card was drawn when citizens, newspapers, and politicians demanded the Creek Indian raids along the Gulf Coast be dealt with.

A turning point in the campaign against the southern tribes occurred on August 30, 1813, when a large war party attacked and massacred civilians at Fort Mims in Alabama. Word of the massacre spread far and wide, causing panic among settlements across the South. Jackson was sent to deal with the Creeks and other southern Indian nations, many of whom had been inspired by the great chief, Tecumseh, and his call for Indian unity and opposition to American settlement of Indian lands. Jackson vowed the massacre at Fort Mims would be avenged with equal brutality. He would soon be given the chance to fulfill his promise.

The governor and legislature of Tennessee organized a large militia to deal with the "Indian problem" on their southern border. Two armies were deployed from Tennessee rather than one, however, for the purpose of trying to satisfy the two main military commanders from the state, both of whom wanted to be in charge. One force of roughly 2,500 men was assigned to General John Cocke and the other, of equal size, was commanded by General Andrew Jackson. In October of 1813, the two armies marched separately to Alabama. Jackson, whose arm was still in a sling from a recent bullet shot, was so weak he had to be lifted onto his horse. The armies would rendezvous in the Mississippi territory and Alabama with an army led by General John Floyd with a force of Georgia militiamen and General Ferdinand Claiborne in command of Mississippi volunteers and the Third Regiment of regulars.[12]

Despite Jackson's delay in marching south and impressive number of men raised, in truth the armies resembled organized mobs rather than disciplined fighting forces. They were not properly equipped and the men had received virtually no training. Many of the supplies promised never arrived and the unruly volunteers itched to attack anyone. Already running low on food, ammunition, and supplies, Jackson's army arrived in Alabama at the end of October, setting up camp in Creek territory in central Alabama near the Coosa River. Word soon arrived that a large number of warriors were nearby at a village named Tallushatchee.

Jackson dispatched his trusted number two—Major General John Coffee—with at least 900 men and Cherokee allies, most of them mounted, for the purpose of destroying the Creek warriors. It did not matter whether the village of Tallassahatchee was home to friendly Creeks or hostile Creeks aligned with Chief Weatherford and his allies. On November 3, Coffee organized his men into two columns and was able to draw the warriors out of the village and into a trap. In the bloody attack that followed, the warriors were surrounded and annihilated, and the village was sacked. Women and children were killed.

The death toll was placed at 186. Davy Crockett, who would go on from the battle to enjoy great fame as a frontier politician, described the scene in barbaric terms, saying, "We shot them like dogs." Only eighty-four women and children survived the massacre, and they were taken prisoner. General Coffee lost only five men and had another forty-one wounded.[13] The campaign against the Red Sticks and other hostile Indian nations in the southeast had begun.

## DEFEATING THE CREEKS

Jackson's scouts then discovered the movements of a Creek war party rough-ly thirty miles away at Talladega. The warriors were attacking both white settlements and Indians allied with the United States. Itching for a fight, Jackson set off immediately to engage the Creeks. His army of 800 cavalry and 1,200 infantry arrived at the hostile Creek village on November 8. A bonus was waiting in the village for Jackson. William Weatherford, the half-white chief who had organized so many bloody raids against white settlers, was there with his braves.

Before sunrise on November 9, Jackson gave the order to attack. In typical Jackson fashion the attack was made head on and with little plan-ning. However, when the Creek warriors began fighting back, some militia units in the middle of Jackson's line broke ranks and ran. The Americans had underestimated the strength of the warriors. Nearly 1,000 warriors joined the fight and the tide of the battle was turning against Jackson. However, Jackson ordered his cavalry to quickly ride to encircle the Indi-ans and he inspired his militia units to stand their ground and fight. The cavalry charge from both sides of the battle prompted the Creek warriors to flee. The Americans carried the day in yet another bloody affair. Jackson reported that nearly 300 Creeks were killed, while his army suffered only seventeen dead and eighty wounded.[14]

The carnage continued. Another American army sacked Hillibee vil-lage on November 18, killing at least sixty Creeks and taking hundreds pris-oner. Brigadier General John Floyd and nearly 1,000 Georgia militiamen attacked Indian villages near Auttose on the Tallapoosa River on November 29, killing hundreds.[15] It was an all-out war on the Creeks of the southeast.

Through November, thousands of Creeks and other Indians were killed. It was a ruthless reprisal for the Fort Mims massacre. The raw recruits constituting the armies from Tennessee and Georgia were poorly supplied, but they fought like demons, exacting a terrible toll on their enemies. However, despite the momentum, poor logistics prevented the campaign from continuing. After a few weeks, the armies ran short on supplies and ammunition. Promised reinforcements—to take over from militia units with short enlistments—never arrived. With the period of enlistment for many of the volunteers completed, men simply picked up and began the long walk back home. Others deserted, leaving only Jackson and a small force in the region.

Unable to prevent his own men from leaving—even though he pulled a pistol on some of them—Jackson marched a much smaller army to support the Georgia militia, setting up camp at Fort Strother.[16] From December through January, Jackson was down to 130 men. After destroying the Creeks, Jackson's small band was now vulnerable to attack.

In mid-January of 1814, roughly 800 new volunteers arrived at Fort Strother. Eager to continue the campaign against the Creeks, Jackson did not even bother to train the raw recruits before marching them out of the fort and into battle. More men arrived from Tennessee and other states. Jackson enjoyed two smaller, but decisive victories, one at Emuckfau Creek in Alabama on January 22, 1814, and another at nearby Enotachopco Creek five days later. As additional recruits arrived, Jackson was eager to finish off his adversaries. He marched his reinforced army in pursuit of the main Creek stronghold at an Indian village named Tohopeka but known to the Americans as Horseshoe Bend.

## HORSESHOE BEND

The Creeks—and especially the Red Stick tribes who were a militant part of the nation—had been a formidable fighting force throughout much of the South, conducting raids at will. This changed in the fall of 1813 when Jackson and other commanders struck numerous Indian villages with bloody results. By 1814, the Creeks found themselves on the run and fighting for their very existence. Even the ferocious Red Sticks, named for the red war clubs they carried, weapons thought to have magical powers, proved to be no match for Jackson's ruthlessness. By summer of 1814, the direction of the war was changing. The Indian resistance in the Northwest Territory had been destroyed with the death of Tecumseh at the Battle of Thames and the Indian campaign in the southeast was decimating the Creek nation. The British were about to taste defeat in the northern theater of the war at Lake Champlain, Plattsburg, and Fort Erie, while their Chesapeake campaign was about to end at Baltimore.

Most of the 4,000 Red Stick warriors who had been raiding villages throughout the South were now on the run. As word of Jackson's victories spread through the Creek nation, Indians knew they were facing a matter of surrendering to Jackson or being killed. Many turned themselves in. But the last remnants of the once-proud nation who were unwilling to surrender holed up at the village of Tohopeka on the Tallapoosa River in Alabama near a bend in the river resembling a horseshoe. Rather than flee or continue their raids on white settlements and small forts, the Creeks fortified themselves on a peninsula roughly 100 acres in diameter where the Tallapoosa River bent at a sharp angle. From there, the remaining 1,200 Creek warriors—mostly Red Sticks under Chief Manawa—dug in, building earthworks and fortifications that resembled those of the armies they opposed. In fact, General Jackson suspected the British or Spanish had aided the Red Sticks in building the structures. It would be their last stand.[17]

Now possessing several thousand new militia recruits from Tennessee and reinforcements from the 39th Regiment, Jackson marched to Tohopeka. He arrived on March 27, 1814, with an army three times the size of the Creek defenders. He was also supported by loyal Creek, Choctaw, and Cherokee warriors. Without organizing a siege, building batteries, or offering the Creeks terms, Jackson hit them immediately. To soften up the defenses, the American artillery bombed the earthworks and defenses for over one hour with 3- and 6-pound cannons. However, the cannons were too small to do much damage to earthen defenses, inspiring the Creeks inside to loudly mock the Americans. This only made Jackson angrier and, at ten-thirty that morning, Jackson ordered his loyal friend, John Coffee, to lead a cavalry unit across the river to begin the attack and to send a flank around the village in order to cut off any route of escape. Coffee's Indian allies swam across the river and cut free the Creeks' canoes. There would be no escape and no surrender.

Jackson led the frontal assault, ordering the 39th Regiment across the river. The cavalry and Jackson's regulars overwhelmed the minimal fortifications in minutes. In the hand-to-hand fighting that ensued, Jackson's men slaughtered everyone they encountered. Huts were set ablaze and fleeing Indians were shot. In the words on one historian "Once [the Americans] were into the horseshoe it was more a massacre than a battle."[18]

In desperation, the Creeks retreated to a small, wooden fortification inside the compound. One of the first Americans to reach the fort was Major Lemuel Montgomery, a descendent of the famed Richard Montgomery who led the assault on Quebec in 1775 during the Revolutionary War. Major Montgomery climbed the wall to the roof of the structure and from that high vantage point rallied his men to follow. He was shot in the head and died on the spot, but his actions motivated the Americans, who quickly overran the fort. His second-in-command was a young Sam Houston, who would later gain fame at the Alamo in Texas. Lieutenant Houston and his men broke through the main door and into the fort. The Americans also surrounded the wooden structure and aimed their muskets through the small holes and gaps between the logs. Those inside had no chance.

With their defenses breached and ruin upon them, many of the Creeks panicked and ran to the river's edge. But their canoes had been sent adrift. As they tried to forge the river, Coffee's cavalry fired down on them. It is estimated that 300 Indians were killed while trying to swim across the river. Behind them, Jackson completed his sweep through the small peninsula, killing an estimated 557 Creeks and destroying all resistance.[19] The general described the sight, saying simply "The carnage was dreadful."[20]

The battle was over quickly. Only three warriors remained alive on the peninsula and roughly 350 women and children were captured. Jackson lost only twenty-six dead and roughly 150 wounded, with perhaps two dozen casualties among his Indian allies in the one-sided battle.[21] Horseshoe Bend was one of the most impressive American victories of the war. The only drawback of the victory was that William Weatherford, the half-Indian chief that had long harassed the Americans, was unaccounted for. He had again slipped through the noose. The battle also helped Jackson move beyond his earlier suspect association with Aaron Burr's scheme for a western empire and positioned him as the leader of the defense of the American South. Of the decisive battle, Jackson justified his decision to not accept surrender, saying, "The fiends of the Tallapoosa will no longer murder our Women and Children, or disturb the quiet of our borders."[22] The future of the southern Indian ended that day.

After the battle, Jackson was promoted to brigadier general and given command of the military district based in Mobile. In that capacity, he set about building forts along the Gulf Coast. He also forced the remaining Creek villages to surrender their lands and even took lands from allied Indian nations, accusing all Indians of disloyalty and treachery, and treating First Americans from across the region with equal brutality. In a treaty signed at Fort Jackson near Montgomery, millions of acres of Indian lands—regardless if they were Creek or Cherokee—through Georgia, Alabama, and Mississippi were confiscated.[23] After the treaty, the Cherokee leader, Chief Junaluska, who fought alongside the Americans against the Red Sticks, said in frustration, "If I had known that Jackson would drive us from our homes, I would have killed him that day at the Horseshoe."[24]

William Weatherford, known also as Chief Red Eagle, finally reappeared. He decided to surrender to Jackson with the words: "My warriors can no longer hear my voice. Their bones are at Talladega, Tallushatchee, Emuckfau, and Tohopeka . . . I now ask for [peace] for my nation, and for myself." It was too late for that.[25]

# ECHOES

"Peace of Ghent 1814 and triumph of America." Acknowledgment: By P. Price, Jr., Philadelphia, 1915; U.S. Library of Congress, Washington, DC (LC-USZ62-3686).

# THE SOUTHERN CAMPAIGN

## GULF COAST

Much of the War of 1812 was fought along the Canadian border, requiring the northern states and their militia units to shoulder a disproportionate amount of the war effort. Yet, a key component of the war was the campaign against the southern Indians, namely the Creek Nation, and Britain's effort to invade America from the Gulf Coast toward the end of 1814. But America's interest in invading Canada drew both attention and resources away from the southern campaign, and many in the South did not feel threatened by either the British or hostile Indians. As such, there was only minimal thought given to coastal defenses or suppressing the Creek uprising in the South, even though James Madison, James Monroe, Henry Clay, and other war leaders were from the region.

The War Department eventually sent General James Wilkinson to command the Gulf Coast. He requested 10,000 men and forty ships, but was given only a few small gunboats and fewer than 1,700 men for the entire region. The Gulf Coast never would be adequately garrisoned or defended. Wilkinson was charged with securing the region and occupying Spanish Florida. A worse pick for the job could not have been made, as Wilkinson was corrupt, incompetent, and on Spain's payroll as a spy against his own government. Wilkinson managed to take West Florida and the port of Mobile in the spring of 1813, not because of superior military tactics, but because the Spanish were abandoning the area. However, the general was reassigned to the Canadian theater of war, which would end up being a blessing in disguise for the Gulf. Once again, though, military operations in the South languished.

All this changed when the Red Sticks and other Creek warriors began slaughtering settlers throughout Alabama and Georgia, and news of the massacre at Fort Mims reached Washington. Through the late fall of 1813,

Andrew Jackson was dispatched to the Gulf Coast, where he proceeded to destroy the Creeks in several brutal battles that November. By the end of March of 1814, the campaign was essentially concluded with the complete destruction of the Creek stronghold at Horseshoe Bend in Alabama.[1]

Jackson had longed to command an army on the Gulf Coast or to be sent to invade Canada. However, the outspoken general had more than his fair share of opponents in high office, none of whom wanted him anywhere near the glory of battle. Old Hickory did his cause little good when he called out other commanders and units as cowards for refusing to march into Canada or for failing to destroy the Creeks in the South. Said the headstrong Tennessean:

> If the government orders . . . (I would) rejoice at the opportunity of placing the American eagle on the ramparts of Mobile, Pensacola, and Fort Saint Augustine, effectually banishing from the southern coasts all British influence.[2]

When Jackson urged President Madison to allow him to send an army to Canada, some of the volunteers he lured to the mission were sent but under the command of William Henry Harrison rather than under Jackson's command. The spirited Jackson was the polar opposite of his cerebral president and Madison both opposed putting the wild duelist in charge of his southern defenses and nearly removed Jackson during the campaign. Had he done so, history might very well have been quite different. Jackson chafed while awaiting his opportunity, frustrated by delays. But this would only end up aiding Jackson during the southern campaign, as it built in him a steely determination to accomplish his mission.[3]

Jackson suspected his earlier association with Aaron Burr and the western empire scheme were to blame for his inaction. Other politicians did not trust Jackson's judgment or his ability to be "controlled." Several southern politicians and War Hawks wanted to seize Spanish Florida, which had been transferred from British control in 1783 as part of the Treaty of Paris that ended the American Revolution. But other political leaders including President Madison understood the risks involved in the effort, lest Spain be brought into the war too. Napoleon had removed Ferdinand VII from the Spanish throne but the Spanish found an ally in Britain. As such, Spain could be counted on to support Britain in America and to allow them free reign in their holdings in Florida and Texas. American war planners fretted over this possible alliance, noting that "Whoever possesses the Floridas held a pistol at the heart of the republic."[4]

Because of the sensitivities involved—the situation required a political scalpel, not a military axe—Jackson was not the right man. One of America's most vicious warriors, but one who openly lobbied for seizing Florida and the whole Gulf Coast, almost did not get into the fight. Eventually, however, with Indian atrocities in the South mounting and American efforts in Canada failing, there was little choice but to send Jackson. Jackson enjoyed a close relationship with the governor of his home state of Tennessee, and his friend put him in command of the state's militia ordered to the Gulf.[5]

The British also understood the strategic importance of the Gulf Coast to securing the Mississippi River and controlling America's trade and access to the frontier settlements. To take the Gulf and "Big Muddy" was to cut America in half. But the necessity of fighting Napoleon in Europe and simultaneously defending Canada prevented Britain from seizing the Gulf and marching up the Mississippi. They had neither the funds nor spare troops for the task.

However, when the Napoleonic campaign began winding down and thanks to Admiral Cochrane's continual agitation, an attack on the Gulf Coast was put in motion in the spring of 1814. Captain Hugh Pigot, aboard the HMS *Orpheus* and supported by the HMS *Shelburne*, was sent to the Gulf, where he gathered intelligence, began planning for the invasion, supplied the Creeks with armaments, and fomented rebellion. A major British offensive was pending. It was a good thing for the Americans that Andrew Jackson and not James Wilkinson was put in charge of the region's defense.

## THE DEFENSE OF FORT BOWYER

On May 10, 1814, British ships dropped anchor by the Apalachicola River. Landing parties brought weapons and supplies ashore for the purpose of arming Indians along the Gulf Coast who were fighting the Americans. One of them was led by Major Edward Nicholls who, with the assistance of 100 Royal Marines, provided stockpiles of arms to Indians, escaped slaves, disaffected Spaniards, and others. He and other British agents even met with and promised pirates operating in the Gulf of Mexico that they would not be harassed (as was the practice of the American navy). When the British field operatives reported back to commanders, they assured them that Britain would have the full support of Indians and pirates in the Gulf and that these allies would inflict damage on the American army. However, by the time the British flotilla arrived to begin the southern invasion in the late fall, the Creek rebellion was crushed and other Indian nations in the region were pacified.[6]

Satisfied with his early reconnaissance, Admiral Cochrane requested a full invasion of the Gulf Coast on June 20, 1814, and decided to lead the attack himself with the support of General Robert Ross. He suggested that a force of 3,000 British regulars striking at Mobile around November "would drive the Americans entirely out of Louisiana and the Floridas."[7] However, driven by his hatred of the Americans, an overconfident Cochrane failed to plan for a number of contingencies and he rushed the invasion in the event peace was achieved. He threatened, "I have it much at heart to give them a complete drubbing before Peace is made."[8] The plan suffered its first setback when General Ross was killed during the failed attempt to sack Baltimore. Cochrane also assumed he would face cowardly commanders and militia units who would run at the sight of the massive British force.

Ultimately, the British invasion plan was expanded to include several thousand additional men from the Napoleonic conflict and a West Indian regiment. They would be joined by Major General John Keane, replacing Ross, with even more troops. The large armies would rendezvous in Jamaica in mid-November, and proceed to New Orleans. Smaller, advance forces were ordered to begin striking at American ports and forts in September.

Andrew Jackson arrived on the Gulf Coast to find defenses at New Orleans, Mobile, and other key sites utterly lacking and the populace in a panic over word of a pending attack by a massive British army. Mobile was a town of less than 1,000 inhabitants. However, it was a critically important location that could be used to support the southern invasion. The town was defended by a small fort roughly thirty miles from the downtown and nestled on the edge of the entrance to Mobile Bay. It was named for the officer who built it a year prior—Colonel John Bowyer. There was no time to build additional forts; Fort Bowyer would have to do.

Mobile had been a Spanish possession, but became part of the United States when the war started. The Spanish abandoned the town in April of 1813, two months before Bowyer assumed control of the site and began expanding the sand, wooden, and earthen stockade with a commanding view of the bay front. Fourteen cannons were placed behind its walls, but

only two of them were large guns, and the fort was still under construction when the British arrived in September. Jackson had the fort garrisoned
with roughly 120 to 160 infantrymen under Major William Lawrence. Fort
Bowyer would soon be faced with the first of two battles in this war, and
it would later be the site of the Civil War naval engagement made famous
by Admiral David Farragut's immortal battle cry: "Damn the torpedoes.
Full speed ahead!"[9]

On September 11—two weeks after Washington was burned and a
day before the British would launch their doomed invasion of Baltimore—
four ships from the Royal Navy set sail from Pensacola in Florida's western
panhandle to begin the invasion of the Gulf Coast. Their destination was
Mobile Bay and the small fort that protected it. In command was Captain
Henry Percey with his flagship the HMS *Hermes*, sporting twenty guns,
and the HMS *Sophie*, HMS *Carron*, and HMS *Childers*, only slightly less
powerful ships. Many of the guns were carronades, which were effective in
short-range situations and thus required the ships to engage Fort Bowyer
at point-blank range. This would be their undoing.

About nine miles east of Fort Bowyer, Captain Percey disembarked
roughly seventy Royal Marines who rendezvoused with 130 loyal Indians.
This small force was under the command of Lieutenant Colonel Edward
Nicholls. However, Nicholls fell ill from dysentery and his force marched
along the beach to the fort without him, hoping to create a diversion on
land while the small squadron attacked the fort by sea. The land force was
now led by Captain George Woodbine, who ordered his marines to build
a battery in the sand dunes outside the fort for their small cannon.

On September 14, the land attack began but was quickly repelled by
the defenders inside Fort Bowyer. The next day the four ships sailed up
to the fort and positioned themselves to bombard the structure. The guns
inside the fort fired first, beginning at roughly three-thirty in the afternoon.
The *Hermes* and *Sophie* returned fire soon afterward, while the other two
ships tried to position themselves without the necessary wind. Without a
strong wind, the other two ships were unable to support the *Hermes* and
*Sophie*. These two ships were on their own and unable to maneuver.

The bombardment lasted over two hours, but the British ships took
the main brunt of the American barrage. An explosion on deck sent shrapnel and splinters flying. The debris hit Colonel Nicholls in the head and
legs, and took out one of his eyes. The sails and rigging of the *Hermes*
were torn apart, the bow was struck by a direct hit, and the anchor line
was ripped from the ship. The wounded ship ran aground near the fort

and her sailors had to be evacuated by rowboats sent from the *Sophie*. All the while, the Americans continued their artillery fire, preventing the crew of the stranded ship from an orderly evacuation. Captain Percey, having lost his flag ship, ordered it burned. When the flames reached the main magazine that evening, the ship blew to pieces on the shoreline.[10]

Embarrassed from the loss of his flagship and with at least thirty-two dead, a few dozen wounded, and his team on land defeated, Percey called off the invasion of Mobile and sailed away. The Americans inside Fort Bowyer suffered only four dead and another four wounded. The small fort prevailed and Mobile was, for the moment, saved. The British assault on the Gulf Coast was dealt another setback. When news of the defeat reached the high command, they delayed the invasion. This only gave Andrew Jackson time to plan his defenses.

## SEIZING PENSACOLA

American commanders received reports that British units were using forts in Spanish Florida. The British captain, George Woodbine, was known to be operating in Florida and meeting with Spanish officials; and in August of 1814, British troops arrived to occupy Fort San Miguel and work with the Spanish at Fort San Carlos. From Florida they had earlier incited hostile Indians to attack American settlements and now could launch the southern invasion of the country. Also, after the defeat of the Creek nation at the hands of Andrew Jackson, many of the vanquished Indians fled to Spanish Florida. As such, Jackson itched to march on Pensacola. Even though it was not his assigned mission, Jackson's aim was to drive the British from the forts, capital city, and from Spanish Florida. Interestingly, a letter ordering the general not to touch Pensacola because of the risk of bringing the Spanish into the war was sent to Jackson. It did not arrive until after the war ended, however.[11]

Jackson's dilemma was that his army remained much depleted due to desertions and the terms of militia enlistments expiring after his campaign across Alabama and major victory at Horseshoe Bend earlier that year. As such, Jackson had to wait for his friend and fellow general, John Coffee, to arrive with additional volunteers. Coffee delivered. In November of 1814, after rendezvousing with Coffee in Alabama, Jackson marched to Pensacola with an army of roughly 4,000 volunteers.

Arriving on the outskirts of the city, Jackson sent Major Henri Piere as a messenger under a white flag to meet with the Spanish governor, Mateo Gonzales Manrique, to discuss terms. But Piere was fired upon. Jackson dispatched a second messenger—a Spaniard—who passed along the demands that the British evacuate Florida. Spain was offered neutrality. From inside the city, Governor Manrique refused. The governor had 500 Spanish soldiers at nearby Fort San Carlos, while the British held Fort San Miguel with 100 men. They were supported by a few loyal Creeks and Seminoles.[12]

At dawn on November 7, Jackson marched most of his army to Pensacola, surrounding the city. The sandy beaches made it difficult to transport their artillery, but Jackson was determined to sack Pensacola with or without his cannons. A battery defended the outskirts of the city and Jackson ordered his men to charge it. It was captured in minutes. As the general prepared to enter the city, Governor Manrique approached his foes under a white flag. The governor surrendered and agreed to any terms Jackson might have as long as the city would be spared. An agreement was reached. Fort San Miguel was given to the Americans, but the British in the fort had fled to Fort San Carlos roughly fourteen miles away.

Jackson then marched his army to San Carlos. However, as he prepared to storm the fort on November 8, the British abandoned it and blew it up. The small British garrison fled to rendezvous with the HMS *Sophie* and the small squadron of warships in the area. They immediately set sail ahead of Jackson's army.

Jackson had taken an important city and driven the British from West Florida with only minimal casualties and fighting. Only seven Americans were dead and another dozen wounded. Jackson accomplished something else too. The Spanish were furious that the British abandoned and destroyed their fort without a fight. Victorious, Jackson returned to Mobile on November 11 and began preparations for the defense of New Orleans. This would be the real test of the southern campaign.

# 34

# THE TREATY OF GHENT

## A CHRISTMAS EVE PEACE

The War of 1812 had never been a very popular war. Much of the citizenry of Britain, Canada, and the United States were opposed to the war from its inception. The unnecessary and unfortunate attacks against civilian populations by both sides as well as the economic hardships resulting from the war further eroded support for the war among the public, press, and politicians. Many people were therefore hopeful a treaty would quickly be negotiated. That was not to be the case.

The British monarch and government were initially opposed to peace talks. The fact that the war seemed to be going their way through 1813 and British pride—they had lost to the upstart colonials before—prevented them from pursuing peace. However, key defeats in 1814 and a growing frustration with the cost and length of the war brought them to the table in earnest. For example, in the early rounds of talks the British sent only low-ranking diplomats. But, as the British commissioner, Henry Goulburn, observed: "If we had either burnt Baltimore or held Plattsburgh, I believe we should have had peace on our terms. But as things appear to be going on in America, the result of our negotiations may be very different."[1]

Although the prospects for an end to the war were doubtful, peace talks continued through the summer and fall of 1814 in the city of Ghent in Belgium. President Madison sent able peace commissioners such as John Quincy Adams, Albert Gallatin, and Henry Carroll. To please his detractors in Congress, he reluctantly agreed to send Henry Clay, the war-mongering Speaker from Kentucky whose inflammatory rhetoric probably did more to rush America into a foolish war than anything else. However, even the hawkish Clay had experienced a change of heart—as much as was possible for him—and now embraced peace.[2]

Months passed with little progress toward peace. No substantive offers of peace were forthcoming from either side, and the peace commissioners met only infrequently. The British demanded territorial concessions. They wanted Maine and free access to the Mississippi River. For their Indian allies, they requested the western Great Lakes and territories in the American South and West. In present-day terms, the Americans would have had to surrender the states of Illinois, Indiana, Michigan, and Wisconsin as well as western Ohio. Obviously, these conditions were unacceptable to most Americans, the administration of James Madison, and especially the expansionists in the frontier and southern states.

The British hard line, however, softened in the fall on account of several major American victories in the war. Gone were the requests for Maine and western Ohio and access to the Mississippi River. The issue of Indian sovereignty and lands was also taken off the table. On November 27, the British also dropped their claim to *uti possidetis*, Latin for "as you possess," a doctrine dating to Roman times allowing a belligerent party to claim territory conquered in war. These more realistic positions allowed the peace talks to move forward.[3]

Even so, the reality that they had failed to win another war against America was painful for most Britons. British newspapers and politicians expressed their shock and dismay at the unfavorable terms in the treaty. The *London Times* opined:

> We have retired from the combat with the stripes yet bleeding on our backs . . . [and] with the recent defeats, at Plattsburgh, and on Lake Champlain, unavenged. To make peace at such a moment . . . betrays a deadness to the feelings of honour, and shows a timidity of disposition, inviting further insult."[4]

Some even worried that America would begin preparing to invade the British Isles. But most Britons had tired of the blood and expenditure halfway across the world and preferred to focus on the post-Napoleonic order in Europe.

On December 24, the treaty was finally agreed upon by both sides in Ghent. The British government signed the treaty just four days later. Interestingly, the issues that caused the war—impressment, sailor's rights, free trade—were not a part of the negotiated peace. In fact, they were not even mentioned in the treaty. After Britain defeated Napoleon, the basis for impressment and trade sanctions were no longer pertinent. The emperor abdicated on April 6, 1814, and the first Treaty of Paris was signed on May 30, 1814, helping to facilitate the terms at Ghent.

## QUESTIONS

Unfortunately, as the peace negotiators in Belgium were concluding their business, a large British flotilla was in the Gulf of Mexico, unloading a massive army headed for New Orleans. Owing to primitive transportation and communication systems, word of the treaty would not arrive in time to prevent the coming fight. But another peace convention held in Connecticut without the blessings of the Madison administration hoped to end the war immediately.

The Hartford Convention began on December 15, 1814, and ran until January 4, 1815. The goals of its organizers included ending the war and the trade embargoes that proved to be so ruinous for New England merchants, shippers, and communities. Attended by New England Federalists who had long opposed what they deemed "Mr. Madison's War," they hoped to end the war by formally preventing their state militias from being used in the continued efforts to invade Canada. At the same time they opposed the invasion of Canada, communities throughout New England wanted their militias protecting the home front when the region was threatened by a British invasion in 1814. Such a prohibition against the use of New England militias was not the only way to end the war. The Convention also opposed a state loan to the federal government to finance the war and leaders such as Roger Griswold, John Lowell, Timothy Pickering, and others suggested New England enter into their own peace treaty with the British.

It nearly happened. Delegates from Connecticut, Massachusetts, New Hampshire, Rhode Island, and Vermont, loyal to the Federalist effort held meetings in secret. This led to the Hartford Convention, whose presiding officer was George Cabot of Massachusetts, a moderate on the war question. He was assisted by Theodore Dwight and Harrison Gray Otis. The delegates at Hartford even considered a resolution to secede from the Union but the moderate, wiser faction was able to defeat the measure. What the Convention did accomplish was to produce a report highly critical of President Madison and the southern and frontier War Hawks who rushed the country into the conflict. The Convention also proposed amendments to the Constitution to limit war powers and the favoritism shown to southern states.[5]

The effort by these "Peace Hawks," however, was undermined by the timing of their final report, which coincided with the announcements that America won a great battle at New Orleans and that peace had been achieved. The timing embarrassed the region and contributed to the demise of the Federalist Party.

Within days, three separate—and very different—messages were dispatched to Washington. Riders from New Orleans would race north to deliver the news of the American victory at New Orleans in January; two of the peace commissioners, Henry Carroll of the United States, and Britain's Anthony St. John Baker, set sail from Europe on the HMS *Favorite* with the treaty in hand; and Harrison Gray Otis and two other delegates from the Hartford Convention headed south with a petition to end the war and express the growing interest in impeaching James Madison if he did not make peace.

Stormy seas prevented the HMS *Favorite* from sailing up the Chesapeake to deliver the treaty to President Madison. Instead, the ship was diverted to New York and did not dock until February 11. On February 4, news had finally reached Washington that the British were defeated at New Orleans. The peace commissioners were thus greeted by a city still in the throes of wild celebrations—not because of peace, but on account of victory in New Orleans. Riders spread out across the country to carry reports of the victory. It was received far and wide by jubilant crowds. Coincidentally, this raised in the peace commissioners' minds, and back in Britain, the possibility that Americans would not want peace and the War Hawks in Congress would pressure the president and their peers not to sign the Treaty of Ghent.[6]

To their relief, when Ghent Commissioners Carroll and Baker arrived to announce that peace had been reached in Ghent, the public's celebration only increased. Bonfires roared across the capital city and cannons signaled salutes. Similarly, across the country church bells rang and people took to the streets to celebrate. In New England, where bitter feelings over the war remained and support for the Hartford Convention was strong, disagreements were put aside to join in the festivities. Peace would prevail. Any concerns Carroll and Baker had about support for their peace treaty seemed misplaced and even underwhelming. Americans seemed more interested in celebrating the victory at New Orleans than in details of the treaty. Moreover, their major announcement had been usurped. Another American delegate from Ghent, Christopher Hughes, had made better time sailing to nearby Annapolis and had delivered news of the treaty on February 8, beating them to the punch.

Not everyone was forgiven. When the Hartford Convention delegates arrived in Baltimore they learned of both the peace treaty in Ghent and the American victory in New Orleans. Their concern was that their bad timing would make them appear to be traitors. Indeed, General Winfield Scott, one of the war's most celebrated heroes, dismissed the delegates as "grievance deputies" and wrote to Secretary of State James Monroe that the convention was no more than "a fine subject of jest and merriment to men of all parties." Sure enough, when they arrived in Washington they were jeered and President Madison refused to even see them.[7]

## WINNING THE PEACE

The "Treaty of Peace and Amity between His Britannic Majesty and the United States of America" stated that the Americans and British were:

> . . . desirous of terminating the war which has unhappily sub-
> sisted between the two countries, and of restoring, upon principles
> of perfect reciprocity, peace, friendship, and good understanding
> between them, have, for that purpose, appointed their respective
> Plenipotentiaries. . . .[8]

The treaty was presented to the Senate, who ratified it on February 16 by a vote of thirty-five to zero. It was signed by President Madison on the 17th. That night, he met with the British envoy, Anthony St. John Baker, for a positive discussion. The next day, the president proclaimed peace and delivered a message to Congress, saying that the war was fought "with a success which is the natural result of the wisdom of the Legislative councils, of the patriotism of the people, of the public spirit of the militia, and of the valor of the military and naval forces of the country."[9]

The treaty consisted of eleven articles. The first three declared a cease fire, the return of all territories, papers, documents, and property (Article I), an end to naval hostilities and a recall of warships (Article II), and the return of all prisoners of war (Article III). Articles four through six gave the United States control of any islands within 20 leagues of the American shoreline (Article IV), established a boundary between the United States and Canada (Article V) and along the middle of Lake Ontario, Lake Erie, Lake Huron, Lake Superior, and all rivers near the border (Article VI). The next three articles created boards of commissioners charged with surveying and negotiating both the ownership of western territories and implementing the details of the treaty. Surprisingly, given the power of the frontier and southern War Hawks, many of whom were slaveholders, Article X stated:

> Whereas the traffic in slaves is irreconcilable with the principles of humanity and justice, and whereas both His Majesty and the United States are desirous of continuing their efforts to promote its entire abolition, it is hereby agreed that both the contracting parties shall use their best endeavors to accomplish so desirable an object.[10]

While the British finally reconciled the need for the peace treaty, they worried about America's response to it and anxiously awaited word not only of whether the treaty had been signed but America's response to the Hartford Convention. No one knew how this surprise event would factor into the larger terms of the peace. At the same time, the British hoped for word that the final campaign of the war had ended in victory. The massive British army was striking at New Orleans with plans to invade northward along the Mississippi River. The overwhelming victory Britain expected would help heal the bitterness of the war. It might also expedite the signing of the Treaty of Ghent or possibly even derail the peace. Victory at the mouth of the mighty Mississippi might also impact the nature of the Louisiana Purchase. Because Britain refused to recognize any actions by Napoleon, they saw the sale of the vast central region of the United States as illegitimate.

On March 9, news finally arrived in Britain that their massive army was annihilated by a much smaller American force under Andrew Jackson. They then discovered that Napoleon had escaped from his incarceration at Elba and was again on the prowl. Just four days later, however, word arrived that the Americans had signed the peace treaty. Britain had no choice but to move beyond the war with America.

It took almost as long for word to spread through the American frontier and Canada. Skirmishes continued through mid-February and Governor Prevost did not hear about the peace until a rider arrived in Quebec on March 1. Long after the Treaty of Ghent, animosities continued between the Americans and British, and border disputes were not uncommon. Negotiations continued between the two countries for many years. In 1817, for example, the Rush-Bagot Convention was signed between Richard Rush, the acting American secretary of state and Charles Bagot, the British Minister to Washington. It was ratified in the Senate a year later. The Convention addressed disarmament on the border and limited both countries to four warships, each of less than 100 tons on the Great Lakes. As time passed, Anglo-American relations warmed and the two powers enjoyed a long peace and prosperous cooperation.[11]

One thing the Treaty of Ghent did not do was deal with the pressing matter in December of 1814 of the massive British army preparing to sack New Orleans and invade the American South.

# 35

# THE BATTLE OF NEW ORLEANS

## PREPARATIONS

After dispatching the Creek nation earlier in the year and seizing Pensacola on November 7, Andrew Jackson moved his army to Mobile Bay, where the small American detachment there had just successfully repelled an attempt by the British to siege the fort guarding the entrance to the bay and city. The general then marched his army to New Orleans on November 22, 1814. There was no time to waste. Reports arrived that the British were preparing a massive third prong to their invasion of the United States. The northern prong had failed miserably at Lake Champlain and Plattsburgh, and the central prong along the Chesapeake, after a crushing victory at Bladensburg and sacking Washington, stalled at Baltimore. British commanders were eager to redeem themselves with one final assault at New Orleans. They planned for the complete destruction of the city and its defenders, as a first step to an invasion from the south [see Map 8 in Appendix].

But they were not the only ones itching for a fight. Jackson had lusted for British blood ever since the Revolutionary War when, as a child, he lost his mother and two brothers to the war. Orphaned at a tender age, Jackson blamed the British for his misery and had looked forward to this confrontation for over three decades.[1]

Arriving in New Orleans on December 1, Jackson observed that the city was completely unprepared to defend itself, much less from an invading force of thousands of battle-hardened British regulars and a large flotilla of warships. Arriving like a conqueror, Jackson declared martial law and took over the city. He put his army, the entire city, and nearby slaves to work preparing earthen defenses, piling up sugar barrels, digging wide ditches, and taking advantage of swamps and the river to enhance his defenses.

339

Jackson also erected eight artillery batteries on the city's perimeter and placed sharpshooters behind trees and behind piles of dirt.

The 47-year-old general also realized that his army of 3,000 volunteers was inadequate in the face of a battle-hardened force that would eventually number close to 14,000 British regulars. He set about enlisting anyone who could fight in the defense of New Orleans. It would end up being one of the most eclectic armies ever to fight—freed slaves, creoles from Haiti, Cajuns from the swamps of Louisiana, Gulf Coast fishermen and merchants, Choctaw warriors, Spanish and French residents of the crescent city, and even Captain Jean Lafitte, his brothers Pierre and Dominique, and their band of motley pirates who operated out of the city were all put into service by Jackson. It brought his force strength to almost 4,000.[2]

Lafitte also provided Jackson with valuable intelligence on the British. It turned out that the British tried to recruit Lafitte, with his knowledge of the waterways of the region, to work against the Americans. But the conniving pirate wagered his men would be better off under American rule and informed Jackson of Britain's plans for New Orleans. Lafitte supported Jackson despite the fact that in September the Americans had commandeered his fleet of vessels. The British commanders also tried to recruit thousands of Creeks, southern slaves, and freed blacks, wrongly assuming they would willingly fight against the Americans. These were but a few of the mistakes and miscalculations the British would make in the disastrous campaign.[3]

Meanwhile, Jackson was preparing his army and the city's residents for the fight of their lives. Inspiring them to repel the invaders or die, Jackson bellowed:

> Fellow citizens of every description! Remember for what you contend. For all that can render life desirable, for a country blessed with every gift of nature, for property, for life, and for liberty. . . .[4]

## SURPRISE ON LAKE BORGNE

On December 10, the British armada arrived in the waters off the Mississippi Delta. The grand army, comprised of veterans of the Napoleonic wars and other battles, expected Jackson and city leaders to surrender.

The invasion was led by Major General Sir Edward Pakenham, a revered military commander, General John Keane, and Vice Admiral Alexander Cochrane. The supremely confident admiral, however, continued to underestimate the Americans despite his defeat at Baltimore. He had hoped that a northern invasion would distract and undermine America's ability to defend its southern border. Even though the northern and central invasions had failed, Cochrane was optimistic and went forward with his invasion of New Orleans. He had a superior fighting force and a powerful navy made up of experienced soldiers and sailors. The admiral toasted the invasion about to get under way with the words "I shall eat my Christmas dinner in New Orleans."[5]

Nearby at Lake Borgne, thousands of British soldiers were gathering for the invasion. An advance force of roughly 1,200 soldiers and sailors under Captain Nicholas Lockyer made their way to the mouth of the Pearl River and anchored near Isle aux Pois (Pea Island), located east of New Orleans on Lake Borgne. However, for the past few days the Royal Navy's movements had been monitored by Lieutenant Thomas A. C. Jones. The young lieutenant observed the British fleet arriving on the morning of December 10, then reconnoitered them from a safe distance. On December 13, it became apparent that the British were sailing to begin their invasion so Jones rushed his five small gunboats to intercept the fleet. It was an act of both utter foolishness and great courage.

The wind did not favor Jones, so he was not able to engage the British fleet until December 14. Jones positioned his gunboats in a line in a mile-wide strip of shallow water near a cluster of small islands named Malheureaux, Ship, and Cat. They were directly in the path of the British. He commanded only 185 sailors and a total of twenty-three cannons on board five gunboats lacking names. His small squadron was known only by the boat numbers: 2, 5, 156, 162, and 163. It was not much of a force.[6]

But Jones thought to account for the lack of strong winds by anchoring and using a winch system with cables that would allow him to turn his boats from side to side in order to deliver accurate fire. When the British fleet arrived around ten-thirty that morning in three columns of forty warships, Jones ordered his men to open up. It was the last thing the British were expecting and the American gunboats hit the larger warships with a flurry of accurate fire, inflicting damage.

Jones and his small squadron never had a chance. In one hour the British were able to knock the gunboats out of commission. Around noon, they boarded the damaged vessels and captured the crews. Jones was severely wounded and it took him months to recover, but early in the battle his men wounded the British commander. The British lost seventeen men, had nearly 100 wounded, and sustained damage to their ships. Jones lost only six men, with roughly three dozen wounded. The surprise on Lake Borgne unnerved the British, who did not expect resistance, much less such a brave stand. When word of the attack reached the commanders, they decided to delay the invasion. Again, this only gave Andrew Jackson the extra time he needed to prepare his defenses.[7]

## SLEEP WELL, LOBSTERBACKS

After the delay ordered as a result of the gunboat attack on Lake Borgne, the Royal Navy's advance scouts looked for areas to land the invasion force. They remained hesitant. The American sailors taken prisoner on Lake Borgne had lied and told their captors that the American army in New Orleans was far larger than it really was. Their stories were corroborated by an American physician named Morel, who had requested permission to treat the wounded prisoners aboard the British ships. Morel also exaggerated the strength of Jackson's forces. Something of a Francis Scott Key—who, with a physician named Dr. Beane, was also held by Admiral Cochrane while Baltimore was being shelled—Morel was not permitted to leave the British ship until after the Battle of New Orleans. Like Key before him, Morel waited impatiently for word of the results of the important battle.

Some of the bayous and waterways that led to or near New Orleans had been blocked by residents and Jackson's troops. Trees were felled and boats sunk in order to prevent ships from navigating through them. One of the waterways free of debris was Bayou Bienvenu. Jackson had ordered that all bayous and canals south of the city be blocked, but Jacque Villere and his son, Gabriel, officers in the local militia, did not want to block a bayou next to their plantation. Major Jacque Villere would nearly be court-martialed after the battle for his failure to comply with the order, but was later acquitted thanks to his bravery and service in the defense of New Orleans.[8]

Bayou Bienvenu led to a canal that emptied into the Mississippi River at a point only a few miles from the city's downtown. Even though it was only 100 yards wide and six feet deep, it was neither blocked nor guarded, and it was a suitable site to disembark the advance guard. Bayou Bienvenu would be the spot.

The British began unloading the first wave of the massive army on December 22. General Keane was set ashore with at least 1,800 troops and marched them through the swamps and forests of the Louisiana coast, aided by a local Spanish fisherman who showed them the way. However, the British army made little progress. Exhausted and frustrated with the ordeal of trying to traverse Louisiana's muck, marshes, and thick cypress forests while pulling cannons and supplies, Keane decided to make camp on the bank of the Mississippi only seven miles from the entrance to the city and by the Villere Plantation. Colonel William Thornton was charged with organizing the camp on the soggy fields of the plantation which nestled up against the Mississippi. With reinforcements who arrived later, the British had roughly 2,500 men in camp. This first wave of the invasion would be joined later by the full army under Sir Edward Pakenham.

Colonel Thornton, who preferred an immediate attack on New Orleans but was overruled by General Keane, had seized the Villere Plantation and arrested Jacque Villere, the owner of the plantation. Once again, delays would end up costing the British. While in camp, Major Villere managed to escape his confinement by killing his favorite dog (he knew it would bark) and jumping out a high window. On discovering that his prisoner had escaped, Colonel Thornton was said to have screamed, "Catch him or kill him!"[9] He should have made sure that was the case because Villere managed to find Andrew Jackson to alert him of the British position.

Never one to wait patiently for a fight, when Jackson heard the British were marching on New Orleans he roared to his soldiers: "By the eternal! The enemy shall not sleep upon our soil!"[10] Rather than wait behind his earthworks at New Orleans, Jackson decided to march a smaller force of his army to find the British camp. Guided by local planters and Villere, who knew the area, Jackson's force crept undetected to the British camp.

A thick bayou fog rolled over the British camp at the Villere Plantation that evening, making it difficult to see more than a few yards in any direction. At the same time as his troops approached the camp, Jackson ordered the schooner, *Carolina*, to float along the river up to the edge of the British camp. It also took advantage of the dark, foggy night. The small ship was observed, but the British thought nothing of a single vessel, perhaps assuming it was a Spanish or French vessel or pleasure craft.

Overconfident, exhausted from the long, difficult march through the lowlands of New Orleans and lacking horses, the British failed to reconnoiter the area or post adequate sentries. At around sunset, Jackson ordered his cannons to fire into the camp. Nearby, the *Carolina* joined the artillery barrage. After two hours of cannon fire, the main attack on the perimeter of the camp was ordered. Coffee's cavalry units and the Tennessee riflemen were sent by Jackson to circle the camp, while he attacked with the main army head-on from the main road leading into the plantation. In the fog and darkness, all battle lines broke down, making it hard to tell friend from foe. Confusion reigned in the nighttime battle.

General John Coffee's cavalry units rode into the camp but dismounted and, using knives and hatchets, attacked the British by hand. A British captain by the name of George Gleig described the brawl, noting, "Many a sword which till tonight had not drunk blood, became in a few minutes crimson enough."[11] The British were unaccustomed to fighting at night and were unprepared for the assault. Moreover, in hand-to-hand fighting, Jackson's volunteers and backwoodsmen, who were joined by about 290 freed blacks and twenty Choctaw braves, prevailed over the British who were trained to form disciplined lines on open battlefields.

Jackson's militiamen did not run like those fighting in Canada and exacted a toll on the British. The British were pushed out of the camp and into the swamps. But, at around three o'clock in the morning, General Keane pushed forward with reinforcements, allowing the British to finally regroup and fire on their attackers. It drove the Americans back. After vicious fighting, Jackson retreated a short but safe distance back toward New Orleans. Over 100 British soldiers were dead and a few hundred others were wounded. The camp was destroyed and dozens of men went missing in the dark. Jackson reported twenty-four men dead and 115 wounded.

Perhaps the main casualty, however, was the psychological blow dealt to the army. Already tired and shocked by the bold attack, the British lost their will to fight. They would get no sleep that night—or the next. The British were afraid to light campfires, lest the American artillery would target them. A shaken Keane again decided to wait for additional reinforcements before marching on New Orleans. The British had not expected the surprise attacks at Lake Borgne or the Villere Plantation.

Over the next few days, thousands of additional reinforcements arrived. Yet, unbeknownst to either army, on Christmas Eve commissioners in Ghent were able to hammer out a peace treaty ending the war. By Christmas Day, General Pakenham had arrived and the British army numbered perhaps 14,000. Pakenham, an aristocrat and brother-in-law of the Duke of Wellington, tried to inspire the bewildered army. But, over the next two weeks while the massive force organized the assault on New Orleans, they were repeatedly hit by small ambushes.

They finally broke camp and headed for New Orleans.

## THE BIG ONE

A sea of bright red uniforms spread out in a great column. In formation, Sir Pakenham's grand army marched in parade formation in three huge columns toward Jackson's defenses on the edge of New Orleans at Chalmette Plantation on the morning of January 8, 1815 [see map 1 in Appendix]. Their bayonets gleamed in the morning light. Pakenham had little choice regarding the direction of the attack. Even if he wanted to outflank Jackson, the swamps, river, and woods on either side of Jackson's earthworks and lines precluded such an attack. Jackson's defensive line stretched one mile from the Mississippi on his right to a cypress swamp on his left. Five-foot high earthen walls shielded the army and cannons.

Rather than rethink the battle, the British came straight on through a large, wide, and open marsh. It proved to be a killing field. The British had hoped to soften up Jackson's defenses with a long cannon attack prior to the infantry attack. But the cannonballs simply disappeared into the deep mud of the marshlands. Jackson rallied his troops by dismissing the British artillery as mere "toys."[12]

As the British advanced, Cajuns and Indians attacked from the edges of the marsh. They inflicted heavy casualties against men stuck shin-deep in the muck. From behind their earthen mounds, Jackson's artillery rained fire down on the battlefield. The warships assigned to provide cover for the British infantry from the flanks were limited by a miraculously timed break in one of the levees that drained the water level to a point too low for the draft of large warships. Realizing they needed forward artillery but unable to pull cannons through the mud, the British sent a force of 1,000 men to seize Jackson's outer artillery batteries. Had they been successful, the British could have turned the guns around to fire on the American defenses. But Jackson's artillerymen repelled the assault. Cannons were loaded with grapeshot, which tore the British infantry to pieces at close range.

Jackson failed to plug a gap in his left flank, which offered the British an opening. But, the conditions under foot made it impossible for them to use cavalry or to rush a flanking unit to take the site. When the British turned in that direction, the few men on the line fought doggedly and pushed the British back.

Elsewhere, the British had planned a flanking attack. Colonel William Thornton, whose men had been beaten at the nighttime attack on Villere Plantation, crossed the Mississippi River with 1,500 men. On the bank on the river, they engaged and defeated 800 Kentucky militiamen and captured the Americans' naval cannons. However, the battle and difficult terrain slowed Thornton's advance to the extent that he never arrived at the site of the main battle in time to support General Pakenham's main assault.

Meanwhile, the main battle raged on and had turned into a rout. Perhaps most effectively, American sharpshooters, recruited from the hunters and outdoorsmen in Jackson's militia, trained their fire on any British soldier wearing gold ornamentation. One by one, the British officers fell in the swamps. General Pakenham died from a cannonball, Major General Samuel Gibbs was mortally wounded, General Keane was shot and nearly died, and other senior commanders were among those hit by sharpshooters. All four major generals leading the invasion were killed or severely wounded.

The swampy conditions under foot, made worse by heavy rains in the days leading up to the battle, made it next to impossible for the British to advance to Jackson's line. Entire units were cut down and soldiers tried in vain to climb over their fallen comrades. Those who made it to the earthworks found muddy moats dug in front of them. Without the necessary ladders required to forge the moats and assault the five-foot walls, the British clawed hopelessly into the rich, Delta mud. From atop the mounds, Jackson's men fired down onto the trapped Redcoats.

The thousands of bayonets fixed for the battle were never used. After two hours, the replacement officers called off the suicide march. Well over 2,000 British soldiers were lost. Countless others went missing in the forests and swamps, and hundreds were captured. A hellish scene covered the battlefield. Piles of dead and wounded Redcoats filled the marsh and the blood spilled stained the ground in every direction. Captain Gleig, a British officer who chronicled the details of the battle, said of the slaughter:

> Of all the sights that I ever witnessed, that which met me there was beyond comparison the most shocking and the most humiliating. Within the narrow compass of a few hundred yards were gathered together nearly a thousand bodies, arrayed in British uniforms . . . An American officer stood by smoking a cigar with a look of savage exultation.[13]

The reports vary, but it appears the Americans suffered only between eight and thirteen dead. Andrew Jackson, orphaned by the British during the American Revolution, and nearly recalled from his command, had handed the British perhaps their worst one-day defeat in history.

## AFTERMATH

Jackson saved New Orleans. It was one of the most impressive and lopsided victories in military history and, even though it occurred after the Treaty of Ghent was signed, the battle provided America with a symbolically significant victory. The battle allowed the nation, which suffered through too many debacles and defeats, to see the war as a victory. For the first time in the young republic's history, a sense of nationalism spread out across the land. Equally important was the fact that any post-treaty designs the British had on their former possession ended with the crushing defeat. Indeed, Sir Pakenham had not only been named by the British as commander of the southern theater of the invasion, but they prematurely also declared him governor of Louisiana.

Sensing the newfound patriotic fervor, Jackson read a message to his victorious army on January 21, celebrating their "undaunted courage, patriotism, and patience, under hardships and fatigues . . ." He noted:

> Natives of different states, acting together, for the first time, in this camp differing in habits and in language, instead of viewing in these circumstances the germ of distrust and division, you have made them the source of an honourable emulation, and from the seeds of discord itself have reaped the fruits of an honourable union.[14]

In the months and years to come, as the two countries negotiated the remaining details of prisoner swaps, borders, and the status of fortifications, the Americans were able to negotiate from a position of strength on account of New Orleans. Even along the Canadian border, it was the news of the disaster at New Orleans as much as word of the Treaty of Ghent that inspired the British to vacate forts and villages. When the British army marched out of Fort Mackinac, the Winnebago chief, Sausamauee, said to his former allies, "Father! You promised us repeatedly that this place would not be given up. It would be better that you had killed us at once, rather than expose us to a lingering death."[15] New Orleans changed everything.

The main British army literally crawled and limped painfully back through the swamps to the flotilla anchored just offshore. They destroyed bridges as they went, in the event the Americans pursued them. The British stayed but a week to treat their wounded. The only senior general alive,

John Lambert, had had enough. He called off any further action. Then the massive armada set sail.

Despite the decisive victory, Jackson and his commanders appear not to have known what the British were doing. Failing to trail the British or post spies at the coast, the Americans remained at New Orleans expecting another attack. At the site of one of their former camps, the British put dummies in red uniforms to trick the Americans into thinking they were sentries. It worked. Over the next few days, Jackson ordered the Americans to occasionally fire cannon shots at the sites and at coastal encampments used by the British to ferry men and equipment out to the ships.

## 36

# THE MAKING OF A NATION

## THE CRUCIBLE OF LEADERSHIP

The War of 1812 was America's first war and the first great challenge the young republic faced. However, many of the Revolutionary heroes were too old or deceased by the time the War of 1812 started. Therefore, the war offered opportunities for a new generation who had come of age after the Revolution and a new set of leaders whose mettle would be forged on the fields of battle. The War of 1812 became the crucible of no fewer than seven U.S. presidents.

The first was Thomas Jefferson, America's third president, who dealt unsuccessfully with impressment of American sailors and restrictions on international trade during both of his terms as president. While Jefferson avoided war with Britain, his actions in response to the British attack on the USS *Chesapeake* and his embargo against British products only temporarily delayed and diffused tensions. To many Americans, 1812 was "Mr. Madison's war." It was Madison, the fourth president, who declared war and presided through its duration. The war nearly ended Madison's presidency and challenged him in ways that no other president could imagine save for Abraham Lincoln. But Madison was reelected and endured the great crisis.

The war helped put five future commanders in chief in the office, including three in a row after the conclusion of the war. The first of them was James Monroe, who served as President Madison's secretary of state and interim secretary of war, and who, in that capacity, even rode at the front of an American army attempting to protect the capital city from invasion. Monroe would be elected after James Madison, serving as the nation's fifth president. Monroe's successor was John Quincy Adams, who served in a diplomatic capacity during the war and was one of the peace commissioners in Ghent who secured the favorable terms that ended the war. However, unlike Jefferson, Madison, and Monroe, all of whom were reelected, the sixth president would serve only a single, frustrating term in office. The reason for his defeat in 1828, however, had less to do with any shortcomings in office than it did his opponent.[1]

Adams lost that election to Andrew Jackson, who had led American forces in the war to numerous victories against the Creek nation and in the American South. In fact, of all the heroes the war produced, "Old Hickory" might have been the most celebrated, having dispatched a massive British invasion at New Orleans at the close of the conflict.

After a single term by Martin Van Buren from 1837 to 1841, another War of 1812 hero assumed the presidency. William Henry Harrison was elected as the ninth president in 1840 representing the new Whig Party. The lore of "Old Tippecanoe's" exploits during the war and his triumph over both The Prophet at Tippecanoe and great chief Tecumseh at Thames helped build an aura around Harrison and was enough to propel him to the nation's highest office on a narrow 150,000 vote margin. Tragically, Harrison, who was already advanced in years and in poor health, gave the longest inaugural address in American history during a cold day in 1841 and caught pneumonia. He died only one month into his term.[2]

The speech that did Harrison in has been widely panned by critics as excessively verbose. Even the famed politician and intellect, Daniel Webster, who helped edit and shorten the president-elect's words, said he had to take a hatchet to the countless flowery and classical references in the address, but that it still managed to kill not just Harrison but "seventeen Roman proconsuls as dead as smelts, every one of them."[3] Others spread the tale that it was not the length of the speech or the weather that did Harrison in but a curse from his long-time adversary, Chief Tecumseh. For killing Tecumseh, Harrison was said to be cursed, along with every American president elected in twenty-year intervals—or so the story goes. Harrison's demise after being elected in 1840, was followed by other presidential deaths: Abraham Lincoln, elected in 1860 and assassinated five years later; James Garfield, elected in 1880 and assassinated the following year; William McKinley, elected in 1900 and assassinated the following year; Warren Harding, elected in 1920 and dead three years later of heart failure; Franklin Roosevelt, elected in 1940 and dead five years later of a cerebral hemorrhage; and John Kennedy, elected in 1960 and assassinated three years later. Ronald Reagan, who was elected in 1980, was shot a few weeks into his presidency but survived, thereby—according to the legend—breaking Tecumseh's curse.[4]

Another military officer, Zachary Taylor, would become America's twelfth president and the last of the War of 1812 generation to end up in the presidency. However, unlike Jackson and Harrison, Taylor was a young officer during the war and not one of the main generals leading the conflict. The war also produced gifted military leaders like General Jacob Brown and General Winfield Scott as well as the British defender of Canada, Sir Isaac Brock. The American commanders, along with their colleagues Andrew Jackson and William Henry Harrison and the British military genius General Brock, however, were relegated to a single theater of fighting in a war that featured many divergent theaters. For this reason, they were never able to put their stamp on the war and thereby gain fame synonymous with other wars in the way other great military generals were able to do such as George Washington, Ulysses Grant, and Dwight Eisenhower.

Shockingly, Winfield Scott and some of the better American commanders were not promoted after the war. Although angry that Madison and Monroe failed to promote him to lieutenant general, Scott would eventually get the fame he sought. He achieved the rank of general-in-chief of the army in 1841, was lauded for his efforts in the war with Mexico, nearly won the presidency in 1852, and, late in life, commanded the Union army briefly during the Civil War. Several other leaders of the war went on to successful careers. Richard Mentor Johnson, who fought at the pivotal Battle of Thames, became Martin Van Buren's vice president in 1837. Albert Gallatin, one of the peace commissioners, served as secretary of the treasury and as a diplomat. The war also produced many future governors and members of Congress.

Of course, the war also had more than its fair share of shameful swindlers who profited from the fighting, colorful poltroons who passed themselves off as military commanders, and corrupt politicians who mismanaged nearly every facet of the conflict. It is a long list but among the worst were Generals Henry Dearborn, William Hull, Stephen Van Rensselaer, and James Winchester, all of whom cost America key battles and numerous lives lost. History has rightly been unkind to them. Henry Clay and his rowdy War Hawks managed to survive the war and many of them enjoyed long political careers, despite their ruinous actions, war-mongering, and divisive brand of politics. Clay served as speaker, a member of both the House of Representatives and Senate, and nearly won the presidency. History has been more generous to Clay than he deserves.

Fate was less kind to many of the British military leaders. Isaac Brock, Robert Ross, and Edward Pakenham, three of Britain's most gifted generals, all died in the war. Sir George Prevost managed to survive the war but was recalled to Britain to face court martial for his disastrous leadership at the Battle of Plattsburgh. However, he died while awaiting the verdict. Many naval commanders who lost battles to the upstart American fleet were similarly brought up on charges and saw their careers end. Admiral Alexander Cochrane survived the war, but was marginalized in British society and his reputation suffered greatly. One of the few British leaders to enjoy success after the war was Admiral George Cockburn, who was assigned to escort Napoleon aboard the HMS *Northumberland* to imprisonment at St. Helena, where Cockburn served as the island's governor. Cockburn went on to attain the rank of First Lord of the Admiralty and served as a Member of Parliament. However, the admiral who long burned with rage toward the Americans was devastated by the peace treaty and never reconciled his frustration at not besting the Americans.

## ITS RIGHTFUL PLACE IN HISTORY

The conflict also produced iconic chapters in the American adventure. It was the War of 1812 that immortalized the warship USS *Constitution*, which earned the nickname "Old Ironsides" after British cannonballs bounced off her sturdy hull. It was the War of 1812 that witnessed General Andrew Jackson's upset victory at New Orleans when he led a rag-tag band of poorly trained militiamen—as well as Cajuns, Indians, slaves, and pirates—in a complete rout of one of the largest, most battle-tested armies ever assembled on the continent. It was during the War of 1812 that outgunned defenders of Baltimore stopped a massive invading force that had just sacked the American capitol. And it was from that same engagement that an American lawyer-poet, while stuck aboard a British warship, was inspired to pen the words "the rockets' red glare, bombs bursting in air" when his countrymen prevailed.

The War of 1812 is one of the least known, most misunderstood events in American history and yet it is one of the most important. It impacted Indian relations, western expansion, the demise of the Federalist Party, who were seen as traitors, and a number of important technological advances. In doing so, the war shaped the political geography of both the United States and the continent. Moreover, at the outset of the conflict, America was a loose collection of bickering states with little in common with one another, spread across vast forests that separated small, isolated villages. By the end of hostilities, however, the country had taken an important step toward nationhood. The famed historian, Robert Remini, suggested, that "in a real sense, the War of 1812 was part of a search for national identity."[5] Albert Gallatin, one of the peace commissioners and Madison's secretary of treasury, wrote to his former boss, Thomas Jefferson of the war: "In every aspect I must acknowledge that the war has been useful . . . The character of America stands now as high as ever on the European continent, and higher than ever it did in Great Britain."[6]

America survived its first real test—political division at home and a second war for independence against a foreign foe. In doing so, the fledgling nation was imbued with confidence at home and legitimacy in the eyes of the world. As a result of the war, a nation emerged on the world stage stronger, more confident, and more united.

So why has so little been written on the war? Why have teachers and textbooks skipped this significant event? Why have military historians often overlooked the war, even though it would be a century before the United States had another major conflict with European powers (aside from the brief Spanish-American War)?[7] One probable answer is that the war in North America that started in 1812 has the misfortune of being sandwiched between, and thus greatly overshadowed by, the earlier Revolutionary War and later Civil War. Also, internationally, it was seen as a mere sideshow to the on-going conflict between Britain and France. In comparison to those conflicts, it has been relatively lost to history.

As wars go, it was also admittedly somewhat short and small, although it was a major conflict from the Canadian perspective and did involve fighting on land and water, and both internationally and across North America. American, British, Canadian, and Indian casualties numbered roughly 25,000, a small number compared to the carnage of the American Revolution and Civil War, as well as the Napoleonic wars in Europe happening at around the same time as the War of 1812. Indeed, on September 7, 1812, at Borodino near Moscow, over 70,000 French and Russian soldiers were killed or wounded, while roughly 60,000 British, French, and Prussian casualties occurred in 1815 at the Battle of Waterloo that ended Napoleon's reign of terror. Several of the battles during the War of 1812 resulted in a handful of casualties and even some of the major engagements had casualty counts in the dozens or maybe the hundreds, by comparison.

But there were casualties. The war resulted in roughly 8,600 British dead, wounded, or missing. The Americans sustained an estimated 11,300 casualties. However, this does not measure the economic costs to any of the countries, the loss of trade, the impact to the American Indian, and other war-related problems. Moreover, the records kept by local militia officers were poor, many records from the war were lost, and some American commanders under-reported casualties to hide the extent of their defeats. It is all but certain that the casualty numbers were far worse than reported.[8]

There are other explanations for the relative disinterest in the conflict. Of course, the misnomer of a war fought over two-and-one-half years but named for just a single year has not helped. Indeed, it was a vastly more complicated conflict. The war's causes and consequences have been largely misunderstood and ignored. No single issue or idea—or motto such as "Remember the Alamo" or "The defense of liberty" or "The abolition of slavery"—defines the War of 1812. This also gives the suggestion that it was an unjust and unsuccessful war, which is somewhat true. Indeed, by the end of the conflict both sides were so sick of war and so eager to reach an agreement that they put all differences behind them. At the negotiations in Ghent, for instance, there was little mention of the tensions and disagreements that caused of the war. The main contentions of impressment of American sailors, of Canada and Indian land claims, and of restrictions on international trade, were never discussed.

## LEGACY

The war means different things to different people. For example, it was a disaster for the American Indian. The war ended Tecumseh's dream of a grand Indian confederation and sealed the tragic fate of all First Americans by opening the American West for settlement and fueling the earliest fires of manifest destiny. Americans would quickly push all the way to the Pacific Ocean. For the British, the war was, at best, a distraction from the main conflicts in Europe against Napoleon and, at worst, an embarrassment that further diminished the British Empire and exacted a terrible toll in lives lost and economic pain. Yet, Britain demonstrated to the world that it would go to war to defend her colonies and that it was still determined to be a global superpower.

For Canadians, the war remains a great source of national pride. Interestingly, while Americans celebrated victories with great gusto and declared many officers to be national heroes, adorning them with medals, hosting parades in their honor, and elevating them to high public office, the Canadian response tended to be calm and introspective toward the war. Although General Isaac Brock was later knighted for his remarkable leadership during the war, even decisive and momentous victories such as Chateauguay, Crysler's Farm, and Beaver Dams were met in Canada and Britain with little fanfare.[9] But the war did initiate events that would later lead to independence and greatly impact Canada's future.

Fighting side by side to fend off the Americans, the English and French communities in Canada enjoyed a temporary improvement in relations, and provinces that had little in common and were separated by great distances were unified. The Canadian historian, Arthur Lower, suggested, that "It therefore does not seem too far out to say that the War of 1812 is one of the massive foundation stones of modern Canada."[10]

The amount of money spent by the British on the war provided opportunities for local merchants and farmers. Many communities prospered economically supplying the army and the villages of Montreal, Quebec, and York, and others grew rapidly and developed into prosperous trading centers. Of course, the United States would never again make a serious effort to take Canada and, after everything was said and done, the American and Canadian borders remained roughly as they were before the war and a long and prosperous peace has ensued between the United States and Canada, and between the United States and Great Britain.

In the months after the Treaty of Ghent was signed, the fighting— mostly in the form of isolated skirmishes—gradually subsided. The border between the United States and Canada essentially returned to its pre-war form, people and products once again crossed the border with regularity, and trade between the Americans and British would soon drive both nations' economies. On one hand, it was as if the war had never happened. On the other hand, it changed the continent and world. One historian deemed the Treaty of Ghent to be "less a shout of triumph than a sigh of relief."[11]

The United States would enter into a long peace, but not all the lessons of the war were heeded. Eventually the horrors of slavery, the reality of sectionalism, and the demands of southern War Hawks would spark a civil war. Yet, the War of 1812 is a coming-of-age story that rebuilt and remade America and American democracy. Although it had been dismissed around the world as a political experiment that would not last, the new republic had emerged on the world stage, gained military experience, now possessed a respectable navy, and controlled the vast frontier on its western border.

It has been two centuries since the War of 1812, which makes for an opportune time to raise the conflict's profile and tell the true history of a war that was simultaneously important but unnecessary. The War of 1812 was a fascinating moment in American history, but one that, at best, has received only cursory study from most scholars, while being wholly ignored by the American press and public. Nevertheless, it was one of the most important formative experiences in American history. It was, it could be said, a costly and complicated tie![12]

# APPENDIX

All maps courtesy of the Department of History, United States Military Academy.

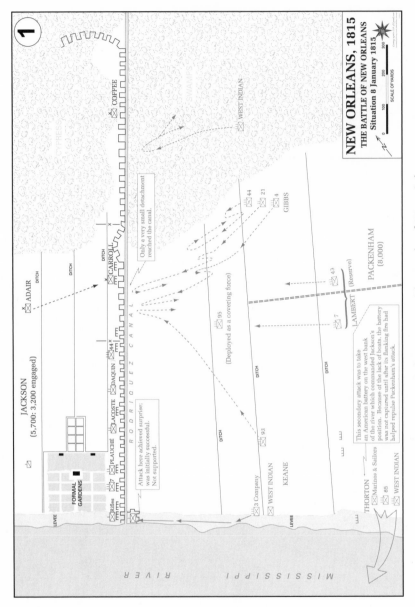

Map 1. New Orleans, 1815: The Battle of New Orleans

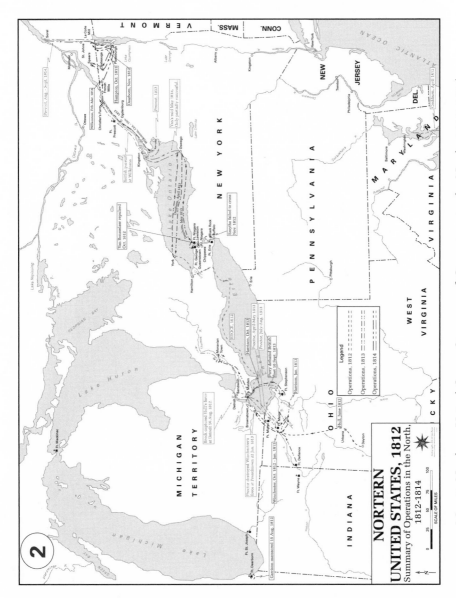

Map 2. Northern United States: Summary of Operations in the North, 1812–1814

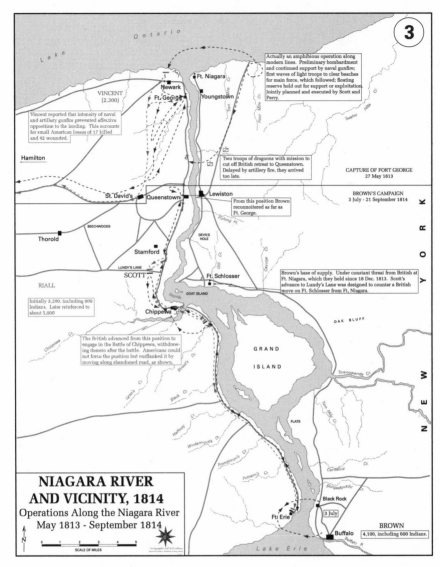

Map 3. Niagara River and Vicinity: Operations along the Niagara River

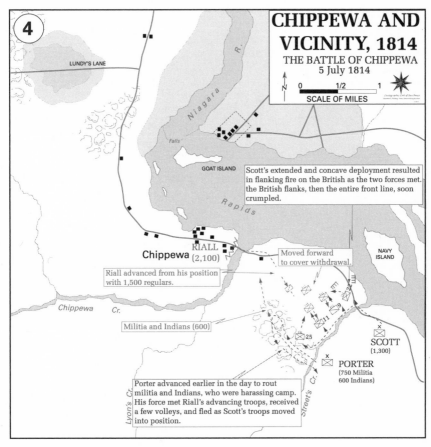

**CHIPPEWA AND VICINITY, 1814**

THE BATTLE OF CHIPPEWA
5 July 1814

0    1/2    1
SCALE OF MILES

4

LUNDY'S LANE

Niagara R.

Falls

GOAT ISLAND

Rapids

NAVY ISLAND

RIALL
Chippewa (2,100)

Scott's extended and concave deployment resulted in flanking fire on the British as the two forces met. the British flanks, then the entire front line, soon crumpled.

Moved forward to cover withdrawal.

Riall advanced from his position with 1,500 regulars.

Militia and Indians (600)

9

11

25

SCOTT
(1,300)

PORTER
(750 Militia
600 Indians)

Chippewa Cr.

Lyon's Cr.

Street's Cr.

Porter advanced earlier in the day to rout militia and Indians, who were harassing camp. His force met Riall's advancing troops, received a few volleys, and fled as Scott's troops moved into position.

Map 4. Chippewa and Vicinity: The Battle of Chippewa

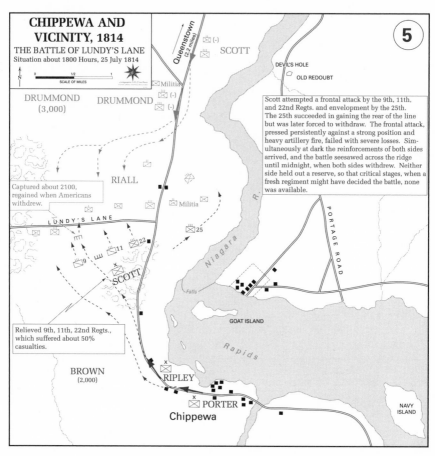

**CHIPPEWA AND VICINITY, 1814**

THE BATTLE OF LUNDY'S LANE
Situation about 1800 Hours, 25 July 1814

SCALE OF MILES
0    1/2    1

Queenstown
(2.2 miles)

SCOTT

DEVIL'S HOLE

OLD REDOUBT

DRUMMOND
(3,000)

DRUMMOND

Militia

Scott attempted a frontal attack by the 9th, 11th, and 22nd Regts. and envelopment by the 25th. The 25th succeeded in gaining the rear of the line but was later forced to withdraw. The frontal attack, pressed persistently against a strong position and heavy artillery fire, failed with severe losses. Simultaneously at dark the reinforcements of both sides arrived, and the battle seesawed across the ridge until midnight, when both sides withdrew. Neither side held out a reserve, so that critical stages, when a fresh regiment might have decided the battle, none was available.

RIALL

Captured about 2100, regained when Americans withdrew.

LUNDY'S LANE

Militia

25

9    11    22

SCOTT

PORTAGE ROAD

Niagara R.

Falls

GOAT ISLAND

Relieved 9th, 11th, 22nd Regts., which suffered about 50% casualties.

Rapids

BROWN
(2,000)

RIPLEY

PORTER

Chippewa

NAVY ISLAND

Map 5. Chippewa and Vicinity: The Battle of Lundy's Lane

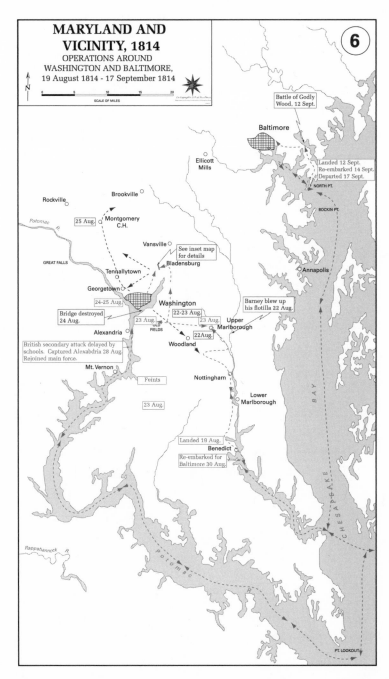

Map 6. Maryland and Vicinity: Operations around Washington and Baltimore

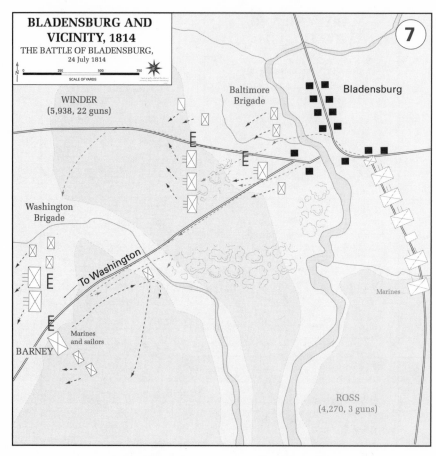

Map 7. Bladensburg and Vicinity: The Battle of Bladensburg

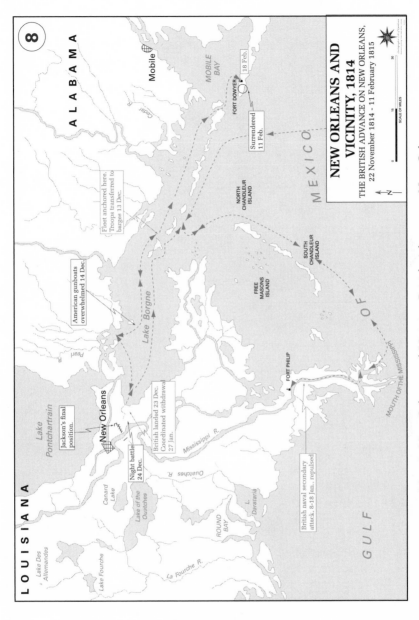

Map 8. New Orleans and Vicinity: British Advance on New Orleans

# NOTES

## CHAPTER 1

1. Nardo, Don, *World History Series: The War of 1812* (Farmington Hills, Mich.: Lucent Books, 1999), see preface; Penner, Mary, "War of 1812 Veterans Left Bountiful Information," Scripps Newspaper Co., (Oct. 4, 2006).

2. Perkins, Bradford, *The First Rapproachment: England and the United States, 1795–1805* (Philadelphia: University of Pennsylvania Press, 1955); Horsman, Reginald, *The War of 1812* (New York: Alfred A. Knoff, 1969), pp. 7–8.

3. Perkins, Bradford, *Prologue to War: England and the United States, 1805–1812* (Berkeley: University of California Press, 1961), p. 1–31; the quote is from Horsman, *War of 1812*, p. 1.

4. Adams, Henry, *History of the United States of America: During the Administrations of James Madison* (New York: Library of America, 1986 reprint), p. 439.

5. Tucker, Glenn, *Poltroons and Patriots: A Popular Account of the War of 1812* (Indianapolis, IN: Bobbs-Merrill, 1954), Vol. 1, p. ix; Tucker maintains that both sides wanted to avoid war, yet drifted into it.

## CHAPTER 2

1. "The War of 1812" (Chapter 6 of the Army Historical Series), *American Military History* (Washington, DC: U.S. Army); see "War of 1812 Statistics" at <www.historyguy.com/war_of_1812_statistics.htm>.

2. Borneman, Walter R., *1812: The War that Forged a Nation* (New York: Harper Perennial, 2004), pages 45–46.

3. Jefferson's quote comes from Malone, Dumas, *Jefferson and His Time: The Sage of Monticello* (Boston, Little Brown, 1977), p. 85.

4. Taylor, R., "The War of 1812: An Introduction," The War of 1812 Website at <http://www.warof1812.ca/intro.html>.

5. The description of the North American conflict as a side show is from Borneman, *1812*, p. 1.

6. Horsman, *The War of 1812*, p. 3.

7. Henry Clay boasted of the ease with which Canada could be taken and that it would be but the first-step in a larger goal. See "Clay to Thomas Bodley, Dec. 18, 1812, in Hopkins, J. F., ed., *Papers of Henry Clay: The Rising Statesman, 1797–1814* (Lexington: University Press of Kentucky, 1959), p. 842.

# CHAPTER 3

1. The spelling of Strachan's name differs depending on the source. It seems likely that it was spelled differently on his identification papers and that he used an alias.

2. Malone, Dumas, *Jefferson the President: Second Term, 1805–1809* (Boston: Little Brown, 1974), pp. 416–419.

3. Black, Jeremy, *The War of 1812 in the Age of Napoleon* (Norman, OK: University of Oklahoma Press, 2009).

4. Perkins, *Prologue to War*, pp. 1–31.

5. Latimer, Jon, *1812: War with America* (Cambridge, MA: The Belknap Press of Harvard University Press, 2007), p. 6.

6. Lord Sheffield ridiculed the law and proclaimed it was "an act for the relief and protection of American seamen." See *Observations on the Commerce of the American States* (Toronto: Gale Ecco—Eighteenth Century Collections Online, 2010), p. 27.

7. Taylor, R., "Standing Interrogatories used by the Royal Navy when Questioning Sailors of Captured Ship in the War of 1812," The War of 1812 Website at <http://www.warof1812.ca/interrogatories.html>.

8. Garraty, John A., *The American Nation: A History of the United States* (New York: Harper & Row, 1966), pp. 189–190.

9. Taylor, "War of 1812: Introduction."

# CHAPTER 4

1. Latimer, *1812*, p. 21

2. Hickey, Donald R., *The War of 1812: A forgotten Conflict* (Urbana, IL: University of Illinois Press, 1989), p. 17.

3. See Thomas Jefferson's "Proclamation in Response to the Chesapeake Affair," July 2, 1807; available through The Miller Center at the University of Virginia <millercenter.org/president/detail/3499>.

4. Tucker, *Poltroons*, Vol. 1, p. 92.

5. MacKenzie, Alexander Slidell, *The Life of Commodore Oliver Hazard Perry*, Vol. I (New York: Harper and Brothers, 1840), pp. 78–79.

6. Taylor, "War of 1812: Introduction."

7. Dumas Malone, *Jefferson the President*, p. 425–426.

8. Berton, Pierre, *The Invasion of Canada, 1812–1813* (Toronto: McClelland and Stewart, 1980), p. 37.

9. This was reported by *The National Intelligencer* on February 26, 1813; the influential newspaper opined that the legislation would help avoid war.

10. Borneman, *1812*, pp. 39–40.

11. Ibid., p. 40.

12. Taylor, "The War of 1812: Introduction."

13. Tucker, *Poltroons*, Vol. 1, p. 42.

14. Ibid., p. 48–51.

15. Hickey, *War of 1812*, pp. 21–22.

## CHAPTER 5

1. Article IV, Section 3, Clause 1 in the U.S. Constitution sets out the process for a territory becoming a state. A comprehensive discussion of the "enabling act" that must take place for this to happen appears in The Green Papers; see <www.thegreenpapers.com/slg/explanation-statehood.phtml#fun>.

2. For information on the Jay Treaty, see the digital archive at Columbia University at <www.columbia.edu/cu/lweb/digitl/jay/jaytreaty.html>; see also the U.S. History Website at <www.u-s-history.com/pages/h455.html>.

3. Two helpful sources on the purposes and impact of the Lewis and Clark "Voyage of Discovery" on the westward expansion are PBS at <www.pbs.org/lewisandclark> and National Geographic at <www.nationalgeographic.com/lewisandclark>.

4. Borneman, *1812*, p. 11.

5. See the letter "Hamilton to McHenry," June 27, 1799 in Syrett, Harold C., ed., *The Papers of Alexander Hamilton*, Vol. 23, April 1799–October 1799 (New York: Columbia University Press, 1976), pp. 227–228.

6. Boreman, *1812*, p. 48.

7. See the letter "Jefferson to Washington," May 23, 1792 in Washington, H. A., ed., *The Writings of Thomas Jefferson* (New York: H. W. Derby, 1861); in the letter Jefferson discussions the possibility of southern secession.

8. See the letter "Wilkinson to Cushing," November 7, 1806 in Wilkinson, James, *Memoirs of My Own Times* (Philadelphia: Abraham Small, 1816), 2 volumes, Appendix 99.

9. The Conway Cabal, <www.ushistory.org/march/other/cabal.htm>.

10. John Randolph described Wilkinson as the only man he knew who "was from the bark to the very core a villain." See Latimer, Jon, *1812: War with America* (Cambridge, Mass.: Belknap Press of Harvard University Press, 2007), pp. 195–196.

11. For a discussion of Burr's conniving and his defeat orchestrated in part by Alexander Hamilton, see Brands, Henry W., *The Heartbreak of Aaron Burr* (New York Random House, 2012); see also Fleming, Thomas, *Duel: Alexander Hamilton, Aaron Burr, and the Future of America* (New York: Basic Books, 2000).

12. See the letter "Merry to Harrowby," August 11, 1804 in Kline, Mary-Jo, ed., *Political Correspondence and Public Papers of Aaron Burr*, Vol. 2 (Princeton, NJ: Princeton University Press, 1983), pp. 891–892.

13. See the entry in Kline, *Political Correspondence*, Vol. 2, p. 950.

14. Remini, Robert V., *Andrew Jackson and the Course of American Empire, 1767–1821* (New York: Harper & Row, 1977), pp. 145–151.

15. Ibid., p. 157.

16. See the letter "Wilkinson to Cushing," November 7, 1806 in Wilkinson, *Memoirs*, Appendix 99.

# CHAPTER 6

1. Latimer, *1812*, p. 25; see also the battlefield sites at <www.fallentimbersbattlefield.com> or <www.ohiohistorycentral.org>.

2. See the letter "Harrison to Secretary of War William Eustis," November 3, 1809 in Esarey, Logan, ed., *Messages and Letters of William Henry Harrison*, Vol. 1, 1800–1811 (Indianapolis, IN: Indiana Historical Commission, 1923), p. 389; see also pp. 359–362.

3. Cleaves, Freeman, *Old Tippecanoe: William Henry Harrison and His Time* (New York: Charles Scribner's, 1939), p. 67.

4. For a good history of the Shawnee being driven off their ancestral lands, see R. David Edwards, *The Shawnee Prophet* (Lincoln: University of Nebraska Press, 1985).

5. Borneman, *1812*, p. 31.

6. Taylor, "War of 1812: Introduction."

7. Tucker, *Poltroons*, Vol. 1, p. 101.

8. Grant, John and Ray Jones, *The War of 1812: A Guide to the Battlefields and Historic Sites* (Buffalo, NY: Western New York Publishing Broadcasting Association, 2011), p. 11.

9. Tucker, *Poltroons*, Vol. 1, p. 100.

10. See Edwards, *Shawnee Prophet*.

11. Grant and Jones, *War of 1812*, p. 10.

12. See the letter "Harrison to Secretary of War Eustis," August 7, 1811 in Esarey, *Messages and Letters*, p. 549.

13. Grant and Jones, *War of 1812*, pp. 10 and 30.

14. See the PBS video "The War of 1812" at <video.pbs.org/video/2089393539> (2011).

## CHAPTER 7

1. See "Pigeon Roost Massacre," in History of Indiana at <www.county history.com/history/095.htm>

2. Peckham, Howard, ed., "An Eyewitness Account of the Siege of Fort Wayne," *Indiana Magazine of History*, Vol. 4 (December 1948), p. 413–416.

3. Latimer, *1812*, pp. 25 and 29.

4. Borneman, *1812*, p. 33.

5. Hickey, *War of 1812*, p. 25.

6. For a comprehensive discussion of the battle at Tippecanoe, see Jortner, Adam, *The Gods of Prophetstown: The Battle of Tippecanoe and the Holy War for the American Frontier* (New York: Oxford University Press, 2011); see also the battlefield site at Tippecanoe County Historical Association at <www.tcha.museum. in.us/battlefield.htm>.

7. Borneman, *1812*, p. 35.

8. Jortner, *Gods of Prophetstown*.

9. Grant and Jones, *War of 1812*, p. 34.

10. Jortner, *Gods of Prophetstown*.

## CHAPTER 8

1. Grant and Jones, *War of 1812*, p. 13.

2. See the letter "Jefferson to Madison," April 26, 1798 and the letter "Thomas Jefferson to James Mdison," June 21, 1798; both use the term and are found in Stimpson, George, *A Book about American Politics* (New York: Harper & Brothers, 1952), p. 55.

3. Latimer, *1812*, pp. 31–32.

4. *Annals of Congress of the United States*, Twelfth Congress, First Session, Dec. 16, 1811, p. 533.

5. Tucker, *Poltroons*, Vol. 1, p. 39.

6. Ibid., p. 36.

7. U.S. Congress, *Annals of Congress*, Eleventh Congress, 1st Session, pp. 578–581.

8. Garraty, John A., *The American Nation: A History of the United States* (New York: Harper & Row, 1966), p. 197; see also Taylor, "War of 1812: Introduction."

9. DeGregorio, William A., *The Complete Book of U.S. Presidents* (Fort Lee, NJ: Barricade Books, 2001), pp. 65–66; see also Watson, Robert P. and Richard M. Yon, eds., *The American Presidents*, 3rd ed. (Pasadena, Calif.: Salem Press, 2006), p. 94.

10. For a good discussion of Madison's diminutive size and his health ordeal, see Marx, Rudolph, "The Health of the President: James Madison," at <www.healthguidance.org/entry/8905/1/the-health-of-the-president-james-madison.html>.

11. Thompson, Richard W., *Recollections of Sixteen Presidents from Washington to Lincoln* (Ann Arbor, MI: University of Michigan Library, 1894), p. 64.

12. Ibid., p. 66.

13. Tucker, *Poltroons*, Vol. I, pp. 362–363.

14. Jacobs, James R., *The Beginning of the U.S. Army, 1783–1812* (Princeton, NJ: Princeton University Press, 1947), pp. 351–353; see also Sprout, Margaret, *The Rise of American Naval Power, 1776–1918* (Princeton, NJ: Princeton University Press, 1939), pp. 55–60.

15. See the letter "Madison to Jefferson," February 7, 1812 in the Madison Papers, Vol. 46, Library of Congress; see also either Horsman, *War of 1812*, p. 19 or Horsman, Reginald, *Causes of the War of 1812* (New York: Barnes, 1962), p. 240 for a discussion of the uncertainty as to whether most soldiers could even be counted on in the event of an invasion of Canada.

16. The article is from the journal *The Boston Patriot*, June 13, 1812; see Tucker, Poltroons, Vol. 1, p. 60.

17. This article is from the journal *The Boston Patriot*, March 23, 184; see Tucker, Poltroons, Vol. 1, p. 55.

18. Pratt, Julius W., *The Expansionists of 1812* (New York: Macmillan Company, 1925), p. 40.

19. *Annals of Congress*, 11, Congress, I Sess., 1283, 1809; see also Pratt, *Expansionists*, p. 35.

20. Madison's War Message to Congress, June 1, 1812 is at Presidential Rhetoric at <www.presidentialrhetoric.com/historicspeeches/madison/warmessage.html>.

21. Hickey, *War of 1812*, p. 44

22. Borneman, *1812*, p. 50.

23. Grant and Jones, *War of 1812*, p. 1; Borneman, *1812*, p. 51.

# CHAPTER 9

1. See the letter "Liverpool to Prevost," May 15, 1812 in the British Colonial Office Archives, Public Records Office, pp. 58–60; see also Horsman, *War of 1812*, p. 25.

2. Horsman, *War of 1812*, p. 25; see also "Sir George Prevost," in The Canadian Encyclopedia at <www.thecanadianencyclopedia.com>.

3. Tupper, Ferdinand Brock, *The Life and Correspondence of Major-General Sir Isaac Brock*, 2nd ed. (London: Kessinger Publishing, 1847), pp. 33–37; see also Horsman, *War of 1812*, pp. 25–26.

4. See the letter "Brock to Liverpool," March 23, 1812 in Tupper, *Life and Correspondence*, p. 7; see also other similar letters on pp. 33–37.

5. See the letter "Brock to his brother," September 18, 1812 in Tupper, *Life and Correspondence*, p. 316.

6. See the letters "Prevost to Liverpool," May 18, 1812 and April 20, 1812 in Tupper, *Life and Correspondence*, pp. 197–202 and pp. 148–151; see also Horsman, *War of 1812*, p. 27.

7. Hitsman, J. Mackay, *The Incredible War of 1812* (Toronto: Robin Brass Studio, 1999), pp. 33–37; see also Horsman, *War of 1812*, p. 27.

8. Hickey, *War of 1812*, p. 80.

9. Risch, Erna, *Quartermaster Support of the Army: A History of the Corps, 1775–1939* (Washington: Quartermaster Historian's Office, 1962), pp. 136–142; see also Hickey, *War of 1812*, pp. 78–79.

10. See the letter "Jefferson to Castlereagh," April 21, 1812 in White, Leonard D., *The Jeffersonians: A Study in Administrative History, 1801–1829* (New York, 1959), p. 217.

11. Brown, Gilbert Patten, "A Sturdy Oak of New England Life," *The Granite Monthly* (October 1903, Vol. 35, No. 4), p. 182; see also the Lane Memorial Library, Hampton, New Hampshire at <www.hampton.lib.nh.us/hampton/biog/henrydearborn3.htm>.

12. See the letter "Tompkins to Macomb," July 12, 1812 in Hastings, Hugh, ed., *Public Papers of Daniel D. Tompkins, Governor of New York, 1807–1817*, Vol. III (Albany, NY: J. B. Lyon, 1902), p. 27.

13. Grant and Jones, *War of 1812*, p. 14.

14. McAfee, Robert Breckinridge, *History of the Late War in the Western Country* (Ann Arbor: University of Michigan microfilms, 1966; originally published by Worsley & Smith in Lexington, Kentucky in 1816), p. 52.

15. Hull, William, *Memoirs of the Campaign of the North Western Army of the United States, AD 1812* (Boston: True & Greene, 1824), p. 17.

16. McAfee, *History of the Late War*, pp. 58–60.

17. Tucker, *Poltroons*, p. 155.

18. Gauthier, Alain, "Quartered in a Far-away Colony, Isaac Brock would Emerge as One of Britain's Most Ablest and Tragic Figures," War of 1812 Website at <www.warof1812.ca/brock.html>.

19. Ibid.

20. Taylor, R., "Battles of Michilimackinac and Fort Dearborn," War of 1812 Website at <www.warof1812.ca/batmac.html>.

21. McAfee, *History of the Late War*, pp. 70–73.

22. Hickey, *War of 1812*, p. 84; see also Latimer, *1812*, p. 69

23. Borneman, *1812*, pp. 66–67; see also Taylor, "Battles of Michilimackinac."

24. McAfee, *History of the Late War*, p. 70.

25. See the letter "Hull to Eustis," August 7, 1812" in Brannan, John, *Official Letters of the Military and Naval Officers of the United States During the*

*War with Great Britian in the Years 1812, 1813, 1814, and 1815* (Washington: Way & Gideon, 1823), p. 36.

26. Horsman, *War of 1812*, p. 39.

27. Hitsman, *The Incredible War*, p. 80.

28. Grant and Jones, *War of 1812*, p. 17.

29. Latimer, *1812*, pp. 67–68.


## CHAPTER 10

1. Henderson, Robert, "Soldier's Families Under Fire: Ambush at Toussant Island 1812," The War of 1812 Website at <www.arof1812.ca/ambush.htm>; the account of the battle was originally published in 1828 by P. Finan, a British child whose father was an officer in the war.

2. Henderson, Robert, "A Tranquil River No More: The Raid on Gananoque," The War of 1812 Website at <www.warof1812.ca/gananoque.htm>.

3. Latimer, *1812*, p. 74.

4. Horseman, *War of 1812*, p. 45.

5. Hickey, *War of 1812*, pp. 86–87.

6. James E. Walmsley, "Alexander Smyth," in Allen Johnson and Dumas Malone, eds., *Dictionary of American Biography*, 20 volumes (New York: Charles Scribner's Sons, 1928–1936), Vol. 27, pp. 373–375.

7. Malcomson, Robert, *A Very Brilliant Affair: The Battle of Queenston Heights, 1812* (Toronto: Robin Brass, 1998), p. 142.

8. Nursey, Walter R., *The Story of Isaac Brock: Hero, Defender and Savior of Upper Canada 1812* (Toronto: McClelland and Stewart, 1923), p. 177.

9. Grant and Jones, *War of 1812*, p. 67.

10. Eisenhower, John S. D., *Agent of Destiny: The Life and Times of General Winfield Scott* (New York: Free Press, 1997), pp. 10, 18.

11. Bornemann, *1812*, p. 74.

12. Eisenhower, *Agent*, p. 39.

13. Grant and Jones, *War of 1812*, p. 68.


## CHAPTER 11

1. Walmsley, "Alexander Smyth," pp. 377–375.

2. Grant and Jones, *War of 1812*, p. 17.

3. See the War of 1812 Website at <war1812.tripod.com/batfman.html>.

4. The archives at the U.S. House of Representatives has information on Smyth's service; see <www.House.gov>; see also <www.govtrack.us/congress/members/alexander_smyth/410120>

5. Hickey, *War of 1812*, p. 88; see also Tucker, *Poltroons*, p. 146.

6. Hickey, *War of 1812*, p. 77.

7. See U.S. Army Center of Military History at <www.history.army.mil/books/sw-sa/eustis.htm>.

8. See the letter "Harrison to Eustis," January 14, 1812 in Carter, Clarence, ed., *The Territorial Papers of the United States*, 16 vols. (Washington, DC: Government Printing Office, 1939–1948), Vol. VIII, pp. 159–160.

9. Hickey, *War of 1812*, pp. 135–139.

# CHAPTER 12

1. See The River Raisin Battlefield Website at <www.riverraisinbattlefield.org/the_battles.htm>.

2. Horsman, *War of 1812*, p. 81.

3. See the letter "Taylor to Harrison," September 10, 1812 in Brannan, *Official Letters*, pp. 61–65.

4. See the War of 1812 Website, "Battle of the Raisen River," at <war1812.tripod.com/batraison.html>.

5. Latimer, *1812*, pp. 119–120.

6. See The River Raisin Battlefield Site at <www.riverraisinbattlefield.org/the_battles.htm>.

7. See The River Raisin Battlefield Site at <www.riverraisinbattlefield.org/the_battles.htm>.

8. See the War of 1812 Website, "Battle of Ogdensburg," at <war1812.tripod.com/batogden.html>.

9. Hickey, *War of 1812*, p. 85.

10. See The River Raisin Battlefield Site at <www.riverraisinbattlefield.org/the_battles.htm>.

# CHAPTER 13

1. See the letter "Armstrong to Cabinet," February 8, 1813 in U.S. Congress American State Papers: Documents and Executive, of the Congress of the United States, Vol. 1, p. 439; see also Adams, Henry, *History of the United States During the Administration of Jefferson and Madison*, Vol. 7 (Chicago: University of Chicago Press, 1979 reprint from New York, 1889–1891), pp. 148–149.

2. See the letters "Dearborn to Armstrong," March 3, 9, and 16, 1813 in Brannan, *Official Letters*; see also Horsman, *War of 1812*, p. 91.

3. Losing, Benton, *The Pictoral Field-Book of the War of 1812* (New York: Harper & Row, 1869) p. 586.

4. Latimer, *1812*, pp. 132–134.

5. Myer, Jesse S., *Life and Letters of Dr. William Beaumont* (St. Louis: C.V. Mosby Co., 1912), p. 44.

6. Hickey, *War of 1812*, pp. 129–130.

7. Cruikshank, E., *The Documentary History of the Campaign Upon the Niagara Frontier in the Year 1813* (Welland, Ontario: Lundy's Lane Historical Society, 1902), pp. 281–282 (part 5).

8. See the letter "Brown to Dearborn, July 25, 1813 in Adams, *History of the Unite States*, p. 735.

9. Malcomson, Robert, *Lords of the Lake: The Naval War on Lake Ontario, 1812–1814* (Annapolis, Md.: Naval Institute Press, 1998), p. 109.

## CHAPTER 14

1. Borneman, *1812*, p. 153.

2. See the letters "Harrison to Armstrong," February 11 and 18 1813 in Horsman, *War of 1812*, p. 99.

3. A story on the fort appeared in the Richmond Enquirer on April 13, 1813; see Mahon, *War of 1812*, pp. 159–161.

4. Grand and Jones, *War of 1812*, pp. 48–49; see also Mahon, John K., *The War of 1812*. (Gainesville: University of Florida Press, 1972), p. 160.

5. Horsman, *War of 1812*, pp. 100–101.

6. See the War of 1812 Website, "Massacre at Fort Meigs," at <war1812. tripod.com/batmeigs.html>.

7. Antal, Sandy, *A Wampum Denied: Proctor's War of 1812* (Carleton, MN: Carleton University Press, 1997), p. 226; see also Sugden, John, *Tecumseh: A Life* (London: Pimlico, 1999), p. 335.

8. See the letter "Proctor to Prevost," July 11 1813 in Wood, W. C. H., ed., *Select British Documents of the Canadian War of 1812*, Vol. 2 (Toronto: Champlain Society, 1920–1928), p.253.

9. See the War of 1812 Website, "Massacre at Fort Meigs," at <war1812. tripod.com/batmeigs.html>.

10. "The History of Fort George," Fort George National Historic Site in Ontario; see The Friends of Fort George Website at <friendsoffortgeorge.ca>.

11. Borneman, *1812*, p. 108.

12. Gilpin, Alec R., *The War of 1812 in the Old North-West* (East Lansing: Michigan State University Press, 1958), pp. 202–207; see also Casselman, Alexander Clark, ed., *Richardson's War of 1812: With Notes and Life of the Author* (Tygers Valley, South Africa: Ulan Press, 2012), pp. 177–179.

13 Borneman, *1812*, p. 156.

14. Horsman, *War of 1812*, p. 102.

15. Hickey, *War of 1812*, p. 136.

## CHAPTER 15

1. Latimer, *1812*, pp. 144–146.

2. Berton, Pierre, *Flames Across the Border in Canada* (New York: Random House, 1981), p. 72–80; see also The Battlefield Museum at <www.battlefieldhouse.ca/billy_scout.asp>.

3. Zaslow, Morris, *The Defended Border: Upper Canada and the War of 1812* (Toronto: Macmillan Co., 1964), p. 58.

4. Berton, Pierre, *Flames Across the Border: The Canadian-American Tragedy, 1813–1814* (Boston: Little, Brown, 1981), pp. 72–78; Stanley, G. F. G., *The War of 1812: Land Operations* (Toronto: Macmillan, 1983), p. 188.

5. Borneman, *1812*, p. 109.

6. Hickey, *War of 1812*, p. 141; Latimer, *1812*, p. 147.

7. Raddall, T. H., *The Path of Destiny* (Toronto: Doubleday, 1958), p. 248; Wood, *Select British Documents*, Vol. 2, see "Memoir of Laura Secord," February 18, 1861, pp. 164–165.

8. Borneman, *1812*, p. 110.

9. Hitsman, *Incredible War*, p. 335; see also Stanldy, George, "The Indians in the War of 1812," in Zaslow, Morris, *Defended Border*, p. 182.

10. Hitsman, *Incredible War*, p. 155.

## CHAPTER 16

1. See the Town of Burnt Corn page at <burntcorn.com/htmfiles/battle.htm>; see also Harrington, Scott, "Burnt Corn," *Mobile Press Register*, May 25, 1985, p. 6-C; see also Hickman, Kennedy, "Creek War: Fort Mims Massacre," Military History Website at <militaryhistory.about.com/od/warof1812/p/creek-war-fort-mims-massacre.htm>.

2. Brannan, *Official Letters*, pp. 202–205; see also Losing, *Pictoral Field Book*, pp. 745–758.

3. McAfee, *History of the Late War*, pp. 461–463; see also Tucker, *Poltroons*, pp. 448–451.

4. Grant and Jones, *War of 1812*, p. 57.

5. Pray, J., and Carl E., "The Contributions of Governor Shelby and the People of Kentucky to the Freedom of Michigan in the War of 1812," *Michigan History Magazine* Vol. 29 (October-December 1945), pp. 522–540; see also Wrobel, Sylvia and George Drider, *Isaac Shelby: Kentucky's First Governor and Hero of Three Wars* (Danville, KY: Cumberland Press, 1974).

6. McAfee, *History of the Late War*, p. 337.

7. Hickey, *War of 1812*, p. 137.

8. Grant and Jones, *War of 1812*, p. 58.

9. Ibid., p. 58.

10. Borneman, *1812*, p. 160.

11. The poem dates to the War of 1812 and the author is unknown.

## CHAPTER 17

1. Horsman, *War of 1812*, p. 52.

2. Ibid., p. 52; see also Roosevelt, Theodore, *The Naval War of 1812*, Vol, 1 (Annapolis, MD: Naval Institute Press, 1987; reprint in 1900 and 1987, original published by G.P. Putnam Sons in 1882), pp. 76–104.

3. Borneman, *1812*, p. 78.

4. A few sources were used for not just boarding enemy ships, but naval weaponry and life aboard warships of the time, including the National Maritime Museum, which is part of the Royal Museums Greenwich at <www.fmg.co.uk>; the U.S. Department of the Navy, Navy Department Library, "Living Conditions in the 19th Century Navy" at <www.history.navy.mil/library/online/living_cond. htm>; and an article on nineteenth-century naval weapons on the U.S. History Website at <www.ushistory.com/19th-century_weaspons_f.shtml>.

5. Horsman, *War of 1812*, p. 57; see also Roosevelt, *Naval War*, Vol. 2, p. 106.

6. Horsman, *War of 1812*, p. 53.

7. Ibid., p. 55.

8. The story appeared in the *London Times*, August 2, 1813; see the Times Archive at <www.thetimes.co.uk/tto/archive>.

9. His Majesty's decree was the "Declaration of his Royal Highness the Prince Regent Relative to the Cause and Origin of the War with America," issued on January 9, 1813 in Hansard, T. C., ed., *The Parliamentary Debates from the Year 1803 to the Present Time Forming a Continuation of the Work Entitled "The Parliamentary History of England from the Earliest Period to the Year 1803,"* 41 volumes (London: T. C. Hansard, 1803–1820), see Vol. 24, p. 375.

10. Waterhouse, Benjamin, *A Journal of a Young Man of Massachusetts* (Boston: Rowe and Hooper, 1816)—reprinted as "Extra No. 18" in the *Magazine of History* (New York, 1911), p. 60; Waterhouse was a surgeon who served on a privateer and was captured by the British.

11. Horsman, *War of 1812*, p. 56.

12. Latimer, *1812*, pp. 91–93.

13. See the article "USS *Wasp* vs. HMS *Frolic*," History of War Website at <www.historyofwar.org/articles/battles_wasp_frolic.html>.

14. Ellis, James H., *A Ruinous and Unhappy War: New England and the War of 1812* (New York: Algora Publishing, 2009), pp. 130–145.

15. See the article "The *Enterprise* vs. the *Boxer*," War of 1812 Website at <http://warof1812.tripod.com/evsb.html>.

16. See the letter "Porter to Hamilton," October 14, 1812 in Dudley, William S. and Michael J. Crawford, eds., *The Naval War of 1812: A Documentary History* (Washington Naval Historical Center, multiple volumes 1985–1992), Vol. 1, p. 528.

## CHAPTER 18

1. See the biography of Captain Isaac Hull, Naval History and Heritage Command, U.S. Department of the Navy Library, at <www.history.navy.mil/bios/hull_isaac.htm>.

2. See the USS *Constitution* at the Naval History & Heritage Command at Charlestown Navy Yard, Charlestown, Massachusetts <history.navy.mil/ussconstitution/history.html>.

3. Grant, Bruce, *Isaac Hull: Captin of Old Ironsides* (Chicago: Pellegrini and Cudahy, 1947), pp. 202 and 225.

4. Borneman, *1812*, p. 83.

5. Grant, *Isaac Hull*, p. 391.

6. Borneman, *1812*, p. 84.

7. Ibid., p. 86.

8. Grant, *Isaac Hull*, p. 391.

9. Ibid., pp. 240–242.

10. Latimer, *1812*, p. 98.

11. Borneman, *1812*, p. 88; the story also appeared in the *London Times*, October 9, 1812. See the Times Archive at <www.thetimes.co.uk/tto/archive>.

12. Mahan, Alfred Thayer, *Sea Power in its Relations to the War of 1812*, Vol. 1 (Boston: Little Brown, 1905), pp. 334–335.

13. Borneman, *1812*, p. 88.

14. See the American Legion Website at <burnpit.legion.org/2010/02/Stephen-decatur-retakes-burns-uss-philadelphia-tripoli-harbor>; see also the Naval History & Heritage Command Website at <www.history.navy.mil/photos/events/barb-war/burn-phl.htm>.

15. See the article on the Barbary Pirate Wars, Naval History and Heritage Command, U.S. Department of the Navy, at <www.history.navy.mil/photos/events/barb-war/burn-phl.htm>.

16. Wilson, Elisabeth, "A Gallnter Fellow Never Stepped a Quarter Deck: The Story of Stephen Decatur," *Founders of America*, at <www.foundersofamerica.org/decatur.html>.

17. See the article "*United States* Captures the *Macedonian*," War of 1812 Website at <war1812.tripod.com/usvsmac.html>.

18. Borneman, *1812*, p. 91.

19. Grant and Jones, *War of 1812*, p. 138.

20. Borneman, *1812*, pp. 94–95; see also Forester, S. C., *Age of the Fighting Sail: The Story of the Naval War of 1812* (Garden City, NJ: Doubleday, 1956), p. 127.

21. See the USS *Constitution* at the Naval History & Heritage Command at Charlestown Navy Yard, Charlestown, Massachusetts <history.navy.mil/ussconstitution/history.html>.

## CHAPTER 19

1. Borneman, *1812*, p. 217.

2. Latimer, *1812.* p. 251

3. Borneman, *1812*, p. 218.

4. Ibid., p. 174.

5. See the letter "Croker to Warren," January 5, 1813 in Dudley and Crawford, *Naval War*, Vol. 2, pp. 14–15.

6. There are two particularly helpful Websites devoted to American privateers during the War of 1812. See the U.S. Merchant Marine page at <www.usmm.org/warof1812.html>; see also a site devoted to privateers with detailed numbers and accounts at <1812privateers.org/>.

7. See the article on George Cockburn on the War of 1812 Website at <www.mywarof1812.com/leaders/cockburn-george.html>.

8. See the U.S. Merchant Marine "American Merchant Marine at War" Website at <www.usmm.org/warof1812.html>.

9. Grant and Jones, *War of 1812*, p. 149.

10. See the U.S. Merchant Marine "American Merchant Marine at War" Website at <www.usmm.org/warof1812.html>.

11. Ibid.

12. Grant and Jones, *War of 1812*, p. 149.

13. For a good source on Boyle, see Hopkins, Jr., Fred W., *Tom Boyle: Master Privateer* (Cambridge, MA: Tidewater Publishers, 1976); a helpful account of the role played by privateers is Maclay, E. S., *History of American Privateers* (New York: D. Appleton, 1899).

14. See the article "Joshua Barney," Office of Naval Records and Library, U.S. Department of the Navy, collection: Joshua Barney ZB file, Navy Department File at <www.navy.mil/bios/barney_jos.htm>; see also the article on Joshua Barney at the War of 1812 Website at <warof1812.net/joshuabarney.com>.

15. Bishop, RoAnn, "The Ups and Downs of a Seafaring Man," <nc1812.wordpress.com/2011/04/07/the-ups-and-downs-of-a-seafaring-man/>.

16. Horsman, *War of 1812*, pp. 59–60; see also Maclay, Edgar Stanton, *A History of American Privateers* (New York: D. Appleton & Co., 1924; reprint from 1899, also available in ebooksread version), pp. 225–228.

17. See the article "Capture of the USS President," The War of 1812 Website at <http://war of1812.tripod.com/presvsendy.html>.

## CHAPTER 20

1. Borneman, *1812*, p. 113.
2. Roosevelt, *Naval War*, p. 178.
3. Ibid., p. 179.
4. Tucker, Poltroons, p. 267.
5. Mahan, Sea Power, Vol. 2, p. 139.

## CHAPTER 21

1. Howell, William Maher, "The Arrival of Dobbins at Erie," *Inland Seas*, Vol. 51 (1995), pp. 32–34; for a source on Dobbins, see Ilisevich, Robert D., *Daniel Dobbins, Frontier Mariner* (Erie, Penn.: Erie County Historical Society, 1993).
2. Hickey, *War of 1812*, p. 156; Latimer, *1812*, p. 168.
3. Borneman, *1812*, p. 123.
4. Ibid., p. 124.
5. Mahan, Sea Power, Vol. 2, p. 77.
6. Borneman, *1812*, p. 132.
7. Scaggs, David Curtis and Gerard T. Altoff, *A Signal Victory: The Lake Erie Campaign* (Annapolis, Md.: Naval Institute Press, 1997), pp. 164–167.
8. Ibid., pp. 164–167.
9. Ibid., p. 180.
10. Ibid., p. 180.
11. Grant and Jones, *War of 1812*, p. 52.

## CHAPTER 22

1. Latimer, *1812*, pp. 44 and 108.
2. Latimer, 1812, p. 72; see also Malcomson, Robert, *Lords of the Lake: The Naval War on Lake Ontario, 1812–1814* (Annapolis, MD: Naval institute Press, 1998), pp. 40–49.
3. For information on Fort Frederick location, history, and defenses, see the article "Fort Frederick" at the Cataraqui Archaeological Research Foundation at <www.carf.info/kingston-past/kingston-archaeology/fort-frederick>.
4. Latimer, *1812*, p. 148.
5. Hickey, *War of 1812*, p. 129.

6. See the Website on the War of 1812 at <war1812.tripod.com/brace.html>.

7. For information on the fort, see the Friends of Fort Ontario at <fortontario.com>; see also the City of Oswego Website at <www.oswegony.org/about_fort.html>.

8. See the Website on the War of 1812 at <war1812.tripod.com/screek.html>.

9. Hickey, *War of 1812*, p. 185.

10. Ibid., p. 184.

11. Elting, John R. *Amateurs to Arms: A Military History of the War of 1812* (New York: da Capo Press, 1995), p. 188; see also Forester, *Age of the Fighting Sail*, pp. 187–188; see also Roosevelt, *Naval War*, pp. 203–204.

# CHAPTER 23

1. Hickey, pp. 169–170, 183; for a helpful source on Wilkinson's scandalous rule in Louisiana, see Linklater, Andro, *An Artist in Treason: The Extraordinary Double Life of General James Wilkinson* (New York: Walker and Co., 2012); for a fun, imagined (but believable) read about Wilkinson's life, see the historical novel by Keith Thompson, *Scoundrel! The Secret Life of General James Wilkinson* (NorLights Press, 2012).

2. For mention of Hampton's incompetence, see the letter "Jacob Brown to Secretary of War," May 8, 1814 in the General Jacob Brown Papers, Library of Congress; see also "Letter from a Congressman," January 8, 1815 in the Lexington *Reporter* (February 8, 1815); see also Hickey, *War of 1812*, p. 305.

3. Borneman, *1812*, p. 167.

4. Ibid., p. 163.

5. Hickey, *War of 1812*, p. 145.

6. See the War of 1812 Website at <warof1812.tripod.com/batcrys.html>.

7. Latimer, *1812*, pp. 201–206.

8. Hickey, *War of 1812*, p. 145.

9. Way, Ronald, in Zaslow, *Defended Border*, p. 64.

10. Graves, Donald E., *Field of Glory: The Battle of Cysler's Farm* (Toronto: Robin Brass Studio, 1999), p. 223.

11. Ibid., p. 272.

12. Borneman, *1812*, pp. 170–171.

13. Henderson, Robert, "The Short List: Ontario's Significant Places and Events in the War of 1812," War of 1812 Website at <www.warof1812.ca/lacolle.htm>.

14. Jacobs, James R., *Tarnished Warrior: The Story of Major-General James Wilkinson* (New York: Macmillan, 1938), p. 296.

15. Tucker, Poltroons, p. 418; the story ran in the *New York Gazette*, January 9, 1814.

## CHAPTER 24

1. Colquhoun, "The Career of Joseph Willocks," *Canadian Historical Review*, Vol. 7 (December 1926), pp. 287–293; Cruikshank, Ernest A., "A Study of Disaffection in Upper Canada in 1812–1815," in Morris Zaslow, ed., *The Defended Border: Upper Canada and the War of 1812* (Toronto: Macmillan, 1964), pp. 208–221.

2. "Merritt, William Hamilton," *Dictionary of Canadian Biography Online* (University of Toronto, 2000) at <www.biographi.ca/009004-119.01-e. php?bioid=38719>.

3. Campbell, Ronald, "The Capture of Fort Niagara: December 19, 1813," Suite 101 at <suite101.com/article/war-of-1812-the-british-capture-fort-niagara-december-19-1813>.

4. See the article on Fort Niagara, War of 1812 Website at <war1812. tripod.com/ftniagara.html>.

5. See the "Proclamation by McClure," October 16, 1813 in Brannan, *Official Letters*, pp. 244–246; see also the letter "McClure to Armstrong," December 13, 1813 in Latimer, *1812*, pp. 223–224.

6. For information on the fort and its history, see Old Fort Niagara at <oldfortniagara.org>; see also the Fort Niagara State Park at <www.nyspark.com/parks/175/details.aspx>.

7. See the letter "Lewis Cass to Drummond," January 12, 1814, in *American State Papers: Military Affairs*, Vol. 1 (Washington: Gales and Seaton, 1832–1861), p. 488; see also Latimer, *1812*, p. 225.

8. Henderson, Robert, "The Storming of Fort Niagara," War of 1812 Website at <www.warof1812.ca/ftniagra.htm>.

9. Campbell, "Capture of Fort Niagara."

10. Latimer, *1812*, pp. 226–227, 269.

11. See the Website for Old Fort Niagara at <www.oldfortniagara.org>.

12. Hickey, *War of 1812*, pp. 142–143.

13. Werbaneth, James P., "British Strategy Toward New York and New England in the War of 1812," paper presented at the War of 1812 in New York and Beyond symposium, March 31, 2012, by the New York Military Affairs Symposium.

14. This poem ran in the New York Gazette in response to the disastrous invasion and the trial of General William Hull; the trial transcript is found at "The Defence of Brigadier General William Hull," Albany, New York (March 1814) at <www.archive.org/stream/defenceofbrigadi00hullw/defenceofbrigadi00hullw_djvu. txt>.

# CHAPTER 25

1. For information on Napoleon's capture and escape from Elba, see Mackenzie, Norman, *Escape from Elba: The Fall and Flight of Napoleon, 1814–1815* (Barnsley, England: Pen and Sword Books, 2007).

2. Latimer, *1812*, p. 367.

3. Borneman, *1812*, p. 178; the comment about the Americans appeared in the *London Times* on May 24, 1814.

4. Hickey, *War of 1812*, p. 182.

5. Borneman, *1812*, p. 185.

6. Eisenhower, *Agent of Destiny*, pp. 80–84.

7. Scott, Winfield, *Memoirs of Lieutenant.-General Scott, LLD*, Vol. 1 (Freeport, NY: Books for Libraries Press, 1970; reprint), p. 134.

8. Roosevelt, *Naval War*, p. 328.

9. Ibid., p. 328.

10. Gilpin, Alec R., *The War of 1812 in the Old North-West* (East Lansing: Michigan State University Pres, 1958), pp 246–247; see also Scanlan, Peter Lawrence, *Prairie du Chien: French, British*, American (Menasha, Wis.: George Banta, 1937), p. 117.

11. For information on the history of the fort, see Mackinac Island State Park at <www.mightymac.com/fortmackinac>; see also <>www.mackinacparks.com/fort-mackinac>.

12. See the article on the Battle of Lundy's Lane on the War of 1812 Website at <war1812.tripod.com/batlundy.html>.

13. Eisenhower, *Agent of Destiny*, pp. 89–90.

14. Borneman, *1812*, p. 192.

15. Scott, *Memoirs*, Vol. I, pp. 139–141.

16. Hickey, *War of 1812*, p. 188.

17. Ibid., p. 188.

18. See the article on the Battle of Lundy's Lane on the War of 1812 Website at <war1812.tripod.com/batlundy.html>.

19. Borneman, *1812*, p. 192.

20. Grant and Jones, *War of 1812*, p. 83.

21. See the letter "Brown to his brother," August 4, 1814 in the Brown Papers, Massachusetts Historical Society; see also Lossing, *Pictoral Field Book*, Chapt 36.

22. Eisenhower, *Agent of Destiny*, pp. 93–95.

23. Mahon, *Sea Power*, Vol. II, p. 313.

24. The account of the situation was given by a man named Mr. James. Fortunately this was one of Campbell's last raids. The source is found in the War of 1812 Website at <war1812.tripod.com/raids.html>.

25. See the War of 1812 webstie at <war1812.tripod.com/raids.html>.

# CHAPTER 26

1. Borneman, *1812*, p. 100.
2. Mahon, *Sea Power*, Vol. 2, pp. 362–363.
3. Hickey, *War of 1812*, p. 190.
4. Mahon, *Sea Power*, Vol. 2, pp. 363–364.
5. Borneman, *1812*, p. 199.
6. Hitsman, *Incredible War*, p. 253.
7. Ibid., p. 255.
8. Borneman, *1812*, p. 208.
9. Macdonough, Rodney, *The Life of Commodore Thomas Macdonough, U.S. Navy* (Boston: Fort Hill Press, 1909), p. 176.
10. See the article on the War of 1812 Website at <www.warof1812trail.com/downie.htm>.
11. See the article on the Battle of Plattsburgh on the War of 1812 Website at <war1812.tripod.com/batplatts.html>.
12. Borneman, *1812*, p. 212.
13. Hitsman, *Incredible War*, p. 267.
14. Hickey, *War of 1812*, p. 193.
15. Roosevelt, *Naval War*, pp. 356–357.

# CHAPTER 27

1. Latimer, *1812*, pp. 308–309.
2. Adams, Henry, History, Vol. 8, pp. 155–162; see also Skeen, Carl Edward, "Monroe and Armstrong: A Study in Political Rivalry," *New York Historical Society Quarterly*.
3. Borneman, *1812*, p. 224.
4. Gleig, George Robert, *The Campaigns of the British Army at Washington and New Orleans* (Totowa, NJ: Rowman and Littlefield, 1972, reprint), p. 54.
5. Borneman, *1812*, p. 225.
6. Latimer, *1812*, pp. 309–310, 313.
7. Hickey, *War of 1812*, p. 198.
8. Adams, *History*, p. 1018.
9. Tucker, *Poltroons*, p. 537.
10. Ball, Charles, *A Narrative of the Life and Adventures of Charles Ball, a Black Man* (New York: John Taylor, 1837), p. 468.
11. Pitch, Anthony S., *The Burning of Washington: The British Invasion of 1814* (Annapolis, MD: Naval Institute Press, 1998), p. 85.
12. See the article on the Battle of Washington and burning of the White House on the War of 1812 Website at <war1812.tripod.com/batwash.html>.

## CHAPTER 28

1. See the letter "S. Burch and J. T. Frost to Patrick Magruder," September 15, 1814 in *Annals of Congress: Debates and Proceedings in the Congress of the United States, 1789–1824*, 42 volumes (Washington, 1834–1856), 13th Congress, 3rd session, p. 207; see also the letter "Magruder to Speaker fo the House," December 17, 1814 in the same source, pp. 953–957.

2. See the article on the battles in Baltimore and Washington on the War of 1812 Website at <war1812.tripod.com/batwash.html>.

3. Ibid.

4. Watson, Robert P., *The Presidents' Wives; Reassessing the Office of First Lady* (Boulder, Colo.: Lynne Rienner Publishers, 2000), p. 45.

5. Dolley's original letters about the burning of the White House no longer exist, but evidence of them does. See Clark, Allen C., *Life and Letters of Dolley Madison* (Washington: W. F. Roberts, 1914), p. 125 and 166; see also the article "At a Perilous Moment Dolley Madison Writes to Her Sister," *Madison Quarterly*, Vol. 4 (January 1944), p. 28; for a discussion of Mrs. Madison's heroics at the White House see Watson, Robert P. *Life in the White House: A Social History of the First Family and the President's Home* (Albany: SUNY Press, 2004), pp. 24 and 231.

6. See also Watson, *Presidents' Wives*, p. 45.

7. Latimer, *1812*, p. 319–320.

8. Adams, *History of the United States*, p. 1015; see also Borneman, *1812*, p. 230.

9. Borneman, *1812*, p. 232.

10. Pitch, Anthony S., *The Burning of Washington: The British Invasion of 1814* (Annapolis, MD: Naval Institute Press, 1998), p. 124.

11. Ibid., p. 142.

12. Clark, *Letters of Dolley Madison*, p. 166.

13. Hickey, *War of 1812*, p. 201; see also Pitch, *Burning*, p. 144.

14. Goebel, Greg, "By the Dawn's Early Light," (April 12, 2001), see 6.2 "Burning of the White House" at <www.vectorsite.net/tw1812_06.html>; see also *The War of 1812*, PBS Video, transcript at <video.pbs.org/video/2089393535/>.

15. Borneman, *1812*, p. 233; see also the letter "Monroe to Cochrane," September 6, 1814 in Brannan, *Official Letters*.

16. The poem by Philip Freneu is reprinted in Lossing, *Pictoral Field Book*, Ch. 39.

## CHAPTER 29

1. Hickey, *War of 1812*, p. 202.

2. Lord, Walter, *By the Dawn's Early Light* (New York: W. W. Norton, 1972), pp. 222–223.

3. Borneman, *1812*, p. 237.

4. Pezzola, John, "Battle of North Point," War of 1812 Website at <www.warof1812.ca/northpoint.htm.>

5. Ibid.

6. Ibid.

7. Borneman, *1812*, pp. 242–243.

8. Ibid., p. 243

9. Gleig *Campaigns of the British*, p. 109.

10. For helpful sources on Samuel Smith, see Pancake, John, *Samuel Smith and the Politics of Business* (Tuscaloosa: University of Alabama Press, 1972); see also U.S. House of Representatives, *Biographical Dictionary of the United States Congress* at <bioguide.congress.gov/scripts/biodisplay.pl?index=s000609>.

11. Pezzola, "Battle of North Point."

## CHAPTER 30

1. For information on Fort McHenry, see the National Park Service Website at <www.nps.gov/fomc>.

2. Latimer, *1812*, p. 326.

3. Borneman, *1812*, p. 245.

4. Magruder, Jr., Caleb Clarke, "Dr. William Beanes, the Incidental Cause of the Authorship of the Star-Spangled Banner," *Records of the Columbia Historical Society*, Vol. 22 (1915), pp. 207–224.

5. Borneman, *1812*, p. 241.

6. George, Christopher T, *Terror on the Chesapeake: The War of 1812 on the Bay* (Shippensburg, PA: White Mane Books, 2000), p. 146.

7. Latimer, *1812*, p. 330.

8. Hickey, War of 1812, p. 203; see also the letter "Cochrane to Croker," September 17, 1814 in *Niles' Weekly Register*, Vol. 7 (December 3, 1814), pp. 199–200. *The Niles Weekly Register* and *The Weekly Register* archives are found in the Cumulative Index (1811–1948) at <nilesregister.com>.

9. See "The Star-Spangled Banner: The Flag that Inspired the National Anthem" exhibit at the Smithsonian Institution's National Museum of American History at <americanhistory.si.edu/exhibitions/star-spangled-banner>.

10. Borneman, *1812*, p. 241.

## CHAPTER 31

1. Carsted, Frederick, "The Siege of Fort Erie," War of 1812 Website at <www.warof1812.ca/forterie.htm>.

2. Hickey, *War of 1812*, p. 188.

3. Hughes, B. P., "Siege Artillery in the 19th Century," *Journal of the Society of Army Historical Research*, Vol. 60 (1982), pp. 129–139; Latimer, *1812*, pp. 334–335.

4. See the letters "Drummond to Prevost," August 12, 1814 and "Prevost to Drummond," August 26, 1814, as well as "Secret Order," August 14, 1814, in Cruikshank, Ernst A., ed., *Documentary History of the Campaigns Upon the Niagara Frontier in 1812–1814*, 9 volumes (Welland, Ontario: Tribune Press, 1896–1908), Vol. 1, pp. 132, 174, 139–142; see also "Instructions to Lt. Col. Fischer," August 14, 1814 in Dunlop, William, *Recollections of the American War, 1812–1814* (Toronto: Historical Publishing, 1905), p. 70

5. Latimer, *1812*, pp. 334–338.

6. Ibid.

7. See the article on the siege at the War of 1812 Website at <war1812.tripod.com/siege.html>.

8. Grant and Jones, *War of 1812*, p. 87.

## CHAPTER 32

1. For a helpful study of Jackson's youth, see Brands, H. W., *Andrew Jackson: His Life and Times* (New York: Anchor, 2006).

2. Grant and Jones, *War of 1812*, p. 171.

3. Watson, Robert P., *Affairs of State: The Untold History of Presidential Love, Sex, and Scandal* (Lanham, Md.: Rowman & Littlefield Publishers, 2012), pp. 172–174.

4. Ibid., p. 173.

5. Remini, *Jackson and the Course*, pp. 182–184.

6. Watson, *Affairs of State*, pp. 178–179.

7. Ibid., p. 176.

8. Ibid., p. 177.

9. See the article "Andrew Jackson vs. Charles Dickinson," Garland County Library, Arkansas; blog post at <garlandcountylibrary.blogspot.com/2011/05/andrew-jackson-vs-charles-dickinson.html, www.garland.lib.ar.us.>

10. Remini, *Jackson and the Course*, pp. 168–169.

11. Ibid., pp. 168–169.

12. Borneman, *1812*, p. 146.

13. For the letter, see Brannan, *Official Letters*, p. 215.

14. See the letters "Jackson to Blunt," November 4 and 15, 1813 in Bassett, John Spencer, ed., *Correspondence of Andrew Jackson*, Vol. 1 (Washington: Carnegie Institution, 1926–1935; 7 volumes), pp. 341 & 348–350.

15. See the letter "Jackson to Armstrong," November 30, 1813 in Parton, James, *Life of Andrew Jackson* Vol. 1 (New York: Mason Bros., 1860), pp. 446–453; the letter is also available in Basett, *Correspondence*, Vol. 1, pp. 355–357

16. Bassett, *Correspondence*, Vol. 1, pp. 345–346 & 354–355; see also Borneman, *1812*, p. 149.

17. Horsman, *War of 1812*, p. 224.

18. Ibid., p. 225.

19. Losing, *Pictorial Field Book*, pp. 777–781.

20. Remini, *Jackson and the Course*, pp. 208–210.

21. See the letter "Jackson to Mrs. Jackson," April 1, 1814 in Bassett, *Correspondence*, Vol. 1, pp. 489–494.

22. Hickey, *War of 1812*, p. 151.

23. See the letters "Armstrong to Jackson," May 22, 1814, and "Jackson to Blount," August 9, 1814 in Bassett, *Correspondence*, Vol. 2, pp. 4 & 24.

24. Borneman, *1812*, p. 152.

25. Remini, *Jackson and the Course*, p. 218.

## CHAPTER 33

1. Hickey, *War of 1812*, pp. 149–151.

2. Parton, *Life of Andrew Jackson*, Vol. 1, p. 372.

3. Hickey, *War of 1812*, pp. 206–207.

4. Dangerfield, George, *The Era of Good Feelings* (New York: Harcourt Brace, 1952), p. 127.

5. Borneman, *1812*, p. 137.

6. Horsman, *War of 1812*, p. 226.

7. See the letter "Cochrane to Croker," June 20, 1814 in Wrottesley, George, *Life and Letters of Burgoyne*, Vol. 1 (London: Richard Bentley, 1874), pp. 304–305.

8. Horsman, *War of 1812*, p. 228.

9. See the "Damn the Torpedoes: Infernal Machines" exhibit at Vicksburg National Military Park, National Park Service at <www.nps.gov/vick/forteachers/upload/torpedoes.pdf>.

10. See the letter "Lawrence to Jackson," September 15, 1814 in Brannan, *Official Letters*, pp. 424–426.

11. Grant and Jones, *War of 1812*, p. 168.

12. Latimer, *1812*, pp. 370–374.

## CHAPTER 34

1. Grant and Jones, *War of 1812*, p. 21.

2. Latimer, *1812*, pp. 222, 362, 392.

3. Ibid., pp. 391–392.

4. Borneman, *1812*, pp. 294–295.

5. Latimer, *1812*, 367.

6. Hawkish British commanders such as Admirals Cockburn and Cochrane, as well as some members of Henry Clay's War Hawks in the southern and frontier states, were still unhappy with the prospects of peace. Both sides still felt they could win the war or at least gain a military advantage late in 1814 so as to influence the talks in Ghent more favorably to their position.

7. Hickey, *War of 1812*, p. 279.

8. A complete transcript of the Treaty of Ghent is available through "Our Documents" at <www.ourdocuments.gov/doc.php?flash=true&doc=20&page=tran script>.

9. *Annals of the Congress of the United States*, Thirteenth Congress, Third Session, February 18, 1815, p. 255.

10. See the transcript at "Our Documents."

11. There were tensions on both sides after the war over the return of property seized during the war including naval ships. It tooks months before forts along the Canadian border were abandoned and to complete prisoner swaps. However, trade between the United States and Canada and with Britain improved almost immediately.

# CHAPTER 35

1. Jackson's father died while his mother was pregnant. His oldest brother died during the Revolutionary War and his middle brother also died during the war after contracting an illness in a British prison, while young Andrew survived the ordeal. Jackson's mother died from the same or similar illness when she went to the prison to beg for the release of other American boys. Jackson blamed the British and harbored a deep grudge against them, one that festered for many years.

2. de Grummond, Jane Lucas, *The Baratarians and the Battle of New Orleans* (Baton Rouge: Lousiana State University Press, 1961); see also Sugden, John, "Jean Lafitte and the British Offer of 1814," *Louisiana History*, Vol. 20 (1979), pp. 159–167.

3. de Grummond, Jane Lucas, *The Baratarians and the Battle of New Orleans* (Baton Rouge: Louisiana State University Press, 1961).

4. Grant and Jones, *War of 1812*, p. 171.

5. See the article on the British landing and invasion on the Battle of New Orleans Website at <battleofneworlens.org/britishland.htm>.

6. See the War of 1812 Website at <www.mywarof1812.com/battles/141214. html>.

7. See the article on the Battle of New Orleans on the War of 1812 Website at <www.mywarof1812.com/battles/141214.html>.

8. Gayarre, Charles Etienne, *History of Louisiana*, Vol. 4 (New Orleans: F. F. Hanswell and Brothers, 1903), pp. 419–423; see also Walker, Alexander, *Jackson and New Orleans: An Authentic Narrative of the Achievements of the American Army under Andrew Jackson before New Orleans* (Cranbury, NJ: Scholars Bookshelf, 2005; reprinted from an old manuscript) pp. 22–28.

9. See the letter of "Eligius Fromentin," December 30, 1814 in *Niles' Register*, Vol. 7 (February 4, 1815), p. 360; see also Latour, *Historical Memoir*, pp. 80–87).

10. Smith, Zachary F., *The Battle of New Orleans* (Louisville, KY: John P. Morton & Co., 1904), available through Project Gutenberg as an ebook (#25699) at <www.gutenberg.org/files/25699/25699-8.txt> (June 5, 2008).

11. Gleig, *Campaigns of the British*; see also The War of 1812, "The Attack at the Villere Plantation," at <www.galafilm.com/1812/e/events/orl_villere.html>.

12. Hickey, *War of 1812*, pp. 210–211.

13. Grant and Jones, *War of 1812*, p. 17.

14. See the "Jackson" letter in Latour, Arsene Lacarriere, *Historical Memoir of the War in West Florida and Louisiana in 1814–15* (Gainesville, University Press of Florida, 2008), p. 337.

15. Grant and Jones, *War of 1812*, p. 173.

# CHAPTER 36

1. John Qunicy Adams was likely the least popular of the group of presidents. Of course, we did not have approval polls back them (thankfully!). However, his "suspect" victory in 1824—when Jackson won the popular vote but Adams won the Electoral College—which was dubbed a "corrupt bargain" and Jackson's popularity limited any chance Adams had of being reelected.

2. Harrison gave the longest inaugural address in history on a bitterly cold day. He was not dressed properly and caught pneumonia. Already advanced in years, he passed away only one month into his term.

3. Webster was appointed as Harrison's secretary of state and even helped him edit his inaugural address. Nevertheless, Webster rightly noted that the unwieldy address—the longest inaugural in history—was not effective. The quote appears on the White House Website at <www.whitehouse.gov/about/presidents/williamhenryharrison%20>.

4. Tecumseh's "curse" is an urban legend that is found in many forms and places. Possibly the first recorded or popular reference to it was in 1931 by the Ripley's Believe It or Not show. To read about the curse, see the American History Website at <americanhistory.about.com/od/uspresidents/a/Tecumseh.htm>.

5. Remini, *Jackson and the Course*, p. 166.

6. Borneman, *1812*, p. 304.

7. The Spanish-American War was in 1898. There were smaller conflicts such as the Mexican-American War and ongoing hostilities against Native Americas in the intervening years.

8. Taylor, R., "Summary of the End of the War of 1812," The War of 1812 Website at <http://www.warof1812.ca/summary.html>.

9. Ibid.

10. Ibid.

11. Dangerfield, George, *The Awakening of American Nationalism* (New York: Harper & Row, 1965), p. 2.

12. Tucker, *Poltroons*, p. ix.

# SELECT BIBLIOGRAPHY

Adams, Henry, *History of the United States of America During the Administrations of James Madison* (New York: Library of America, 1986, reprint from 1889–1891, 9 volumes).

*Annals of Congress of the United States: Debates and Proceedings in the Congress of the United States, 1794–1824,* 42 volumes (Washington: 1834–1856).

Antal, Sandy, *A Wampum Denied: Proctor's War of 1812* (Carleton, MN: Carleton University Press, 1997).

"The Argus vs. The Pelican," The War of 1812 Website; <http://war1812.tripod.com/avsp.html>.

Babcock, Louis, *The War of 1812 on the Niagara Frontier* (Buffalo, NY: Buffalo Historical Society, 1927).

Ball, Charles, *A Narrative of the Life and Adventures of Charles Ball, a Black Man* (New York: John Taylor, 1837).

Barbuto, Richard. Niagara, *1814: America Invades Canada* (Lawrence: University of Kansas Press, 2000).

"The Battle of Thame's River," The War of 1812 Website; <http://warof1812.tripod.com/batthames.html>.

Bassett, John Spencer, ed., *Correspondence of Jackson* (Washington: Carnegie Institution, 1926–1935; 7 volumes).

Berton, Pierre, *Flames Across the Border: The Canadian-American Tragedy, 1813–1814* (Boston: Little, Brown, 1981).

Berton, Pierre, *The Invasion of Canada, 1812–1813* (Toronto: McClelland and Stewart, 1980).

"Biographies in Naval History: Captain Isaac Hull," Naval Historical Center, Isaac Hull ZB file, Navy Department Library <http://www.history.navy.mil/bios/hull_isaac.htm>.

"Biographies in Naval History: Captain Stephen Decatur," Naval Historical Center, Stephen Decatur ZB file, box 62, Navy Department Library, <http://www.history.navy.mil/bios/decatur.htm>.

"Biographies in Naval History: Captain William Bainbridge," Naval Historical Center, William Bainbridge ZB file, Navy Department Library <http://www.history.navy.mil/bios/bainbridge_wm.htm>.

Bishop, RoAnn, "The Ups and Downs of a Seafaring Man," <http://nc1812. wordpress.com/2011/04/07/the-ups-and-downs-of-a-seafaring-man/>.

Black, Jeremy, *The War of 1812 in the Age of Napoleon* (Norman: University of Oklahoma Press, 2009).

Borneman, Walter R., *1812: The War that Forged a Nation* (New York: Harper Perennial, 2004).

Brands, H. W., *Andrew Jackson: His Life and Times* (New York: Anchor, 2006).

———, *The Heartbreak of Aaron Burr* (New York Random House, 2012).

Brannan, John, *Official Letters of the Military and Naval Officers of the United States During the War with Great Britian in the Years 1812, 1813, 1814, and 1815* (Washington: Way & Gideon, 1823), p. 36.

Brenton, E. B., "Some Account of the Public Life of the Late Lieutenant-General Sir George Prevost, Bart. Particularly of his Services in the Canadas . . . ," *The Quarterly Review* (Kindle Locations 1687–1691).

Brooks, Charles, *The Siege of New Orleans* (Seattle: University of Washington Press, 1961).

Brown, Gilbert Patten, "The Physician of Two Wars: Gen. Henry Dearborn, M.D.,"

*The Granite Monthly*, Vol. 35, No. 4 (October 1903), p. 183. <http://www. hampton.lib.nh.us>.

"Captain George Cockburn," Saint Vincent College, UK, Heritage site <http:// www.stvincent.ac.uk/heritage/1797/people/cockburn.html>.

"The Capture of the 'Julia' and the 'Prowler,' " The War of 1812 Website; <http:// war 1812.tripod.com/Julia.html>.

"Capture of the USS President," The War of 1812 Website; <http://war of1812. tripod.com/presvsendy.html>.

Carter, Samuel, *Blaze of Glory: The Fight for New Orleans 1814–1815* (London: Macmillan, 1971).

Casselman, Alexander Clark, ed., *Richardson's War of 1812: With Notes and Life of the Author* (Tygers Valley, South Africa: Ulan Press, 2012).

"The Chesapeake vs. The Shannon," The War of 1812 Website; <http://war1812. tripod.com/chvssh.html>.

Clark, Allen C., *Life and Letters of Dolley Madison* (Washington: W. F. Roberts, 1914).

Cleaves, Freeman. *Old Tippecanoe: William Henry Harrison and His Time* (New York: Charles Scribner's, 1939).

Coles, Harry L., *The War of 1812* (Chicago: University of Chicago Press, 1965).

Collins, Gilbert, *Guidebook to the Historic Sites of the War of 1812* (Toronto: Dundurn, 2006).

"Commodore David Porter, USN," Naval Historical Center, U.S. Department of the Navy, Washington Navy Yard, Washington, DC. <http://www.history. navy.mil>.

"Commodore Isaac Chauncey, USN," Naval Historical Center, U.S. Department of the Navy, Washington Navy Yard, Washington, DC. <http://www.history.navy.mil>.

Cruikshank, Ernest A., *The Documentary History of the Campaign Upon the Niagara Frontier in the Year 1813* (Welland, Ontario: Lundy's Lane Historical Society, 1902; Welland, Ontario: Tribune Press, 1896–1908).

Dangerfield, George, *The Awakening of American Nationalism* (New York: Harper & Row, 1965).

Dangerfield, George, *The Era of Good Feelings* (New York: Harcourt, Brace, 1952).

de Grummond, Jane Lucas, *The Baratarians and the Battle of New Orleans* (Baton Rouge: Louisiana State University Press, 1961).

"Delaware Military History," Military Heritage. <http://militaryheritage.org/macdonough.html>.

Dillon, Richard, *We Have Met the Enemy: Olivery Hazard Perry* (New York: McGraw-Hill, 1978).

Dudley, William S., and Michael J. Crawford, eds., *The Naval War of 1812: A Documentary History* (Washington: Naval Historical Center, multiple volumes 1985–1992).

Dunlop, William, *Recollections of the American War, 1812–1814* (Toronto: Historical Publishing, 1905).

Edwards, R. David, *The Shawnee Prophet* (Lincoln: University of Nebraska Press, 1985).

Eisenhower, John S. D., *Agent of Destiny: The Life and Times of General Winfield Scott* (New York: Free Press, 1997).

Ellis, James H., *A Ruinous and Unhappy War: New England and the War of 1812* (New York: Algora Publishing, 2009).

Elting, John R. *Amateurs to Arms: A Military History of the War of 1812* (New York: da Capo Press, 1995).

"The Enterprise vs The Boxer," The War of 1812 Website; <http://warof1812.tripod.com/evsb.html>.

Esarey, Logan, ed., *Messages and Letters of William Henry Harrison*, Vol. I, 1800–1811 (Indianapolis: Indiana Historical Commission, 1923).

Fleming, Thomas, *Duel: Alexander Hamilton, Aaron Burr, and the Future of America* (New York: Basic Books, 2000).

Forester, S. C., *Age of the Fighting Sail: The Story of the Naval War of 1812* (Garden City, NJ: Doubleday, 1956).

Fredriksen, John C., *Free Trade and Sailors' Rights: A Bibliography of the War of 1812* (Westport, CT: Greenwood Press, 1985)

Frost, John, *The Commodores: Stephen Decatur* (Jazzybee Publishing; Kindle Edition, Kindle Locations 9–18).

Garraty, John A., *The American Nation: A History of the United States* (New York: Harper & Row, 1966).

Gayarre, Charles Etienne, *History of Louisiana*, Vol. 4 (New Orleans: F. F. Hanswell and Brothers, 1903).

George, Christopher T, *Terror on the Chesapeake: The War of 1812 on the Bay* (Shippensburg, PA: White Mane Books, 2000).

Gilpin, Alec, *The War of 1812 in the Old North-West* (East Lansing: Michigan State University Press, 1970).

Gleig, George Robert, *The Campaigns of the British Army at Washington and New Orleans* (Totowa, NJ: Rowman and Littlefield, 1972, reprint).

Grant, Bruce, *Isaac Hull: Captain of Old Ironsides* (Chicago: Pellegrini and Cudahy, 1947).

Grant, John, and Ray Jones, *The War of 1812: A Guide to the Battlefields and Historic Sites* (Buffalo, NY: Western New York Publishing Broadcasting Association, 2011).

Graves, Donald E., "The Hard School of War: The Collective Biography of the General Officers of the United States Army in the War of 1812," War of 1812 Magazine (Napoleon Series, Issue 2, 2006) <http://www.napoleon-series.org/military/warof1812/2006/issue2/c_generals.html>.

Graves, Donald E., "Old Salt Indeed: The Amazing Career of Lieutenant Provo Wallis of HMS *Shannon*," The War of 1812 Website; <http://www.warof1812.ca/wallis.htm>.

Graves, Donald E., *Field of Glory: The Battle of Crysler's Farm* (Toronto: Robin Brass Studio, 1999).

"Hartford Convention," The War of 1812 Website; <http://war1812.tripod.com/hartford.html>.

Hastings, Hugh, ed., *Public Papers of Daniel D. Tompkins, Governor of New York, 1807–1817*, volume 3 (Albany, J.B. Lyon, 1902).

Heine, William, *96 Years in the Royal Navy* (Hantsport, Nova Scotia, 1987).

Henderson, Robert, "'Not Merely an Article of Comfort': British Infantry Greatcoats During the War of 1812," The War of 1812 Website at <www.warof1812.ca/greatct.htm>.

———, "Soldier's Families Under Fire: Ambush at Toussant Island 1812," The War of 1812 Website at <www.arof1812.ca/ambush.htm>.

———, "A Tranquil River No More: The Raid on Gananoque," The War of 1812 Website at <www.warof1812.ca/gananoque.htm>.

Hickey, Donald R., *War of 1812: A Forgotten Conflict* (Urbana: University of Illinois Press, 1989).

"Historic Fort Gaines on Dauphin Island, AL," Archive of Historical Data, Books, Maps and Other Materials, Dauphin Island History Archive <http://www.dauphinislandhistory.org>.

Hitsman, J. Mackay, *The Incredible War of 1812: A Military History* (Toronto: Robin Brass Studio, 1999).

Hopkins, J. F., ed., *Papers of Henry Clay: The Rising Statesman, 1797–1814* (Lexington: University Press of Kentucky, 1959).

Hopkins, Jr., Fred W., *Tom Boyle: Master Privateer* (Cambridge, MA: Tidewater Publishers, 1976).

Horsman, Reginald, *The Causes of the War of 1812* (New York: Barnes, 1962).

———, *The War of 1812* (New York: Random House, 1969).

Hull, William, *Memoirs of the Campaign of the North Western Army of the United States* (Boston: True & Greene, 1824).

Ingraham, George, "The Story of Laura Secord Reevisited," *Ontario History* (volume 57, 1965).

Jacobs, James R., *The Beginning of the U.S. Army, 1783–1812* (Princeton, NJ: Princeton University Press, 1947).

———, *Tarnished Warrior: The Story of Major-General James Wilkinson* (New York: Macmillan, 1938).

Jortner, Adam, *The Gods of Prophetstown: The Battle of Tippecanoe and the Holy War for the American Frontier* (New York: Oxford University Press, 2011).

"The journal kept on board the U.S. frigate Constitution, by Captain Edward Preble, U.S. Navy," from Friday August 3, 1804 and Saturday, August 4, 1804; *Naval Documents Related to the United States Wars with the Barbary Powers*. Vol. 4 (Washington: U.S. Government Printing Office, 1942), pp. 336–338.

Kline, Mary-Jo, ed., *Political Correspondence and Public Papers of Aaron Burr*, two volumes (Princeton, NJ: Princeton University Press, 1983).

Latimer, Jon, *1812: War with America* (Cambridge, MA: Belknap Press of Harvard University Press, 2007).

Latour, Arsene Lacarriere, *Historical Memoir of the War in West Florida and Louisiana in 1814–15* (Gainesville: University Press of Florida, 2008; reprint from 1999 edition edited by Gene Allen Smith).

Linklater, Andro, *An Artist in Treason: The Extraordinary Double Life of General James Wilkinson* (New York: Walker and Co., 2012).

Lord, Walter, *By the Dawn's Early Light* (New York: W. W. Norton, 1972).

Losing, Benson J., *The Pictorial Field-Book of the War of 1812* (New York: Harper & Row, 1869).

Macdonough, Rodney, *The Life of Commodore Thomas Macdonough, U.S. Navy* (Boston: Fort Hill Press, 1909

Madison, Dolley, "At a Perilous Moment Dolley Madison Writes to Her Sister," *Madison Quarterly*, Vol. IV (January 1944), pp. 27–29.

MacKenzie, Alexander Slidell, *The Life of Commodore Oliver Hazard Perry*, Vol. 1 (New York: Harper and Brothers, 1840).

Maclay, Edgar Stanton, *A History of American Privateers* (New York: D. Appleton & Co., 1924; reprint from 1899, also available in ebooksread version).

Maclay, E. S., *History of American Privateers* (New York: D. Appleton, 1899).

Mahan, Alfred Thayer, *Sea Power and Its Relations to the War of 1812*, two volumes (Boston: Little, Brown, 1905).

Mahon, John K., *The War of 1812*. (Gainesville: University of Florida Press, 1972).

Malcomson, Robert, *Lords of the Lake: The Naval War on Lake Ontario, 1812–1814* (Annapolis, MD: Naval institute Press, 1998).

Malcomson, Robert, *A Very Brilliant Affair: The Battle of Queenston Heights, 1812* (Toronto: Robin Brass, 1998).

Malone, Dumas, *Jefferson the President: Second Term, 1805–1809* (Boston: Little Brown, 1974).

———, *Jefferson and His Time: The Sage of Monticello* (Boston: Little, Brown, 1974).

McAfee, Robert Breckinridge, *History of the Late War in the Western Country* (Ann Arbor: University of Michigan microfilms, 1966; originally published by Worsley & Smith in Lexington, Kentucky in 1816).

Molotsky, Irvin, *The Flag, the Poet, and the Song: The Story of the Star-Spangled Banner* (New York: Dutton, 2001).

Nardo, Don, *World History Series: The War of 1812* (Farmington Hills, MI: Lucent Books, 1999).

Nursey, Walter R., *The Story of Isaac Brock: Hero, Defender and Saviour of Upper Canada, 1812* (Toronto: McClelland and Stewart, 1923)

Parton, James, *Life of Andrew Jackson* (New York: Mason Bros., 1860).

Perkins, Bradford, *The First Rapprochement: England and the United States, 1795–1805* (Philadelphia: University of Pennsylvania Press, 1955).

Perkins, Bradford, *Prologue to War: England and the United States, 1805–1812* (Berkeley: University of California Press, 1961).

Pitch, Anthony S., *The Burning of Washington: The British Invasion of 1814* (Annapolis, MD: Naval Institute Press, 1998).

Pratt, Julius W., *The Expansionists of 1812* (New York: Macmillan Company, 1925).

Pray, J., Carl E., "The Contributions of Governor Shelby and the People of Kentucky to the Freedom of Michigan in the War of 1812," *Michigan History Magazine* Vol. 29 (October–December 1945).

Raddall, T. H., *The Path of Destiny* (Toronto: Doubleday, 1958).

Remini, Robert V., *Andrew Jackson and the Course of American Empire, 1767–1821* (New York: Harper & Row, 1977).

Rickard, J. "Major-General Sir Roger Hale Sheaffe," *History of War* (Nov. 25, 2007) <http://historyofwar.org/articles/people_sheaffe_roger.html>.

Risch, Erna, *Quartermaster Support of the Army: A History of the Corps, 1775–1939* (Washington, DC: Quartermaster Historian's Office, 1962).

Roosevelt, Theodore, *The Naval War of 1812* (Annapolis, MD: Naval Institute Press, 1987; reprint in 1900 and 1987, original published by G.P. Putnam Sons in 1882).

"Rush-Bagot Convention," The War of 1812 Website; <http://war1812.tripod. com/rushbaghot.html>.

Scanlan, Peter Lawrence, *Prairie due Chien: French, British*, American (Menasha, WI: George Banta, 1937).

Scott, Winfield, *Memoirs of Lieutenant.-General Scott, LLD*, Vol. 1 (Freeport, NY: Books for Libraries Press, 1970 reprint).

Shomette, Donald, *Flotilla: The Patuxent Naval Campaign in the War of 1812* (Baltimore: Johns Hopkins University Press, 2009).

Skaggs, David Curtis, and Gerard T. Altoff, *A Signal Victory: The Lake Erie Campaign* (Annapolis, MD: Naval Institute Press, 1997).

Skeen, Carl Edward, *Citizen Soldier in the War of 1812* (Lexington: University of Kentucky Press, 1999).

Smith, Zachary F., *The Battle of New Orleans* (Louisville, KY: John P. Morton & Co., 1904).

Sprout, Margaret, *The Rise of American Naval Power, 1776–1918* (Princeton, NJ: Princeton University Press, 1939).

Stanley, G. F. G., *The War of 1812: Land Operations* (Toronto: Macmillan, 1983).

"Star-Spangled History," Maryland War of 1812 bicentennial Commission <http:// starspangled200.org/history/pages/beanes.aspx>.

Stimpson, George, *A Book about American Politics* (New York: Harper & Brothers, 1952).

Sugden, John, *Tecumseh's Last Stand* (Norman: University of Oklahoma Press, 1985).

———, *Tecumseh: A Life* (London: Pimlico, 1999).

———, "Jean Lafitte and the British Offer of 1814," *Louisiana History*, Vol. 20 (1979), pp. 159–167.

Syrett, Harold C., ed., *The Papers of Alexander Hamilton*, 23 volumes (New York: Columbia University Press, 1976).

Taylor, R., "The Battle of Maguaga," The War of 1812 Website; <http://www. warof1812.ca/batmag.html>.

———, "The Battle of Tippecanoe," The War of 1812 Website; <http://www. warof1812.ca/tipcanoe.html>.

———, "The Capture of Detroit," The War of 1812 Website; <http://www. warof1812.ca/batdetroit.html>.

———, "Naval Battle: *Constitution* vs. *Guerriere*," The War of 1812 Website; <http://www.warof1812.ca/cvsg.html>.

———, "Sea Battle: *President* vs. *Belvidera*," The War of 1812 Website; (http:// www.warof1812.ca/pvsb.html).

———, "Summary of the End of the War of 1812," The War of 1812 Website; <http://www.warof1812.ca/summary.html>.

———, "Standing Interrogatories used by the Royal Navy when Questioning Sailors of Captured Ship in the War of 1812," The War of 1812 Website; <http://www.warof1812.ca/interrogatories.html>.

————, "The War of 1812: An Introduction," The War of 1812 Website; <http://www.warof1812.ca/intro.html>.

Thompson, Richard W., *Recollections of Sixteen Presidents from Washington to Lincoln* (Ann Arbor: University of Michigan Library, 1894).

Tucker, Glenn, *Poltroons and Patriots: A Popular Account of the War of 1812*, two volumes (Indianapolis: Bobbs-Merrill, 1954).

Tupper, Ferdinand Brock, *The Life and Correspondence of Sir Isaac Brock* (Public Domain Books; Kindle Locations 81–90.)

"The War of 1812 Revisited," Canada.com (September 27, 2007); <http://www.canada.com/story_print.html?id=b294d588-07a0-43c3-bbd4-09e361b8f5fe&spo...>.

Walker, Alexander, *Jackson and New Orleans: An Authentic Narrative of the Achievements of the American Army under Andrew Jackson before New Orleans* (Cranbury, NJ: Scholars Bookshelf, 2005; reprinted from an old manuscript).

Washington, H. A., ed., *The Writings of Thomas Jefferson* (New York: H. W. Derby, 1861).

Watson, Robert P., *Affairs of State: The Untold History of Presidential Love, Sex, and Scandal* (Lanham, MD: Rowman & Littlefield Publishers, 2012).

————. *Life in the White House: A Social History of the First Family and the President's Home* (Albany: SUNY Press, 2004), pp. 24 and 231.

————, *The Presidents' Wives; Reassessing the Office of First Lady* (Boulder, CO: Lynne Rienner Publishers, 2000).

White, Leonard D., *The Jeffersonians: A Study in Administrative History, 1801–1829* (New York, 1959).

Wilkinson, James, *Memoirs of My Own Times*, two volumes (Philadelphia: Abraham Small, 1816).

Wood, William, ed., *Select British Documents of the Canadian War of 1812* (Westport, CT: Greenwood Press, 1968; four volumes originally published in Toronto by the Champlain Society, 1920–1928).

Wrobel, Sylvia, and George Drider, *Isaac Shelby: Kentucky's First Governor and Hero of Three Wars* (Danville, KY: Cumberland Press, 1974).

Wrottesley, George, *Life and Letters of Burgoyne*, Vol. 1 (London: Richard Bentley, 1874).

Zaslow, Morris, *The Defended Border: Upper Canada and the War of 1812* (Toronto: Macmillan Co., 1964).

# ABOUT THE AUTHOR

Robert P. Watson, PhD, has published over 30 books, two encyclopedia sets, and hundreds of scholarly articles, chapters, and essays on American politics and history. A frequent media commentator, he has been interviewed by outlets throughout the United States and internationally, was for many years a Sunday columnist with the *Sun-Sentinel* newspaper, and serves as the political analyst for WPTV 5, south Florida's NBC affiliate. He is also the recipient of numerous awards for his community service, contributions to the study of the American presidency, and his teaching, including "Distinguished Professor of the Year" at both Florida Atlantic University and Lynn University twice, where he currently serves as Professor of American Studies.

# INDEX